Zen Classics

Zen Classics

Formative Texts in the History of Zen Buddhism

EDITED BY STEVEN HEINE AND
DALE S. WRIGHT

OXFORD
UNIVERSITY PRESS

2006

OXFORD
UNIVERSITY PRESS

Oxford University Press, Inc., publishes works that further
Oxford University's objective of excellence
in research, scholarship, and education.

Oxford   New York
Auckland   Cape Town   Dar es Salaam   Hong Kong   Karachi
Kuala Lumpur   Madrid   Melbourne   Mexico City   Nairobi
New Delhi   Shanghai   Taipei   Toronto

With offices in
Argentina   Austria   Brazil   Chile   Czech Republic   France   Greece
Guatemala   Hungary   Italy   Japan   Poland   Portugal   Singapore
South Korea   Switzerland   Thailand   Turkey   Ukraine   Vietnam

Copyright © 2006 by Oxford University Press, Inc.

Published by Oxford University Press, Inc.
198 Madison Avenue, New York, New York 10016

www.oup.com

Oxford is a registered trademark of Oxford University Press

Library of Congress Cataloging-in-Publication Data
Zen classics: formative texts in the history of Zen Buddhism /
edited by Steven Heine and Dale S. Wright.
p.   cm
Includes bibliographical references and index.
Contents: The concept of classic literature in Zen Buddhism /
Dale S. Wright—Guishan jingce and the ethical foundations of Chan practice /
Mario Poceski—A Korean contribution to the Zen canon the Oga hae scorui /
Charles Muller—Zen Buddhism as the ideology of the Japanese state /
Albert Welter—An analysis of Dogen's Eihei goroku /
Steven Heine—"Rules of purity" in Japanese Zen /
T. Griffith Foulk—Zen koan capping phrase books /
Victor Sogen Hori—Imagining Indian Zen /
Michel Mohr—Meditation for laymen and laywomen / David Riggs.
ISBN-13 978-0-19-517525-7; 978-0-19-517526-4 (pbk.)
ISBN 0-19-517525-5; 0-19-517526-3 (pbk.)
1. Zen literature—History and criticism. 2. Zen Buddhism.
I. Heine, Steven, 1950– II. Wright, Dale S.

BQ9264.2.Z455 2005
294.3'85—dc22   2004066287

Printed in the United States of America
on acid-free paper

Acknowledgments

We thank Cynthia Read and Oxford University Press for their interest in the project. We are also grateful for the support provided by our respective institutions in the preparation of the manuscript. Special thanks go to several assistants who worked on the manuscript, including Sandy Avila, Kelly Kuylen, Adiene Rodas, and Cristina Sasso.

Contents

Abbreviations, ix

Contributors, xi

Introduction: The Concept of Classic Literature in
Zen Buddhism, 3
Dale S. Wright

1. *Guishan jingce* (*Guishan's Admonitions*) and the Ethical
   Foundations of Chan Practice, 15
   Mario Poceski

2. A Korean Contribution to the Zen Canon: The *Oga
   Hae Seorui* (Commentaries on Five Masters on the
   Diamond Sūtra), 43
   Charles Muller

3. Zen Buddhism as the Ideology of the Japanese State: Eisai and
   the *Kōzen gokokuron*, 65
   Albert Welter

4. An Analysis of Dōgen's *Eihei Goroku*: Distillation
   or Distortion? 113
   Steven Heine

5. "Rules of Purity" in Japanese Zen, 137
   T. Griffith Foulk

6. Zen Kōan Capping Phrase Books: Literary Study and the Insight "Not Founded on Words or Letters," 171
   G. Victor Sōgen Hori

7. Imagining Indian Zen: Tōrei's Commentary on the *Ta-mo-to-lo ch'an ching* and the Rediscovery of Early Meditation Techniques during the Tokugawa Era, 215
   Michel Mohr

8. Meditation for Laymen and Laywomen: The *Buddha Samādhi (Jijuyū Zanmai)* of Menzan Zuihō, 247
   David E. Riggs

   Appendix:
   Pinyin–Wade-Giles Conversion Table, 275

   Index, 281

Abbreviations

T   *Taishō shinshū daizōkyō* [Japanese Edition of the Buddhist Canon] (Tokyo: Daizōkyōkai, 1924–1935).

Z   *Zoku zōkyō* [Dai Nihon zokuzōkyō] (Kyoto: Zōkyō shoin, 1905–1912).

XZJ   *Xu zangjing* (Taipei: Xinwenfeng, 1968–1970; reprint of *Dai Nihon zokuzōkyō*).

Contributors

T. GRIFFITH FOULK is professor of religion at Sarah Lawrence College and co-editor-in-chief of the Soto Zen Translation Project based in Tokyo. He was trained in both Rinzai and Soto Zen monasteries in Japan and has published extensively on the institutional and intellectual history of Chan/Zen Buddhism.

STEVEN HEINE is professor of religious studies and history and director of the Institute for Asian Studies at Florida International University. Heine has published numerous books and articles dealing with the life and thought of Dōgen and the history and philosophy of Zen Buddhism, including *Dōgen and the Kōan Tradition: A Tale of Two Shōbōgenzō Texts* (1994), *The Zen Poetry of Dōgen: Verses from the Mountain of Eternal Peace* (1997), *Shifting Shape, Shaping Text: Philosophy and Folklore in the Fox Kōan* (1999), *Opening a Mountain: Kōans of the Zen Masters* (2001), and *Zen Canon: Understanding the Classic Texts* (co-edited with Dale S. Wright, 2004).

G. VICTOR SŌGEN HORI, a former monk in the Daitokuji branch of Japanese Rinzai Zen, is associate professor of Japanese religion in the Faculty of Religious Studies at McGill University in Montreal. He has published *Zen Sand: The Book of Capping Phrases for Kōan Practice*, a translation with commentary of the Rinzai Zen monks' handbook of capping phrases for kōans (2003), and is active in the Montreal Buddhist communities.

MICHEL MOHR presently works as a lecturer at the University of Doshisha in Kyoto. He obtained a doctorate in 1992 from the University of Geneva (Switzerland), where he was working as an assistant of the Japanese Department between 1987 and 1992. His publications include *Traité sur l'Inépuisable Lampe du Zen: Tōrei (1721–1792) et sa vision de l'éveil* [Treatise on the Inexhaustible Lamp of Zen: Tōrei and his vision of awakening], 2 vols. (1997).

CHARLES MULLER is professor, Faculty of Humanities, Toyo Gakuen University (Japan). His publications include *The Sutra of Perfect Enlightenment: Korean Buddhism's Guide to Meditation* (1999), and *Patterns of Religion* (1999) [co-author]. He is also the founder and managing editor of the H-Buddhism Buddhist Scholars Information Network (http://www2.hnet.msu.edu/~buddhism/) and Chief Editor of the online Digital Dictionary of Buddhism (http://www.acmuller.net/ddb).

MARIO POCESKI is an assistant professor of Buddhist studies at the University of Florida. His research focuses on the history of Buddhism in late medieval China. Currently he is finishing a book on the history and doctrines of the Hongzhou school of Chan. His earlier publications include *Manifestation of the Tathāgata: Buddhahood According to the Avatamsaka Sūtra* (1993) and *Sun-Face Buddha: The Teachings of Ma-tsu and the Hung-chou School of Ch'an* (2001).

DAVID E. RIGGS is currently a researcher at the International Center for Japanese Studies in Kyoto. He has taught at the University of California Santa Barbara and the University of Illinois. He received his Ph. D. from the University of California Los Angeles, where his dissertation was entitled "The Rekindling of a Tradition: Menzan Zuihō and the Reform of Japanese Soto Zen in the Tokugawa Era."

ALBERT WELTER is associate professor of religious studies at the University of Winnipeg, specializing in Chinese and Japanese Buddhism. His previous publications include articles on Chinese Ch'an, and a book-length study of the Ch'an scholiast Yung-ming Yen-shou. He is currently preparing several manuscripts for publication, including a translation of the *Kōzen gokokuron*.

DALE S. WRIGHT is David B. and Mary H. Gamble Professor of Religious Studies and Asian Studies at Occidental College. His area of specialization and research is Buddhist philosophy, particularly Hua-yen Buddhism and Ch'an/Zen Buddhism. His publications include *Philosophical Meditations on Zen Buddhism* (1998), *The Kōan: Texts and Contexts in Zen Buddhism* (co-edited with Steven Heine, 2000), and *Zen Canon: Understanding the Classic Texts* (co-edited with Steven Heine, 2004), as well as numerous articles in *Philosophy East and West, Journal of the American Academy of Religion, History and Theory*, and elsewhere.

Zen Classics

Introduction: The Concept of Classic Literature in Zen Buddhism

Dale S. Wright

Zen Classics is a sequel to *The Zen Canon,* published by Oxford University Press, in which we began to explore the variety of influential texts in the history of Zen Buddhism. In *Zen Classics* we continue that exploration by shifting our primary focus from the Chinese origins of Zen to the other East Asian cultures where the Zen tradition came to fruition in subsequent eras. Here we invite scholars doing original research on Chinese, Korean, and Japanese Zen literature to survey a single work or genre of works that, because of its power and influence, has helped shape the Zen tradition and cause it to be what it is today.

It has by now become clear to those of us studying the Zen tradition of Buddhism that in spite of the powerful rhetorical opposition mounted against the written word, the volume, variety, and influence of Zen literature are enormous. Zen literature is one of the primary ways in which the tradition communicates its teachings and is perhaps the most important way that it extends itself into future historical contexts. Zen texts come in a range of genres. Primary among these are the "recorded sayings" of famous Zen masters; the "transmission of the lamp" histories, which string together important stories and biographies into a lineage structure; *kung-an* or *kōan* collections, which evolved out of these earlier literatures and sought to bring the teachings into finer focus; monastic codes enunciating rules of conduct for the life of Zen monks and nuns; and a wide variety of commentarial literature related to all of these primary genres. From its early origins in the language of medieval China, Zen literature spread to Korea, Japan, and Vietnam, where it slowly worked its way into the languages of those cultures, and subsequently into virtually every language and culture in the world today. A few of these works, by virtue of their transformative influence, have come to be regarded as classics, such as the *Platform Sutra* attributed to Hui-neng and Dōgen's *Shōbō-genzō*.

What, then, is a classic text? Common sense presents us with several options. A classic text might be the original motivating statement of a tradition, the earliest formulation of its truth. Yet we tend to use the word "classic" not just for initial founding texts but for important subsequent writings as well. Another option might be that classic texts illuminate the heart or the core of a tradition, whenever in the history of the tradition it was written, and this definition probably comes closer to the meaning we seek here. Yet, if we are careful and honest in the way we examine the history of a tradition, we can see that what practitioners within a tradition might regard as its heart or core shifts significantly throughout its long life. The primary or most urgent point in one era will become passé in the next, precisely because of the way it was stressed in the earlier era. Traditions are fluid, fully historical in their way of being, and over time become too complex to be reduced to a single core statement.

So, pressing further, we might attempt to define a classic text as one whose power or skill in evoking insight or persuasion transcends the era in which it was written. This definition avoids the difficulty of placing the classic in the epoch of origins of a tradition. This is important, since the identification of a text with the past undermines its ability to be forceful in subsequent times. To be a classic is to persist in the present setting, to be powerful now and not simply at some moment in the past. This understanding of "classical" also manages to avoid defining a classic text in terms of a timeless doctrinal position that is not subject to the influences and turns of history. As we can now see, all cultural artifacts are produced within a temporal and cultural context and are therefore subject to the particular movements of that setting. But even though no single doctrinal position will be adequate in all epochs of cultural history, there are texts—those that have come to be regarded as classics—that somehow manage to communicate forcefully and persuasively in historical periods beyond the ones in which they were produced. Their ideological position is certainly not timeless, but their powers of communication seem to carry on long beyond the typical shelf life of cultural products. They appear, in other words, to evoke reflection, insight, and motivation not just in the setting imagined by their authors but in some important way beyond that as well.

Designating a text a classic, therefore, is not just a statement about its position in the past; it is more importantly a statement about how it fares in the present, and in the series of previous "presents" that have arisen between a text's origins and the present moment. Calling something a classic means that in addition to its having been important or powerful in the past, the text can still wield power in the present. It is not so much that the text is, by virtue of that power, "timeless," because, first of all, there may very well have been historical periods when it did not possess that capacity, and second, the idea in the text or the segment of it that currently holds sway may differ significantly from the idea or segment that once did. It would be better to say that a classic text is "timely" because its timeliness consists in the fact that it can manage to provoke insight in very different times even if the insight or the understanding of it differs.

The classic therefore, exists in the variety of insights that it evokes in different times and places. In a new and different setting, the function of a classic text is not so much to preserve an original message as it is to speak forcefully and pointedly to a new set of cultural issues. Although not as old as the Buddhist tradition of which it is a part, the Zen portion of Buddhism has come to be what it is today through lengthy processes of cultural evolution. Zen institutions began with one set of concerns and motivations and quickly transformed into others as they came to take a different and more established role in China. And whatever concerns had motivated the Chinese creators of Zen could not have been shared in exactly the same way by later Zen leaders in other East Asian cultures. A classical text is classical precisely by virtue of its power to speak effectively in new cultural and historical settings and to address new and unanticipated concerns, rather than by virtue of its being irrevocably moored in the past and in univocal meanings. And if each classic text constitutes some kind of advancement for the tradition, then the tradition as a whole certainly cannot be conceived in static and ahistorical terms. This, at least, is the direction of understanding for the term "classical" that would allow us to take advantage of the obvious strengths of contemporary historical thinking.

Just as important, understanding "classical" in a way that is flexible and open to change helps make it cohere with the Buddhist tradition, which stresses the principles of impermanence and dependent origination. These basic features of the earliest Buddhist worldview work against the static conception of history that we tend to assume if we have not thought deeply about it. They also make it possible for us to see that the principles of Buddhism apply just as much to Buddhism itself as they do to other entities in the world. Buddhism not only articulates the doctrine of impermanence, it is itself impermanent. What it is in any setting depends on a myriad of historical factors. In fact, there is in the repertoire of Buddhist concepts one that captures our conception of a "classic" very well. This is the Mahayana concept of skill-in-means, the idea that, in order to be effective and transformative in a wide variety of social and historical settings, the teachings of Buddhism will need to be flexible, malleable, and not inalterably fixed in meaning. And it has indeed been true that in Buddhist history, the most successful and effective teachings and texts have been those that appear to have the virtue of flexibility, those that are open to be shaped in a variety of directions in order to meet the needs of different people in unique situations and contexts. Classic texts are skillful in this respect. They seem to be able to stretch themselves far enough to accommodate the demands of different times and do not therefore come to be inalterably associated with the particular issues and concerns at the time of their original composition.

As we know from reading great Zen texts, however, Zen masters appear to have been much less concerned about simply being Buddhist than about establishing an atmosphere within which an awakening might take place. This concern would be just as true for texts that articulate a stern, disciplinary atmosphere of rule-following as it is for those Zen texts that mock such rigidity. It is this diversity of literary approach that makes Zen texts so difficult to classify. Some Zen texts, indeed some of the most famous, refuse to mean anything at all. They provoke, they challenge, and they raise questions that can be answered only through extraordinary insight. Indeed, it may very well be that the question is the most basic form of Zen discourse, rather than pronouncements, proclamations, or statements.

Moreover, some Zen texts feature comedy as a form of discourse that has liberating effects. Comedy evokes and celebrates moments of freedom from mental bondage, which was at times one way to articulate the goal of the practice. Other Zen texts take a critical point of view; they ridicule artificial conceptions of the practice and belittle forms of practice that aim at anything short of full awakening. Sometimes these negative tracts function to make the traditional language of the Buddhist tradition look stiff and shallow in comparison to the Zen language that demystifies and deconstructs them. Zen masters were, more than most Buddhists, enthralled with the power of language to transform the mind, even if their criticism of ordinary language was devastatingly pointed. These few examples of forms of discourse in Zen demonstrate the refined focus that we find in its texts on the overarching concern for liberating insight.

That the kinds of insight a single classic text evokes over its lengthy history might change is a realization required by the study of both Buddhist history and Buddhist thought. Zen practice has always entailed the practice of meditation, although the form that this contemplative exercise takes has changed. Textual meditation is certainly one such form, and it has been practiced by serious Zen practitioners since the beginning of the tradition. In the context of such practice, the primary goal of reading would not have been an accurate interpretation in the sense of accord with the intentions of the original author. The goal would have been awakening, and this would be made possible only when the reader comes to see where he or she stands in the world by means of the vision offered in the text. It is not necessary to decide whether the meaning of the text resides in the author, or the original context, or the reader, or his or her context, because the insight afforded by the text occurs always in the interaction between those elements. In each case, the classic texts allow the reader to see him or herself and what matters in light of the text, while simultaneously the readers inevitably understand the text in light of their own context.

The reading of classic texts in the Zen tradition inevitably included the traditional practices of imitation and emulation. The texts themselves, and the ideal figures represented in them, served for subsequent eras as exemplary models for how practitioners should shape themselves. When the classics functioned in this authoritative way, the reader was not so much a productive agent acting on the text as someone who sought to appropriate what it had to say in an open posture of listening and responsiveness. In this sense, the classic Zen texts served as a factor favoring continuity and stability as practitioners in various times and places would seek to fashion themselves out of meditative dialogue with these same texts. In each case, however, practitioners would have read differently, each in light of their own contexts and issues, and in their interpretations they would have added something significant to the tradition. Considered in this light, the Zen tradition would resemble an ongoing conversation between readers of the classic texts in a lineage of historical periods, each adding to the tradition what the cultural situation in his or her time made possible.

All the essays in this volume are written in the style of contemporary historical inquiry. They seek to discover how each text or genre of texts came to be what it is, and how each influenced the tradition to take the shape that it did. Readers interested primarily in cultural history will find the essays to be superb examples of this contemporary science. Other readers, however, those interested primarily in Zen practice or its fundamental conceptions of the self and the world, will wonder what this historical approach contributes to their quest. Does the study of Zen history contribute to or distract from the study of Zen as a spiritual inquiry? The question is important for readers to ponder and, at the same time, to ask, why? Here are just a couple of thoughts to get you started.

Most, although perhaps not all, of the great Zen masters mentioned in these pages assumed the vital significance of Zen history. Understanding this history in the form of genealogy, and referring to it regularly in *dharma* talk of various kinds, these Zen visionaries understood how vital this form of self-knowledge is, and that ignoring it entails great risks to the tradition. According to the Buddhist principle of dependent origination, we understand what something is, including Zen, through our grasp of the lineage of factors that have brought that something into being. The less we understand about the history of anything, the more likely we are to assume that it has a fixed essence, that what it appears to be right now is what it really is, always has been, and always will be. The more we understand about the history of Zen, the more open our minds will be to nuances and complexities in the tradition, and the more open we will be to newly emerging possibilities for its future in our own lives and beyond. Historical understanding helps to loosen our conceptual grip on things; it allows us to see the reality in which we live as "impermanence," and in that way it restricts our natural tendencies toward rigid or dogmatic understanding. This openness of mind and historical sensitivity can be found in profound ways in virtually all of the Zen masters whose innovations in Zen conception and practice produced one of the most interesting traditions of spirituality that the world has ever seen.

Does the study of Zen history contribute to the study of Zen as a spiritual inquiry? Yes, clearly. But it would be unproductive and unfair not to pose the opposite question offered above: Does the study of Zen history distract or detract from the study of Zen as a spiritual inquiry? Listening attentively to the Zen masters again, we would have to respond again in a qualified affirmative. Although historical study doesn't *necessarily* detract from a Zen spiritual quest, there is a sense in which it might do so. Perhaps most important is that historical understanding might mistakenly be conducted as though it were an end in itself, something that does not need to be set into a larger context of its meaning for our lives. In fact it cannot be such an end, but rather needs to serve a larger vision of the reality within which we live. If we lose sight of that larger vision of the present, we engage in historical study as antiquarian attachment to the past. Historical understanding can fulfill its mission only by looking through the past that is uncovered to its implications for the present in which we live, and by pointing beyond the past to some new future that the past will serve or illuminate. If the practice of Zen is meant to enlarge our vision, to deepen our understanding of who we are and how we are to live, then it will need to carefully consider the ways that historical study of Zen is included within it. But that mindfulness is precisely what Zen practice seeks to inculcate, and where it succeeds, the practitioner is likely to have a profound sense of the importance of the tradition's history. The opposite failure, although all too common in religious settings, is truly disabling—the refusal to accept the truth of history, the inability to take its lessons into account, the perverse need to alter the historical record to maintain an ideology that fears the facts. These are the risks of avoiding the historical study of Zen in the context of its practice, and the reasons why the study of Zen history cannot over time be excluded from the authentic study of Zen.

The essays chosen for this volume offer careful historical studies of texts that have earned the right to be called classics. The texts are taken from different cultures and different historical periods and fall into a variety of Zen genres. What follows is a brief introductory summary of the eight essays in this volume.

Chapter 1. "*Guishan jingce* (*Guishan's Admonitions*) and the Ethical Foundations of Chan Practice"

Mario Poceski's study of *Guishan's Admonitions,* a ninth-century Chinese Hongzhou Chan text attributed to Guishan Lingyou, a disciple of Baizhang, sheds light on a dimension of this famously iconoclastic Zen tradition that surprises Zen scholars, east and west. This interesting and unusual text, the only Hongzhou school text discovered in the Dunhuang caves, places its primary focus on monastic discipline and the place of morality in Chan practice. This emphasis contrasts sharply with the overall point of view that we associate with Hongzhou Chan, whose best-known writings tend to disparage the conservative orientation of codes of monastic discipline and moral training. But Guishan's text is clearly a response to tension in the relationship between Chan monasteries and the wider society within which they existed, especially the larger political milieu which regularly cycled between support for Buddhist monasticism and serious doubts about it.

As Poceski shows, *Guishan's Admonitions* calls for serious reform to purify the moral and spiritual practices of monks, while simultaneously describing the monastic ideal toward which they ought to strive. Rejecting the image of the Chan iconoclast, the *Admonitions* depict a Chan monasticism that is largely indistinguishable from Chinese Buddhist monasticism as a whole. Guishan's image of the paradigmatic Chan monk is simply a good Buddhist, and Poceski concludes by highlighting the pragmatic and realistic implications of this position. *Guishan's Admonitions* is therefore best understood as a Chan attempt to place a realistic model of Buddhist monastic discipline before the minds of practitioners in order to provide them with actual practices to guide their daily lives. Although this image has not been given pride of place in Japanese or Western Zen in the modern period, we can certainly imagine historical circumstances arising in which Guishan's text might prominently reappear.

Chapter 2. "A Korean Contribution to the Zen Canon: The *Oga Hae Seorui* (Commentaries on Five Masters on the *Diamond Sūtra*)"

Charles Muller's essay offers insight into the working of a classic Mahāyāna *sūtra*–the *Diamond Sūtra*–within the Korean Sŏn monastic community. The *Diamond Sūtra,* one of the most condensed and therefore easily accessible Mahāyāna classics, inspired dozens of commentaries in every Mahāyāna Buddhist culture. Muller's essay analyzes Gihwa's subcommentary on five classic *Diamond Sūtra* commentaries. In Gihwa's text, therefore, we have three layers of reflection: the original *sūtra*, commentaries by five famous Chinese masters, and Gihwa's unifying vision that makes the *Oga Hae Seorui* coherent as a functional monastic meditation tool. This text from Gihwa, himself the pre-eminent Buddhist figure of his time, became the central conceptual training tool in Sŏn monasteries and has retained that status for the past six centuries. Muller's essay shows how this text provided the conceptual core for Korean Sŏn, which avoided the provocative anti-textual histories that have defined Chinese Chan and that surfaced periodically in Japanese Zen. Because the *Diamond Sūtra* addresses the prominent Buddhist theme of language and its relationship to the nonlinguistic world, how practitioners have understood this *sūtra* makes an enormous difference in how linguistic practices are positioned in the full range of Buddhist meditations. The influence and power of Gihwa's effort to collect the best Chinese *Diamond Sūtra* studies, arranging and interpreting them for the purposes of Korean monastic training, qualifies the *Oga Hae Seorui* for the status of a classic text itself.

Chapter 3. "Zen Buddhism as the Ideology of the Japanese
State: Eisai and the *Kōzen Gokokuron*"

Albert Welter's careful study of Eisai, the founding figure of Japanese Rinzai Zen, and his principal text, the *Kōzen gokokuron,* shows us how the twists and turns of history establish the grounds upon which a text will either gain and maintain power and influence or fail to do so. The *Kōzen gokokuron* was already a classic text by the end of its own Kamakura period. It defined for the newly emerging Zen sect, and for other Buddhists as well, how the monastic system would position itself with respect to the state. The text outlined for monks and for government officials the vital role Buddhist thought and practice played in maintaining the moral and spiritual core of Japanese culture. To do this, of course, it would need to focus heavily on the importance of Buddhist moral precepts within the overall practices of Buddhism and to show how this moral emphasis served the interests of the state. Against other Zen ideologies, therefore, Eisai was conservative in allying Zen practice to broader social and governmental concerns and was positioned in opposition to the antinomian character of certain dimensions of the Chinese Ch'an heritage. When the reform tradition of "pure Zen" took hold in Tokugawa Japan, however, Eisai's standing, and that of the *Kōzen gokokuron,* would inevitably fall. The former "classic" text was submitted to critique and fell into obscurity. Throughout his analysis, Welter shows how the fate of the text is clearly linked to broader historical developments, which either set the stage for its use and valorization or undermine it. Perhaps, like Mario Poceski's *Guishan jingce,* Eisai's text awaits a new era in which its themes will once again be pertinent to the central concerns of Zen history.

Chapter 4. "An Analysis of Dōgen's *Eihei Goroku*: Distillation or Distortion?"

Steven Heine takes up a Sōtō Zen text that has been instrumental in shaping the tradition of Dōgen Zen in order both to analyze what it is and to ask whether it accurately summarizes Dōgen's *Eihei Kōroku* (examined in *The Zen Canon*) or whether, in the process of distilling it, it actually distorts it. The importance of the question is brought forth by Heine's reminder that the texts abbreviating the writings of Dōgen were more influential than the texts from which they were drawn. To get an interesting take on this issue, Heine asks how the pattern of abbreviation stood in the traditions of Dōgen and Ch'an/ Zen literature. Here he finds "minimalist expression" a powerful and impor- tant theme, although in the end Heine concludes that linguistic expansion rather than compression is a more adequate symbol of Dōgen's work. The essay continues to survey the controversy in Japan over the accuracy of the *Eihei Goroku* and concludes, with Ishii Shūdō, that the *Eihei Goroku* is far from a mirror image of Dōgen's original *Eihei Kōroku*. Whether that alteration through the course of Zen history is a problem to be addressed by returning to the original source, or instead is a perfectly appropriate sign of the imper- manence and contextuality that Dōgen so powerfully conceived, is the impor- tant question that concludes Heine's essay.

Chapter 5. "'Rules of Purity' in Japanese Zen"

In this essay, T. Griffith Foulk continues the research on the Chinese monastic regulations genre that he had completed for *The Zen Canon*, here providing an excellent overview of how Song-style Buddhist monasteries came to be estab- lished in Japan through the extensive study and use of this genre of Zen lit- erature. This body of literature, the "Rules of Purity" (C. *qinggui*; J. *shingi*), established for Japanese Zen what it meant to be a monastery, and how, exactly, an authentic monastery ought to be constructed, structured, and governed. Given the significance of Zen monastic institutions in Japan from the Kama- kura period down to the present, the importance of this literature for Japanese culture generally is paramount. Because Chinese monastic codes continued to develop from the Song through the Yuan and Ming dynasties, Zen monasteries in Japan would periodically be compelled to rewrite the codes of monastic structure to adapt to new influences from the mainland as well as new needs and situations that had arisen in Japan.

The result of these extensive import and adaptation efforts is an impressive corpus of literature, from early travelers such as Eisai, Enni, and Dōgen down to the contemporary Japanese debates on monastic practice that are affecting the way "Zen centers" all over the world organize their activities. Through the interesting histories told here, two theses stand out. One is Foulk's well-supported claim that neither the arrangement of "Chan" monasteries nor the "rules of purity" that governed them were the exclusive inventions or possessions of the Chan School of Chinese Buddhism. The other is that in spite of the dominance of Mahayāna traditions of Buddhism in East Asia, pioneers in the Chan tradition were part of a larger movement to revive strict monastic regulations based on the Hīnayāna *vinaya* codes. Both of these developments are seen as having shaped Japanese monastic codes, including those produced in Japan beginning in the thirteenth century.

Chapter 6. "Zen Kōan Capping Phrase Books: Literary Study and the Insight 'Not Founded on Words or Letters'"

G. Victor Sōgen Hori's thesis in this essay—that Zen kōans derive from an ancient tradition of Chinese literary games—holds great promise for our understanding of the origins and history of Zen practice. Zen phrase books, Hori explains, should be understood as a subgenre of Zen kōan literature, but also as a category of texts that derives from the ancient Chinese tradition of proverbs, sayings, and allusional poetry. In their Zen institutional setting, phrase books have two primary sources: the wordless insight that is "not founded on words and letters," and the tradition of Chinese literary games. In this ancient poetic tradition, skilled poets would challenge each other's powers of memory and composition by presenting a verse and challenging an opponent to recall the second line or follow the allusion to another poem. This tradition can be traced to early Chinese sources wherein the ancient *Book of Songs,* the Confucian *Analects,* and early Taoist texts such as the *Tao te ching* would be pressed into playful, poetic use in literary games. Following Hori's lead, one can see the connection between these games and the kinds of exchanges that are found inscribed in some of the most famous kōans—both contain mysterious language, both allude to profound traditions beyond what is occurring in the present moment, and both lead to a flash of insight, something like a "mind-to-mind transmission." The use of Zen phrase books as sources of "capping phrases" for the kind of mental discipline that develops in monasteries is revealed by Hori's analysis to be part of a much older tradition than Zen, and a very significant genre of East Asian literature.

Chapter 7. "Imagining Indian Zen: Tōrei's Commentary on the *Ta-mo-to-lo ch'an ching* and the Rediscovery of Early Meditation Techniques during the Tokugawa Era"

Michel Mohr's essay provides an introduction to two seminal texts, a fifth-century meditation sūtra and a commentary on the sūtra by Japanese Zen master Tōrei, which help shape early modern Zen. The *Ta-mo-to-lo ch'an ching* is a Chinese canonical treatise on meditation techniques, which is possibly translated from Indian sources but about which no traces beyond the Chinese appear to exist. Although the word "Ch'an" or Zen appears in the title, the text predates the origins of the Zen school and therefore represents an earlier stage of Chinese Buddhist meditation tradition. Mohr traces the uses of this text in the Zen school of the Sung dynasty, and then through a series of developments in Japan leading up to Tōrei's commentary. What we gain, therefore, is a close look at a seminal meditation classic through many layers of Zen tradition as a background for Tōrei's commentary and early modern use of it. As Mohr shows us, Tōrei's commentary amounts to a quest for the roots of Zen practice in early Buddhist meditation as a way for him to propose reform for the Zen school in his time.

Chapter 8. "Meditation for Laymen and Laywomen: The *Buddha Samādhi* (*Jijuyū Zanmai*) of Menzan Zuihō"

David Riggs's essay on Menzan's *Buddha Samadhi* provides an analysis of how and why this text has held so prominent a position in Sōtō Zen monasteries for the past two and a half centuries. Menzan, a leading figure in Sōtō Zen in eighteenth-century Japan, composed the *Buddha Samadhi* to provide informal orientation to Zen meditation for laymen and women. Riggs shows how the text manifests the reforms sweeping through the Sōtō tradition in the eighteenth century by focusing exclusively on Dōgen, Sōtō's founding figure. Rather than offering step-by-step instruction in *zazen*, however, the *Buddha Samadhi* uses Dōgen's *Bendōwa* to explain how meditation practice is related to the ultimate vision of the Zen and Buddhist tradition. In this sense, Menzan's informal text *is itself* a meditation, not just *about* meditation. Neither technical nor philosophically abstract, the *Buddha Samadhi* has become a classic statement of the point of Sōtō Zen, functional and inspiring at a variety of levels of comprehension. Its central theme—the practice of realization—would provide the power for Menzan's text to retain its usefulness and status throughout the modern period.

Note on Transliteration of Chinese Terms and Names

Aware that there are two acceptable systems of scholarly transliteration for Chinese (Pinyin and Wade-Giles), each at this point rather well known, the editors of this volume have allowed authors to work in the system of transliteration that they feel most suitable. Please see the appendix for Pinyin–Wade-Giles conversion table.

I

Guishan jingce (Guishan's Admonitions) and the Ethical Foundations of Chan Practice

Mario Poceski

The historical relationship between Chan and Buddhist monasticism is typically discussed in reference to the putative establishment of a unique system of "Chan monastic rules" during the Tang period (618–907). The creation of such new monastic structures and regulations—commonly identified as the Chan "Pure Rules" or "Rules of Purity" (C. *Chan jinggui*; J. *Zen shingi*)—is traditionally ascribed to Baizhang (749–814), chief disciple of the renowned Mazu (709–788) and a leading figure in the Hongzhou school, which was at the forefront of the transition from early to classical Chan. The story about the emergence of distinctive Chan institutions and models of monastic practice is part of a sectarian narrative that depicts the development of the classical Chan tradition, especially the Hongzhou school, as an unambiguous shift away from the established norms, teachings, and institutional structures of earlier Indian and Chinese Buddhism. Supposedly an integral part of that process was the repudiation of long-established monastic mores and institutions.

Recent Chan scholarship has increasingly challenged this interpretation of Tang Chan's attitudes toward received monastic traditions by showing that it is based on tenuous and unreliable evidence, and by gradually unmasking its uncritical reliance on interpretative schemata that reflect the ideologies of later (i.e., post-Tang) Chan/Zen traditions in both China and Japan. This chapter focuses on a key record from the Tang period that undermines the idea that late Tang Chan rejected established ethical norms and monastic ideals. The text in question is *Guishan jingce (Guishan's Admonitions)*, a significant part of the Hongzhou school's limited literary output that, so far, has been ignored by Chan/Zen scholarship. It was composed by Guishan Lingyou (771–853), Baizhang's foremost disciple and leading representative of the Hongzhou school's third generation. With its primary focus on monastic discipline and the place of morality in the Chan path to spiritual awakening, this text is unique among Tang-period Chan documents. It sheds unique light on Tang Chan's rather conventional attitudes toward monastic ideals and mores and brings into question the prevalent view about the iconoclastic turn that Chan supposedly took under the Hongzhou school. By extension, the chapter also serves as a preliminary study of the attitudes toward monasticism and conventional morality within the classical Chan tradition.

The chapter first introduces the text and its author and places them in the broader historical context of ninth-century China. A brief discussion of *Guishan jingce*'s provenance and structure is followed with basic biographical data about its author and an overview of the historical circumstances that shaped the views and sentiments expressed in the text. It then presents an analysis of the text's central ideas about the ideals of monastic life. The chapter ends with preliminary reflections on the Chan tradition's attitudes toward received monastic mores and institutions, and on the relationship between Chan practice and ethical observances.

Text and Author in Historical Context

Provenance of the Manuscript

The oldest manuscript of *Guishan jingce* was recovered from among the Dunhuang documents that were discovered during the early twentieth century. Its title is *Dagui jingce* and it is part of a manuscript kept in Paris in the Peliot collection of Dunhuang materials (catalogue no. 4638). As such, it is the only text associated with the Hongzhou school found among the Dunhung documents. The text is incorporated into a larger collection entitled *Yan heshang ji* (*Reverend Yan's Collection*).[1] The text of *Dagui jingce* is immediately followed by *Xinxin ming* (*Inscription on Faith in Mind*), the famous poem traditionally attributed to Sengcan (d. 606?), the putative third Chan patriarch.[2] *Xinxin ming*'s verses follow *Guishan jingce*'s final verse section without any interruption or any explicit marker that separates the two texts. The poem's title is altered to *Xinxin xinming* (by adding the character *xin*, "faith"), so that its beginning appears as another four-character line in the final verse section of *Guishan jingce*. As was pointed out in Tanaka Ryōshō's study of the text, the quality of the handwritten manuscript is not very good and it contains numerous copying errors.[3]

The dating of the Dunhuang manuscript can be established from a document on the back of the manuscript, which is dated 936 (third year of the Qingtai era of the Latter Tang dynasty).[4] We can presume that *Yan heshang ji* was copied on the back of this document at about that time, probably because of a scarcity of paper. The identity of Reverend Yan, the compiler of the collection, is not entirely clear. Tanaka identifies five monks as possible candidates and concludes that the most likely choice is Chan teacher Yan of Guishan, a disciple of Guishan whose name is listed in the table of contents of fascicle 11 of *Jingde chuandeng lu* (*Record of the Transmission of the Lamp from the Jingde [Era]*).[5] Considering the great distance between Guishan's monastery in Hunan and Dunhuang, and in light of the political developments during the Tang-Five Dynasties transition, a copy of *Guishan jingce* probably reached Dunhuang before the fall of the Tang in 907, perhaps even before the start of Huang Chao's (d. 884) rebellion in 878, which is within a couple of decades of Guishan's death.[6]

In addition to the Dunhuang manuscript, there are three other versions of *Guishan jingce* in the following collections: *Quan tang wen, Taishō shinshū daizōkyō*, and *Xu zang jing*.[7] The *Taishō* version is part of *Zimen jingxun*, a collection of mostly Chan texts compiled during the Ming dynasty (1368–1644). The *Xu zang jing* version, entitled *Zhu guishan jingce* (*Commentary on the Guishan jingce*), includes a commentary written by Shousui (1072–1147), a monk associated with the Caodong school.[8] Published in 1139, this is the earliest commentary. Subsequently, *Guishan jingce* and Shousui's commentary were incorporated into *Fozu sanjing chu* (*Commentaries on Three Scriptures of the Buddhas and Patriarchs*), a collection comprised of three texts used as manuals in the training of novices.[9] Another commentary of *Guishan jingce* is Daopei's (1615–1702) *Guishan jingce zhinan*, which forms a part of his *Fozu sanjing zhinan* (*Primer of Three Scriptures of the Buddha and the Patriarchs*) written during the early Qing dynasty (1644–1912).[10]

Guishan and the Text

Guishan was born in the Zhao family, whose ancestral home was in Zhangqi, Fuzhou prefecture (present-day Fujian Province).[11] He became a novice at the age of fifteen at Jianshan monastery in his native province. Sometime during his late teens he traveled north to Hangzhou (Zhejiang Province), where he was ordained at Longxing monastery. During his stay there, Guishan studied the Buddhist scriptures and the *vinaya*.[12] In 793, at the age of twenty-two, he traveled to northern Jiangxi, an area that was a stronghold of the Hongzhou school. During a visit to Letan monastery on Shimen mountain, where Mazu was buried six years earlier, he met Baizhang, who at that time was residing close to his teacher's memorial pagoda. Guishan became Baizhang's disciple and later followed him to Baizhang mountain.[13] He ended up staying with Baizhang for well over a decade.

In about 810, Guishan moved to Dagui mountain (also known as Gui mountain, in Hunan Province), where he spent the rest of his life; its name is commonly used to refer to him.[14] Gradually a number of monks came to study with him and his Tongqing monastery became one of the main centers of the Chan school. During Guishan's long and successful teaching career his monastic disciples included famous Chan teachers such as Yangshan Huiji (807–833) and Xiangyan Zhixian (n.d.). He also attracted a number of noted lay supporters, including the prominent official and lay Buddhist Pei Xiu (787?–860).[15]

During the anti-Buddhist persecution instigated by emperor Wuzong (r. 840–846), Guishan had to flee his monastery, which was seriously damaged, and disguised himself as a layman. During the early stage of the restoration of Buddhism, initiated after the next emperor, Xuanzong (r. 846–859), ascended the throne, Pei Xiu (a civil governor of Hunan at the time) offered support to Tongqing monastery. At the time he also received religious instructions from Guishan.[16] Other noted officials who were Guishan's supporters included Li Jingrang (n.d.), who probably met Guishan while serving as a civil governor of Shannan-dao during the Dazhong era (847–860),[17] and Cui Shenyou (n.d.), who was a civil governor of Hunan.[18] The author of Guishan's first stele inscription—which was subsequently lost—was Lu Jianqiu (789–846),[19] and the calligraphy for the inscription was done by the famous poet Li Shangyin (812–858).[20] By the tenth century, Guishan and Yangshan were acknowledged as the putative "founders" of the Guiyang school of Chan, the earliest of the so-called five Chan schools that were recognized in post-Tang Chan.[21]

Guishan jingce is the only text that is directly attributed to Guishan. Other records that are traditionally regarded as representing his teachings are a few transcripts of excerpts from his sermons and a larger selection of dialogues which were included in his record of sayings compiled during the early Ming dynasty (1368–1644).[22] Some of these materials are also incorporated in his hagiographies in various collections in the transmission of the lamp genre. Although there is no conclusive evidence that Guishan wrote *Guishan jingce*, there is little to suggest that the traditional attribution is problematic. It is true that Guishan's stele inscription makes no mention of it, but such omission is not uncommon in records of that type.[23] Moreover, Guishan's authorship is suggested by internal evidence. As will be seen, the depiction of Chan practice presented in the text's fourth section closely resembles other Hongzhou texts written during the same period and includes passages that can be found in Guishan's sermons. Furthermore, the tone of urgency and the self-critical attitude evidenced in the text suggest that it was written around the time of the Huichang era's persecution of Buddhism, when Guishan and his contemporaries faced Wuzong's far-reaching purge of the monastic order and when there was a sense that Buddhism faced the threat of obliteration.

Structure and Contents

Guishan jingce consists of two parts: a prose section, which is the main part of the treatise, followed by verses that recapitulate the principal ideas expressed in the prose portion. This kind of literary format, in which a longer expository prose section is followed by a shorter verse summary, is often found in translations of Buddhist scriptures and it also appears in the writings of medieval Chinese monks. The original text lacks any explicit division into separate parts, although in Daobei's commentary the main body of the text is subdivided into five sections. [24] According to him, the five sections deal with these topics:

1. Discussion of the perils and problems associated with physical existence.
2. Reprimands about various abuses of monastic life.
3. Clarification of the correct reasons for "leaving home" (i.e., becoming a monk).
4. Discussion of the shortcut for "entering the Way" (i.e., the practice of Chan).
5. Concluding advice and exhortations.

This division of the text is quite useful and I will allude to it in the following pages. Nonetheless, such division also tends to impute to the original text greater structural coherence than is really merited. The whole text is quite repetitive and lacks a clearly articulated thematic structure and carefully developed line of argument. For example, recurring injunctions about varied abuses of monastic life not only are found in the second section but are dispersed throughout the text. In fact, critiques of monks' wayward ways, juxtaposed with implorations/encouragements to live according to hallowed monastic ideals, are principal themes. The final verse section consists of thirty-six four-character lines and constitutes less than ten percent of the entire work. It does not contain anything new but merely recapitulates key points made in the previous sections.

The tone of Guishan's treatise is direct, and often quite personal. This approach indicates that its contents were intended for the monks at his monastery. On the other hand, the issues of monastic discipline and practice discussed in the text have broad relevance beyond the confines of a particular monastic community. In fact, they touch upon key issues pertinent to the whole monastic order in ninth-century China. Guishan probably was concerned about both the quality of monastic life in his own monastery and the overall state of the Buddhist clergy at the time.

Guishan's stated agenda is to expose and rebuke prevalent abuses of monastic life and articulate a set of guidelines for following a purposeful religious vocation. These twin objectives—to critique monastic transgressions and to evoke the lofty ideals of Buddhist monasticism—are interwoven and reinforce each other. These kinds of critiques of monastic vice and praises of exemplary conduct are common tropes in Buddhist literature. In that sense, Guishan's text is on familiar ground and accords with established models, even if it has a distinctive tenor and occasionally adopts elements of the Chan school's pe-culiar idiom. The text is also unique for its brief discussion of Chan soteriology, which is integrated into its overall argument about the importance of ethical observances and monastic discipline.

Historical Context

Guishan's comments about monastic life deal with perennial issues and ideals, but they are also related to the state of Buddhism during the middle part of the ninth century. That was a period of flourishing religiosity, during which Buddhism attracted large followings among all segments of the population and received broad support and imperial patronage. Nevertheless, the large Bud-dhist establishment also faced serious internal and external problems. Accord-ing to its detractors, the Buddhist church's amassing of vast economic re-sources and its far-reaching influence on Tang society were accompanied by a sense of complacency, moral decay, and institutional corruption. As Buddhist institutions grew in size and wealth, they attracted increasing numbers of in-dividuals who entered the monastic order for reasons other than religious piety. The result was the overall downgrading of the quality of the clergy, a situation that was by no means unique in the long history of Buddhism.

Under the Tang, in order to become a proper monk one had to receive ordination in accord with the *vinaya*. The ordinations were sanctioned and controlled by the state, which appropriated the right to decide who could join the monastic order. In theory, in addition to receiving ordination, monks were also expected to possess proper religious motivation and lead pious lives gov-erned by monastic rules and customs. In actual practice, as Guishan's texts make clear, the system that regulated entry into the clergy was not effective in making sure that only people with proper religious motivation entered the order. Many people received ordination certificates without strong religious commitment and willingness to submit themselves to the rigors of monastic practice and discipline.

Accounts about monastic abuses recounted in historical documents—in-cluding Emperor Wuzong's edicts concerning Buddhism and the anti-Buddhist memorials presented to the throne by literati-officials—gave a picture of the Buddhist church beset with dereliction and corruption.[25] Notwithstand-ing the evident bias of such records, they do reflect real problems in terms of both reality and perception, and they shed light on strains in the relationship between the state and the church. Moreover, similar criticism can be found in the writings of Buddhist authors. For example, critiques of corrupt Buddhist clergy appear in the poems of the eighth-century Buddhist recluse and poet

Hanshan (n.d.). In one of his poems Hanshan mocks monastic greed and hypocrisy, evoking images similar to those found in Guishan's text. In another poem Hanshan contrasts virtuous monks with brazen impostors who enter the order without religious aspirations, and whose greed, ignorance, and evil acts will surely lead to rebirth in hell, a description that also parallels some of Guishan's critiques.[26]

Even though the problem of monastic corruption was a perennial issue and not unique to the ninth century, there was a sense of a steady worsening of the quality of the clergy that was related to the increase in its size. Part of the problem can be traced back to government's policy of selling ordination certificates in order to raise cash for its treasury.[27] Although the policy was introduced in 755 as an expedient measure after the outbreak of the An Lushan rebellion in order to raise revenue for military expenditures, the practice became widespread and had long-lasting ramifications. In the long run, the policy had serious adverse effects for both the state's finances and the well-being of the Buddhist church. Until the end of the dynasty, subsequent governments were unable to resist the lure of quick money, even though the release of large numbers of able-bodied adults from tax obligations had disastrous long-term effects on the economy and the state treasury. To make matters worse, unscrupulous local officials, who expanded their power and independence during the post-rebellion period, joined in the lucrative business of selling ordination certificates to anyone who could afford them.

The harsh realities that governed the lives of most people and the lack of opportunities for social advancement, coupled with the privileged status of the Buddhist clergy, caused many to enter the monastic order for reasons that had little to do with religious piety. A huge influx of people joined the Buddhist order simply to avoid paying taxes and being subjected to corvée labor.[28] The presence of large numbers of such fraudulent "monks" reinforced existing perceptions about monastic laxity and corruption. They posed a serious problem in terms of public perceptions of Buddhism, especially evident during the Huichang-era (841–846) persecution, when Wuzong was able to implement his harsh anti-Buddhist policies without strong opposition from the bureaucracy or the general public.

The contents of Guishan jingce reflect the gravity of such predicaments. The text acknowledges problems in the condition of the monastic order and draws attention to the need for serious reform, offering prescriptions and corrective measures that would lead to the improved quality of the clergy. Its somber and urgent tone reflects the quandary Buddhism found itself in during the Huichang-era persecution and its aftermath. The text acknowledges the pervasive problem of monastic laxity and corruption, but it also tries to make a case for the ultimate worth of monastic life and its value for society. These themes suggest that the text was probably created either during the early buildup to the persecution after Emperor Wu's ascent to the throne, when the monastic community was facing increased criticism, or during the persecution's aftermath, when Buddhist leaders were reflecting on the reasons for the maltreatment their religion was subjected to and were trying to make sure that key problems within the monastic community were properly addressed.

Ideas and Ideals

Critiques of Monastic Delinquency

Guishan's critiques of monastic abuses and wayward behavior are expressed against a backdrop of basic Buddhist teachings about karma, rebirth, and spiritual cultivation, even as they reflect the socioreligious peculiarities of Tang China. The text starts by evoking a basic Buddhist idea: the impermanence (C. *wuchang*; Skt. *anitya*) of physical existence. The first paragraph underscores the compounded nature of the physical body and the fact that change is the only permanent feature of human life. The same theme reappears in a number of later passages:

> Having received a body because of being bound by karma, one is not yet [able to] escape the troubles associated with physical existence. The body received from one's parents is formed by a multitude of causes. Although it is sustained by the four elements, they are constantly out of harmony with each other.[29] The impermanence of old age and illness does not await anyone. What has existed in morning is gone by evening. The world changes in an instant. [Physical existence] is like spring frost or morning dew, disappearing all of a sudden. Like a tree planted on a [river] bank or rattan growing in a well, how can it last for a long time?[30] Thoughts are flashing by quickly, within an instant, and with the passing of [each] breath there is new life.[31] How can you then peacefully and comfortably pass [your time] in vain?[32]

According to traditional Buddhist teachings, in order to break away from the cycle of mundane existence or *samsara* (*shengsi*), one needs to experience spiritual awakening and attain liberation. Customarily monastic life is regarded as the best venue for the cultivation of the spiritual virtues, experiences, and insights that bring about that realization. The text highlights the monastic distinction, pointing to the renunciation of normal family ties and social obligations as key markers of entry into the religious order:

> [Monks] do not supply their parents with tasty foods, and they steadfastly leave behind the six relations.[33] They cannot pacify their country and govern the state. They promptly give up their family's prop-

erty and do not continue the family line [by their failure to produce a male heir]. They leave far behind their local communities, and they shave their hair and follow their [religious] teachers. Inwardly they strive to conquer their thoughts, while outwardly they spread the virtue of noncontention. Abandoning the defiled world, they endeavor to transcend [the mundane realm of birth and death].³⁴

Reflecting the socioreligious milieu of late medieval China, the text acknowledges that a monk's choice to leave secular life and practice religion is a "privilege" granted by the ruler and the wider society, not an undeniable right to which individuals are automatically entitled. Monastic life is a viable vocation for those with spiritual aspirations only because the government and the general public offer support to the monastic order. Aware of the hackneyed criticism that monks eschew traditional Confucian-inspired duties toward the family and the country—which was leveled ad nauseam throughout the history of Buddhism in China—the text resorts to an equally conventional response by arguing that the monks' rejection of social conventions is justified by the lofty religious purpose of their renunciation. Even as monks turn their backs to time-honored social norms and values, by leading authentic religious lives they bring spiritual benefits to their families and the wider society. In light of those considerations, Guishan reminds his monastic audience of its indebtedness to others, and he strongly criticizes monks who abuse the privileges bestowed on them by failing to approach their religious vocation conscientiously:

> How can you declare "I am a monk" [C. biqiu; Skt. bhiṣsu] as soon as you receive the monastic precepts? The lay donors [C. tanyue; Skt. dānapati] provide the daily necessities and the monastery's permanent property [changzhu]. Without understanding or properly considering where they come from, you [mistakenly] assume they are supplied in a natural way, as a matter of fact. Having finished your meal, you gather in groups and noisily engage in rambling talk about worldly things. However, as you experience ephemeral pleasures, you do not know that pleasure is the cause of suffering. For a very long time you have been following defilements and have not yet tried to reflect inwardly. Time is passing in vain; months and years are wasted to no avail. You are receiving abundant offerings and sumptuous donations. In this way, years pass by without your intending to abandon [this way of life]. The [defilements] you accumulate grow more and more as you maintain the illusory body.³⁵
> The Guide [i.e., the Buddha] issued an injunction in which he admonished and encouraged the bhikṣus to progress along the way, be strict with their bodies, and [not be too concerned about] not having enough of the three requisites [of robes, food, and shelter]. Here, a

lot of people are addicted to favors without any repose. As days and months pass by, like the sound of the passing wind, they become white-haired [without noticing it].[36]

In a society where Buddhist institutions are entrenched and receive wide public support, entry into the monastic order automatically guarantees a certain level of economic security and removes the uncertainties of daily survival that characterize the existence of common people. In principle, such arrangements enable monks to lead pious lives dedicated to the pursuit of spiritual perfection. Nonetheless, that position can easily be abused and exploited for personal advantage. A number of passages in Guishan's treatise depict individuals who misuse monastic life by straying from the proper pursuit of their religious vocation and leading an indolent existence. Here is one of the early examples:

> Without having yet grasped the meaning of the teachings [of Buddhism], they cannot awaken to the recondite way. As they become old and accumulate monastic seniority, they become pretentious despite their poor abilities. Unwilling to draw near and rely on excellent [spiritual] mentors [lit. "friends"], such persons know of nothing else but being rude and conceited. Without being versed in the Dharma and the vinaya, they have no inhibitions whatsoever. Sometimes, with loud voices they engage in [useless] talk without any restraint. They do not respect their seniors, peers, or juniors. They are not different from a gathering of brahmins. [During meals] they make noise with their alms bowls, and they rise up first as soon as they have finished eating. As they leave in disorder or return in an inappropriate manner, their appearance is not at all that of monks. Rising from their seats in an agitated manner, they disturb other people's minds.[37]

According to Guishan, the failure of corrupt monks to learn the Buddhist teachings and acquire proper religious values posed serious structural problems for the monastic order. Under the monastic rules concerning seniority, which were further reinforced by the traditional Chinese respect for old age, such pseudo-monks eventually assumed positions of seniority in the monastic hierarchy, despite their lack of appropriate spiritual qualities. Such situations predisposed them to be even less malleable to positive influences, as they became arrogant and hopelessly set in their undisciplined ways. The text describes such monks as being without self-discipline or a sense of appropriate demeanor. Behaving in ways contrary to proper monastic decorum, the reader is told, such pseudo-monks created discord and problems for the entire monastic community:

Because [such corrupt monks] do not observe the small regulations and the minor rules of deportment, they cannot guide the new generation [of monks, as a result of which] new students have no one to emulate [as a model of proper behavior]. When others reprimand them, they say, "I am a mountain monk." Since they are unfamiliar with the sustained practice of Buddhism, their disposition and actions are constantly unbecoming and crude. When viewed in this way, should beginners become lazy and greedy persons, as time slowly slips by they will eventually become abominable persons. Unaware, they will in due course start staggering and become old and useless. When they encounter various circumstances, they [will not know what to do], like someone facing a wall. When asked [about the teachings of Buddhism] by younger students, they have no words of guidance. Even when they have something to say, their words do not accord with the scriptures. Sometimes, when younger monks speak lightly to them, they reprimand the younger monks for not having good manners. They become angry and rancorous, and they vent their anger on others.[38]

The situation described here had serious ramifications for the condition of Buddhism and the image of monks in Tang society. Monastic training is a gradual process in which younger monks learn by observing the examples and absorbing the instructions of their seniors. If senior monks are ignorant about the doctrines and practices of Buddhism, the younger generations of monks have nobody to learn from and are left without proper models to follow. Thus the failure to learn and abide by the teachings of Buddhism is not only a personal downfall but also a dereliction of the monks' duty to ensure the transmission of Buddhism to later generations. It is noteworthy that in the passages just cited, as well as in other places, the scriptures and the monastic code of discipline are identified as key sources of religious authority and legitimacy. This concept reflects Guishan's, and by extension the Chan school's, acceptance of a mainstream view prevalent in Tang Buddhism.

In a number of places the text reminds its audience of the dire consequences awaiting those who indulge in the kinds of reprehensible behaviors just described. Here is one example from the second section of the text:

One morning they will wake up lying sick in their beds, bothered and constrained by a multitude of ailments. From dawn until night they will keep on thinking, while in their minds there will be confusion and fear. The road ahead will be unclear, and they will not know where they are going. Even if, at that point, for the first time they become aware and remorseful of their faults, it will be of no avail; [being too late,] that is like digging a well after one becomes thirsty. They might have self-regret for not having practiced earlier and for having many faults and demerits at their old age. At the point of departure, having squandered [their whole life], they will tremble with fear and will be filled with panic. When someone crosses away from the living, like a sparrow flying away, his consciousness follows its karma. As when a person incurs debts, he will first come under pressure to pay back those who are powerful. In the same way, though there are many kinds of mental states in the mind, one inclines to descend into [a specific rebirth according to] the predominant part [of the defiled mind].[39] The murderous demon of impermanence does not stop for an instant. Life cannot be extended and time waits for no one. Nobody among the human beings and the gods living in the three realms of existence can escape this kind of destiny.[40] In this manner, one [is reborn and] receives a [new] body for untold eons.[41]

In a typical manner, the text describes the unfortunate circumstances that surround the end of a life that has been wasted in unworthy pursuits. According to the doctrines of karma and rebirth, an evil person who has led an immoral life while pretending to be a monk cannot expect to be reborn amid happy and favorable circumstances. In the preceding paragraph and elsewhere, Guishan uses popular teachings about the law of karma in a way familiar from Buddhist literature. He is urging rectification of immoral or improper behavior by restating traditional Buddhist views about the dire consequences of unwholesome acts. These are rather basic Buddhist teachings, reminding us that Chan teachers dealt with real people, with all their problems and failings, not just with the spiritual virtuosi whose images populate later writings about Tang Chan.

Exemplary Monastic Ideals

Much of Guishan's text focuses on censure of sundry abuses of monastic life, but its critiques are juxtaposed and contrasted with positive images of lofty monastic ideals. The text valorizes the religious act of "leaving home" and becoming a monk (C. *chujia*; Skt. *pravrajita*) and adopts a traditional image of monks as individuals who have left the mundane life in order to single-mindedly pursue the quest for spiritual perfection. Echoing traditional sentiments, the exemplary monk is depicted as an otherworldly ascetic dedicated to his practice and oblivious to the pull of material things and worldly pleasures. The image of monks presented in the text was familiar in Tang society. Such broadly defined standards of model religious behavior were recognized by both

the monastic order and the general public, even if they were not always followed in actual practice.

In keeping with received traditions and prevailing customs, Guishan contends that monastic identity and practice are intimately related to the observance of the *vinaya* (*lü*), the monastic code of discipline. The text describes the
role of monastic discipline as follows:

> The Buddha first established the *vinaya* and began to enlighten [his
> disciples]. The monastic regulations and the rules of dignified de-
> portment are pure like ice and snow. By observing the precepts and
> ceasing transgressions, [monks] control their initial [spiritual] re-
> solve. The detailed regulations correct all that is crude and unwhole-
> some. When someone has not yet gone to the teaching site of the
> *vinaya* [*pini faxi*],[42] how can he evaluate the superior vehicle of the
> definitive meaning [*liaoyi shangsheng*]? It is such a pity when a whole
> lifetime is passed in vain. Regretting afterwards about missed oppor-
> tunities will be of little avail.[43]

Here the *vinaya* is presented as the foundation of authentic religious life.
Following a long-established tradition, the text affirms that observance of the
monastic precepts leads to a lifestyle that is conducive to the development and
maintenance of proper religious aspiration. Ethical observance is also described as an essential condition for realizing the highest doctrines of Buddhism, including the ultimate teaching of the "superior vehicle." Guishan
having established the importance of monastic discipline, in the third section
of the text is found this explanation of the correct reasons for "leaving home"
and becoming a monk:

> Those who have left home [i.e., monks], having set off toward the
> transcendental direction, differ from laypeople in both their mind
> and their external appearance. They cause the seed of sanctity [i.e.,
> the seed of Buddhahood] to continue to flourish and make Mara's
> armies tremble with fear.[44] They repay the four kinds of benevolence
> and save those living in the three worlds.[45] If you are not like that,
> then you falsely pretend to be a member of the monastic order.[46]

The monastic distinction implies a clear line of separation between monks
and ordinary people. Monks differ in their external appearance, their values,
and the goals to which they dedicate their lives. In the preceding paragraph,
the text offers another brief rejoinder to the previously noted criticism that
monks are not filial and properly socialized in a conventional (namely Confucian) sense. It does so by adopting a standard Buddhist argument, namely
that through their spiritual practice monks repay the depth of gratitude they
owe to four key constituencies: their parents, the ruler, the people who sup-

ported them, and the Buddha. By embodying and actively propagating the teachings of Buddhism, they ensure their continued transmission and aid the spiritual salvation of their fellow human beings. Guishan then goes on to offer some practical advice about how to cultivate a genuine monastic disposition:

> Having left your relatives, when with a determined [spiritual] resolve you put on the monastic robes,[47] where are your thoughts and aspirations directed? Think about it from dawn until night—how can you afford to pass your time procrastinating? A person of great ability who has set his mind on the Buddha's teachings becomes an exemplar to the latecomers [to religious life]. [But even if] you are always like that, you will still not be able to [fully] accord [with the truth]. When speaking, your words should accord with the scriptures. In conversation, you should depend on the examination and study of the records of ancient exemplars. Your appearance and conduct should be outstanding, and your spirit should be lofty and peaceful.[48]

The text continues to reiterate familiar monastic themes and ideals. Again, we find monks described as individuals who have left secular life and are concerned solely with the quest for enlightenment. We are also once more reminded that the basic criteria of proper spiritual understanding are the Buddhist scriptures. Individual behavior is to be modeled on the actions and sayings of ancient exemplars of Buddhist perfection, as recorded in Buddhist literature. All of these statements are those of a person with deep respect for tradition, someone who defines the monastic vocation in fairly conventional terms. Here we are far removed from the familiar figure of the Chan iconoclast, who is usually portrayed as someone who flaunts tradition and rejects conventional religious authority. The significance of the monastic tradition, and especially the central role of spiritual teachers, is further described in the following paragraph:

> A journey to a distant place should be undertaken with the help of good friends, and one needs to purify one's ears and eyes again and again. When journeying and when stopping, one must select [suitable] companions, always listening to [teachings] he has not heard before. Therefore, it has been said, "I was born by my mother and father, but I was perfected by my [spiritual] friends."[49] Drawing close to and associating with the virtuous is like walking in mist or dew—though the clothes do not become wet, there is always dampness. Becoming influenced by those who are evil leads to the increase of evil knowledge and views. Performing evil from morning to night, one directly meets retribution, and after death one drowns and perishes [to be reborn in the evil realms]. Once the human body is lost,

it [might be] impossible to regain it for myriad eons. Sincere words
are not pleasing to the ear, but how can you fail to inscribe them in
your hearts. Then you can cleanse your mind [of defilements] and
cultivate your virtue, retire into obscurity and conceal your name,
and collect your spirit, so that there is an end to all [mental] noise.[50]

Here the text stresses the importance of spiritual mentors (or friends, C.
shan zhihshi; Skt. *kalyāṇa-mitra*),[51] which typically refers to monks' spiritual
teachers. By extension, the term can also be applied to other monks who provide support and guidance along the path of practice and realization. Such a
sense of monastic camaraderie is notably expressed in the text's final exhortations, which include the following passage: "When you deeply know your
faults and suffering, then you can encourage each other to persevere with your
practice. Make a vow that for the next hundred eons and thousand lives you
will everywhere be spiritual companions [*falü*] to each other."[52]

Echoing comparable passages in the *agamas* and the Mahayāna scriptures,
Guishan advises his monks to associate with spiritual mentors and be constantly willing to learn from them. Likewise, he advises them to avoid evil
people, lest they are influenced by them and led astray from the path. In case
the audience forgets, they are again reminded about the workings of the law
of karma and the unfortunate consequences of unwholesome actions. Similar
sentiments are reiterated in the text's concluding exhortations. There Guishan
yet again implores his monastic audience to engender an ardent determination
to practice the teachings of Buddhism, and he urges them to examine and
perfect their daily conduct:

I sincerely hope that you will establish a determined [spiritual] aspiration and will engender an exceptional frame of mind. In terms of
your conduct, you should emulate those who are superior to you
and do not arbitrarily follow those who are mediocre and superficial.
You must make a resolution [to achieve liberation] in this lifetime,
and you should presume that no other person could do it for you.
Putting your mind to rest and forgetting external conditions, do not
oppose the various defilements. When the mind is empty and external objects are quiescent, one cannot pass through only because of
being stuck for a long time [into deeply ingrained habitual patterns].
You should earnestly read this text and exhort yourself at all times.[53]

Here monks are once more advised to set their minds on lofty religious
goals and model their behavior on suitable exemplars. As they emulate those
who embody genuine spiritual virtues, they are also to dissociate themselves
from those who lack such attributes. The last quoted passage also offers brief
instructions about how to deal with mental defilements that are reminiscent
of passages in other Chan texts. Monks are advised that opposing or trying to

obliterate mental defilements is futile, because such effort is based on misapprehension of the nonsubstantial and illusory nature of the defilements. Instead of trying to obliterate essentially nonexistent defilements, which reifies them even more, one is simply to put the mind to rest and let it return to a pristine state of purity, which is the mind's original condition before the bifurcation of dualistic thoughts set in. That notion leads to a key issue: the connection between the ethical norms and monastic ideals described in the text and the practice of Chan.

Chan Practice and Realization

So far there has been hardly anything in the text that is distinctive of the Chan school. Its descriptions of the monastic ideal resonate with those in other Indian and Chinese works on morality and monasticism. Guishan's views about monastic life come across as fairly conventional and are in general agreement with mainstream notions prevalent at the time. It is only in the fourth section that the text introduces ideas and concepts that are characteristic of Chan. The section starts with a brief exposition of Chan practice as a path that leads to direct realization of reality:

> If you want to practice Chan and study the Way, then you should
> suddenly go beyond the expedient teachings. You should harmonize
> your mind with the arcane path, explore the sublime wonders,[54]
> make final resolution of the recondite [meaning], and awaken to the
> source of truth. You should also extensively ask for instructions
> from those who have foresight and should get close to virtuous
> friends. The sublime wonder of this teaching [zong] is difficult to
> grasp—one must pay attention very carefully. If someone can sud-
> denly awaken to the correct cause, then he is at the stage of leaving
> defilement behind. He then shatters the three worlds and twenty-
> five forms of existence.[55] Such a person knows that all phenomena,
> internal and external, are not real—arising from mind's transforma-
> tions, they are all provisional designations. There is no need to an-
> chor the mind anywhere. When feelings merely do not attach to
> things, then how can things hinder anyone? Let the nature of other
> things flow freely, without [interfering by] trying to break apart or
> extend anything. The sounds that one hears and the forms that one
> sees are all ordinary; whether being here or there, one freely re-
> sponds to circumstances without any fault.[56]

This description of the Chan path accords with formulations found in other texts associated with the Hongzhou school. Its conception of practice and awakening is reminiscent of Guishan's record,[57] and it also resonates with passages from the sermons of Mazu, Baizhang, and Huangbo. A number of terms used at the beginning of the paragraph—such as "practice Chan" (*can-chan*), "study the Way" (*xuedao*), "harmonize the mind" (*xinqi*), "awaken to the source of truth" (*wu zhenyuan*), "sudden awakening" (*dunwu*)—also appear in the sermons of other Chan teachers. Likewise, key ideas expressed in the paragraph—such as the unreal and mind-created nature of phenomena, and the keeping of an unattached mind that does not interfere with the natural flow of things—are familiar themes to students of Tang Chan. What is more, parts of this paragraph parallel passages from one of Guishan's sermons.[58] For example, the expression "feelings do not attach to things" (*jing bufu wu*) appears in both texts, while the sentence, "The sounds that one hears and the forms that one sees are all ordinary" is similar to a sentence from the sermon, which states: "What one sees and hears at any time is ordinary."[59]

Guishan jingce describes the teachings of Chan as an apex of Buddhist religiosity. In the previous quotation we are told that the practice of Chan leads to sudden awakening, through which one transcends the realm of ignorance and realizes the true nature of reality. The text then goes on to draw connection between the realization of Chan's soteriological goal and the points about monastic attitudes and aims made in the previous sections:

> When someone acts in this manner, he does not put on the monastic robe in vain. Furthermore, such a person repays the four kinds of benevolence and liberates those living in the three worlds. If lifetime after lifetime he can continue [practicing] without giving up, it is definitely plausible to expect that he will reach the stage of Buddhahood. As a guest who keeps on coming and going in the three realms, appearing and disappearing, he serves as a model for others. This one teaching is most sublime and most profound. Just discern the affirmation of your own mind and you will certainly not be deceived.[60]

The monk who perfects the Chan path is presented as a paradigmatic exemplar of authentic religiosity, someone who embodies the monastic ideals described in the previous pages. Having achieved a measure of sanctity, finally he repays the depth of gratitude he owes to others, is able to offer expert spiritual guidance, and serves as a model of religious excellence. It is noteworthy that in contrast to the subitist rhetoric evidenced in the previous paragraph, here we are presented with a more realistic assessment of the human ability to realize spiritual perfection. The text accedes that Buddhahood can be realized if one practices diligently, but it also notes that the realization of that ultimate goal might take a number of lifetimes. Apparently ninth-century monks acknowledged that in reality only a few exceptional individuals were able to achieve the main goals of spiritual practice within a single lifetime. Those who did so were deemed to have joined the ranks of Buddhist saints.

Chan teachers commanded great respect precisely because their spiritual accomplishments were considered to be exceptional, notwithstanding the recurring rhetoric about the accessibility of the experience of enlightenment found in Chan literature.

From such a perspective, sudden awakening is only the beginning of a long and essentially gradual process of spiritual cultivation that culminates with the realization of Buddhahood. This paradigm evokes the theory of sudden enlightenment followed by gradual cultivation advocated by Zongmi (780–841).[61] A similar idea also appears in Guishan's record, where he states that a person who has experienced sudden awakening still needs to continue his spiritual cultivation so that he can gradually remove ingrained karmic tendencies and habitual mental patterns:

> There was a monk who asked the Master [i.e.. Guishan], "Does a
> person who has had sudden awakening still need to continue with
> cultivation?" The Master said, "If one has true awakening and at
> tains to the fundamental, then at that time that person knows for
> himself that cultivation and noncultivation are just dualistic oppo
> sites. Like now, though the initial inspiration is dependent on condi
> tions, if within a single thought one awakens to one's own reality,
> there are still certain habitual tendencies that have accumulated over
> numberless kalpas which cannot be purified in a single instant. That
> person should certainly be taught how to gradually remove the kar
> mic tendencies and mental habits: this is cultivation. There is no
> other method of cultivation that needs to be taught to that person."[62]

In contrast to other Chan texts, in which lofty subitist rhetoric is dissociated from actual everyday behavior and experience, Guishan's treatise displays sensitivity to the realities of religious life. Its main concern is not to present an idealized vision of a spiritual path for the religious virtuosi—in Chan parlance referred to as those of "highest abilities"—in which there is sole emphasis on immediate insight into the nature of reality. Rather, the text shows concern for all those who do not belong to that exalted category, namely the actual monks of Guishan's and other monasteries, many of whom had trouble observing even the basic injunctions of religious life. In contrast to the encounter-dialogue stories about sudden and spontaneous experiences of awakening that are the best-known parts of Chan literature, Guishan's text presents a more realistic picture of religious life and offers practical exhortations about the immediate concerns of ordinary monks.

Chan teachings about sudden awakening might serve as inspiring religious ideals and may perhaps animate spiritual practice, but for most people they remain remote ideas that do not necessarily tally with their everyday experiences. Notwithstanding the Chan school's efforts to demystify and bring down to earth the experience of enlightenment, for most that is still an abstract ideal that offers little practical guidance about actual daily conduct and practice. For monks who do not belong to the highest-ranking category of spiritual virtuosi capable of making the sudden leap into the recondite realm of enlightenment—which is to say, for most monks—the text offers the following advice:

> Those of average abilities, who have not been able suddenly to go beyond [the expedient teachings], should pay attention to the doctrinal teachings [jiaofa]. They should review and rummage in the palm leaves of the scriptures and thoroughly inquire into their principles. [Furthermore, they should also] hand them down to others from mouth to mouth and should expound and make them known, thus guiding the younger generations and repaying the Buddha's benevolence. They should, moreover, not waste their time in vain, but they must in this manner uphold [the teachings of Buddhism]. When someone has dignified conduct in all postures and activities, then he is a monk who is worthy and able to receive the teachings. Have you not seen dolichos leaning on a pine tree, rising upward for a thousand xun?[63] When someone depends and relies on superior causes, then he can obtain extensive benefits.[64]

Ordinary monks are advised that the expedient teachings of traditional Buddhism provide the best approach to religious cultivation. Monks unable to "suddenly transcend the expedient teachings" are encouraged to study and reflect on the doctrines of Buddhism, as presented in the scriptures. They are also advised to become involved in the propagation and transmission of Buddhism and are reminded that they should lead exemplary lives worthy of respect. Although all practices are forsaken at the moment of awakening, those who had not attained such a level of spiritual attainment are urged to cultivate traditional practices such as those noted earlier. At the end of its brief discussion of Chan practice in the fourth section, the text returns to its main theme, the importance of morality and monastic discipline:

> Earnestly practice the pure precepts, without deception, deficiency, and transgression. From lifetime to lifetime there are outstanding and sublime causes and effects. You cannot afford to pass your days aimlessly, letting time go by in a haze. It is a pity when time is wasted without seeking [spiritual] progress. Consuming the offerings of the faithful from the ten directions in vain, such people also fail to repay the four kinds of benevolence. They accumulate [evil karma] and [their ignorance] gets progressively deeper, while their minds' impurities are apt to obstruct [their spiritual development]. Whichever way they try to go, they come to a standstill, and they are disparaged and ridiculed by other people. Therefore it has been said, "He is already a man, and so am I; there is no need to belittle one-

self and shrink back."⁶⁵ If someone is not like that, then he has entered the monastic order in vain; as he lets his whole life to slip by, really he obtains no benefit whatsoever.⁶⁶

At the end of the fourth section, the text again underscores the importance of monastic rules, practices, and observances. It encourages monks not to shrink back from the challenging religious task that awaits them. They are also reminded—with a quotation from Mengzi!—that the Buddha and other great monks of the past were not special or supernatural beings. Ancient sages faced the same obstacles, but they were able to overcome them with wholehearted effort and persistent practice. Only through emulation of their example, declares the text, does a monk's entry into the monastic order acquire true value and meaning, and can he bring benefit to himself and to others.

Attitudes toward Discipline and Morality

Generally speaking, the rules of monastic discipline fulfill several basic functions. First, they serve as communal precepts that regulate the monks' daily life and ensure good working order in the monastery. In that sense, they form a communal charter that organizes monastic life by facilitating an environment and institutional setting that reflect received religious values, beliefs, and doctrines. Thereby the rules codify an institutional system that is conducive to monks' communal pursuit of their vocation. In addition, monastic rules also serve as guidelines for proper individual conduct, molding each monk's internal and external attitudes and reinforcing his commitment to a religious way of life.⁶⁷ As such, monastic rules provide a broad contextual framework for spiritual life and practice, fostering an appropriate mind-set and nurturing mores conducive to pursuit of hallowed religious goals, as understood and accepted by the whole community.

Besides prescriptions for virtuous behavior, monastic regulations also contain proscriptions and punishments for acts deemed improper and unbecoming for a monk. Punishments for monastic transgressions are a feature common to both *vinaya* literature and the additional systems of rules devised by medieval Chinese monks, which were meant to supplement the *vinaya* regulations. A prominent example is Zhiyi's (538–597) *Li zhifa* (*Establishing Regulations*), written for his community on Tiantai mountain. Punishments mentioned in the text include ritual bowing for lesser infractions and expulsion from the community for serious offenses.⁶⁸ Similar punishments are also prescribed in Xuefeng Yicun's (822–908) *Shi guizhi* (*Teacher's Regulations*), the oldest extant monastic rule composed by a Chan teacher.⁶⁹

As was already noted, *Guishan jingce*'s entreaties and instructions about how to lead a disciplined life dedicated to the study, practice, and realization of the truths of Buddhism indicate that its author largely conceived of monastic life in traditional, mainstream terms. In the treatise is found concern for both the communal and personal facets of monastic life. There is an emphasis on the harmonious functioning of the whole monastic community, but also a stress on the purity of an individual monk's religious aspiration and his commitment to a disciplined way of life. The communal and personal aspects are not really separable, given that smooth operation of the monastic community depends on an individual monk's espousal of shared religious values and his commitment to a collective pursuit of the tradition's ideals. As Guishan's text makes clear, such unity of purpose was apparently not easy to achieve, especially in light of the large number of people with diverse motives and predilections who entered the monastic order. The text exemplifies some of the difficulties and challenges faced by Guishan and other monastic leaders in ninth-century China as they tried to fashion and guide communities that in both spirit and practice embodied the central values of Buddhist monasticism.

Guishan jingce provides us with valuable information about the relationship between monastic precepts and conventional morality on the one hand and Chan's soteriological program on the other. The text presupposes a two-tiered path of practice and realization. The higher level, associated with the teachings of Chan, is centered on the notion of radical detachment and transcendence of the mundane realm of delusion and defilement. As described in the text's fourth section, at that level the adept perfects complete detachment, which leads to an immediate, nonconceptual realization of reality. The notion of sudden awakening thus plays a pivotal role in Chan's soteriological schema, serving as a guiding principle and denoting a key spiritual experience. Reflecting an outlook prevalent within Chan circles, awakening is understood as a pinnacle of the Path, a high point when diverse spiritual qualities and practices are merged into a holistic whole, which implies a balance between spiritual insight and everyday activity.

Notwithstanding the call for radical transcendence invoked by the Chan ideal, the text repeatedly makes it clear that normative monastic practices and observances are the foundation of authentic spirituality. Together with other traditional practices, such as study and reflection on the scriptures, they form a comprehensive and progressive regimen of spiritual cultivation. As such, they constitute the second, conventional level of the Path. This level is meant for all those who are unable to "suddenly go beyond the expedient teachings" and directly realize the ultimate truth. Monastic observances and traditional practices, according to the text, enable an aspiring monk to develop spiritually and thus validate his existence, perhaps even reaching a point where he can make the final jump into the abstruse realm of awakening.

Guishan jingce presents a religious vision in which monastic discipline is integrated into Chan practice by simultaneously asserting and collapsing two levels of religious discourse: the radical nondualism of Chan doctrine on the one hand, and conventional teachings about monastic practices and observance on the other. The conception of Chan soteriology implied here revolves around the relationship between these two approaches, which can be termed "sudden" and "conventional," or perhaps "gradual," following the terminology popularized by the sudden versus gradual debates. Traditionalist interpretations of Tang Chan, especially of the Hongzhou school, as an iconoclastic tradition presuppose a wide and potentially unbridgeable gap between the two approaches. That is based on the notion that the "sudden" method inevitably implies a rejection of all "expedient means," including traditional moral observance and spiritual practices.

The contents of *Guishan jingce* make it clear that such interpretation is not tenable. According to the text, these two methods are not diametrically opposed or mutually exclusive. Both of them constitute viable approaches to spiritual cultivation, which complement and reinforce each other. Such outlooks resonate with prior Chan texts, including the earliest records of the Hongzhou school. Its conceptual scheme is also reminiscent of Bodhidharma's treatise on two entrances and four practices, *Erru sixing lun*, regarded as the first text of proto-Chan. There the sudden-like approach of "entry through principle" (*liru*) and the more conventional approach of "entry through practice" (*xingrui*) are both presented as viable methods of spiritual cultivation.[70]

According to *Guishan jingce*, the realization of awakening is not divorced from the broader context of monastic life. The text concurs that at the moment of awakening the adept transcends all beliefs, doctrines, and practices, but such experience takes place within the context of disciplined monastic life. Chan practice is therefore integrated within the overall religious principles and institutional structures of Buddhist monasticism. Admittedly, there is a seeming sense of incongruity with Chan school's radical subitist rhetoric, especially its call to transcend conventional practices as well as the injunction to observe monastic discipline. However, such contradictions are more apparent than real. According to the present text and other documents from the Tang period, it was understood in Chan circles that the detachment and transcendence associated with the experience of awakening did not imply an antinomian abandon and rejection of conventional moral norms (although there were exceptions to that rule, such as the Baotang school in Sichuan). With the attainment of spiritual realization, ethical norms are simply internalized and integrated into a state of heightened awareness and insight.

In contrast to a popular view of late Tang Chan as an iconoclastic tradition, *Guishan jingce* shows how the Hongzhou school's conception of Chan practice was grounded in the religious and institutional milieus of medieval monasticism. The moral basis of practice was constituted by the precepts and mores of Buddhist monasticism. In terms of their attitudes toward ethical observances, Chan teachers and their followers did not depart significantly from time-honored monastic norms and ideals. In that sense, the contents of *Guis-*

han jingce provide evidence in support of a broader argument about the close relationship between Chan monasteries and other forms of Buddhist monasticism in ninth-century China.

We might conclude that monastic discipline and Chan practice were perceived as two complementary aspects of a comprehensive religious system. Each of them addressed a particular facet of religious life, together forming an integrated vision of a progressive path of practice and realization. On a communal level, monastic discipline provided an institutional context for the quest for spiritual awakening. On a personal level, ethical observances instilled attitudes that reinforced religious commitments and sustained spiritual cultivation. In a sense, the sudden awakening paradigm was complementary to the monastic regimen, providing a soteriological framework that imbued everyday life with a higher sense of purpose. That implied the integration of Chan's particular soteriological scheme with the values and practices of the broader monastic tradition.

For Guishan and his contemporaries, adherence to monastic mores and observances was an essential part of their tradition. Far from rejecting traditional monasticism, late-Tang Chan was very much an integral part of it. Therefore, in order to make sense of Chan doctrine and practice, we must take into account the institutional and religious contexts that produced and sustained them, which point to no other than the medieval world of Chinese Buddhist monasticism.

ABBREVIATIONS

CDL   *Jingde chuandeng lu.* 30 *chüan,* in T 51, 2076.
JTS   *Jiu tangshu* (Beijing: Zhonghua shuju, 1975).
QTW   *Quan tangwen* (Shanghai: Shanghai guji chubanshe, 1990).
SGSZ   *Song gaoseng zhuan,* in T 50, 2061
XTS   *Xin tangshu* (Beijing: Zhonghua shuju, 1975).

NOTES

1. For a photographic reproduction of the original manuscript, see *Dunhuang baozang,* no. 134:91–92 (Taipei: Xinwenfeng chuban gongsi, 1981–1986).

2. This rendition of *Xinxin ming* is also the oldest extant version of this popular text. For the standard version, see T no. 48:376–377. For more information about the Dunhuang version of *Xinxin ming,* see Tanaka Ryōshō, *Tonkō zenshū bunken no kenkyū* (Tokyo: Daitō shuppansha, 1983), pp. 297–300.

3. Tanaka, *Tonkō zenshū bunken no kenkyū,* pp. 337–338 (see also idem, "Genoshoshu to sareru Tonko hon *Daii kyosaku* ni tsuite," *Indogaku bukkyōgaku kenkyū* 22/2 [1974], pp. 630–635, which is the original article on which that chapter is based). The other two versions of the text—in QTW and XZJ—are quite similar. Noting a large number of different characters in the Dunhuang manuscript when compared with the later versions, Tanaka suggests two explanations for those discrepancies: copying er-

rors in the Dunhuang manuscript, or the possibility that the editors of the later versions changed the text at certain places in light of their own views about Chan doctrine.

4. Tanaka, *Tonkō zenshū bunken no kenkyū*, pp. 300, 339–340.

5. See CDL 11, T no. 51:281c, and Tanaka, *Tonkō zenshū bunken no kenkyū*, p. 341. Unfortunately, virtually nothing is known about this monk. The other four monks identified by Tanaka are: (1) Chan teacher Xuanquan Yen of Huaizhou, (2) Ruiyan Shiyan of Taizhou, (3) Yaoshan Zhongyan, and (4) Pengyan of Anguo Zhangshou temple in Suzhou.

6. This scenario is postulated in view of the warfare and strife that surrounded the gradual collapse of the Tang dynasty, and the ensuing political divisions during the early decades of the tenth century.

7. QTW no. 919:4243b–44b; T no.48:1042b–43c, and XZJ no. 111:142c–48d. A Japanese translation of *Guishan jingce* can be found in Kajitani Sōnin, "Isan kyōsaku," in Nishitani Keiji and Yanagida Seizan, eds., *Zenka goroku*, vol. 2 (Tokyo: Chikuma shobō, 1974), pp. 141–151. Kajitani has another Japanese rendition with the same title in Nishitani Keiji, ed., *Zen no koten: Chūgoku* (Tokyo: Chikuma shobō, 1968), pp. 151–174. There is also an earlier rendition in Tomitani Tyūkei, trans., "Butsuso sankyō kōgi," in *Sōtō-shū kōgi*, vol. 3 (Tokyo: Kokusho kankōkai, 1975; orig. ed. published in 1928), pp. 175–243. Kajitani and Tomitani both do not offer proper Japanese translations of the text. Instead, they present *yomikudashi* readings of the original, followed by notes and running commentaries, both of which are much more extensive in Tomitani's work. There are also English translations in Mario Poceski, "The Hongzhou School During the Mid-Tang Period" (Ph.D. diss., UCLA, 2000), pp. 456–485, and Melvin M. Takemoto, "The Kuei-shan ching-ts'e: Morality in the Hung-chou School of Ch'an" (M.A. thesis, University of Hawaii, 1983), pp. 79–90.

8. For the text of Shousui's *stupa* inscription (accompanied with a Japanese translation), see Ishii Shūdō, *Sōdai zenshūshi no kenkyū* (Tokyo: Daitō shuppansha, 1987), pp. 479–490. Shousui's commentary is rather brief and not particularly helpful.

9. The other two texts included in the collection are two popular scriptures, *Fo yijiao jing* (*Scripture concerning the Buddha's Bequeathed Teaching*) and *Sishier zhang jing* (*Scripture in Forty-two Sections*), which are also accompanied by Shousui's commentaries.

10. XZJ no. 59:185c–91c. This text contains the same three texts found in Shousui compilation. Daopei is also known as the compiler of *Huayanjing shulun*, which includes the eighty fascicles translation of the *Huayan* scripture together with the two famous commentaries written during the Tang dynasty, by Li Tongxuan (635–730) and Chengguan (738–839).

11. The main source for Guishan's life is Zheng Yu's (n.d.) stele inscription, *Tanzhou Daguishan Tongqingsi Dayuan chanshi beiming bingxu*, in QTW no. 820:3832c, and *Tang wencui* no. 63:6b–8b (Hangzhou: Zhejiang renmin chubanshe, 1986; vol. 2). The inscription was composed in 866, thirteen years after Guishan's death, following the bestowal of imperial title to him in 863 and the construction of his memorial pagoda in 865. Other sources are his biographies in SGSZ 11, T no. 50:777a–b, CDL 9, T no. 51:264b–66a, and *Zutang ji* 16 (Changsha: Yuelu shushe, 1996), pp. 359–363.

12. CDL 9, T no. 51:264b.

13. According to the *Zutang ji* biography, before his journey to Jiangxi, Guishan briefly visited Tiantai mountain and Guoqing monastery, the center of the Tiantai school. There he met with Hanshan and Shide, the two famous recluses and poets. *Zutang ji* 16, p. 360. The same story is also recorded in Guishan's biography in SGSZ 11, T no. 50:777b.

14. Following the CDL biography. However, according to the SGSZ biography, he resided in Changsha until about 820, when he moved to the nearby Gui mountain (also located in Changsha prefecture).

15. Guishan's stele inscription states that Pei Xiu and Guishan met in 846. For Pei's official biographies, see JTS no. 177:4592–4593, and XTS no. 182:5371–5372. For a study of his life that places substantial emphasis on his Buddhist activities, see Yoshikawa Tadao, "Hai Kyū den: Tōdai no ichi shidaifu to bukkyō," *Tōhō gakuhō* 64 (1992): 115–277.

16. According to *Tanzhou daguishan zhongxing ji*, included in *Shimen weizi chan*, *Zenshū zensho* 95, p. 282a, Pei Xiu donated a landed estate to Guishan's monastic community to supply the monks with food provisions. Relevant passages from this text are also quoted in Yoshikawa, "Hai Kyū den," p. 165. See also *Tangwen cui* no. 63: 7a (vol. 2); QTW no. 820:3832c; CTL 9, T no. 51:264c, and Jeffrey Broughton, "Kuei-feng Tsung-mi: Convergence of Ch'an and the Teaching" (Ph.D. diss., Columbia University, 1975), p. 35.

17. See SGSZ 11, T no. 50:777c. It was in response to Li's petition that the court granted the name Tongqing to Guishan's monastery. See SGSZ 11, T no. 50:777c, and Yoshikawa, "Hai Kyū den," p. 164. For Li's biographies, see JTS no. 187b:4891–4892, and XTS no. 177:5290–5291.

18. For Cui, see JTS no. 177:4577–4580.

19. Biographies in JTS no. 163:4271–4273 and XTS no. 177:5284–5285. Lu was also the author of the stele inscription for Mazu's disciple Yanguan Jian; see QTW no. 733:3354b–c, and *Wenyuan yinghua* no. 868:4578a–4579a (Beijing: Zhonghua shuju, 1966).

20. Li's biographies are in JTS no. 190c:5077–5078 and XTS no. 203:5792–5793. He was also the author of an inscription that commemorates Mazu, Xitang, Wuxiang, and Wuzhu; see QTW no. 780:3608b–3609c. Lu's composition of Guishan's inscription and Li's writing of the calligraphy are also noted in Guishan's biography in SGSZ 11, T no. 50:777c.

21. The earliest mention of Guiyang as a separate Chan lineage (*pai*) is in Fayan Wenyi's (885–958) *Zongmen shigui lun*, XZJ no. 110:439d, where it is mentioned along with the Deshan, Linji, Caodong, Xuefeng, and Yunmen lineages.

22. For Guishan's record of sayings, see *Tanzhou Guishan Lingyou chanshi yulu*, T no. 47:577–582, and XZJ no. 119:425c–430c. It is part of *Wujia yulu*, a collection of the records of sayings of the putative "founders" of the five schools of Chan that were recognized during the early Song period.

23. For example, Huangbo's hagiographies contain no mention of his *Chuanxin fayao*, even though the text was compiled by Pei Xiu soon after Huangbo's death and was subsequently circulated within Chan circles.

24. See XZJ no. 59:185d. Kajitani and Tomitani also follow this division of the text.

25. The following passage from a decree issued in 731 is typical of the criticisms aimed against the monastic order: "[Monks] benefit from the privileges of their class and, thus shielded, enrich themselves. It is to no avail that they are exempted from taxes and covrée services. They pile up deception. They are roaming laymen who go about the business of magicians, straining their discourse and thinking" (*Cefu yuangui* no. 159: 17a). Translation adapted from Jacques Gernet, *Buddhism in Chinese Society: An Economic History from the Fifth to the Tenth Centuries*, trans., Franciscus Verellen (New York: Columbia University Press, 1995), p. 198. For Wuzong's anti-Buddhist edicts, see Stanley Weinstein, *Buddhism Under the T'ang* (Cambridge, Mass: Cambridge University Press, 1987), pp. 126–129.

26. Iritani Sensuke and Matsumura Takashi, trans., *Kanzan shi* (Tokyo: Chikuma shobō, 1970), pp. 370–375. See also Robert G. Henricks, trans., *The Poetry of Hanshan: A Complete, Annotated Translation of Cold Mountain* (Albany, N.Y.: State University of New York Press, 1990), pp. 372–373.

27. For a discussion of the sale of ordination certificates during the Tang period, see Chikusa Masaaki, *Chūgoku bukkyō shakaishi kenkyū* (Tokyo: Dōhōsha, 1982), pp. 19–27.

28. See Weinstein, *Buddhism Under the T'ang*, pp. 59–69. For Buddhist clergy's exemption from taxes and corvée labor, see Gernet, *Buddhism in Chinese Society*, pp. 30–36.

29. The four elements are water, air, fire, and earth.

30. The simile of a tree precariously standing on a riverbank comes from the "Shouming" chapter of the *Nirvāṇa Scripture* (reference comes from Tomitani, trans., "Butsuso sankyō kōgi," p. 174). The simile of the rattan growing in a well comes from *Bintoulu wei wang shuofa jing*, T no. 32:787a.

31. An alternative translation of the final clause reads, "With the last breath a new life begins."

32. T no. 48:1042b; XZJ no. 111:142d–143b.

33. The six relations are mother, father, elder brothers (siblings), younger brothers (siblings), wife, and children.

34. T no. 48:1042b–c; XZJ no. 111:143b.

35. The first part of the sentence can also be interpreted to mean "the [material possessions] you accumulate grow more and more."

36. T no. 48:1042c; XZJ no. 111:143–144a.

37. T no. 48:1042c; XZJ no. 111:144b–c.

38. T no. 48:1042c; XZJ no. 111:144c–d.

39. The translation is tentative. The literal translation of the original text is, "they have a tendency to sink into the heavy part."

40. The three realms of existence (also referred to as the "three worlds") are the realm of desire, the realm of form, and the formless realm. According to Buddhist beliefs, everyone is reborn in one of the three realms in circumstances that are dictated by his or her previous karma.

41. T no. 48:1042c; XZJ no. 111:144d–145b.

42. Meaning he has not yet learned the *vinaya* and put it into practice.

43. T no. 48:1042c; XZJ no. 111:144a–b.

44. Mara is the Buddhist personification of evil. He is usually depicted as trying to interrupt or prevent the spiritual progress of Buddhist practitioners.

45. The four kinds of benevolence are directed toward the Buddha, the ruler of the country, one's parents, and one's donors. Sometimes they are also defined as benevolence toward one's parents, all living beings, the rulers of the country, and the three treasures of Buddhism (the Buddha, the Dharma, and the *Sangha*).

46. T no. 48:1043a; XZJ no. 111:145c.

47. Literally "puts on black," the color of the robes Chan monks wore at that time.

48. T no. 48:1043a; XZJ no. 111:146a.

49. The quotation is based on a passage from the biography of Guan Zhong in *Shiji* no. 62:2136. Guan Zhong and Yan Ying, whose biographies form fascicle 62 of *Shiji*, were the two famous ministers of the state of Ji during the Warning States period (c. 403–221 B.C). The same quote also appears in Yaoshan's biography in *Zutang ji* 4, p. 106, where it is attributed to Baizhang.

50. T no. 48:1043a; XZJ no. 111:146a–c.

51. The importance of spiritual mentors is strongly stressed throughout the various Buddhist traditions. For examples from the Pali canon, see the *Anguttara Nikaya* (*Pali Text Society edition*), vol. 1, pp. 8, 15, and vol. 2, p. 9. In China, the best-known description of the role of spiritual mentors is the story of the pilgrimage of Sudhana, told in the last chapter of the *Huayan Scripture*, "Ru fajie pin" (Entering the Realm of Reality), T no. 9:676a–788b and T no. 10:319a–444c.

52. T no. 48:1042b; XZJ no. 111:147d–148b.

53. T no. 48:1043b; XZJ no. 111:147d.

54. The three Japanese versions of the text read *jingyao* (essentials) instead of *jingmiao* (sublime wonders). See Kajitani's renderings in *Zen no koten*, p. 166, and *Zenka goroku*, p. 147, and Tomitani's in "Butsuso sankyō kōgi," p. 214.

55. The twenty-five forms of existence represent the totality of all forms of existence in the three realms, from the deepest hells to the highest heavens.

56. T no. 48:1043a–b; XZJ no. 111:146c–147a.

57. See CDL 9, T no. 51:264c–265a.

58. It should be pointed out that the earliest version of the sermon is in the CDL, compiled some 150 years after Guishan's death.

59. CDL 9, T no. 51:264c.

60. T no. 48:1043b; XZJ no. 111:146c–147b.

61. See Peter N. Gregory, *Tsung-mi and the Sinification of Buddhism* (Princeton, N.J.: Princeton University Press, 1991), pp. 192–196.

62. CDL 9, T no. 51:264c. Translation from Cheng-chien, trans., *Sun-Face Buddha: The Teachings of Ma-tsu and the Hung-chou School of Ch'an* (Berkeley, Cal.: Asian Humanities Press, 1993), pp. 24–25.

63. *Xun* is an ancient measure of length, roughly equivalent to 182 cm.

64. T no. 48:1043b; XZJ no. 111:147b.

65. The quotation is a paraphrase from a passage in the "Duke Wen of Teng" (Teng wen gong) chapter of *Mengzi*. The original passage reads, "He is a man, and I am a man. Why should I stand in awe of him?" See Zhu Xi, *Sishu zhangju jizhu* (Beijing: Zhonghua Shuju, 1983), p. 251. The same quotation also appears in other Chan text, such as *Zongjing lu* 76, T no. 48:839a (where it is part of a verse attributed to the Buddha); CDL 26, T no. 51:429a (in Guizong Huicheng's biography); and Dahui's *Zheng fayan zang*, XZJ no. 118:20b.

66. T no. 48:1043b; XZJ no. 111:147c.

67. For parallels in medieval Christian monasticism, see Talal Asad, *Genealogies of Religion: Discipline and Reasoning Power in Christianity and Islam* (Baltimore: John Hopkins University Press, 1993), p. 137.

68. See T no. 46:794a and Ikeda Rosan, *Makashikan kenkyū josetsu* (Tokyo: Daitō shuppansha, 1986), pp. 274–277.

69. See XJZ no. 119:486d–487b, and Yanagida Seizan, ed., *Zengaku sōsho*, vol. 3, pp. 278–279; for a free Japanese translation, see Ishii Shūdō, *Chūgoku zenshū shiwa* (Kyoto: Zen bunka kenkyūjō, 1988), pp. 480–482.

70. For the text of *Erru sixing lun*, with a Japanese translation, see Yanagida Seizan, ed., *Daruma no goroku: Ninyū shigyō ron* (Tokyo: Chikuma shobō, 1969), pp. 31–47. For English translations, see John R. McRae, *The Northern School and the Formation of Early Ch'an Buddhism* (Honolulu: University of Hawaii Press, 1986), pp. 103–105, and Jeffrey L. Broughton, trans., *The Bodhidharma Anthology: The Earliest Records of Zen* (Berkeley, Cal: University of California Press, 1999), pp. 9–12.

2

A Korean Contribution to the Zen Canon: The *Oga Hae Seorui* (Commentaries of Five Masters on the *Diamond Sūtra*)

Charles Muller

Scriptural Orientations in Korean Seon

Despite the relative vitality of its modern *saṅgha* and its pivotal historical role in East Asian cultural history, Korean Buddhism still remains a seriously neglected field within the broader realm of Buddhist studies.[1] Thus the well-ingrained custom of interpreting Korean Seon according to the models of Japanese Zen or Chinese Chan has also changed little over time. With Korean Seon regularly being seen through the lens of caricaturized views of Tang-Song Chan with its radical nonscriptural tendencies and focus on encounter dialogue, or a Japanese Sōtō/Rinzai model, where textual studies are limited largely to the *Shōbōgenzō* and Zen poetry and where meditative practices consist of either *shikantaza* ("just sitting") or a graduated series of hundreds of kōans and perhaps some sort of cultural admixture with the martial or fine arts. While Chinese Chan and Japanese Zen do have certain fundamental features in common with Korean Seon, the Korean tradition is in significant ways unlike the "meditation schools" of its two neighboring cultures.

One of the more interesting distinctive aspects of Korean Seon, especially as compared with Japanese Zen, is the character of its core literature. While the teaching records of the earliest founders of the "nine mountain" schools tend to reflect the anti-text rhetoric imported from Chinese Chan, as the Seon school developed during the Goryeo period (918–1392),[2] it maintained a distinct scriptural-scholastic component. Although in the case of Japan, this tendency may be found in a school like Tendai, it was certainly not exhibited by the Zen tradition as a whole—at least not to the extent seen in Korea. It is true that we can also see in the sermons and private teaching records of many Seon masters through the Goryeo and Joseon (1392–1910) periods the typical shouting, striking, and exhortation toward investigation of the *hwadu*, (J. *watō*) that one would associate with classical Chan. At the same time there is a substantial amount of attention paid to scriptural study, recitation, and exegesis. Nonetheless, this study and exegesis is of a different character than the doctrinal work carried out in China and Korea during the Tang and Silla periods in that it has a distinct "Chan" orientation, both in literary style and in the choice of topic texts.

Goryeo and Joseon scholastic works tend to be clustered around a narrowly defined set of texts. The collection includes: the *Flower Adornment Sūtra* (K. *Hwaeomgyeong*; C. *Huayan jing*), the *Awakening of Mahayana Faith* (K. *Daeseung gisinnon*; C. *Dacheng chixin lun*), *Sūtra of the Heroic March Concentration* (*Śūraṅgama-sūtra*), *Sūtra of Perfect Enlightenment* (K. *Weongakgyeong*; C. *Yuanjue jing*), *Platform Sūtra* (K. *Yukso dangyeong*; C. *Liuzu danjing*), and the *Diamond Sūtra* (K. *Geumgang gyeong*; C. *Jingang jing*). All together these texts marked an influence on the early formation of Chinese Chan. The concentration on this particular set of texts is readily apparent when one reads through the Goryeo/ Joseon Seon teaching records, where they are regularly cited, or when one peruses catalogues and indices of Korean Buddhist commentarial works and essays of these two periods.

The impact of each of these texts can be correlated with distinct themes within the discourse of Korean Seon. In terms of the influence on the fundamental tendency in Korea toward syncretism and interpenetration, one would cite the *Hwaeomgyeong* and perhaps the *Awakening of Mahayana Faith* [AMF]. In terms of *tathāgatagarbha*, original enlightenment doctrinal influence, one would cite the *AMF* and the *Sūtra of Perfect Enlightenment* [SPE]; in terms of subitistic influences, the *SPE* and the *Platform Sūtra*. But in overall direct influence on the lives of practitioners in terms of exposure in lectures and recitation, there is no text in Korean Seon that has held an influence equal to that of the *Diamond Sūtra*, which is still by far the most popular text in the Korean tradition.

The *Diamond Sūtra* in Korea

The *Diamond Sūtra* is cited everywhere in the Seon teaching records of the Goryeo. Beyond its distinctive thematic orientations, the extent of its influence in Korea also is related to its central role in the myth of the creation of the *Platform Sūtra*, which story provides the source for the very name of the Jogye school.[3] The *Diamond Sūtra* also has its own special thematic affinity with Chan practice, since it is seen throughout the Mahayāna schools of East Asia as the *locus classicus* of what is arguably the most fundamental teaching/practice of Chan: "nonabiding" (K. *muju*; C. *wuzhu*). The *Diamond Sūtra*, in the course of describing the implications of nonabiding, simultaneously leads its reader through an exercise of nonabiding through its repetitive affirmation, negation, and differential reaffirmation. Finally, the *Diamond Sūtra* is, aside from the *Heart Sūtra*, the shortest popular scripture in the East Asian meditative tradition. Since its length allows it to be chanted in about forty minutes, it can be memorized without superhuman effort and has been one of the most popular chanting texts throughout the history of Joseon Buddhism, even to the present day. Upon visiting the temple stores and other Buddhist bookstores in South Korea, one can find an array of tapes and CDs featuring the *moktak* monks— accompanied voices of the Jogye sect's most popular intoner—melodiously chanting the *Diamond Sūtra*. Lay practitioners buy these tapes, and thus the sūtra's influence extends widely to the lay community as well as monastics.

As has been noted, an important dimension of Seon's exegetical tradition is the degree to which it is suffused with and circumscribed by "Chan" tendencies, both in the choice of subject texts and in terms of commentarial style. Whereas the previously mentioned cluster of texts had naturally come to be the focus of studies through the Goryeo and early Joseon periods, the *Śūraṅgama-sūtra*, AMF, *Diamond Sūtra* (in its "five commentaries" version, discussed later in the chapter), *Sūtra of Perfect Enlightenment*, and *Avataṁsaka-sūtra* were formally institutionalized through their inclusion in the Jogye monastic study course. This development is attributed to the Joseon Seon Master Hwanseong Jian (1664–1729). Still today, more than two and a half centuries later, they form the advanced curriculum, or *Sagyo gwa* (*Four Scripture Course*) for the textual studies course in Korean Jogye monasteries.[4] Among these, the *Diamond Sūtra* with the five commentaries, the *Geumgang gyeong oga hae seorui* (*Commentaries of Five Masters on the Diamond Sūtra*), stands out as a native Korean work.

This work, known in Korean by the short title *Oga hae*, is an arrangement of commentaries on the *Diamond Sūtra* that was assembled by the eminent Goryeo/Joseon monk Gihwa (1376–1433).[5] Gihwa selected five important classical commentaries on the *Diamond Sūtra*, collated them according to the passages of the sūtra, and added his own commentary. The range of perspective and style of the five different commentators provides a provocative mixture of interpretations on any given passage, exhibiting an array extending from traditional scholastic doctrinal exegesis to poetic Chan linked verse, satisfying a broad range of readership.

Gihwa (1376–1433)

The lifetime of Gihwa (also known by the monastic name Hamheo Deuktong) coincided with one of the most dynamic periods of social, political, and religious upheaval on the Korean peninsula. The Goryeo regime, which had endured for over four centuries but had become corrupt in its latter period, was on the verge of collapse. Since Gihwa was the leading Buddhist figure of his generation, many of the episodes in his career had to do with his dealings with the epochal events of this juncture in history.[6] Gihwa addressed a wide variety of Buddhist and non-Buddhist religious themes in his writings, but one of his favorite topics was the renewal of Jinul's argument for the essence-function connection of Seon and Gyo, which he addresses primarily within the *Oga hae*. Besides this commentary on the *Diamond Sūtra*, Gihwa also wrote the major Korean commentary to the *Sūtra of Perfect Enlightenment*,[7] a commentary on Xuanjue's *Yongjia ji*,[8] and an essay on the intrinsic unity of the "three teachings" of Buddhism, Confucianism, and Daoism that is considered to be a landmark work in Korean intellectual history, entitled *Hyeonjeong non* (*Manifesting the Correct*). He also wrote a separate essay on the theme of the *Diamond Sūtra*, entitled *Geumgang banya baramilgyeong yun gwan* ("The Penetrating Thread of the *Diamond Sūtra*"), as well as a number of shorter essays and versified works on various doctrinal and meditation-related topics.

Gihwa can be seen as a model example of the Korean Seon master according to the ideal established by Jinul (1158–1210): he was a monk who was steeped in meditative *gong'an* (J. *kōan*) practice, who at the same time demonstrated a thorough mastery of the scriptural tradition, making substantial use of the scriptures in his teaching. Reading through Gihwa's teaching record (*Hamheo dang Deuktong hwasang eorok*) reveals an ample number of sermons in which the master is depicted in the typical Imje (C. Linji) mode of shouting at and striking students while liberally dropping *gong'an* phrases. Yet at the same time the teaching record contains extensive comments made on Buddhist scriptures, as well as on Confucian and Daoist texts.

Gihwa should be seen as the major reviver of Jinul's argument against exclusivist positions taken by certain members of the meditative, mind-to-mind transmission-oriented "Seon" school as opposed to the text-oriented, doctrinal stance of Gyo.[9] Although during the late Silla and early Goryeo the influential Gyo faction had indeed made matters uncomfortable for the newly arising Seon circle, by the time of Gihwa's life, the members of the Gyo faction (typified by Hwaeom, Tathāgatagarbha, and Yogacara scholars) were no longer making any serious challenge to the Seon position, since the Seon schools had clearly been the predominant Buddhist force in Korea for several centuries. While Gihwa was a Seon monk with a strong meditation-oriented perspective to religious cultivation, at the same time he also felt that the denigration of Gyo study methods by Seon extremists was unnecessary and even harmful. Gihwa's interest can be seen in the revalorization of scriptural study both in direct prose addressing the issue and in the fact of his extensive exegetical work.

The Structure of the *Oga hae*

The *Oga hae* is the product of Gihwa's further annotation to his collation of five commentaries to the *Diamond Sūtra*. These commentaries include Zongmi's (780–841) *Jingang jing shulun zuanyao* (T 33, no. 1701:154–169), Huineng's (638–713) *Jingang jing jieyi* (Z 24, no. 459:517–535), Fu Dashi's (497–569)[10] *Liangzhao Fu da-shih song jingang jing*, Yefu Daochuan's[11] *Jingangjing zhu*,[12] and Yuzhang Zongjing's *Jingangjing tigang*.[13] Interwoven with these commentaries and the text of the sūtra itself is Gihwa's own subcommentary.

Gihwa utilizes the commentary of the erudite Zongmi to supply the sūtra's philological details and doctrinal background, as well as to define its technical terms. Zongmi's exegesis compares passages from the various extant translations of the sūtra and cites the important earlier commentaries—mainly those by Asanga and Vasubandhu—which are cited extensively elsewhere. While pointing out the variations in the Chinese rendering of particular passages and then explaining their doctrinal implications, Zongmi also provides detailed definitions of original Sanskrit terms and an analysis of the traditional breakdown of the sūtra itself. The Huineng commentary is used to provide a more flowing philosophical discourse on the doctrinal implications of particular passages but does not yet move into a purely poetic mode.

Fu Dashi's commentary, being from the sixth century, is the earliest and is composed in structured verse. Zongjing's commentary, written during the Song Dynasty, is composed in the colloquial prose Chan style of that period. Most distinctive among the commentators is Yefu Daochuan, a minimalist Chan poet in whose exegesis Gihwa takes great delight. Whereas Gihwa adds occasional comments here and there following Zongmi or one of the other commentators, Yefu's terse, clever, and evocative comments repeatedly inspire Gihwa to poetic outpouring. Yefu's metaphors are based on the story of a legendary emperor in a couplet from the *Shijing*, a line from the *Zhuangzi*, or a famous Chan proverb. These in turn inspire Gihwa to link up with a verse of his own, in imitative style.

The Preface to the *Oga hae*

The *Oga hae* has been studied as a central text in the Korean monastic tradition from the time of Gihwa up to the present, and it is a part of the monks' core curriculum in contemporary Korean Seon. Its status may have been enhanced by the attention paid to it by the influential Yi dynasty monk Hyujeong (1520–1604; popularly known as Seosan Taesa), who alludes to it in the opening paragraph of his influential work, the *Seon'ga Gugam*,[14] by citing its introductory passage.

The profound prefaces attached to commentaries form their own distinctive subgenre in the East Asian classical exegetical tradition. The poetic character of these "preface/introductions" (K. *seo*; C. *xu*) is quite different from that seen in the modern scholarly preface, in that the writer was not thinking to provide explicit referential background material concerning the composition of the text, or any sort of a rational outline of matters to be discussed. The *xu* were composed in verse, in which the main gist of the sūtra or treatise was captured in condensed form. While there is ample evidence for the importance of the role of these prefatory passages throughout the East Asian literary tradition as a whole (not only in Buddhism), it is also obvious that the composition of these opening statements was a practice highly valued by Korean Buddhist monks.[15] In this type of preface the exegete would attempt not only to capture poetically the gist of the entire subject text in a brief paragraph, but at the same time to include the greatest amount possible of literary allusion to important antecedent texts. Gihwa opens up his *Oga hae* with this sort of preface—which is in turn cited by Seosan in the preface to his own *Seon'ga Gugam*.[16] It reads as follows:

> There is One Thing
> Which cuts off names and marks
> right here;
> Yet still penetrates past and present.
> While abiding in a particle,
> It embraces the entire universe.
> Within, it contains all marvels,
> While adapting externally to every type of being.
> It is the master of the three agents,[17]
> The ruler of a myriad phenomena.
> So vast! It is beyond compare,
> So high! It has no peer.
> Is it not divine?
> Although it is bright and clear for those who gaze in its space
>   up and down,
> It is concealed to those who search for it with their eyes and ears.
> Is it not mysterious?
> Although it is prior to heaven and earth, it has no beginning.
> Although it goes after heaven and earth, it has no end.
> Is it empty? Existent?
> I do not know its way of being. (HBJ 7:10b–11b)

Allusions to the first chapter of the *Daode jing* will be obvious to students of East Asian thought, and those familiar with Weonhyo's work will notice the stylistic and thematic similarities between this passage and Weonhyo's opening paragraph in his *Commentary on the Awakening of Faith*.[18]

Aspects of Gihwa's Commentary

Gihwa's commentaries differ from those composed by the earlier systematic scholars of the Tang and Silla dynasties in that they lack philological references and doctrinal categorization. In the *Oga hae*, Gihwa brings up Zongmi's teaching classifications only for the purpose of debunking them with the assertion that these compartmentalizations are untenable under close scrutiny. One of Gihwa's and Yefu's favorite lines, which is repeated throughout *Oga hae*, is "all buddhas possess the same realization: the eyes are horizontal and the nose is vertical" (a Chan metaphor for equality in nature). Gihwa sees no limit in hermeneutic possibilities in the same text, in the same passage, even in the same line. He says of the *Diamond Sūtra* that it "contains the entire content of the Thirty-nine–chapter *Huayan jing*" and that the *Diamond Sūtra* (usually classified in the *panjiao* or hierarchical classification systems as something like "early Mahāyāna") can also be called the Perfect Doctrine and the Sudden Doctrine (HBJ 7:118a). The only correct way to characterize the *Diamond Sūtra*, he maintains, is as the "sūtra of no-characteristics" (HBJ 7:118b21).

Gihwa's "exegesis," like Yefu's, usually takes the form of a restatement of the prior passage in his own poetic language. The sources for Gihwa's commentarial tropes can be from almost anywhere: Weonhyo, Jinul, Confucius, the *Yijing*, *Zhuangzi*, the *Shijing*, or Zongmi.

Key Themes of the *Oga hae*

Since the *Diamond Sūtra* deals directly with the problem of language and the relationship of language to reality, it is the perfect vehicle for Gihwa to express his understanding of the intrinsic unity of Seon and Gyo and his belief in the relevance of scriptural study in attaining the Seon goal of enlightenment. The famous dictum of the *Diamond Sūtra* states, "X is not X, therefore it is X," meaning that X is not actually what our senses and conceptualizing faculties have perceived it to be,[19] and therefore we should not continue to naively understand things to exist in a reified manner and try to appropriate them. This exercise in perspectival adjustment, however, when adhered to in earnest, has a tendency to lead the practitioner to see things as being inexistent. What the *Diamond Sūtra* is saying, however, is that since (1) a view of inexistence also does not describe things as they truly are, and (2) we cannot function in a world where no names exist, we have no alternative but to apply names to things. But when we do so, it must be with the correct, nonappropriating awareness. Since X does not exist, paradoxically the appellation X can (and needs to be) applied to it. This formula also can be understood as a way of expressing the truth of the middle way: "neither X nor not-X." In the context of actual meditation practice (as distinguished from a more logical or rhetorical formulation), this position is termed nonabiding, that is, not being trapped by one-sided notions of existence or inexistence.

While this exercise can be applied to any object, physical or mental, the target concepts of the *Diamond Sūtra* are not just anything that may come to mind. Coming under the critique of the *Diamond Sūtra* are the most subliminally held notions that one might attach to: self, lifetime, personality; early Buddhist notions of the stages of the path; the notion of bodhisattvahood, the transcendent practices, perfect enlightenment, *Tathāgata*-hood, and so forth.

The discourse of the *Diamond Sūtra* can be seen as a critique of the status of language itself, and it is this overall issue that Gihwa takes up in his commentary, seeing the sūtra as expressing the gist of the problematic relationship between Seon and Gyo. The issue of whether language is an admissible vehicle for the transmission of the *buddhadharma* has continually been at the fore of the discourse of the East Asian meditative schools of Buddhism. And this point is particularly relevant for Gihwa, since he is the descendant of the characteristically anti-textual tradition of Linji Chan, which had carried with it into Korea many of Chan's better-known self-characterizations, such as the school that "transmits directly from mind to mind," or "the special transmission outside of words and letters." The degree of continued popularity of such slogans at the time of Gihwa is reflected in his frequent quotation of them in this commentary on the *Diamond Sūtra*. Yet while Gihwa, by the very existence of his commentarial works, acknowledges the viability of the role of scriptural study in Buddhist education, he at the same time does not abandon Chan's acute concerns regarding the pitfalls of language. Hence, Gihwa's treatment of the Seon—Gyo issue is fluid. He says early in the *Oga hae*:

> An ancient said, "The Three Vehicles and Twelve Divisions of the
> Teaching embody the principle and grasp the mystery." This being
> the case, what is the special significance of the ancestral teacher's
> [Bodhidharma's] coming from the West? And the separately trans-
> mitted teaching should also not be found outside of the scriptures.
> But since that which is contained in the worded teaching has re-
> mained hidden and undisclosed, now the patriarchs reveal and
> spread its truth, and not only is the meaning of the doctrine made
> clear but the "separately transmitted teaching" is also fully disclosed.
> Since there has been named such a thing as "the transmission of
> direct pointing," how could this be something that is contained in

the doctrinal teaching? If we merely reflect on the story of Caoxi of Huangmei,[20] this can readily be seen! (HBJ 7:12c5–10)

Gihwa writes with this kind of shifting perspective throughout the *Oga hae*. Certain that the Chan of the patriarchs and the sermons of the Buddha manifest the same reality, he shifts back and forth in acknowledging their merits. Later in the commentary he again points out the usefulness of the worded teaching but warns against attachment to it:

> The dharma that the Buddha has taught is absolute and is relative. Since it is relative, liberation is none other than written language. Since what was taught in the East and taught in the West for forty-nine years[21] is absolute, written language is none other than libera-tion;[22] yet in over three hundred sermons Śākyamuni never ex-plained a single word. If you are attached to the words, then you see branches of the stream but miss their source. If you do away with words, you observe the source but are ignorant of its branch streams. When you are confused about neither the source nor its streams, then you enter the ocean of the nature of experienced real-ity. When you have entered the ocean of the nature of experienced reality, the no-thought wisdom is directly manifested. The no-thought wisdom being directly manifested, whatever is faced is no impediment, and you penetrate wherever you touch. (HBJ 7:42c.21–43a.5)

Although words cannot be denied, one also cannot be attached to words. Implied in the source-streams simile is the essence-function formula. To forget words and become absorbed in the wordless is to forget the phenomenal world (function, K. *yong*) and be attached to the essence (K. *che*). According to Gihwa, this is not an acceptable Buddhist position. Yet Gihwa also counsels along the lines of the better-known Chan theme: that an unbalanced attachment to words can lead to an obstruction of Buddhist realization. What remains is the "middle path," which means continuous avoidance of abiding in one-sided positions. This is "entering the ocean of the dharma-nature," which results in the man-ifestation of no-thought wisdom that penetrates (*tong*) everything with which it comes into contact.

Gihwa's comments on the sūtra and on the other commentators' work repeats this neither-nor position on language. Gihwa makes the same point in another passage from the *Oga hae*. This is in the section of the sūtra where the arhat-interlocutor Subhūti is asked by the Buddha to qualify the status of the teaching itself:

> "Subhūti, what do you think? Does the Tathāgata have a teaching to be explained or not?"

Subhūti answered the Buddha, saying, "World-honored one, the
Tathāgata has no teaching to be explained." (T 8, no. 235:750a.15–16)

Yefu, the poetic commentator who so stimulates Gihwa, says, "Quietly,
quietly." Gihwa adds, "The Buddha has nothing to explain; this is certainly
true. But saying nothing is also not the Buddha's original intention. That is
why Yefu says 'Quietly, quietly.' One should not claim one-sidedly that there is
nothing to be said." A bit further on he adds, "Therefore it is said, 'Even though
you also do not rely on the path of verbal teaching, you should also not be
attached to verbal explanations'" (HBJ 7:56b.24–c.10).

Gihwa has ample opportunity to raise this issue in commenting on the
Diamond Sūtra, since "nonabiding" is the main theme that the sūtra is at-
tempting to express. It is also clear that Gihwa considers the *Diamond Sūtra*
to be so valuable exactly because he considers nonabiding to be the key of all
Buddhist practices. Again invoking the essence-function framework, he says:

> *Nonabiding* is the great essence of the myriad practices, and the
> myriad practices are all the great function of nonabiding. The teach-
> ing of the compassionate saint [the Buddha] takes nonabiding as its
> abode. With the great essence shining, one cannot but be aware of
> the great function. (HBJ 7:36.a.10–13)

Concerning the relationship of the *Diamond Sūtra* to the practice of nonabiding, Gihwa states:

> *Prajna's* divine source is vast, lacking all kinds of characteristics. It
> is extensive, yet lacks an abode. It is empty and not existing; it is
> profound and unknown. Now this single sūtra takes *this* as its core
> teaching and as its essence. Although there is no awareness, there is
> nothing that it does not know. Although there is no abiding, there is
> no place where it does not abide. Although lacking characteristics, it
> does not obstruct any characteristics. This is the function of marvel-
> ous existence. What all Buddhas have realized is exactly the realiza-
> tion of this. What all the patriarchs have transmitted is exactly the
> transmission of this. Their means of awakening people is also ex-
> actly through this. (HBJ 7:14a.15–22)

In the *Diamond Sūtra*, nonabiding is equated with the lack of attachment
to any characteristic (K. *sang*, C. *xiang*). Therefore, the *Diamond Sūtra's* teaching of "no-characteristics" (K. *musang*; C. *wuxiang*) is synonymous with nonabiding. The *Diamond Sūtra's* discussion, as in the case of other texts of the
prajñā-pāramitā genre, carries out a systematic refutation of the abiding in
characteristics, and most important, the characteristics of selfhood and thing-
hood. The *prajñā-pāramitā* writers made targets of the most seminal Buddhist
concepts, such as: "Tathāgata," "dharma," "bodhisattva," and so on, to make

the attack most effective. If one continues to abide in these concepts, then she has not yet been able to let go of her mistaken adherence to the self-imputed reality of conceptual objects. This means that the person has not experienced or turned to the path of Buddhist "faith" (K. *sin*; C *xin*). In order truly to be able to practice nonabiding, one must have faith. To have faith, one must be able to make the transition to the habit of nonabiding. To put it yet another way, nonabiding and Buddhist faith are two aspects of the same thing.[23] The Buddha and Subhūti discuss the arousal of faith in the sūtra, and Gihwa comments as follows:

> Subhūti asked the Buddha, saying, "World Honored One, if sentient beings are able to hear these words, phrases, and passages, will they be able to arouse true faith?"
> The Buddha answered Subhūti: "Do not say such a thing. Even five hundred years after my passing away there will be people who hold the precepts and cultivate goodness, and who will be able to arouse the mind of faith in these passages by regarding them as the truth."[24]

Gihwa comments:

> The above question and answer directly clarify the inner meaning of nonabiding and no-characteristics. Since this inner meaning of non-abiding and no-characteristics is extremely deep and difficult to understand, it cannot be approached by the discriminations of ordinary people. This being the case, as the time of the passing away of the Sage becomes more and more distant, might there not be the possibility of a lack of faith? This is why Subhūti asks the question. However, this reality is certainly not something different from the daily activities of sentient beings, and it penetrates past, present and future. Because of this, even if a man lives in an age of degeneration of the dharma, if his faculties are sharp, he should arouse faith by taking this inner meaning of nonabiding and no-characteristics and regarding it as true. (HBJ 7:38c.12–37a.9)

On Exegesis and Editing

An unusual facet of Gihwa's commentary in the *Oga hae* is his extended discussion of the enterprise of editing and exegesis in itself—the correction of the errors that creep in during the process of translation and commentary. In looking at this discussion, we should be reminded of the difficulty of maintaining and disseminating texts in ancient times before the invention of the printing press. Buddhist sūtras written in classical Chinese (of which there were inevitably various translations) needed to be continually recopied by hand for continuity and further dissemination. This copying was one of the major activities of Buddhist monks of the prepress era. In the process of the copying of intricate CJK logographs, many of which can be indistinguishable from each other in their cursive writing form, chances of error were high. Furthermore, in the case of the Mahayāna sūtra, the operative logic[25] is profound and often quite opposite from what would be seen in a secular argument, and the possibility for an overworked or inattentive copyist to make an error was high. Also, in reading the text, thinking that it did not make sense as it was, or perhaps feeling that the arrangement of the text did not agree with his own sectarian positions, he might very well decide to alter it.

There is a distinctive flavor to Gihwa's admonishments in this section in the degree to which they reflect his Seon orientation. When Gihwa encourages proper scholarly discipline in the handling of a canonical text, he does not stop with the demand for technical care and thorough disciplinary philological preparation. In fact, he places primary emphasis on the development of the commentator's meditative insight which should be brought to bear on the scholarly work. Hence, while we can say that Gihwa has, in other ways, worked for an institution of Gyo into Seon, he is here integrating the "Seon" meditative experience into "Gyo" scholarly activity. The exegete needs to possess not only scholarly training but also the continual deepening of his own meditative experience, so that he will not introduce mistaken interpretations into the text. Thus he is required not only to read the subject text deeply enough to penetrate its key themes, but also to meditate in order to have the necessary mental purity and "wisdom eye" to carry out the work. Gihwa addresses this topic in the introductory section of the *Oga hae*. He first stresses the importance of seriousness regarding the project, since words are the tools for the expression of the Way:

> Written words are the tools for the expression of the Way and the
> means for guiding people. The actual and the overall themes should
> support each other; the theme should penetrate the text throughout
> and be fully contained down to its minutest details. Only when
> omissions, superfluous words, inversions, and errors do not confuse
> its points can the text awaken people's understanding and can it be-
> come a norm for a thousand generations. If this is not the case,
> then not only will the text not open people's eyes, it will become an
> instrument of beguilement. (HBJ 7:13b3–8)

The Huayan principle of mutual containment is operating here through the formula of essence and function. The inner meaning of a canonical text, which is the "essence" (*che*), should be fully manifested in its outward appearance or "function" (*yong*); conversely the external text ("function") should correctly express the internal/invisible essence: they should penetrate each other.

"Penetration" (*tong*) again can be used as a metaphor to describe the action of the mind of the Seon exegete, whose commentarial and editorial work depends upon his meditative preparation.

The task of correcting an error-laden text is not to be carried out lightly by someone who lacks sufficient clarity. Therefore "if you lack the wisdom eye, you cannot but be confounded by arrogance and error" (HBJ 7:13b11–12). Nevertheless, one who initially lacks the sharpness to overcome these mistakes can still treat a text well with the proper meditative preparation: "Although you may lack the wisdom eye, if you silence your discriminations in order to apprehend the point, then the incongruities between the sentences and the theme can be grasped and straightened out" (HBJ 7:13b16–17). The responsibility is heavy, since the exegete is passing on the dharma for future generations:

> If you have understood that the text's errors are like "gnarled roots and knotted bark"[26] and that the meaning is obstructed and not penetrating, and, wary of criticism from others, if you perceive these errors and do not correct them, then how can you reflect the compassion of the Buddha? Later generations, unavoidably receiving the transmissions of error-laden texts, will in turmoil produce forced interpretations in order to make sense of the text. If it is done in this way, then the uncorrected errors become attached to the words of the buddhas and the patriarchs and they will unavoidably become mixed up. This is something that cannot be done by the man of excellence and the thoroughgoing scholar. (HBJ 7:13.c.16–24)

One would think that given the extent and explicitness of this justification for correction of canonical texts in the preface of a commentary to the *Diamond Sūtra*, we would see some suggestions for correction here in this commentary, but there are none. On the other hand, in his commentary to the *Sūtra of Perfect Enlightenment*, Gihwa engages in extensive editing of the sort suggested by this passage,[27] which makes one wonder if this passage has not somehow been misplaced and actually belongs somewhere in that other commentary.

Translation of Section 7 of the *Oga hae*: No Attainment, No Teaching

The *Oga hae* has been studied intensely in the Korean monastic tradition from the time of Gihwa up to the present, and it is an integral part of the monks' core curriculum in contemporary Korean Seon.[28] It is a rather large text, occupying about one hundred pages of the *Hanguk bulgyo jeonseo*, which means that a full annotated translation would be a project of several hundred pages. But the value of such a work would no doubt be great. Access would be provided to the combined exegeses of Zongmi, Huineng, and three other formidable scholars, along with Gihwa, on one of the most influential texts in the East Asian Buddhist tradition. The philosophical merits of such a study would be high, gaining even greater relevance in view of ongoing postmodern concerns with the ontological status of language, which is a central topic of discussion in the *Diamond Sūtra*.

To provide a greater sampling of the *Oga hae* beyond the few isolated citations given earlier, I offer a translation of one complete section of the text. This section, which is the seventh of its thirty-two traditional divisions, is especially relevant to the topic of this chapter in that it addresses the problematic status of the verbal teaching, given the fact that the ultimate realities of other categories have up to this point in the sūtra been rejected. In this section we have access to sufficient representative writings of each of the five commentators, as well as Gihwa. This includes the text running from HBJ 7:43b to 7: 45b.

SŪTRA *"Subhūti, what do you think? Does the Tathāgata attain peerless perfect enlightenment? And does he have a teaching that he explains?"*

ZONGMI The Buddha is asking if Subhūti got it or not, with the expectation that he didn't. That's why Asanga says, "This shows that he has, after all, ended up clinging to [the notion of] perfect enlightenment." In the second sentence he answers in accordance with the reality principle.

SŪTRA *Subhūti said: "As I understand the implications of what the Buddha has explained, there is no determinable phenomenon called peerless perfect enlightenment. And there is also no set teaching that can be expounded by the Tathāgata."*

GIHWA The fact is that all the terms such as thusness, the buddha-nature, enlightenment, and nirvāṇa as well as the transcendent practices [pāramitās], the [four] truths, and the [twelvefold] dependent origination and so forth that are used in application to the capacities of sentient beings are [merely] designations that have not been adequately understood. If you observe from the vantage point of reality, there is, from the start, no such problem. Then again, at the appropriate time there is the teaching of the selflessness of phenomena and persons.

ZONGMI The transformation buddha is not the real buddha; he also does not teach the dharma.

HUINENG *Anuttara* [the unsurpassed] is not gotten from the outside, yet whenever there is no thought of "mine" in the mind, this is exactly it. Medicines are made only to fit the disease, and the teaching is delivered according to the differing faculties of sentient beings. How could there be such a thing as a set teaching? The Tathāgata teaches that the mind of the unsurpassed correct teaching originally lacks attainment.

But you also cannot say that it is not attainable. It is just that since that
which sentient beings see is not the same; the Tathāgata adjusts to their
faculties and natures. Using various skillful means, he awakens and
guides them.

Enabling them to be free from all attachments, he shows them that
the deluded mind of all sentient beings arises and ceases without pause,
chasing after the objective world. Once the prior thought arises slightly,
the subsequent thought responds in its awareness. Awareness does not
abide; views also do not remain. Since it is like this, how could there be
a set teaching that the Tathāgata could expound? [The phoneme] *an* [of
anuttara-samyak-sambodhi] indicates the mind's absence of deluded
thought. *Uttara* indicates the mind's absence of conceit. *Sam* means that
the mind is always in a state of correct concentration. *Yak* means that
the mind is always in a state of correct wisdom. *Sambodhi* means that
the mind is always empty and quiescent. When in one thought-moment
the dull mind of regular people is suddenly removed, one sees the buddha-
nature.

YEFU   When it's cold, say it's cold. When it's hot, say it's hot.

GIHWA   It is because there are two vehicles that we say there are two
vehicles. It is because there is a great vehicle that we say there is a great
vehicle. According to the capacities of sentient beings, one acts expedi-
ently without a set teaching. Following conditions, one stands on reality
and escapes the cage [of passions and distorted cognitions].

YEFU   When the clouds rise on the Northern Mountains, it's raining in
the Southern Mountains.
An ass, it's called, with a horse's label. How many kinds *are*
there?
Seeking the vast oceans, there is no water.
In some places, you accord with the direction; in some places,
you are complete in yourself.

GIHWA   Depending on the state of mind, one teaches the [four] truths
or [twelvefold] dependent origination—or perhaps one elaborates the six
transcendent practices. Since the abilities [of sentient beings] are not the
same, the teaching is also not determined. From this, one articulates a
myriad of words and uses nonconceptual wisdom to respond to each
person's state of spiritual maturity, explaining in both prolix and terse
language the halfway and fully explained teachings, the partial and complete. [Yet] in the prolix and terse explanations, there has never been one
word offered to expound the doctrine.

ZONGMI   The third part explains the articulation of the indeterminate
teaching.

SŪTRA   *Why? The teachings explained by the Tathāgata can be neither appropriated nor explained. There is neither a teaching nor a nonteaching.*

GIHWA   When the Buddha expounds the teaching, sometimes he says there are signs, and sometimes he says there are no signs. He speaks freely without impediment and is never obstructed by holding to one extreme. Therefore we cannot attach to his words. [Afterthought:] As far as the Buddha's teaching is concerned, you can't say that it is a teaching, and you can't say that it is not a teaching. If there is definitely not a teaching, then it is necessary to use a raft to cross the river. If you say that there definitely is a teaching, then you can reach the other shore without needing a boat. Hence, by availing yourself of the Way at the proper time, you reach the truth with a single word, cast out the worldly conditioned mind, and accomplish sagehood. Availing yourself of the Way at the proper time, you use three vehicles and twelve divisions of the canon. What is this? The "scream at the hot bowl" and the "elaboration of the golden shit" are also made based on this.

ZONGMI   Asaṅga says: " 'Cannot be appropriated' refers to the time when one is listening correctly. 'Cannot be explained' refers to the time when one is explaining correctly. 'No teaching' [or 'no phenomena'] is because of the nature of discrimination. 'No nonteaching' [or 'no non-phenomena'] is because of the selflessness of phenomena" [T 25, no. 1510a:761a25–27]. Vasubandhu says: "This 'teaching and nonteaching' is an explanation made based on a knowledge of reality. [The expression] 'nonteaching' [is articulated] because all phenomena lack essence and marks. 'No nonteaching' is articulated because the real marks of selfless thusness exist. Why is it that only verbal expressions are said not to be realized? As soon as there are verbal expressions, they give form to meaning. If they are not realized, then one cannot express them" [T 25, no. 1511:784c1–4].

HUINENG   It is because the Tathāgata is concerned that people will attach to the words, phrases, and sentences that form the content of his exposition and, not awakening to the markless principle, deludedly give rise to understandings. Therefore he says, "cannot be appropriated." Since the Tathāgata gives consideration to each being according to his individual capacities, how can there be any determination in regard to what he teaches? Practitioners, not understanding the Tathāgata's profound intention, simply chant the teaching that the Tathāgata has expounded without fathoming their own original minds, and in the end do not achieve enlightenment. Therefore he says that it is inexplicable. When one chants with one's mouth and the mind does not actualize it, then this is the nonteaching. When one chants with one's mouth and the mind actualizes it, fathoming its unobtainability, then this is no non-teaching.

FU DASHI   Enlightenment is free from verbal explanations.
The person who has up to now been unable to attain this
Relies on the principle of two kinds of selflessness
To realize the body of the dharma-king.
Existence and mind are both delusions.
Not being attached is called "reality."
When you understand no nondharma,
You course out beyond the six objects.

YEFU   What is it?

GIHWA   The teaching expounded by the Buddha is like a gourd sitting on top of the water: with the slightest touch it turns immediately. There is no set teaching that can be appropriated, and there is no set teaching that can be expounded. If a set teaching existed, how could it be inexistent? If the set teaching is inexistent, how could it be non-inexistent? Since there is already no such thing as an existent or inexistent teaching, in the end, what is it? [Afterthought:] Since the claims for the teaching and the nonteaching are already both negated, in the end, what is it?

YEFU   "There is originally nothing to attain;" and "not being so is not held to."[29] In the clear and vast sky, a bird flies, leaving no tracks. Bah! Clearing away delusion and opening up enlightenment, one falls back to spinning. South, north, east, and west naturally come and go.

GIHWA   The existence and nonexistence of a set [teaching] is unaffirmed. Don't look for the Daoist view in the four phrases, because the Daoists don't sit in their midst. Not sitting in the four phrases, a bird flies in the sky without leaving any tracks. Bah! One must again look within the bird's path for self-transformation to be attained for the first time. South, north, east, and west are the same heaven and earth. Don't divide the world and automatically come and go. [Afterthought:] The teaching and the nonteaching—both are unaffirmed; both views are contrary to the Buddha's original intention. Simply look into the sky and seek the bird's track. Bah! Even if it is like this, this is also not the Buddha's original mind. If we really understand the Buddha's original mind, we will say that his teaching is also not obstructed, and we'll say that his nonteaching is also not obstructed.

ZONGMI   Fourth is the reasoning for the teaching of not clinging to explanations.

SŪTRA   *How can this be? All the enlightened sages are distinguished [from worldly teachers] by indeterminate phenomena.*

GIHWA   The teachings actualized by all enlightened sages are all distinguished by means of the unconditioned, and these distinctions are none other than the unconditioned. [People] course out far beyond the middle space into the two extremes, and thus when the unconditioned teaching of a single taste is seen from the perspective of the direct disciples [śrā-vakas], it is called the four noble truths. When seen from the perspective of solitary realizers [pratyeka-buddhas], it is called dependent origination, and when seen from the perspective of the bodhisattvas, it is called the six transcendent practices. Each of the six transcendent practices, dependent origination, and the four noble truths lack a way to be held and are ineffable.

ZONGMI   The Wei translation[30] says: "All sages are named as such based on the unconditioned teaching" [T 8, no. 236:753b22)]. The [Vasu-bandhu] Treatise says: "The sages rely on nothing other than thusness and purity to be called such. It is not that they attain some special dharma" [T 25, no. 1511:784c7]. Therefore there is neither grasping nor explanation, and yet there is differentiation. The Treatise says: "Thusness is replete, and purity distinguishes purity."[31] Asaṅga says: " 'Unconditioned' means 'nondiscrimination.' Hence the bodhisattvas get their name based upon their application of practices, while the Tathāgatas get their name based upon their nonapplication of practices. The first occurrence of the term 'unconditioned' refers to that which is manifested at the overcoming of mental disturbances. The second 'unconditioned' is referred to the peerless enlightenment in regard to the ultimate truth" [T 25, no. 1510:761a28–762a01]. Since the sages of the three vehicles all cultivate and realize the unconditioned, they are set apart together as a group.

HUINENG   That which is understood by those who have the natures and abilities of the three vehicles is not the same. Their insight [varies in terms of] deep and shallow, and hence we say that there are distinctions. When the Buddha expounds the unconditioned teaching, this is none other than that of nonabiding. Nonabiding is none other than signlessness; signlessness is none other than nonarising; nonarising is none other than noncessation. Void, empty, quiescent, with illuminating function gathering all equally, discerning awareness is unobstructed. This is truly none other than the liberated buddha-nature. "Buddha" is none other than "enlightenment;" "enlightenment" is none other than "intelligent illumination;" "intelligent illumination" is none other than "insight;" "insight" is none other than transcendent wisdom.

FU DASHI   "Person" and "phenomena" are both called attachment.

But when fully fathomed, they are the two kinds of
   unconditioned.
While bodhisattvas are able to realize both equally,
The direct disciples can only get one.
When the cognitive and afflictive hindrances are
   exhausted
There is, in the void, no more basis.
Constantly able to maintain this observance
One attains realization, definitely, without doubt.

YEFU   A hair-breadth's difference at the beginning opens up to a distance as vast as that between heaven and earth.

GIHWA   Even though the teaching is of a single taste, there are a thousand distinctions in viewpoint. Those thousand distinctions are contained in merely a single thought. A difference in a single thought opens up a space as vast as that between heaven and earth. Yet even though it is like this, heaven and earth join to become one. In this way, then, when gold becomes a thousand utensils, each utensil is gold. Sandalwood is broken into ten thousand pieces, yet each piece is aromatic.

YEFU   A correct man expounds an errant teaching and the errant teachings all return to correctness. An errant man expounds the correct teaching and the correct teachings all end up being wrong. The river in the north produces tares; the river in the south produces tangerines. Spring arrives and flowers spring forth everywhere.

GIHWA   The unconditioned teaching of a single taste can be correctly or deviantly transmitted. One kind is distinguished into North and South. North and South have the same blooming of flowers.

ZONGJING   Attainment is denied and teaching is denied. The mental function of the compassionate one is like a bolt of lightning—you can't grasp it, and you can't let it go. The tongue born of emptiness is originally rolling out [its words]. Well, let's just say it: the unconditioned teaching has distinctions like this. "In the ancient blue depths, the sky encloses the moon; after three attempts at scooping it and sifting it, you should understand what's actually going on."

GIHWA   Attaining without attainment; expounding without elocution. His function is marvelously spiritual—a lightning flash is difficult to grab with your hand; grasping, you can't get it; releasing, you can't let go. Enjoyable words roll out continuously like powerful waves, able to go high and low. From this point of view, it is like the unconditioned teaching, which ends up having these kinds of distinctions. Now you want to cognize the unconditioned principle without separating from a thousand differences and ten thousand distinctions. Even though it is like this, you still know the mind of the moon and sky in the deep pool. Why be like a foolish monkey exhausting yourself?

ZONGJING   The clouds wrap up the autumn sky as the moon stamps the pond; the cold light is boundless; with whom will you consult? Seeing through the earth with the penetrating heavenly eye; the great way is made clear without availing oneself to consultation.

GIHWA   If you use the sky and moon without stamping them on the water, how can you say that the cold light is vast without limit? Illuminating heaven and earth, including myriad forms without limit; with whom will you consult on this taste? Still, on the top of your head you are able to merge your eyes into one. Where should you look next to search out the profound principle?

ABBREVIATIONS

HBJ   *Hanguk bulgyo jeonseo* (*The Collected Texts of Korean Buddhism*) (Seoul: Dongguk University Press, 1984).

NOTES

1. Note on Korean transliteration: Most of the earlier works cited in this chapter used the older McCune-Reischauer romanization system. Since I have elected to use the new romanization system recommended by the South Korean Ministry of Culture, there are often differences between the romanization systems used in older citations (e.g., Kihwa) and those seen in newly written material (e.g., Gihwa).

2. This is the period of the development of the Jogye school, the descendant of which exists today in Korea.

3. Jogye in Chinese, *Caoxi* is originally the name of a stream southeast of Shaozhou, Guangdong, which became an appellation for the Chan Sixth Patriarch Huineng.

4. Robert E. Buswell, *The Zen Monastic Experience* (Princeton, N.J.: Princeton University Press, 1992), pp. 95–102. Also Hee-Sung Keel, *Chinul: The Founder of the Korean Seon Tradition* (Berkeley, Cal.: Buddhist Studies Series, 1984), pp. 175–178.

5. The *Bussho kaisetsu daijiten* erroneously identifies Gihwa as a Ming Chinese monk. See vol. 3, p. 466a.

6. For details regarding Gihwa's life and works, see my Ph.D. dissertation, "Hamhŏ Kihwa: A Study of His Major Works" (SUNY at Stony Brook, 1993).

7. See my translation of this commentary along with *The Sūtra of Perfect Enlightenment: Korean Buddhism's Guide to Meditation (with the commentary by Seon Monk Gihwa)* (Albany, N.Y.: SUNY Press, 1999).

8. The *Seonjong yeonggajip gwaju seorui* (*Annotation of the Redaction of the Text and Commentaries to the Compilation of Yongjia of the Chan School*), by Gihwa.

9. Surveys of Korean Buddhism to date, both in and outside of Korea, have repeatedly ignored Giwha's pivotal role as transmitter of Jinul's Seon–Gyo unification,

instead usually crediting Hyujeong (1520–1604) as being the most important sustainer of this discourse. However, Gihwa, who lived almost exactly midpoint between these two, wrote in far greater quantity and more directly on the topic than did Hyujeong. Furthermore, one can see in Hyujeong's writings an obvious reliance on Gihwa's works. One can guess that Hyujeong's prominent stature as a cultural hero (he organized the monks' army that was instrumental in thwarting the Japanese invasion by Hideyoshi) may have led scholars to pay greater attention to his role. See Jae Ryŏng Shim, "The Philosophical Foundation of Korean Zen Buddhism: The Integration of Sŏn and Kyo By Chinul (1158–1210)" (Ph.D. diss., University of Hawaii, 1979).

10. Also known as Shuanglin Fu, from Tongyang in Qi. He is named as the preceptor for the Buddhist conversion of Emperor Wu of Liang and is recorded as having established the Shuanglin Temple as well as having supervised one of the earlier editions of the Chinese canon.

11. Daochuan was a Song-period (12 c.) Linji monk, also known by the mountain name of his residence, Yefu. A native of Jiangsu, he first studied under Dongzhai qian and underwent a major awakening experience. After various travels, he returned to Dongzhai, where his famous comments to the Diamond Sūtra were recorded as he responded in verse to questions regarding the sūtra. His dates of birth and death are not known.

12. Contained separately in Z 24, no. 461:536–565 and T no. 2732.

13. According to the Busshō kaisetsu daijiten (vol. 3, p. 460c), this work is extant only in the Oga hae, and my investigations have not yet turned up anything to add to this. I have been unable to locate any biographical information on Zongjing other than the fact that he was a Song monk. Seeing that all other commentators are of Chan affiliation, one would assume that he was from the same tradition. The Busshō kaisetsu daijiten also attributes to him six other works—all exegetical works dealing with the Diamond Sūtra.

14. See HBJ 7:634c–635a.

15. Two of the most famous prefaces in the Korean Buddhist tradition are those composed by Weonhyo in his commentary; see Sung Bae Park, "Wŏnhyo's Commentaries on the Awakening of Faith in Mahayana" (Ph.D. diss., University of California Berkeley, 1979), republished in Peter H. Lee, ed., Sources of Korean Civilization (New York: Columbia University Press, 1993), pp. 157–159. Also Jinul's opening statement to his Hwaeomnon jeoryeo (Essentials of the Treatise on the Huayan jing; HBJ 4:768a).

16. For other citations of this preface, see Han Gidu, Han'guk Seon sasang yeon'gu [Studies in Korean Seon Thought] (Seoul: Ilsasa, 1991), pp. 142, 201.

17. Heaven, earth, and man.

18. The opening passage of the Gisinnon so by Weonhyo (T 44, no. 1844:202a.26-b.4) reads:

> The essence of the Mahayāna is generally described as being completely empty and very mysterious. However, no matter how mysterious it may be, how could it be anywhere but in the world of myriad phenomena? No matter how empty it may be, it is still present in the conversations of people. Although it is not anywhere but in phenomena, none of the five eyes can see its form. Although it is present in discourse, none of the four unlimited explanatory abilities can describe its shape. One wants to call it great, but it

enters the interiorless and nothing remains. One wants to call it infinitesi-
mal, but it envelops the exteriorless without exhausting itself. One might say
it is something, yet everything is empty because of it. One might say it is
nothing, yet the myriad things arise through it. I do not know how to describe it; therefore, I am compelled to call it "Mahayāna." (Sung Bae Park,
trans., "Wŏnhyo's Commentaries," p. 63)

19. We mistakenly perceive things to be inherently existent, rather than depend-
ently originated, and we believe they exist exactly in the form that our senses have
interpreted.

20. More commonly known as Huineng, the Sixth Patriarch.

21. The length of Sākyamuni's teaching career.

22. In the above two sentences Gihwa is alluding to the famous dictum from the
Heart Sūtra, "form is emptiness, emptiness is form."

23. A Buddhist faith that is equivalent to "nonabiding" can be equated with the
"immovable" Patriarchal Faith described by Sung Bae Park, *Buddhist Faith and Sudden
Enlightenment* (Albany, N.Y.: SUNY Press, 1983), pp. 35, 45. According to Park, Patriarchal Faith is a faith that, because of its grounding in *śunyatā*, "lacks an object" and
thus cannot abide anywhere. But it is called "immovable" when contrasted to object-
based forms of faith, which are unstable.

24. T 8, no. 235:749a.26–29. Also see my full translation of the sūtra at http://
www.hm.tyg.jp/~acmuller/bud-canon/diamond_sutra.html.

25. That is, a logic that is based on an understanding of emptiness, which often
produces semantic relationships that are opposite from ordinary logic.

26. A metaphor for confusion.

27. Gihwa's rewrites of the *Sūtra of Perfect Enlightenment* are examined in detail
in my full translation of his commentary and the sūtra, entitled *The Sūtra of Perfect
Enlightenment: Korean Buddhism's Guide to Meditation (with the commentary by the Sŏn
Monk Gihwa)* (Albany, N.Y.: SUNY Press, 1999).

28. For a description of the modern Jogye curriculum, Robert E. Buswell, *The
Zen Monastic Experience* (Princeton, N.J.: Princeton University Press, 1992), p. 99.
Also see Hee-Sung Keel, *Chinul: The Founder of the Korean Sŏn Tradition* (Berkeley,
Cal.: Buddhist Studies Series, 1984), pp. 175–178.

29. These are the third and fourth of the "six teaching phrases" of the Linji
school.

30. The "Wei Translation" is Bodhiruci's translation of the *Diamond Sūtra*, T
no.236.

31. This line is not contained in Vasubandhu's treatise, nor elsewhere in the
Taishō.

3

Zen Buddhism as the Ideology of the Japanese State: Eisai and the *Kōzen gokokuron*

Albert Welter

Toward a Reappraisal of Eisai and the *Kōzen gokokuron*

Eisai (1141–1215, also known as Yōsai)[1] is a major figure in the Japanese Zen tradition, known for introducing Zen and winning major political support for it in the newly formed Kamakura *bakufu*.[2] In spite of the major role Eisai played in changing the course of Japanese Buddhism and establishing Zen as an independent institution, his accomplishments have been obscured by modern developments affecting Zen ideology. In the modern period, Eisai's work has been generally ignored, and his image tends to languish in relative obscurity. The situation into which Eisai and his principal work, the *Kōzen gokokuron*, have fallen is well summarized by Yanagida Seizan, in his introductory essay to the modern Japanese edition and translation of the *Kōzen gokokuron* text:

> It seems that the work entitled *Kōzen gokokuron* has hardly ever been read in earnest. To a remarkably great extent, it has been treated as nothing more than nationalistic propaganda. Such bias is deeply rooted even at present. Frankly speaking, it is hard to find any appeal in this work when it is compared with Dōgen's *Shōbōgenzō* or Shinran's *Kyōgyōshinshō*. . . . [And] this exceedingly low opinion that people have is not restricted to the *Kōzen gokokuron* but is directed at Eisai as well. Aside from the bias that the *Kōzen*

gokokuron advocates a national Buddhist ideology (*kokka bukkyō*), the fact that Eisai sought [government sponsored] robes and titles of recognition for himself, degenerated in his later years to a clerical functionary for the Kamakura *bakufu*, and was nothing more than a construction entrepreneur who envisioned the rebuilding of Tōdaiji and Hōshōji, and so on, completely undermines his image as the founder of a school.[3]

As Yanagida explains, the common perception of the *Kōzen gokokuron* in Japan is that it is a work of "nationalistic propaganda," unworthy of serious reading.

To the extent that Eisai is known to us at present, it may be more likely as "the father of tea cultivation in Japan"[4] than for any achievements in transferring Zen teaching to Japan. As a Zen master, Eisai's reputation was seriously tarnished, according to modern interpretation, by his willingness "to compromise . . . by assuming a reconciliatory attitude toward the Tendai and Shingon."[5] According to this view, Eisai's compromising, syncretistic attitude is a corruption of the ideals inherent in the "pure" Zen tradition.[6]

Serious problems arise when Eisai is judged from the perspective of "pure" Zen, not least of which is the extent Eisai's aims coincide with those of the later "pure" Zen tradition. "Pure" Zen is predicated on the notion that Zen is essentially beyond intellectual comprehension, so that any attempt to treat it historically must be preceded by an understanding of Zen "as it is in itself."[7] In this view, Zen ideally is aloof from the messy world of politics and unsullied by historical circumstances. There is no question that Eisai fairs poorly when subjected to these kinds of criteria. "Pure" Zen cherishes, above all, the defiant masters of the T'ang Zen tradition, who eschewed (at least in legend) political and social contacts in favor of an enlightenment experience, the essential nature of which was deemed ineffable and beyond rational determination. This interpretation leads one to ask whether Eisai has been treated fairly as a historical figure, suggesting that the current perception of the *Kōzen gokokuron* has been determined by a later tradition that emphasized "pure" Zen as the only legitimate expression of Zen teaching and practice.

The current reputation of Eisai stands in marked contrast with the way the Japanese tradition has regarded him. Kokan Shiren awarded Eisai the most prominent place in the *Genkō shakusho*, the collection of Japanese Buddhist biographies completed in 1322, as the first to transmit the Zen teaching of the Rinzai faction to Japan.[8] Eisai also enjoyed a great, if controversial, reputation among his contemporaries. Politically, he had important connections with the Heian court, and he won the respect and patronage of significant figures in the Kamakura *bakufu* government.[9] Religiously, Eisai had been a respected advocate of Tendai esotericism before his conversion to Zen. His monastery in Kyoto, Kenninji, became an active training center for the new Zen movement. Eisai's reputation among his contemporaries was also reflected in his capacity as head of Jufukuji in Kamakura and the support received from the military rulers there, the Hōjō family. The significance of Eisai in religious circles is further reflected in the attraction of prominent students to his reform movement, including no less a person than Dōgen Zenji (1200–1253).

As founder of the Sōtō faction in Japan, Dōgen would later be sharply distinguished as Eisai's sectarian rival, but neither the facts of Dōgen's own life nor his reported statements concerning Eisai substantiate the antipathy between Dōgen and Eisai predicated on later sectarian divisions. Dōgen received early training in Zen at Kenninji, under the direction of Eisai's successor, Myōzen (1184–1225). The example Eisai provided for rigorous training at Kenninji left a lasting impression on Dōgen. In Dōgen's *Shōbōgenzō zuimonki*, Eisai's words are invoked to authorize Zen practices and his collection of sermons are remembered as "the most splendid of words." Elsewhere, Dōgen remarks that "Students today would do well to reflect on the excellence of Eisai's attitude" and that "the nobleness of purpose and profundity of Eisai must certainly be remembered."[10] Dōgen's itinerary while on pilgrimage in China with Myōzen, moreover, consciously followed in Eisai's footsteps.

Nevertheless, Eisai's understanding of Zen was based on different assumptions. In order to distinguish these, I will examine features associated with Eisai's Zen reform movement within the context of assumptions common to late Heian and early Kamakura Buddhism. The focus is on the *Kōzen gokokuron*, Eisai's most important work. The aim is to reveal significant aspects of Eisai's thought in light of the context in which it was written and to examine these against precedents upon which the content of the text was based. The study demonstrates how Eisai and his contemporaries shared certain ideas expressed in the *Kōzen gokokuron* that are overlooked or poorly understood at present. This commonality suggests an alternative way to read the text and the possibility of a more balanced appraisal of Eisai and the *Kōzen gokokuron*.[11]

To reassess Eisai and the message of the *Kōzen gokokuron*, this chapter addresses Eisai's motivations from a number of perspectives. It begins with an inquiry into the theoretical conception of the Buddhist state common to medieval Japanese Buddhism and adopted by Eisai by examining aspects of the *Ninnō kyō* (*Sūtra of Benevolent Kings*), a text central to Eisai's theoretical vision. The discussion emphasizes not only the ideological sway that this text had over Eisai, but also how Eisai conceived of the practical implementation of the text's ideological vision in terms of the Ch'an institutions and practices he observed in Sung China. To understand Eisai's attempt to reform the Japanese Buddhist state along the lines suggested by the model of Sung Ch'an, the study examines the *Kōzen gokokuron* in terms of three leading ideas around which Sung Ch'an had been formed: lineage, institutional organization, and conceptions of Ch'an *vis-à-vis* the Buddhist tradition as a whole. This discussion includes a comparison of the "combined practice" (*kenshū*) or the Zen-based syncretism of the *Kōzen gokokuron* with the influential Sung Ch'an syncretist Yung-ming Yen-shou, whose works exerted broad influence over both Sung Ch'an and Kamakura Zen, notably in the teachings of Dainichi Nōnin and the Daruma faction.[12] This examination concludes with a comparison of how Yen-shou was understood in the *Kōzen gokokuron* and the *Jōtō shōgakuron*, a text associated with Nōnin and the Daruma faction, a leading early contender for the mantle of establishing a separate Zen "school" in Japan. Bringing Yen-shou's interpretation into the analysis at this juncture shows how different the Ch'an (or Zen) of Nōnin, Eisai, and their contemporaries was from that depicted by modern scholars.

The Utopian Vision in Medieval Japan: An Examination of the *Ninnō kyō* [*Sūtra of Benevolent Kings*]

Eisai's argument in the *Kōzen gokokuron* was predicated on widely held assumptions in medieval Japan regarding the role of Buddhism as an essential component of a civilized society. In Japan such notions date from the time of Shōtoku Taishi (574–622), who formally introduced Buddhism as a leading component in the affairs of the country.[13] At this time the Buddhist religion, hitherto dominated by certain clans, was promoted as a unifying force for the Japanese state, newly conceived under Shōtoku's inspiration.

The importance of Buddhism for affairs of state in Japan was reaffirmed in the Nara (710–794) and Heian periods (794–1185), when three Buddhist scriptures provided the cornerstones of state Buddhist ideology in Japan: the *Myōhō renge kyō* (*Sūtra of the Lotus Blossom of the Fine Dharma*, better known simply as the *Hokke kyō*, the *Lotus Sūtra*),[14] the *Konkōmyō kyō* (*Sūtra of the Golden Light*),[15] and the *Ninnō gokoku hannya kyō* (the *Prajñāpāramitā Sūtra Explaining how Benevolent Kings Protect Their Countries*, or simply, the *Ninnō kyō*).[16] These three scriptures became collectively known in Japan as the "three *sūtras* for the protection of the country" (*chingo kokka no sambukyō*).[17] Eisai's treatise calling on the rulers of Japan to promote Zen for the protection of the country shared the widely accepted ideological background that these scriptures provided.

Among the three scriptures for the protection of the country just mentioned, the *Ninnō kyō* assumed the most importance for Eisai.[18] This importance is based on Eisai's admission in the Preface to the *Kōzen gokokuron* that his reason for titling his work *The Promotion of Zen for the Protection of the Country* is that it is consistent with the ideas originally taught by the Dharma King (*hō-ō*), the Buddha, to the Benevolent Kings (*ninnō*).[19] It is also confirmed by the frequency and prominence with which the *Ninnō kyō* is cited by Eisai in the *Kōzen gokokuron*.[20] A review of the *Ninnō kyō* reveals the ideological assumptions of Eisai's Zen reform program in the *Kōzen gokokuron*, based in the *prajñā* (wisdom) tradition of Mahayāna Buddhism.

Most of the topics addressed in the *Ninnō kyō* are well known to anyone familiar with Mahayāna Buddhism, especially to the *Prajñā-pāramitā* (J. *hannya*; perfection of wisdom) literature. Among them are emptiness, the Tathāgata, the bodhisattva path, the two levels of truths, miraculous events, and so on. The appearance of the benevolent kings (*ninnō*) distinguishes the contents of the *Ninnō kyō*, particularly their concern for establishing secular authority based on Buddhist principles. The message contained in chapter 5, "Protecting One's Country" (*gokoku*), together with that of concluding chapters 7, "Receiving and Upholding [the *Ninnō kyō*]," and 8, "[The Buddha] Entrusts [the *Ninnō kyō* and the Three Treasures: the Buddha, Dharma, and *sangha*] to the [Benevolent] Kings," where this concern is most explicitly revealed, draws the content of the *Ninnō kyō* closely to the *Kōzen gokokuron*.[21]

In terms of the message that the *Ninnō kyō* wishes to convey, however, the first four chapters are more than a prelude. They affirm the primary importance that the Buddha Dharma, namely *prajñā*-teaching and those practitioners who are devoted to it, have for the welfare of the state. The first priority of the state, following this logic, is to seek not its own preservation but the preservation of Buddhism. Later the kings learn that the preservation of Buddhism is inextricably bound to the preservation of their own country. This was a powerful message for Buddhist monarchs looking to Mahayāna teaching as a basis and justification for their own rule: spiritual aims and secular interests coincide in support for Buddhism.

In chapter 5 the terms for protecting countries are specified in terms of support for the teachings contained in the *Ninnō kyō* (i.e., *prajñā*-teaching). The Buddha advises that whenever the destruction of a country is imminent, regardless of the cause, the king should sponsor a ritual recitation of the *Ninnō kyō*. In addition, the Buddha recommends that the kings commission daily recitations of the *Ninnō kyō*, as a matter of course, to invoke the assistance of native deities and spirits in protecting their countries. *Ninnō kyō* recitation is also said to be useful for obtaining a number of practical benefits, both material and spiritual, including protection against countless afflictions that plague one during the course of human existence. In short, *Ninnō kyō* recitation is characterized as having unquestionable salutary effects over numerous unseen forces that determine human destiny, particularly the destiny of a ruler and his kingdom. The chapter spells out in concrete terms the methods to be employed by kings to protect their countries, win material and spiritual benefits, and alleviate personal afflictions. It assures kings of the actual benefits to be obtained if they follow ritual procedures focusing on the recitation of the *Ninnō kyō*, and it provides a contrast between the altruistic virtue of the righteous Buddhist monarch and the petty greed of the power-hungry ruler.

The end of chapter 5 is taken up with two exemplary tales that illustrate the chapter's message. The first involves Śakra, who by recourse to the methods just described, was able to repel invading armies seeking his destruction and the destruction of his kingdom. The second relates how the crown prince of a country called Devala conspires to win succession to the throne by offering the heads of a thousand kings in sacrifice to the local god These means were suggested to the crown prince by a non-Buddhist priest, presumably one dedicated to the local god in question. The prince succeeds in capturing 999 kings and transports them to the shrine of the local god, where they are to be sacrificed. One king shy of his goal, the prince encounters his last prospective victim, a king called Universal Light.

Prior to transporting Universal Light before the local god to be sacrificed, the prince grants the king's last request, which is to supply food and drink to Buddhist monks and pay his final respects to the three Buddhist treasures, the Buddha, Dharma, and *Saṅgha*. When the monks recite the *Ninnō kyō* on the king's behalf, Universal Light is able to extricate himself from harm. Upon his arrival in Devala, Universal Light instructs the other 999 kings how to save themselves through recitation of the verses from the *Ninnō kyō*, just as it was originally uttered by the monks he assembled. The recitation ultimately succeeds in converting the crown prince himself, who confesses his wrong and sends all of the assembled kings back to their homes, instructing them to have Buddhist priests in their kingdoms recite verses from the *Ninnō kyō*.

The point of the story is that without the benefit of Buddhist virtue, the non-Buddhist ruler is consumed by the drive for power. This drive is marked by extreme insensitivity and barbarity. Moreover, in this story, local religious authority sanctioned this barbarity. In opposition, Buddhism is presented as a universal religion of compassion, which, through the teaching of the *Ninnō kyō*, offers rulers a vision of peaceful co-existence predicated on a higher law. In short, the *Ninnō kyō* promotes the cause of Buddhist right over sheer force or might.

The concluding chapters of the *Ninnō kyō* describe further the responsibilities incumbent upon righteous monarchs for implementing the cause of Buddhist virtue in their kingdoms. Chapter 7, "Receiving and Upholding (the *Ninnō kyō*)," reinforces the message presented in chapter 5 and supplements the methods suggested to kings for protecting their countries. The *Ninnō kyō* is described here as "the spiritual source of the mind of buddhas, bodhisattvas, and all sentient beings" and "the father and mother of all kings." It is also referred to as a divine charm, the mirror of heaven and earth, a treasure for driving away demons, for obtaining one's desires, and for protecting a country,[22] descriptions that highlight the *Ninnō kyō*'s utility for both religious and political matters.

A principal feature of the *Ninnō kyō* is the responsibility it places on kings for managing Buddhism and ensuring its continued existence. In return for the protection that the *Ninnō kyō* offers them and their kingdoms, the kings are responsible for perpetuating the Dharma here on earth. The Buddha tells King Prasenajit, the chief interlocutor among the benevolent kings, that after his (Buddha's) death, when the extinction of the Dharma is imminent, the king should uphold the *Ninnō kyō* and extensively perform Buddhist ceremonies based on it. The security of every king and the happiness of all the people are said to depend completely on this. For this reason, the Buddha continues, the *Ninnō kyō* has been entrusted to the kings of various countries and *not to the Buddhist clergy or faithful*. The preservation of the Buddha Dharma under such circumstances is thus the primary responsibility of the king, not the *saṅgha*.[23]

Chapter 7 also describes in detail the misfortunes that recitation of the *Ninnō kyō* serves to combat. Topping the list are calamities resulting from disruptions in the celestial and natural order.[24] In East Asian countries influenced by the Confucian doctrine that terrestrial power depended on Heaven's mandate, disruptions in the normal patterns of the heavens were viewed as ominous warnings to the ruler. These signs were potentially threatening to the ruler's prestige and position, giving him ample cause to consider them with extreme gravity.[25] To avoid calamities stemming from disruptions in the celestial and natural (including human) order, the *Ninnō kyō* stipulates ritual recitation of its contents according to a prescribed format.[26]

The *Ninnō kyō* closes with chapter 8, "[The Buddha] Entrusts [the *Ninnō kyō* and the Three Treasures] to the [Benevolent] Kings," and a warning reinforcing the responsibility incumbent upon kings for maintaining Buddhism. In particular, it is stated that at such times when the Buddha, Dharma, and *Saṅgha*, as well as the Buddhist faithful, are absent from the world, the *Ninnō kyō* and the three treasures will be entrusted to kings.[27] It is the responsibility of the kings to initiate the path of wisdom (i.e., *prajñā*-teaching) by having members of the Buddhist assembly recite and explain the *Ninnō kyō* to sentient beings. In other words, the kings are responsible for reconstituting Buddhist teaching in the world; the *Ninnō kyō*, representative as it is of *prajñā*-teaching, is to serve as the basis for this reconstitution.

There are important implications for the model of Buddhist kingship provided in the *Ninnō kyō*. Essentially, the power of the king described here is unambiguous. Although the royal power may be misused in some cases when it is united with the Dharma, and the *Ninnō kyō* is used as a guide, it serves as an indisputable force for good. It is the hallmark, one might say, of the benevolent monarch implementing Buddhist righteousness in the world. The message of the *Ninnō kyō* is particularly appropriate when the decline of the Law (*mappō*) is anticipated, as was the case in late Heian Japan. The *Ninnō kyō* is the prescribed Buddhist antidote for such times.

The *Ninnō kyō* played an extensive role in medieval Chinese and Japanese Buddhism, influencing both state ideology and ritual practices. It constituted an accepted feature of the East Asian Buddhist tradition and commanded a particularly wide following in medieval Japan. The *Kōzen gokokuron* was written within this context. In the first place, the *Kōzen gokokuron* affirmed the *Ninnō kyō*'s vision for the role of Buddhism within the Japanese Buddhist state. It questioned, however, the way that this role had hitherto been fulfilled, and it proposed that certain reforms were necessary in order for the traditional hegemony of Buddhist ideology and secular authority to be properly conceived and executed. The central feature of this reform was predicated on the assumption that Zen teaching represented the legacy of the Buddha's enlightenment and the true teaching of the Buddha. As a result, only Zen teaching could fulfill the ideological quotient of the true Buddhist state.

The model of Buddhist kingship provided in the *Ninnō kyō* thus reflected the long-held aspirations of the Japanese ruling elite and the Buddhist establishment, affirming the accepted model of how the relationship between the secular establishment and the Buddhist clergy was envisioned. This model, in turn, established the parameters for the reform proposals in the *Kōzen gokokuron*.

Ninnō kyō Ideology and Zen Teaching in the *Kōzen gokokuron*

Treatises with overtly political overtones are a unique feature of Japanese Buddhism. On this point, it is useful to contrast Japan with China. When Buddhism was first introduced, China already had an established civilization with well-defined moral and social principles. In the Chinese context, discussions of Buddhist morality thus tended to conflict with nativist sentiments. A persistent tendency among the Chinese was to regard Buddhism as the ideology of an alien people, essentially distinct from the principles and beliefs governing Chinese civilization. As a result, Buddhist treatises on the value of native Chinese traditions tended to be either positively self-assured in the superiority of Buddhism, or apologetically inclined, in search of harmony between native Chinese and Buddhist teachings.[28] By adopting Chinese Buddhist and Confucian ideologies at the same time, Japan tended to fuse Buddhist and Confucian principles into a single harmonious ideology which formed the basis for Japan's definition of civilization.

Aside from the initial objections of the Mononobe warrior clan and the Nakatomi family of Shinto priests in the sixth century, Buddhism was immune from the wrath of antiforeign temper until the rise of Japanese nativism in the Tokugawa (Edo) period.[29] The reason for this immunity is clear. Until Tokugawa rule, Buddhism was the acknowledged core of Japanese civilization. The common refrain among the Japanese ruling elite who determined the course of Japanese civilization was: "When the Buddhist law flourishes, so does the secular order."[30] Because of this belief and until the rediscovery of Chinese Confucianism along with their "pure" Shinto heritage, Buddhism was not regarded as a foreign ideology that had either to proclaim its superiority or to apologize for its presence, as was the case in China. As a result, ideological debates in Japan tended to be sectarian, that is, between different factions that shared a common vision, rather than cutting across fundamental ideological boundaries. Since Buddhism was not relegated to a private domain of exclusively spiritual matters but was viewed as the rationale for state policy and the existence of government institutions, many Buddhist sectarian debates were politically inspired.[31] The decline of authority in the late Heian era exacerbated the need for sectarian debate focusing on political concerns.

The end of the Heian era brought political and ideological challenges to the Heian ruling elite. Ideologically, the Heian decline resulted in challenges to the position of the Tendai school as the spiritual and moral authority of the Japanese state. Politically inspired Buddhist treatises calling for reform were a natural development in this environment. Such works represent a period of new competition within Buddhism, with new factions vying for the honor of displacing Mount Hiei as the "Chief Seat of the Buddhist Religion for Ensuring the Security of the Country."[32]

The most prominent attempt to redefine the Japanese Buddhist state during this period was the *Kōzen gokokuron*. The aim of the work was twofold: to reaffirm the central role of Buddhist ideology as the spiritual and moral core of Japanese civilization, and to challenge the validity of the way this goal was being carried out under the auspices of the Tendai school. The work was set squarely within the context of Tendai reform. Like Luther in sixteenth-century Christendom, Eisai saw Zen not as a revolutionary teaching that would undermine Tendai, but as a reform doctrine that would reestablish Buddhist and Tendai credibility.

The *Kōzen gokokuron* text is divided into a preface and ten sections, concluding with a brief summary. The aim of each section is indicated by its title:

1. Ensuring the Lasting Presence of Buddhist Teaching
2. Protecting the Country (with the Teachings of the Zen School)
3. Resolving the Doubts of the People of the World
4. Verification (Provided by) Virtuous Masters of the Past
5. The Transmission Lineage of the Zen School
6. Scriptural Authorization for Enhancing Faith (in Zen)
7. Outlining Zen Doctrines for Encouraging Zen Practice
8. The Program of Rituals for Protecting the Country at Zen Monasteries
9. Explanations from Great Countries
10. Initiating the Vow to Transfer Merit

Rather than exclude Tendai, Eisai sought to reform it by redefining it in terms of its relation to Zen. In order to understand how Eisai sought to meld Tendai with the Zen tradition, one needs also to understand how Eisai conceived of Zen teaching and how he associated it with *Ninnō kyō* ideology. We can begin by placing Eisai's eventual identification with Zen in the context of his original quest.

When Eisai set out from Japan on his second pilgrimage, his intended destination was not China but India, the homeland of the Buddha and Buddhist teaching.[33] His goal was to personally set foot on the "diamond ground" where the Buddha had attained enlightenment. This plan underscores Eisai's commitment to reform on the pretext that Heian-era decline was rooted in Japan's deviation from correct Buddhist teaching. Only after Eisai's request to continue on to India was denied by Chinese authorities did he focus his attention on the study of Chinese Ch'an.[34] With the possibility of studying authentic Buddhist teaching in the Buddha's homeland thwarted, Eisai turned to a ready alternative: the purported "living" transmission of the Buddha's teaching in the Sung Ch'an masters around him. Sung Ch'an represented a viable alternative to Eisai for a number of reasons.[35] On one level, it is easy to imagine how impressed Eisai must have been with the world of Sung Ch'an, with its grand monasteries, institutional structure, and state support. The stability and prosperity of the Sung world stood in marked contrast to the brutality and chaos into which Japanese civilization had fallen. The revitalization of Mount T'ien-t'ai and its transformation into a Ch'an center during the Sung would have also made a deep impression on Eisai, suggesting the model for reform and revitalization in Japan. The most important influence that Sung Ch'an had on Eisai, however, went beyond these circumstantial factors associated with the splendor of Sung civilization. It was the new synthesis that Zen teaching suggested, integrating crucial aspects of Buddhism for Eisai—Tendai and *prajñā*-teaching, meditation practice and concern for morality, and *Ninnō kyō* ideology—into a single, seamless whole.

Eisai saw Zen teaching in terms that pertained directly to *Ninnō kyō* ideology. In the preface of the *Kōzen gokokuron*, Eisai depicts Zen as the Mind teaching, the essence of enlightenment, and the "actual teaching of the former Buddhas" transmitted through Śākyamuni "from master to disciple via the robe of authentic transmission."[36] The *Ninnō kyō* conceived itself in comparable terms as "the spiritual source of the mind of buddhas, bodhisattvas, and all sentient beings."[37] This depiction accounts for Eisai's view of the *Ninnō kyō* as an integral part of the Zen school's Mind teaching.

In terms of Buddhist scriptures, the Mind teaching is revealed in two forms according to Eisai. "Externally, the Mind teaching conforms to the position taken in the *Nirvāṇa-sūtra* [J. *Nehan kyō*] that the Buddha-nature, through the aid of the precepts, is always present."[38] In this regard, Eisai stands staunchly in the Tendai tradition established by the Chinese T'ien-t'ai master Chih-i, who emphasized upholding the Buddhist precepts as the basis from which wisdom arises.[39] This external emphasis on the precepts is joined to an internal perspective, "the view of the *Prajñā sūtra* [J. *Hannya kyō*] that awakening is attained through wisdom." Taken together, these two perspectives on the Mind teaching indicate the teaching of the Zen school reflecting the trans-sectarian perspective of the inherent harmony between Zen and Buddhist scriptures and doctrines.

The two forms of the Mind teaching referred to by Eisai indicate two med-itation traditions that he attempted to harmonize and integrate. One is the Zen teaching of the *Nirvāṇa-sūtra* and the T'ien-t'ai school, with its emphasis on the precepts. The other is the Zen teaching of the *Prajñā sūtra* and the Ch'an school, with its emphasis on wisdom.[40] I will later examine Sung precedents for the integration of these two Chinese "Zen" traditions.

The emphasis on morality and the precepts emerges in the first section of the *Kōzen gokokuron*, beginning one of the major bases for Eisai's argument: monastic reform. According to *Ninnō kyō* teaching, the survival of both Bud-dhist and secular institutions is predicated on the moral character of a country, typified by the monastic discipline of the Buddhist clergy. This discipline has important consequences regarding the status of Buddhism in society and the role that Buddhism performs in legitimizing state authority. In effect, the be-havior of the Buddhist clergy serves as a moral barometer of the country, de-termining the credibility of Buddhism in the eyes of the state and the country as a whole. By extension, corruption undermines the status of Buddhism and its claim to authority. The Buddhist monastery, whether as the repository of virtue or the beacon of enlightenment, depends on the moral discipline of its members, in this view, for both spiritual and social justification. Practically speaking, the social support given to Buddhism, and ultimately its very exis-tence as a temporal institution, is intricately connected to the moral discipline of its members. In this regard, the opening section of the *Kōzen gokokuron* begins with a quote from the *Sūtra on the Six Perfections* (J. *Roku haramitsu kyō*): "The Buddha said, 'I preached the rules governing moral training [*vinaya*] so as to ensure the lasting presence of Buddhism [in the world],'"[41] marking the temporal aim of Eisai's treatise to preserve the existence and integrity of the Buddhist order. This concern for moral reform is the theme of the first section, and continues to appear throughout the treatise.[42] It is also evident from Eisai's conservative approach toward the Buddhist precepts. In complete defiance of the Japanese Tendai tradition established by Saichō, which estab-lished its identity in part by liberating its members from the stricter, more rule-oriented discipline of early Buddhism, Eisai demanded that Zen monks ob-serve the stricter *Hīnayāna* precepts in addition to *Mahayāna* ones. Eisai's position on monastic reform, moreover, was not a personal, idiosyncratic con-ception. It specifically reflected the model of Buddhism that Eisai had wit-nessed in Sung China. In the *Kōzen gokokuron*, this connection is apparent in the following citation from the *Ch'an-yüan ch'ing-kuei* (J. *Zen'en shingi*, "The Regulations for Pure Conduct at Zen Monasteries"), the official record of reg-ulations observed at Ch'an institutions in Sung China:

The ability to spread Buddhist teaching throughout the world of unenlightened people most assuredly rests on strict purity in one's moral training. As a result, observing the Buddhist rules governing moral behavior [kairitsu] takes precedence in the practice of Zen and the investigation of the Way. Without the insulation and protection from transgressions and errors [provided by the monastic rules], how will one ever become a Buddha or a patriarch? . . . Through reading and reciting the monastic rules and understanding the benefit they provide, one is well versed in the differences between upholding the rules for moral behavior and violating them, and on what behavior is permissible and impermissible . . . [Monks of the Zen School] rely completely on the sacred utterances issued from the mouth of the golden one, the Buddha; they do not indulge their fancies to follow ordinary fellows.[43]

The political aim of Eisai's reform is expressed directly when he states, "In our country, the Divine Sovereign [the Japanese Emperor] shines in splendor, and the influence of his virtuous wisdom spreads far and wide."[44] Recall that Eisai specifically stipulated the Kōzen gokokuron, the "Treatise on the Promotion of Zen for the Protection of the Country," as being consistent with the teaching of the Buddha to the Benevolent Kings (i.e., the Ninnō kyō). For Eisai this meant that Zen, as the legitimate interpretation of Buddhist teaching and practice, represented the means through which Ninnō kyō ideology could be implemented. The basis for Japan's future glory, Eisai asserted, rested in state sponsorship of Zen teaching.

Much of Eisai's confidence stemmed from his belief in Japan's destiny as one of the preeminent Buddhist kingdoms in the world. Eisai is quick to show how this belief is based on scriptural authority, on the Buddha's assertion recorded in the scriptures that in the future "the most profound teaching of Buddhist wisdom" [prajñā] will flourish in the lands to the northeast.[45] For Eisai, "the most profound teaching of Buddhist wisdom" is none other than Zen teaching. The lands to the northeast where this teaching is destined to flourish are China, Korea, and Japan. Since the transmission of Zen teaching to China and Korea has already been accomplished, only the transformation of Japan remained. The clear implication is that Japan's natural destiny as a preeminent Buddhist country can be fulfilled only by the adoption of Zen teaching.[46] The Mind teaching of the Zen school, in conjunction with the vision of the ideal Buddhist state in the Ninnō kyō, thus constitutes the basis for Japan's future glory.

The ideology of the Ninnō kyō played an important role not only in determining the primary position of Buddhist moral teaching in the affairs of the country but also in determining where primary responsibility lay for carrying out such reforms. Recall in this regard the provision, advanced in the Ninnō *kyō*, that rulers of states—not the Buddhist clergy or faithful—were responsible for managing Buddhism and ensuring its continued existence. The preservation of Buddhism in this conception, it should be remembered, is intricately connected with the ruler's own self-interest in preserving his state. Thus, since the state is primarily a moral order based on Buddhist teaching, the moral integrity of the Buddhist clergy lies at the core of the state's identity.[47]

The declining social and political situation at the end of the Heian era provided Eisai's message with a great sense of urgency. Here too the *Ninnō kyō* served as a primary source of inspiration. On the one hand, recall that the *Ninnō kyō* characterizes itself as "the father and mother of all kings" (i.e., rulers), and as a treasure for driving away demons and protecting a country. More specifically, recall the admonition in the *Ninnō kyō* that it be entrusted to rulers especially at such times when the credibility of Buddhist teaching and the Buddhist clergy have been exhausted. The clear implication is that the *Ninnō kyō* should serve as the ruler's model for reestablishing the authority of Buddhist institutions and the moral character of his country. As a result, there is a strong sense in the *Kōzen gokokuron* that the *Ninnō kyō* speaks directly to the political and moral decay of the time. Witness the following passage from the *Ninnō kyō*:

> Oh Great Monarch, when Buddhist teaching has degenerated to the
> point where its doctrines alone survive but it is no longer practiced
> [*masse*] . . . , the king and his chief ministers of state will frequently
> engage in illicit activities [that contravene Buddhist Law]. They will
> support Buddhist teaching and the community of monks only for
> their own selfish interests, committing great injustices and all sorts
> of crimes. In opposition to Buddhist teaching and in opposition to
> the rules governing moral behavior, they will restrain Buddhist
> monks as if they were prisoners. When such a time arrives, it will
> not be long before Buddhist teaching disappears.[48]

In accordance with *Ninnō kyō* teaching, the ruler of the country is best situated to reestablish the credibility of Buddhist teaching and the moral order of the state. Given the political turmoil and competition among claimants to the imperial throne, on one hand, and the rising importance of the military in government affairs and the competition between different warrior families, on the other, the position occupied by any ruler was extremely tenuous. Eisai's response to this state of affairs seems to be reflected in a passage from the *Scripture on the Perfection of Wisdom of the Victorious Ruler* (*Shō-tennō hannya kyō*):

> Suppose that when a bodhisattva who had studied the Buddhist
> teaching on wisdom [i.e., the *prajñā-* teaching of the Zen school] be-
> came the ruler of the country, mean despicable sorts of people came

to slander and insult him. This ruler would defend himself without making a display of his majesty and authority, saying, "I am the ruler of the country. I rule exclusively by the authority vested in me through the Buddhist teaching [on wisdom]."[49]

This statement suggests that the *Ninnō kyō* was important to the message of the *Kōzen gokokuron* in two ways. In terms of its overall message, the *Kōzen gokokuron* was conceived within the framework of *Ninnō kyō* ideology. This is its fundamental significance. In terms of the social and political context, the historical situation within which the *Kōzen gokokuron* was created, the passages cited from the *Ninnō kyō* suggested concrete solutions to specific issues. In this latter instance, the *Ninnō kyō* is not unique but fits a general pattern guiding the references to scriptures in the *Kōzen gokokuron*. Because of the overall importance of *Ninnō kyō* ideology for the *Kōzen gokokuron*, however, the references to the *Ninnō kyō* merit special attention.

From the preceding we can see how Zen teaching suggested a program of reform for Eisai. In Eisai's interpretation, the Zen-based reform program was necessary to realize Japan's destiny as a great Buddhist country. Zen represented moral reform through increased vigilance in following the precepts (*kai*), the essential teaching on Buddhist wisdom (Skt. *prajñā*, J. *hannya*) transmitted through the masters of the Zen school, the meditation traditions (*zen*) of both the T'ien-t'ai/Tendai and Ch'an/Zen schools, and the method to achieve the ideal Buddhist state advocated in the *Ninnō kyō*. In Eisai's interpretation, Zen clearly had the potential to serve as the multidimensional ideology that Japan required, encompassing the political, moral, soteriological, philosophical, and utopian aims of the country. The *Ninnō kyō*, we have seen, played a significant role in establishing the political and utopian aims, as well as the parameters for carrying them out.

Zen Monastic Ritual and *Ninnō kyō* Ideology

The implications of Eisai's adaptation of *Ninnō kyō* ideology in terms of the practices engaged in at Zen monasteries are drawn in section 8 (The Code of Conduct at Zen Monasteries) of the *Kōzen gokokuron*.[50] Eisai's alleged inspiration for this section is the monastic code used at Sung Ch'an monasteries, the *Ch'an-yüan ch'ing-kuei* (J. *Zen'en shingi*),[51] as well as works used to guide monastic practice (i.e., *vinaya* rules) in "great Buddhist countries." In effect, the section outlines a plan explaining how the program of activities at Zen monasteries serves the interests of the state. The plan is discussed in two parts. The first part discusses what the program of activities depends on, and the second details the annual rituals to be observed at Zen monasteries.

The most noteworthy feature in Eisai's discussion of activities at Zen monasteries is the emphasis on moral conduct.[52] Strict observance of the monastic code constitutes the basis for the revival of the country conceived in terms of *Ninnō kyō* ideology. When monks are "armed externally with the rules for correct behavior [i.e., the precepts of the small vehicle], creating a field of blessings for human beings and gods, and sustained internally by the great compassion of bodhisattvas [i.e., the precepts of the great vehicle], acting as sympathetic fathers to sentient beings, His Majesty the emperor, the highly esteemed treasures [of the country],[53] and the skilled physicians of the country [i.e., Buddhist monks] rely exclusively on them." The revival of the country is thus tied to the strict moral conduct of Buddhist monks.

A second feature of note is the rigor of monastic discipline at Zen monasteries. This is presented in terms of the daily and nightly rituals that monks are required to follow. Four sessions (totaling roughly eight hours) are devoted to *zazen* meditation. In comparison, roughly four hours are devoted to sleep. This schedule too is rationalized in terms of *Ninnō kyō* ideology:

> Through their constant meditation [*nen-nen*], [the monks] repay the country's kindness [*koku-on*]. Through their constant activity [*gyōgyō; a reference to Buddhist practices*], [the monks] pray for the enhancement of the [country's] treasure [i.e., the emperor] [*hōsan*].[54] In truth, [the constant meditation and constant activity of the monks] is the result of the eternal glory of imperial rule [*teigo*] and the perpetual splendor of the *dharma*-transmission lamp [*hōtō*].[55]

Again, the revival of imperial glory is connected to the strict moral discipline of the Zen school.

Other provisions are designed to ensure that the public conduct and dress of Zen monks are in keeping with the traditions established for members of the Buddhist clergy. These provisions confirm an image of the Zen monk as a devoted practitioner, observing strict conduct and moral discipline and commanding public respect in his dress and demeanor. An additional provision stipulates that members of Zen monasteries are *not* self-sufficient but are supplied through the alms of the community. "[Zen] monks do not engage in tilling the fields or rice cultivation, because they have no time to spare from *zazen* meditation." The point here is that Zen monastic institutions preserve the well-established, reciprocal relationship between the clergy and lay communities; Zen monks do not rely on independent means that might deprive the society at large of a primary source of blessings (i.e., giving alms). This condition also coincides with an image of moral authority that a well-disciplined Zen clergy commands. Eisai's image of the Zen monastery, it should be noted, contradicts the prevailing view championed in Rinzai orthodoxy that Pai-chang initiated the hallowed principle of self-sufficiency practiced at Zen monasteries.[56]

The annual ritual observances at Zen monasteries, the second part of Eisai's discussion in section 8, further ensure that Zen fulfills its social obligations as the official religion of the state. These obligations, on the whole, are directed at a sociopolitical order maintained through moral virtue, which, following the rationale employed in this context, is cultivated through specific ritual observances. The rationale for several of these observances is connected to the preservation of the emperor and the country. It is no accident, moreover, that these observances head the list.

The first are rituals commemorating the emperor's birthday. Buddhist sūtras are recited for a thirty-day period prior to the emperor's birthday to pray that the emperor enjoy "boundless longevity" (seijū mukyō). Sūtras specified for recitation at these rituals include most prominently the "four scriptures for protecting the country," the *Dai hannya kyō* (Skt. *Mahāprajñapāramitā sūtra*),[57] in addition to the *Myōhō renge kyō*, *Konkōmyō kyō*, and the *Ninnō gokoku hannya kyō* mentioned previously.[58] This establishes, at the outset, the commitment of Zen institutional resources to the traditional Buddhist ideology of the Japanese state in terms that had prevailed in Japan through the Heian era.

The second set of rituals refers to formal ceremonies conducted on six days each month for invoking the buddhas' names and reciting scriptures. At the top of the list of aims that these ceremonies are meant to accomplish is the spread of "the August virtue of His Majesty" (ōfū) and the enrichment of imperial rule (teidō).[59]

There were also ceremonies held on the last day of each month specifically aimed at repaying the kindness of the emperor. These ceremonies featured lectures on the *Prajñāpāramitā sūtras*. Ceremonies held at mid-month in honor of the previous emperor featured lectures on the *Mahā-parinirvāṇa sūtra*. All of the rituals considered thus far indicate the persistent dedication of Zen monks, as representatives of Buddhist teaching, to dispatch their political obligations to the state (i.e., the emperor).

In addition are ceremonies, held two days each month, designed to enlist the support and protection of native (i.e., non-Buddhist) gods for the Buddhist cause. Since Buddhism was considered the ideology of the state, providing the moral pretext for social and political order, support for Buddhism by regional deities was perceived as having obvious implications for the welfare of the country as a whole.

Other rituals and ceremonies conducted at Zen monasteries were associated with the role that Buddhism played in society. Among these were vegetarian banquets held on memorial days to seek merit on behalf of the deceased. In theory, anyone could sponsor such a banquet, but in practice only elite members of the society commanded the resources necessary to sponsor one, and members of the imperial family were noteworthy sponsors. In addition, provision was made for additional vegetarian banquets at Zen monasteries, sponsored by government officials. The reasons for these are unspecified but are presumably related to the potential efficacy of merit accumulated on such occasions for affairs of state.

The annual rituals and ceremonies served other purposes as well. On the one hand, they address further the concern that Zen monks be morally rigorous in their discipline. In addition, they address the issue of whether the Zen approach is exclusive or syncretic. This issue is resolved in two ways. First, it is resolved through rituals that demonstrate that Zen teaching includes the entire corpus of Buddhist scriptures, and second, through an institutional affirmation of the practices associated with other Buddhist schools, namely Shingon and Tendai. In addition to the meditation hall, Eisai's Zen monastic compound included a Shingon Hall devoted to the performance of Mikkyō ceremonies (to pray for blessings and earn merit for the deceased) and a Cessation and Contemplation (*shikan*) Hall for cultivating Tendai-based meditation practices. According to the activities that he sanctioned, there is no doubt that Eisai came down heavily on the side of syncretism at the practical level as well as the theoretical one. Syncretism also figures prominently in Eisai's adoption of Sung Ch'an precedents.

The Nature of Zen Teaching and the Meaning of Zen Practice: Sung Ch'an Precedents for the *Kōzen gokokuron*

By the beginning of the Sung period, Chinese Buddhism was driven by three concerns. The incorporation of these concerns led to a new conception of Buddhism in China championed by dominant lineages or "houses" of Ch'an. The first concern was associated with the question of lineage itself, the importance it assumed in conferring status, and the distinct form that it took in the Ch'an school. The second concern related to Ch'an's self-definition during the Sung period, particularly the relationship between Ch'an teaching and the teaching of other schools of Buddhism. The third concern was the importance of Buddhist practice to Sung Ch'an's self-definition, particularly as it related to moral discipline and the observation of the *vinaya* rules. Each of these concerns is crucial for understanding Eisai's conception of Zen in the *Kōzen gokokuron*. They distance Eisai substantially from the criteria he is usually subjected to by those evaluating his contributions to the development of Zen in Japan.

As the first Japanese master to transmit directly the teaching of the Rinzai (C. Lin-chi) faction to Japan, Eisai is often subjected to the criteria of a supposed "pure" Zen tradition that originated with T'ang dynasty Lin-chi masters. Subjecting Eisai to T'ang Ch'an rhetoric should be avoided for two reasons. First, such an evaluation mistakes the role of lineage in the Ch'an tradition, assuming that it carries an unassailable ideological agenda when in fact its main function is to confer status upon an individual as a legitimate master.[60] Second, it assumes that Lin-chi faction orthodoxy in the Sung period had the same ideological assumptions as the Rinzai faction later on in Japanese history. This later account of Lin-chi/Rinzai teaching does stem from the canonical literature of the T'ang Ch'an tradition, to be sure. Nevertheless, the compilation of the "recorded sayings" (C. *yülu*, J. *goroku*) upon which the contemporary understanding of Lin-chi/Rinzai ideology is based is almost exclusively a post-T'ang phenomena. At the time of Eisai's visits to China at the end of the twelfth century, it was the Lin-chi lineage that had come to dominate the Ch'an world, not the Lin-chi ideology.[61]

The difference between Eisai's understanding of Zen and what would later become the accepted ideology of the Lin-chi school is suggested in the following example. According to a famous story related in the *Platform Sūtra*, when Emperor Wu asked Bodhidharma whether his lifetime of building temples, giving alms, and making offerings had gained merit for him or not, Bodhidharma rebuked his suggestion. The Sixth Patriarch explained Bodhidharma's rebuke by differentiating the search for blessings (*fu*) from the search for merit (*kung-te*). "Building temples, giving alms, and making offerings are merely the practice of seeking after blessings. . . . Merit is in the *Dharmakāya*, not in the field of blessings."[62] In other words, conventional Buddhist practices aimed at seeking blessings are at best peripheral to Ch'an teaching. The real essence of Ch'an practice lies in "seeing into your own nature" and cultivating a "straightforward mind." This concept is far removed from the *Ninnō kyō* model of the Buddhist ruler who actively promotes a flourishing Buddhist practice in his realm, centering on the very "practices aimed at seeking blessings" denigrated in the *Platform Sūtra*.

One might argue, however, that the actual effect of the *Platform Sūtra* distinction between merit and virtue was only to separate what is essential in Buddhist practice from what is secondary. In this formulation, meditation is essential because it provides merit, the enlightenment experience of "seeing into your own nature." Other, externally driven practices such as building temples, giving alms, and making offerings, "seeking after blessings," may be regarded as complementary but unessential. It follows that meditation and monastic discipline would constitute the integral components of Ch'an practice, the basis from which the enlightenment experience is realized. Yet, contrary to expectation, it is precisely here that we encounter the famous Ch'an denial of conventional forms of Buddhist meditation and monastic discipline that were the particular hallmarks of Lin-chi-faction rhetoric: "Even for those who keep the rules regarding food and conduct with the care of a man carrying oil so as not to spill a drop, if their Dharma-eye is not clear, they will have to pay up their debts."[63] Lin-chi characterizes his monastery as a place where the monks "neither read sūtras nor learn meditation."[64] This is a far cry from the stern emphasis on monastic discipline and conventional meditation as prerequisite for Buddhist practice advocated by Eisai.

The *Liu-tsu t'an ching* (J. *Rokuzu dankyō*; "Platform Sūtra of the Sixth Patriarch") and the *Lin-chi lu* (J. *Rinzai roku*; "Record of Lin-chi"), unassailable classics according to later tradition of Ch'an teaching, are conspicuous by their absence in the *Kōzen gokokuron*. Nor can one find reference to any of the hallowed masters of the recorded sayings tradition. This absence suggests that Eisai looked elsewhere for his interpretation of Zen in spite of his lineal affiliation. But where should the model for Eisai's Zen be sought, if not in these "classic" works? Eisai's conception of Zen bears the strong imprint of concerns that drove Ch'an in the early Sung period. Although the interpretation of Sung Ch'an by Ta-hui Tsung-kao (1089–1163), a leading master of the Lin-chi faction who emphasized *k'an-hua* and *kung-an*, or kōan-introspection—the terms that came to characterize much of Ch'an teaching and practice—was in place by the time of Eisai's study in China; there is no evidence of its influence in the *Kōzen gokokuron*. In spite of his factional affiliation, Eisai's definition of Zen is indebted to masters who were neither associated with the Lin-chi lineage nor sympathetic to positions that defined Lin-chi ideology.

Prior to the ascendance of the Lin-chi faction in the early Sung, Ch'an was dominated by masters associated with the revival of Buddhism in the Wu-yüeh region.[65] The majority of these masters were descendants of Fa-yen Wen-i. They dominated the temples of Ch'ien-t'ang, the political center of the region that later became the Southern Sung capital of Hang-chou, and were responsible for the revival of Mount T'ien-t'ai as a Buddhist center. The rulers of Wu-yüeh, rather than the clergy, played the leading role in planning the revival.[66] Much of the enterprise of the Wu-yüeh rulers was naturally aimed at restoring Mount T'ien-t'ai, the spiritual center of the region, which had fallen into decay as a result of neglect and destruction in the late T'ang period. It also involved dispatching envoys to Japan and Korea to retrieve lost works of the T'ien-t'ai school. These events, aimed at reviving the past glory of T'ien-t'ai as a center for Buddhism, also influenced the type of Ch'an teaching that flourished in the Wu-yüeh region. This legacy was particularly attractive to Eisai, who saw in Ch'an the remedy for the reform of Japanese Tendai. Eisai's whole presumption of Zen as both the lost source and the fulfillment of Tendai teaching seems predicated on the Wu-yüeh revival of Mount T'ien-t'ai as a Ch'an center. The interpretation of Ch'an developed by Fa-yen lineage monks from this region, rather than Lin-chi orthodoxy, had the greatest influence over Eisai's understanding of Zen.

Concerns about Ch'an lineage, the relation between Ch'an and Buddhist teaching, and the observance of Buddhist discipline ran particularly high in the early Sung period. The resolutions suggested by leading Buddhist masters at this time played an important role in determining the shape of the Ch'an tradition from the Sung period on. In the following, I examine Eisai's positions in the *Kōzen gokokuron* regarding these three concerns against precedents established at the beginning of the Sung period. In particular, Eisai's positions are discussed in reference to resolutions for the concerns suggested in the works of three masters from the Wu-yüeh region: Tao-yüan (Dōgen; fl. c. 1000), compiler of the *Ching-te ch'uan-teng lu* (J. *Keitoku dentōroku*; Ching-te era Record of the Transmission of the Lamp);[67] Yung-ming Yen-shou (J. *Eimei Enju*; 904–975), compiler of the *Tsung-ching lu* (J. *Sugyō roku*; Records of the Source-Mirror) and *Wan-shan t'ung-kuei chi* (J. *Manzen dōki shu*; Anthology on the Common End of Myriad Good Deeds);[68] and Tsan-ning (J. *Sannei*; 919–1001), compiler of the *Sung kao-seng chuan* (J. *Sō kōsoden*; Sung Biographies of Eminent Monks) and the *Seng shih-lüeh* (J. *So shiryaku*; Outline History of the Saṅgha).[69] In each of their respective ways, these three masters set precedents that came to characterize Sung Ch'an. These were not the only precedents for Ch'an teaching and practice during the Sung period. Under the later influence of Lin-chi Ch'an masters, Ch'an's interpretation took a decidedly different direction, emphasizing the archetypal Ch'an persona recorded in *kung-an* and *yü-lu* collections. In spite of Eisai's affiliation with the Lin-chi lineage, his understanding of Ch'an bears a marked resemblance to these earlier precedents.[70]

The identification of Buddhist identity in terms of lineal associations was one of the conventions that characterized Sung Buddhism. Lineage association was already an established mark of Buddhist, including Ch'an sectarian, identity by the T'ang, but it did not go without challenge as a means of designating identity. Nonsectarian collections of Buddhist biographies, the *Kao-seng chuan* (Biographies of Eminent Monks) and *Hsü kao-seng chuan* (Biographies of Eminent Monks, Continued), provided the most valued format for interpreting the lives of noteworthy monks prior to the Sung. The early Sung period exhibited ambivalence between two different approaches for recording the biographies of exemplary Buddhist monks. This ambivalence is reflected in the nearly simultaneous appearance of two works: the *Sung kao-seng chuan* (988), which is committed to the established patterns for recording the biographies of monks in Chinese Buddhism, and the *Ching-te ch'uan-teng lu* (1004), which became the widely accepted precedent for recording the identities of Ch'an monks in the Sung period.[71] The different approach of each work is reflected conceptually in the way the basic identity of a monk is defined and in the regard for sectarian lineage.

The difference between the *Sung kao-seng chuan* and *Ching-te ch'uan-teng lu* approach to biography centers on the essential identity of individual monks and the criteria determining that identity. In the *Sung kao-seng chuan* works, events associated with particular monks were recorded according to standardized categories of "expertise," regardless of sectarian affiliation.[72] The category of "expertise" indicated the essential identity of the monk, the mark of a monk's "eminence." The *Ching-te ch'uan-teng lu*, on the other hand, was a sectarian work of the Ch'an school. Its purpose was to promote the lineage of the Fa-yen (J. *Hōgen*) faction over rival factions as the heir to Ch'an mind transmission. Rather than a broad-based nonsectarian approach that recognizes different categories of expertise, the *ch'uan-teng lu* (J. *dentōroku*) approach determined a monk's worth according to narrowly defined sectarian criteria decided by the Ch'an school.[73] Both approaches influenced Eisai's characterization of Zen in the *Kōzen gokokuron*.

Ching-te ch'uan-teng lu's influence on the *Kōzen gokokuron* is most evident in section 5, "The Transmission Lineage of the Zen School," where Eisai aligns himself with the Huang-lung (J. ōryō) line of the Lin-chi (J. Rinzai) faction of Ch'an, substantiating his claim with a detailed record of the transmission lineage of the Ch'an school extending to Eisai himself. In the *Kōzen gokokuron*, the authorization is backed by a formal statement certifying the transmission of the Mind teaching to Eisai from his mentor, Hsü-an Huai-Ch'ang (J. Kian Eshō) of Wan-nien (J. Mannen) Temple on Mount T'ien-t'ai.[74]

The lineage recorded by Eisai in the *Kōzen gokokuron* was a standard one in the Ch'an tradition, consisting of three parts. The first part associated the origins of the Ch'an lineage with the former Buddhas of the distant past, culminating with the "seven Buddhas of the past" which begins with Vipassin (J. Bibashi) and ends with Śākyamuni (J. Shakamon). The second part listed the twenty-eight Indian patriarchs adopted in the Ch'an lineage, from Mahākāśyapa (J. Makakasho) to Bodhidharma (J. Bodaidaruma). The list adopted by Eisai is identical to the one first adopted in the *Pao-lin chuan* (compiled 801).[75] The *Pao-lin chuan* (J. *Hōrinden*; Transmission of the Treasure Grove) lineage of patriarchs was accepted without variation in the important Ch'an works of the Sung period, including Tao-yüan's *Ching-te ch'uan-teng lu* and Yen-shou's *Tsung-ching lu*.[76] The third part included the list of Chinese patriarchs, from Hui-k'o (J. Eka) through Hui-neng (J. Enō) and Lin-chi (J. Rinzai), founder of the Lin-chi (J. Rinzai) faction, and through the Sung Ch'an master Huang-lung Hui-nan (J. ōryō Enan), founder of the Huang-lung (J. ōryō) branch, and ending with Eisai's teacher Hsü-an Huai-chang, followed by Eisai.

There is no doubt that this certification of transmission represented a crucial component in Eisai's claim as legitimate heir and direct descendant of the Buddha's teaching. In the context of early Kamakura Japan, Eisai's claim countered a similar claim by a contemporary, Dainichi Nōnin (?–1196?), a self-proclaimed representative of the Daruma faction.[77] To bolster his claim, Nōnin sent disciples to China to procure acknowledgment for his status as interpreter of Zen. The Sung Ch'an master Te-kuang (1121–1203), upon receiving a letter and gifts sent by Nōnin, is reported to have "gladly attested to Nōnin's awakening and sent him a Dharma robe, a name, and picture of Bodhidharma with a verse-in-praise inscribed."[78] The direct and personal (i.e., authentic) transmission between master and disciple claimed by Eisai stood in marked contrast to Nōnin's indirect (i.e., inauthentic) transmission.

In this context, Eisai claimed that authentic transmission was a prerequisite for government support of Zen. Eisai contends that the reason the Lin-chi faction is the most prosperous of the five factions of Ch'an in China is that it receives official authorization from the Sung government.[79] This claim suggests that Eisai's promotion of Zen, specifically the Huang-lung branch of the

Lin-chi faction, is closely connected to his support for a similarly inspired government revival of Buddhism in Japan. The Sung Ch'an model suggested that authentic Buddhism was based on direct transmission from master to disciple, a claim that Eisai verifies in his own case.

In spite of Eisai's identification with lineage transmission in the *Kōzen gokokuron*, his sectarian identity was not exclusive. The narrower sectarian approach identifying one exclusively on the basis of lineage was a product of the later Kamakura period and was foreign to Eisai.[80] Eisai, as was seen earlier, recognized the validity of the T'ien-t'ai *ch'an* tradition in addition to that of the Ch'an school. In this regard, Eisai's view of Ch'an is not exclusively tied to Ch'an sectarian identity, but is part of a broader movement within Buddhism encompassing the Ch'an and T'ien-t'ai meditation traditions. This view of Ch'an more closely resembles that of the early Sung *vinaya* master, Tsan-ning, and the Ch'an syncretist, Yen-shou.

Although Tsan-ning was not a member of the Ch'an school, he lived in an age and an area in which Ch'an influence was pervasive. Tsan-ning's view of the Ch'an school is interesting in light of his own position as a high-ranking member of the Sung bureaucracy and a monk trained in the *vinaya*, at a time when Ch'an was establishing itself as the most influential school of Buddhism in China. In addition to similarities in the way Tsan-ning and Eisai understood Ch'an lineage, discussed later, a link between Tsan-ning and the *Kōzen gokokuron* can be drawn in three ways. In the first place, direct citations from Tsan-ning's *Sung kao-seng chuan* appear in the *Kōzen gokokuron*.[81] Furthermore, Tsan-ning and Eisai shared certain temporal goals regarding the restoration and preservation of Buddhism. In the conclusion to the *Seng shih-lüeh*, Tsan-ning provides his reason for writing in terms of "hope for the revival of Buddhism" and "to ensure the lasting presence of the True Law" (*cheng-fa*),[82] phraseology repeated nearly verbatim in the title of section 1 of the *Kōzen gokokuron*, "Ensuring the Lasting Presence of Buddhist Teaching [or Law]." Third, Tsan-ning was a proponent of Buddhist ritual at the Sung court. He advocated that Buddhist institutions and rituals be viewed as legitimate expressions of the Chinese state. He specifically promoted use of *Jen-wang ching* (J. *Ninnō kyō*) inspired rituals by the imperial court.[83] Government support for Ch'an institutions during the Sung was heavily indebted to the case Tsan-ning made for Buddhism at the early Sung court. These links between Tsan-ning and the *Kōzen gokokuron* can also be extended more specifically to the question regarding Ch'an lineage.

Tsan-ning was an avid supporter of Ch'an but sought to incorporate it within the Buddhist tradition as a whole. Tsan-ning viewed Ch'an as the fulfillment of the Buddhist meditation tradition, not as an independent transmission of Buddhist teaching at odds with the traditions that preceded it. His major reservation was with those who promoted Ch'an as an independent movement that excluded other Buddhist teachings and schools. Tsan-ning's inclination to view Ch'an as the fulfillment of the Buddhist meditation tradition is evident from the way in which he accepts the traditional lineage of the Ch'an school in relation to that of the T'ien-t'ai school.

The fact that Tsan-ning accepts in principle the lineage of the Ch'an school is clear from his comments recorded in the *Sung kao-seng chuan*.[84] There, he runs through the conventional list of Chinese Ch'an patriarchs from Bodhidharma, through Hui-k'o, Seng-ts'an, and Tao-hsin. After Tao-hsin, the lineage divides into two branches, that of Hung-jen and that of Niu-t'ou Fa-jung. Although Hung-jen also produced two branches, that of Shen-hsiu and that of Hui-neng, it was Hui-neng who passed on the robe of transmission and it was his school that flourished thereafter. In contrast to the Ch'an lineage, Tsan-ning also presents the lineage of the T'ien-t'ai school in an abbreviated form: the masters Hui-wen, Hui-ssu, and Chih-i. The T'ien-t'ai masters are credited with furthering Ch'an methods in China (specifically the "three contemplations" of emptiness, provisional existence, and the middle way between these two; and "cessation and contemplation" (*chih-kuan*)) through the Sui dynasty (581–618). The important point here is that T'ien-t'ai is presented in such a way that it represents *ch'an* prior to the Ch'an movement that traced its origins to Bodhidharma. The *ch'an* of the Ch'an school that flourished in the T'ang represents, in Tsan-ning's arrangement, the fulfillment of T'ien-t'ai *ch'an*. Tsan-ning thus affirmed the validity of Fa-yen Ch'an in Wu-yüeh, where Fa-yen Wen-i's disciple, T'ian-t'ai Te-shao, converted Mount T'ien-t'ai into a center for Ch'an training (albeit with a heavy dose of T'ien-t'ai teaching added). The appeal of this situation for Eisai is obvious.

The assumptions underlying Tsan-ning's view of Ch'an parallel those of Eisai in the *Kōzen gokokuron*. This is particularly evident in Eisai's characterization of Tendai in relation to Zen. In the first place, Eisai treats Tendai adaptations of *ch'an* in section 4 of the *Kōzen gokokuron*, just prior to his discussion of Zen school *ch'an* in section 5. This parallels the order with which Tsan-ning treats T'ien-t'ai and Ch'an in the *hsi-ch'an* commentary of the *Sung kao-seng chuan* mentioned previously. Following the Japanese Tendai tradition recorded in the *Isshin-kai* of Saichō, moreover, Eisai maintained that direct contact (i.e., legitimate transmission) occurred between Bodhidharma and Hui-ssu, which became the basis for a lineage of *ch'an* transmission within the T'ien-t'ai school.[85] Doing so allowed Eisai to reconstruct the history of *ch'an* transmission in China in a way that agreed with Tsan-ning yet also went a crucial step further. It asserted that T'ien-t'ai *ch'an* was more than merely *ch'an* prior to the Ch'an movement emanating from Bodhidharma. Since Tsan-ning contended that T'ien-t'ai *ch'an* and the *ch'an* of the Ch'an school could be traced from the same source, the Ch'an master Bodhidharma, this meant that the direct transmission from Bodhidharma was not the exclusive prerogative of the Ch'an school but also included T'ien-t'ai. This was a suitable pretext for one advocating Zen as the basis for Tendai reform.[86]

Two important points in section 4 of the *Kōzen gokokuron* confirm Eisai's interpretation of Zen. The first is the aforementioned proposition that Sung Ch'an represents the legitimate legacy of both Ch'an and T'ien-t'ai teaching and that the essence of this tradition is embodied in the Buddhist practice authorized in the Sung Ch'an monastic code, the *Ch'an-yuan ch'ing-kuei*.[87] In conjunction with the actual lineage in section 5, it established Eisai as legitimate heir to this Sung Ch'an tradition. The second point is reflected directly in Eisai's concluding remarks to the section: "In terms of the main point raised here, the scriptures, monastic rules, and treatises preached by the Buddha throughout the five periods of his teaching career are all essential teachings of the Buddha's *zen*."[88] The point here is that Eisai viewed Zen teaching within the context of the Buddhist tradition as a whole—*zen* is seen as the inspiration for the entire Buddhist tradition and not as an exclusive teaching fundamentally opposed to that tradition. The Buddhist tradition, one should add, is here framed in terms of the interpretation given to it in the T'ien-t'ai *p'an-chiao* (J. *hankyō*) doctrine.[89]

While Eisai's position on Zen within Buddhism parallels that of Tsan-ning, it is more notably framed within principles of Ch'an syncretism associated with Yung-ming Yen-shou. Yen-shou played a leading role in defining Buddhism and the meaning of Buddhist practice in the post-T'ang period. His influence spread to Korea and Japan, as well as China. In this respect alone, Yen-shou cast a wide shadow over the development of the "world of Zen" as Ch'an movements spread throughout East Asia. Although most commonly associated with developments in Chinese Ch'an and Korean Sŏn, Yen-shou's influence was strongly felt in early Japanese Zen as well. His model served as an inspiration for Dōgen,[90] and his works were frequently cited in Japanese Buddhist circles.[91] More significantly for the present context, Yen-shou's writings figured directly in the dispute between Eisai and Nōnin's *Daruma-shū* regarding the correct understanding of Zen (discussed here later). As a result, Yen-shou was a central figure in the struggle to define Zen in early Kamakura Japan.

Yen-shou's influence in the *Kōzen gokokuron* is exhibited in two interrelated ways: through specific reference to his writings, and through the general adoption of his ideas. The *Tsung-ching lu* is cited in various contexts in the *Kōzen gokokuron*. In section 3, for example, it is cited in response to concerns that Zen practitioners adhere to a false view of emptiness or an obscure realization, based on their prized independence from words and letters.[92] It is also cited in connection with a question about Zen practitioners' alleged reluctance to follow the monastic rules and conventional Buddhist practices, or to engage in such common practices as the recitation of Buddha names or making offerings to relics.[93] In section 7, "Outlining Zen Doctrines and Encouraging Zen Practice," it is cited as the basis for the first of the three methods considered, "[viewing Zen] from the perspective of conventional Buddhist teaching" (C. *yüeh-chiao*; J. *yakukyō*).[94] In brief, Eisai relies on Yen-shou to verify that Zen is harmonious with rather than antagonistic toward established Buddhist doctrines and practices.

One work of Yen-shou in which his syncretic tendencies are made abundantly clear is the *Wan-shan t'ung-kuei chi*.[95] In this work, a wide range of activities are advocated as constituting Buddhist practice: worshipping Buddhas and bodhisattvas; venerating *stūpas*; chanting *sūtras*; preaching the *dharma*; practicing repentance, the *pāramitās*, and the eightfold path; defending orthodoxy; contemplation; practicing the recitation of Buddha names (*nien-fo*); building temples; and even practicing self-immolation.[96] This broad range of Buddhist activities may be linked to the context of an early Sung Buddhist revival that is pluralistic in nature. The problem for Yen-shou was how to justify the inclusion of such diverse practices in one system. The diversity of his "myriad good deeds" (*wan-shan*) did not fit well with the narrower concerns of established Buddhist schools. The focal point around which the myriad good deeds are advocated in the *Wan-shan t'ung-kuei chi* is often connected with the *Fa-hua ching* (J. *Hokkekyō*) and T'ien-t'ai teaching. The *Fa-hua ching* is the principal scripture mentioned in connection with *sūtra* chanting and Dharma lectures. It is the basis for practicing repentance and figures prominently in Yen-shou's contemplation practice as well. It provides the principal inspiration for self-immolation. Yen-shou's much heralded *nien-fo* practice is also based on it.

To justify the pluralistic array of practices, Yen-shou looked to theoretical conceptions common to Buddhism, particularly the T'ien-t'ai and Hua-yen traditions. Significantly, the *Wan-shan t'ung-kuei chi* begins with the claim that all good deeds (*shan*) are ultimately based on (*kuei*) the absolute, true form (*shih-hsiang*) (i.e., the true reality of all forms, true suchness, the ultimate) of fundamental principle (*tsung*). The point here is that extensive and active practice is necessary and that one should not cling foolishly to aimless sitting and thereby obstruct true cultivation. The reason for this precept is provided in the nature of interaction between the abstract and particular as conceived through *li* (noumena) and *shih* (phenomena), central conceptions in the Hua-yen tradition. In addition, Yen-shou draws from a number of theoretical constructions that parallel *li* and *shih*: the real and the expedient, absolute truth and worldly truth, nature and form, substance and function, and emptiness and existence. This parallel also extends to the title of the work. For Yen-shou, the meaning of *wan-shan* (the myriad good deeds) is closely connected to the meaning of *shih* (phenomena) and all of its associated meanings. The meaning of *t'ung-kuei* (the common end), the realm of the absolute, is closely associated with *li* (noumena) and all of its counterparts.

Yen-shou's syncretism and his promotion of Buddhist pluralism in the *Wan-shan t'ung-kuei chi* is dependent on the theoretical dichotomy of *li* and *shih*. According to Yen-shou, the relationship between these two aspects of reality is one of identity, but because Buddhist practitioners insist on stressing the *li* side of the equation as the real source of enlightenment, the myriad good deeds or the *shih* side of the equation have fallen into disrepute and tend to be either rejected or neglected. Rather than being seen as disturbances to the realm of Truth, the activity of the myriad good deeds should be regarded as manifestations of one's realization and confirmation of enlightenment attained. In the correct relationship between the theoretical and practical, both are awarded equal emphasis and neither is neglected at the expense of the other. The basis for this relationship is implicit in the structure of reality itself. The equal emphasis accorded theory and practice represents a reflection of the same relationship that exists between the absolute and the myriad good deeds, *li* and *shih*, and so on.

It is clear that Eisai agreed with Yen-shou's approach. Stylistically, the *Kōzen gokokuron* has much in common with the *Tsung-ching lu* and the *Wan-shan t'ung-kuei chi*. Yen-shou's methodology, outlined in his preface (*hsü*) to the *Tsung-ching lu*, combines three elements: first, establishing the correct teaching (*cheng-tsung*); second, responding to questions to dispel doubts; and third, citing scriptural authority to support one's claim.[97] This methodology is prominent in the *Kōzen gokokuron* as well, where Eisai's indebtedness to Yen-shou's method in the *Tsung-ching lu* is openly acknowledged.[98] The application of Yen-shou's method in the *Kōzen gokokuron* can also be demonstrated as follows. The expressed aim of the *Kōzen gokokuron* is to establish Zen as the correct interpretation of Buddhist teaching (i.e., establishing the correct teaching).[99] The longest section of the *Kōzen gokokuron*, section 3, "Resolving the Doubts of the People of the World," is presented in a question-and-answer format reminiscent of that employed by Yen-shou (i.e., responding to questions to dispel doubts). Even a cursory glance at the *Kōzen gokokuron* reveals the importance of scriptural passages for authorizing the positions taken (i.e., citing scriptural authority to support one's claims).[100]

As we have seen, Eisai's syncretism is indebted in various ways to Sung precedents. What is surprising is not Eisai's indebtedness to Sung Ch'an, but the sources that he relied on most for his understanding. His opposition to an interpretation of Zen as an isolated and independent tradition places him both at odds with Rinzai orthodoxy and in agreement with Sung Ch'an syncretism as championed by monks from Wu-yüeh affiliated with the Fa-yen faction. In Yen-shou's case, the influence on Eisai extended beyond coincidental similarity. Yen-shou's syncretism figured prominently in the battle to define early Kamakura Zen.

The Role of Syncretism in Early Japanese Zen: Yen-shou's
Influence on Eisai's *Kōzen gokokuron* and the
Daruma-shū of Nōnin

In addition to the general influence of Yen-shou's writings on Sung and Kamakura Buddhism, his writings formed the background for a major dispute
in early Kamakura Zen. Ishii Shūdō has called attention to the influence of the
Tsung-ching lu on the content of *Jōtō shōgakuron* (*Treatise on the Bodhisattva's
Attainment of Enlightenment*), an important work of the Japanese Daruma faction, Eisai's main rival for the Zen banner.[101] Ishii has shown clearly the close
relationship between large portions of the *Jōtō shōgakuron* and the *Tsung-ching
lu*, demonstrating the Daruma faction's dependence on Yen-shou's text. Given
the Japanese Daruma faction's reliance on the *Tsung-ching lu*, Eisai's rivalry
with Nōnin and the impact Yen-shou had on the *Kōzen gokokuron*, it is important to establish more clearly the relationship between Yen-shou's syncretism
and the position adopted by Eisai in the *Kōzen gokokuron*.

The discussion here begins with a review of Ishii's characterization of the
issue.[102] As Ishii notes, Yanagida Seizan maintains that in a brief document,
the *Mirai ki*,[103] written a year prior to the *Kōzen gokokuron* (in the eighth year
of the *Kenkyū* era, 1197), Eisai rejected the claims of Kakua (b. 1142) and Nōnin
(?–1196) as transmitters of the Zen school to Japan.[104] Yanagida concludes that
Eisai's aim in compiling the *Kōzen gokokuron*, moreover, was to distinguish his
position regarding Zen from that of Nōnin and the Daruma faction. According
to Yanagida, Eisai's insistence on aligning Sung Ch'an teaching and Sung
Buddhist precept practice makes sense in terms of his need to distinguish his
aims from those of the Daruma faction, whose own interpretation of Zen emphasized its antinomian character. In accomplishing this purpose, Eisai created
another problem. His strict precept practice included following the rules of the
Hīnayāna *vinaya*, something that Saichō, the founder of Japanese Tendai, rejected. For political reasons, to establish Tendai independence from the Nara
Buddhist schools, Saichō insisted that Mt. Hiei monks follow only the less
rigorous bodhisattva precepts.[105] As a result, Eisai found himself maintaining
a precarious balance, promoting a strict style of Zen to counter the Daruma
faction that challenged the spirit of Saichō's reform and jeopardizing his own
Zen as a Tendai reform movement.

How does Eisai's criticism of the Daruma faction square with the fact that
both the *Kōzen gokokuron* and the *Jōtō shōgakuron* exhibit strong influence from
the seminal figure of Sung Ch'an, Yung-ming Yen-shou? Ishii maintains that
although Nōnin and Eisai were both heavily influenced by Yen-shou's syncretism, Nōnin tended toward a "naturalistic, heretical Zen" (*shizen gedōteki zen*)
based on the contention "Mind itself is Buddha" (*sokushin zebutsu*), whereas
Eisai interpreted the *Tsung-ching lu* in terms of Yen-shou's moralism based on

adherence to the Buddhist precepts (*jiritsu shūgi*).[106] The former position refers to the Daruma faction's alleged rejection of the precepts and conventional Buddhist practice on the assumption that "from the outset there are no pas-sions; from the beginning we are enlightened."[107] As a result, conventional practice is essentially useless. While stated in a highly condensed form, the main thrust of this position, I might add, is in agreement with later Rinzai Zen orthodoxy. Eisai, on the other hand, is deeply indebted to Yen-shou's con-ception of Zen as the "Mind school" and to Yen-shou's insistence that the Buddhist precepts and conventional Buddhist methods are necessary prereq-uisites for and accompaniments to true Zen practice. And, as Ishii points out, this view accounts for Eisai's insistence on the importance of the *Zen'en shingi* in the transmission of Zen teaching and practice to Japan.[108]

Behind Ishii's characterization of Eisai's Zen is the acknowledgment that Eisai's experience in Sung China extended beyond the influence of Yen-shou and the early Sung period. Yen-shou's influence on Eisai was filtered through the Sung Lin-chi (J. Rinzai) lineage interpretation of Ch'an with which Eisai identified. This identity, as was previously mentioned, was formally asserted in section 5 of the *Kōzen gokokuron*, which placed Eisai as a fifty-third–gener-ation heir of the Huang-lung (J. *Ōryō*) faction of the Lin-chi school, dating from the seven Buddhas of the past. Ishii is correct in asserting that this con-nection had a great impact on Eisai's understanding of Zen, including his perspective on the Zen-based Buddhist syncretism promoted by Yen-shou. The influence of the Lin-chi faction on Eisai's position in the *Kōzen gokokuron*, however, needs to be assessed carefully.

The normative position of Lin-chi Ch'an is often characterized in terms of four verses attributed to Bodhidharma: "A special transmission outside the teachings" (C. *chiao-wai pieh-ch'üan*; J. *kyōge betsuden*); "Do not establish words and letters" (C. *pu-li wen-tzu*; J. *furyū monji*); "Directly point to the human mind" (C. *ch'ih-chih jen-hsin*; J. *jikishi ninshin*); and "See nature and become a Buddha" (C. *chien-hsing ch'eng-fo*; J. *kenshō jōbutsu*). Although the individual use of each of these phrases predates the Sung dynasty, they were not estab-lished as a normative set of expressions until well into the Sung.[109] The latter three verses appear in the *Kōzen gokokuron*, where they are attributed to Bod-hidharma, and are referred to as the "gateway of Zen" (*zenmon*).[110] The first verse, "A special transmission outside the teachings," is noticeably absent. This omission further aligns Eisai with Tsan-ning and Yen-shou, whose understand-ing of Ch'an also included the latter three verses but not the first.[111] Together, they represented a Ch'an/Zen tradition that did not identify itself as "a special transmission outside the teachings" and was the prevailing interpretation of Ch'an at the outset of the Sung.

While broad agreement existed between Eisai's Zen syncretism and early Sung Ch'an, there were also differences regarding the actual form such syn-cretism might take. Section 7 of the *Kōzen gokokuron*, "An Outline of the Principal Methods for Practicing Zen," points to the specific form of Eisai's Zen syncretism.[112] This section classifies Zen teaching into three types. The first is the type, described earlier, associated with Yen-shou and the *Tsung-ching lu*, "[viewing Zen] from the perspective of conventional Buddhist teaching (C. *yüeh-chiao*; J. *yakukyō*)."[113] In this section, Eisai maintains that these methods are aimed at "dull-witted, ordinary people"; nevertheless, they are considered "skillful means for initiating the cultivation [of Zen]."

The second type, "[viewing Zen] from the perspective of Zen" (C. *yüeh-Ch'an*; J. *yakuzen*), is reminiscent of assumptions commonly encountered in the sectarian exclusiveness of the "pure" Zen tradition. Methods here aimed at "the most talented people" are "not confined to words and letters [i.e., the Buddhist textual tradition] and not concerned with mental thought [i.e., conventional meditation practices]." They represent methods of practice that are "free from mental deliberation" and methods of study that "transcend the ways of either common people or sages."

The third type refers to "[viewing Zen] from the aspect that conventional Buddhist teaching and Zen teaching hold in common" (C. *yüeh tsung-hsiang*; J. *yaku sōsō*).[114] This type points to a higher level of synthesis for Eisai than that represented by Yen-shou. It is based on a common assumption pervading Mahayāna Buddhist thought that anything implicated in name and form has only a provisional existence and is ultimately unreal. This metaphysical reductionism is here applied to whatever one may practice or study, including conventional Buddhist teaching and Zen teaching. In the end all conceptions, even "enlightenment" or *nirvāṇa*, are nothing more than designations for provisionally existing things and are essentially unreal. This is the ultimate standpoint (i.e., that there is no standpoint) of Zen (and for that matter, Buddhist) teaching and practice. In the end, Eisai concludes:

> The [teaching of the] Zen school is independent of what is articulated in names and words, independent of mental deliberations and distinctions, incapable of comprehension, and ultimately unobtainable.[115] The so-called "Law of the Buddha" is not a law that can be articulated and is only [provisionally] named the Law of the Buddha.[116] What is currently referred to as Zen marks this as a conspicuous feature of its teaching. Since the above three methods are all [articulated in terms of] provisional names, anyone who claims that Buddhist Zen teaching depends on words and letters and is articulated verbally is actually slandering the Buddha and slandering the Law.[117] Because of this, the patriarch-master [Bodhidharma] referred to the Zen approach [in terms of] "do not rely on words and letters, directly point to the human mind, and see one's nature and become a Buddha." Anyone who [tries to understand Buddhism] by grasping names and words is ignorant of the Law, and anyone who [tries to

understand Buddhism] by grasping at the appearances [of names and forms] is even more deluded. [The state that] is inherently immovable, where there is nothing to be obtained, is what is referred to as seeing the Law of the Buddha [in the true Zen approach].[118]

Eisai's syncretism thus rejected the exclusivity of "pure" Zen as an independent teaching apart from scriptural tradition, while accepting the superiority of Zen's interpretation of Buddhism. In other words, Eisai's Zen does not stand in opposition to the Buddhist tradition but represents its fulfillment and crowning achievement. It represents the legitimate, "true," and full understanding of Buddhist teaching, as opposed to the legitimate but partial and incomplete interpretations that preceded it.

Ultimately, the *Kōzen gokokuron* reflects Eisai's experience with Sung Ch'an. This experience, like the characterization of Zen in the *Kōzen gokokuron*, is informed and influenced by, but not confined to, the stamp that Yen-shou placed on post-T'ang Buddhism. In this respect, Eisai's Zen syncretism may be aligned with two of Yen-shou's concerns. The first is that Zen be understood within the broader context of Buddhist teaching; Zen and Buddhist teaching share a fundamental unity in outlook. The second is that Zen practice be firmly based in the Buddhist tradition of moral discipline and that it encompasses conventional Buddhist practices. These two concerns aligning Eisai and the *Kōzen gokokuron* with Yen-shou's syncretism, moreover, sharply distinguish Eisai's approach from that associated with Dainichi Nōnin and the Daruma faction.

In addition, Eisai's syncretism deviates from that of Yen-shou in significant ways. Rivalry between Eisai and Nōnin and the latter's dependence on Yen-shou made it advantageous for Eisai to provide some distance between his position and Yen-shou's. This may be a contributing factor in Eisai's categorization of Zen teaching in section 7 of the *Kōzen gokokuron* discussed previously, which relegates Yen-shou's understanding of Zen to an inferior status.

Scriptural references reveal doctrinal differences between Eisai and Yen-shou. A review of the sources either cited or referred to by Yen-shou in the *Wan-shan t'ung-kuei chi* reveals that scriptures and treatises associated with the T'ien-t'ai and Hua-yen schools were the most important influences on his thought.[119] *Prajñā-pāramitā* scriptures constituted a third major influence. A similar tabulation of sources in the *Kōzen gokokuron* reveals that scriptures and treatises associated with the T'ien-t'ai (J. Tendai) school are most frequently cited, followed by *Prajñā-pāramitā* scriptures and scriptures from the *Vinaya* (J. *ritsu*).[120] This fact suggests an important difference between Yen-shou's and Eisai's syncretism. Whereas Yen-shou's syncretism was constructed around T'ien-t'ai and Hua-yen, reflecting the influence of T'ang Buddhist scholasticism, Eisai's syncretism was constructed around Tendai and *prajñā* thought, reflecting the influence of the Japanese Tendai school and the Zen (C. Ch'an) tradition, particularly of the Sung Lin-chi faction, which Eisai affiliated with *Prajñā-pāramitā* literature. The emphasis on T'ien-t'ai/Tendai is a common feature in both Yen-shou and Eisai's syncretism. The emphasis on Hua-yen doctrine in Yen-shou's syncretism is almost totally absent from the *Kōzen go-kokuron*, which instead emphasizes *prajñā* sources.

The *prajñā* tradition was also important for Eisai as an ideology supporting the rulers of a Buddhist state. For Eisai, this ideology was particularly represented by the *Prajñāpāramitā Sūtra, on Explaining How Benevolent Kings Protect Their Countries* (*Ninnō gokoku hannya kyō*). The *prajñā* tradition thus provided an essential link for Eisai in connecting both the spiritual and political aims of Zen Buddhism in a single ideological framework.

Ultimately, what we have in the *Kōzen gokokuron* is a philosophy based on the Buddhist nominalism of the *prajñā* tradition, insisting that things exist in name only but not in actuality. This includes the Zen of Bodhidharma and the Chinese Lin-chi masters, whose descendants Eisai associated with in China. Combined with this philosophy is a practice based on the strict moral code of the Buddhist *vinaya* tradition, insisting that *zen* practice and the enlightenment experience are predicated on the observance of the precepts. This is the conservative Zen based on Buddhist principles of moral conduct. For Eisai, strict adherence to the Buddhist precepts is a necessary condition upon which the enlightenment experience (*prajñā*) is based. The following formulation from section 7 of the *Kōzen gokokuron* is inspired by the *Tso-ch'an i* (J. *Zazengi*) section of the *Ch'an-yuan ch'ing-kuei* (J. *Zen'en shingi*):[121]

> Any practitioner who wants to cultivate the teaching of the Zen
> school amounts to a bodhisattva studying *prajñā*. They should . . . be
> devoted to the cultivation of *samādhi* [and] maintain the wondrous
> purifying precepts of great bodhisattvas. . . .
>   The *Sūtra on Perfect Enlightenment* says, "All unobstructed pure
> wisdom arises from *zen* meditation [C. *ch'an-ting*; J. *zenjō*]." From
> this we know that to transcend common existence and enter the
> realm of the sacred, one must engage in [meditation] to quell the
> conditions [that cause vexations]. It is most urgent that one rely on
> the power of meditation [in all activities], whether walking, standing,
> sitting, or lying down. If one wants to realize [the power of] medita-
> tion, one must carry out the practice of the *vinaya* [precepts]. Those
> who carry out *zen* meditation practice in the absence of the stipu-
> lated provisions of the *vinaya* precepts have no basis for their prac-
> tice . . . Therefore, if one wants to realize the method for Zen medi-
> tation described here, one will uphold the *vinaya* purely so that one
> is free of any blemish.[122]

Or, as Eisai states later in the section, "It means that when one enters the ranks of the Thus Come Ones, one practices in the style implicit in their enlightenment and sagely wisdom. This is the form that [the practice of] Zen takes."[123] In this regard, Eisai's position in the *Kōzen gokokuron* stands in marked contrast to the following statements in the *Jōtō shōgakuron*:

> Further, the *vinaya* rules are to control the activities of the mind [C. *sheng-hsin*; J. *seishin*]. With the elimination of mental activity [C. *wu-hsin*; J. *mushin*], one transcends [the need for] the *vinaya*.[124] . . . Originally, there are no *vinaya* rules to practice, much less the cultivation of good deeds.[125]

Rather than the experience of *prajñā* being predicated on *vinaya* practice (i.e., wisdom being based on morality), the *Jōtō shōgakuron* passages suggest that the experience of *prajñā* precludes the need for *vinaya* practice (i.e., wisdom being beyond moral considerations). In this regard, Eisai clearly deviates from the Daruma faction of Nōnin and approximates the position advocated by Yen-shou in affirming the salutary effects of conventional Buddhist practice and morality.

Yen-shou's description of Ch'an as the "Mind Teaching," the essence of all Buddhist teaching, regardless of scriptural, scholastic, or sectarian affiliation, was attractive to all, including Eisai, who viewed Ch'an in connection with conventional Buddhist teaching. The Japanese context out of which Eisai arrived added to this appeal but shaped it in unique ways. What distinguished Eisai's syncretism from Yen-shou's was the way in which the former defined Zen teaching in accordance with the exigencies of his age. Circumstances in Japan determined a definition of Zen compatible with T'ien-t'ai teaching strongly tinged with *mikkyō* (esoteric) rituals.[126] But what distinguished Eisai's definition above all was his identification of Zen teaching with the *prajñā* ideology of the *Ninnō kyō*. It was not enough for Eisai to reform Buddhism by identifying Zen as the culmination of Buddhist teaching, or as a pretext for promoting myriad good deeds. For Eisai, the identification of Zen and the promotion of Buddhist practice were specifically drawn in terms of the *Ninnō kyō*.

In short, Yen-shou's approach acknowledged the legitimacy of Buddhist pluralism and sought to establish a basis for a multitude of Buddhist practices. It was aimed primarily at the private world of the individual practitioner. In Eisai's reform movement the private world of the practitioner was intricately bound to the fate of the country as a whole in a way that was unambiguous. The practitioner's activities were interpreted primarily in terms of their implications for the moral fiber of Japanese society and Japan's political destiny. The social and political dimension into which Zen practice was drawn in the Japanese context derived from the respect that *Ninnō kyō* ideology commanded.[127]

Eisai's Zen Reform Program: Conventional Buddhism
on the Sung-Kamakura Continuum

The *Kōzen gokokuron* promoted Zen as a reform doctrine for Japan. There are two basic assumptions implicit in Eisai's message. The first is that the current state of Buddhism in Japan is corrupt and in need of reform. The second is that the fate of Japan as a country is threatened by the corrupt state into which Buddhism has fallen. Within the context of these assumptions, Eisai's message naturally held important implications for the leaders of the Japanese government and the Heian Buddhist establishment.

Eisai called on the Japanese elite to realize their destiny as the leaders of a great country and enlightened Buddhist civilization. The terms of this ideal were drawn in specific reference to scriptures in the Buddhist canon that served to "protect a country" (*gokoku*). Japanese rulers had long acknowledged the salutary effects of these scriptures. They served as a focal point for services and ceremonies conducted at the imperial court and at Buddhist temples throughout the land, conducted upon imperial request and with government support. Because of Eisai's identification of the Buddhist *prajñā* tradition with Zen teaching, he was particularly drawn to the *Ninnō kyō*, one of the most important scriptures for "protecting a country." Classed among the *prajñā* literature, the *Ninnō kyō* and the ideology that it represented set the parameters within which Eisai's reform program was cast.

A careful examination of the *Kōzen gokokuron* clarifies its reliance on the *Ninnō kyō* and the ideals permeating ancient and medieval Japanese civilization. This raises the question of why the association between the *Kōzen gokokuron* and the *Ninnō kyō*, so central to Eisai's understanding of the role of Zen in Japan, has been overlooked and excused whenever the subject of Eisai and the *Kōzen gokokuron* are raised. Aside from an association with Japanese nationalism, a subject long avoided in the postwar period, the marginalization of Eisai and the *Kōzen gokokuron* may be attributed to the ideology of "pure" Zen that has prevailed in modern Zen interpretation.

Eisai's understanding of Zen was based on different assumptions. In order to distinguish these, the present study suggests an alternative way to read the text and understand its content. It also indicates the direction from which a more balanced appraisal of Eisai and the *Kōzen gokokuron* might come, one more in keeping with the historical circumstances of his life and the actual content of his thought.

The search for the source of misinterpretation of Eisai and the *Kōzen gokokuron* leads one to suggest an association of Zen masters in the respective "golden ages" of Ch'an in China and Zen in Japan. The combination of these "golden ages" evokes what might be termed a "T'ang-Tokugawa alliance." This alliance, based on the common belief that a tradition of T'ang and Tokugawa

Zen masters epitomizes the essence of a "pure" Zen tradition, bears the stamp of modern Rinzai orthodoxy, which considers that the truest heirs of the great T'ang Zen tradition of Hui-neng, Ma-tsu Tao-i, Pai-chang Huai-hai, Huang-po Hsi-yün, Lin-chi I-hsüan, and so on were Tokugawa Rinzai masters such as Bankei (1622–1693) and Hakuin (1685–1768).[128] In this interpretation, Zen irrationalism reigns supreme as the quintessential expression of *satori* (enlightenment).

A general reason precipitating this T'ang-Tokugawa alliance may also be suggested. The alliance was due to more than coincidence or simple recognition of spiritual kinship. It was precipitated in large part by the renewed identity of Zen masters in the Tokugawa period as political outsiders, when the Tokugawa shoguns officially replaced Zen (and for that matter, Buddhism) as the official ideology of the Japanese state with "Sung Learning" (*Sōgaku*), or Neo-Confucianism. According to this interpretation, as the Confucian "Ancient Learning" (*kogaku*) and Shinto "National Learning" (*kokugaku*) schools came to dominate political debate, Zen found its true voice as political outsider, echoing the "pure" Zen of its T'ang predecessors.[129]

The point, finally, is this: the kind of Zen master Eisai has been portrayed as has been determined by notions about Zen that Eisai himself did not adhere to. It is clear that when judged in terms of the criteria stemming from the Tokugawa Rinzai tradition, Eisai and the *Kōzen gokokuron* have not faired well. This fact suggests important differences separating Eisai from both his legendary T'ang predecessors and the Tokugawa masters who came after him. In short, Eisai held a different set of assumptions. In contrast to the T'ang–Tokugawa alliance of "pure" Zen, the *Kōzen gokokuron* reflects the assumptions of a syncretistic-oriented Zen that can be placed on what might be termed a "Sung-Kamakura continuum."

This syncretic style of Zen formed the basis for the thought of Yen-shou, the major figure of Ch'an–Buddhist syncretism in the post-T'ang period.[130] We have also seen how the syncretic style of Zen is important for the correct understanding of Eisai and the *Kōzen gokokuron*. Moreover, Yen-shou and Eisai were not isolated cases. The popularity of Zen syncretism is also reflected in the teaching of Enni Ben'en (1201–1280), who has been judged "the pivotal figure in the history of Zen in Japan during the thirteenth century."[131] Zen syncretism was also the leading teaching in Korean and Vietnamese Zen.[132]

In a search for a more balanced appraisal of Eisai and the *Kōzen gokokuron*, alternate criteria for interpreting Eisai's message of reform are needed. The emphases of Eisai's Buddhist reform program in the *Kōzen gokokuron* can be summarized in terms of wisdom (Skt. *prajñā*; J. *hannya*), the quintessential insight of Buddhist teaching, morality (Skt. *śila-vinaya*; J. *kairitsu*), the monastic discipline on which the Buddhist livelihood is based, and meditation (Skt. *samādhi*; J. *zen*). This formulation comes straight from the common tripartite division of the Buddha's eightfold path as *śīla*, *samādhi*, and *prajñā*. It is affirmed specifically by Eisai in the *Kōzen gokokuron*:

> The destruction of evil depends on the purification of wisdom. The purification of wisdom depends on the purification of meditation. The purification of meditation depends on the purification of the monastic precepts.[133] The Buddha possesses four kinds of positive methods for winning enlightenment. The first is the monastic precepts [*kai*]. The second is meditation [*zen*]. The third is wisdom [*hannya*]. The fourth is a mind free of impurities [*mujoku shin*].[134]

Among these four, Eisai notes, Zen meditation is the most important because it includes the other three. What this means is that far from being a radical, antiestablishment movement, Zen for Eisai was the banner for reform-minded Buddhist conservatism. This conservatism influenced Eisai's conception of Zen teaching and practice, his acceptance of the Buddhist scriptural tradition, and his promotion of moral discipline. It also presumed that Eisai would take a conciliatory approach in an attempt to win the support of government officials.

In the end, this approach suggests that what has passed under the name of Ch'an or Zen is historically conditioned. The question of which interpretation of Zen is "correct"—"pure" Zen or "syncretic" Zen—is not at issue here. What is at issue is coming to a more contextualized understanding of how Zen was perceived and characterized within the continuum of Sung and Kamakura Buddhist masters. Conceptions of Ch'an and Zen have been shaped differently in diverse historical contexts. Earlier conceptions do not always agree with the criteria imposed by later sectarian tradition. Important figures in the history of Ch'an, Zen, and East Asian Buddhism (like Eisai) tend to be marginalized by the later criteria. This marginalization, in turn, has obscured the real nature of their teachings as well as their true impact. Through an examination of select aspects of the *Kōzen gokokuron*, this essay has shown that only by our adopting the assumptions of the materials in question, rather than imposing our own, can the true ramifications of the tradition of Zen syncretism be properly addressed. Such investigations might well yield striking results for our understanding of Buddhism in the East Asian context and lead to significant reinterpretations of the way it has been traditionally presented.

NOTES

1. I would like to thank the Social Science and Humanities Research Council of Canada for supporting research upon which this study is based. The study was initially delivered as a paper at a conference on "Medieval Chan/Zen in Cross-Cultural Perspective" held at Hsi Lai Temple, Los Angeles (1992). An initial report on my re-

search on Yōsai and the *Kōzen gokokuron,* "Buddhist Nationalism and the Origins of Zen in Japan: Toward a Reappraisal of Yōsai and the *Kōzen gokokuron,*" appeared in *Proceedings of the 33rd International Conference on Asian and North African Studies, Contacts Between Culture 4, East Asia: History* (Lewiston, N.Y.: Edwin Mellen Press, 1992), pp. 356–362. A brief introduction and translation of some sections of the *Kōzen gokokuron* appeared in George J. Tanabe, ed., *Religions of Japan in Practice* (Princeton, N.J.: Princeton University Press, 1999), pp. 63–70. I would also like to thank Dr. Barbara Sciacchitano for carefully reading the manuscript and for making numerous suggestions to improve its style.

2. The *bakufu,* or "tent government," refers to the assumption of power by overlords connected with the Hōjō family who established their shogunate in Kamakura in 1185. This is a major turning point in Japanese history, marking the rise of the samurai class and decline of the aristocracy. For a general description, see such sources as G. B. Sansom, *Japan: A Short Cultural History* (New York: Appleton-Century-Crofts, rpt., 62), pp. 270–326.

3. Yanagida Seizan, "Eisai to *Kōzen gokokuron* no kadai," in *Chūsei zenka no shisō* (*Nihon shisō taikei* 16), ed. Ichikawa Hakugen, Iriya Yoshitaka, and Yanagida Seizan (Tokyo: Iwanami Shoten, 1972), p. 439.

4. D. T. Suzuki, *Zen and Japanese Culture* (Princeton, N.J.: Princeton University Press, 1959), p. 272. In the Tokugawa era, Zen nationalism was replaced by a growing Japanese interest in Neo-Confucianism, and later a revived Shinto, both of which offered an alternative basis for state ideology. With the unification of Japan under a Shinto banner during the Meiji period and the effects of militant nationalism during the 1930s and 1940s, Eisai's Zen-based Buddhist nationalism came to be viewed as an anachronism at best. In a climate where the Zen contribution to Japanese artistic and cultural life, the private rather than public arts, was still esteemed, Eisai's work encouraging the positive aspects of tea drinking, the *Kissa yōjōki,* came to be regarded as his most important contribution.

5. Suzuki, *Zen and Japanese Culture,* p. 62.

6. The subject of "pure" Zen and its impact on modern Zen interpretation have received a lot of recent attention, particularly in relation to the writings of D. T. Suzuki and other writers responsible for shaping the contours of modern Zen. See Robert H. Sharf, "The Zen of Japanese Nationalism," in Donald S. Lopez, Jr., ed., *Curators of the Buddha* (Chicago: University of Chicago Press, 1995), pp. 107–160; and Bernard Faure, *Chan Insights and Oversights* (Princeton, N.J.: Princeton University Press, 1993), pp. 52–88.

7. The designation "pure" Zen here derives from D. T. Suzuki, "Zen: A Reply to Hu Shih," *Philosophy East and West* 3/1 (1956): 25–46.

8. *Genkō shakusho* (ch. 2), *Dai nihon bukkyō zensho* 62:75c–77c. Koken Shiren (1278–1346) was a member of the Shōichi branch (after the posthumous title of Enni Ben'en) of the Rinzai faction. His study included a period at Jufukuji in Kamakura, a temple founded by Eisai in the second year of the Shōji era (1200), two years before the founding of Kenninji in Kyoto.

9. On this, see Martin Collcutt, "The Zen Monastery in Kamakura Society," in Jeffrey P. Mass, ed., *Court and Bakufu in Japan: Essays in Kamakura History* (New Haven, Conn.: Yale University Press, 1982), pp. 204–206.

10. *Shōbōgenzō zuimonki* I.6, V.6, II.6, and II.2; Reihō Masunaga, trans., *A Primer of Sōtō Zen: A Translation of Dōgen's Shobogenzo Zuimonki* (Honolulu: University of Hawaii Press, 1971), pp. 10–11, 31, 28, 82.

11. For a full discussion of the current state of our knowledge of Eisai's life and the circumstances surrounding it, see John McRae, "Reconstituting Eisai (1141–1215): The 'combined practice' as an authentic interpretation of the Buddhist tradition," paper presented at the conference "Medieval Chan/Zen in Cross-Cultural Perspective," Hsi Lai Temple, Los Angeles (1992).

12. On Nōnin's role in establishing Zen in Japan, see Bernard Faure, "The Darumashū, Dōgen, and Sōtō Zen," *Monumenta Nipponica* 42/1 (1987): 25–55. On the importance of Yen-shou's writings for Nōnin and Eisai's interpretation of Zen, see Ishii Shūdō, "Dainichi Nōnin, the Daruma Sect, and the Origins of Zen in Japan," paper presented at the conference "Medieval Chan/Zen in Cross-Cultural Perspective," Hsi Lai Temple, Los Angeles (1992).

13. The second article of the seventeen-article document (often referred to as the "Seventeen Article Constitution") attributed to Shōtoku Taishi confirms the importance of Buddhist teaching. The Constitution is contained in the *Nihon shoki* and is translated in William Theodore de Bary et al., *Sources of Japanese Tradition*, vol. 1 (2001), p. 54; de Bary, *East Asian Civilizations: A Dialogue in Five Stages* (New York: Columbia University Press, 1988), pp. 27ff., also discusses the Buddhist sentiment inherent in the largely Confucian tenor of the Shōtoku's document.

14. In Sanskrit, *Saddharma-puṇḍarīka-sūtra*; among several translations of the *Hokke kyō* in Chinese, the one by Kumarajiva in A.D. 406 (T 9, no. 262) is standard.

15. In Sanskrit, *Suvarnaprabhasottama-sūtra*. Three Chinese translations exist (T 16, nos. 663–65). It was promoted at the court of Emperor Temmu (r. 672–686) on the pretext, asserted in the *sūtra*, that the Four Deva Kings (*shi-tennō*) would protect the ruler who followed its teachings. The complete version, the *Konkōmyō-saishō kyō* (*Golden Light Sutra of the Most Victorious Kings*, no. 665), was translated by I-ching (Japanese, Gijo 635–713) in the early eighth century. I-ching's version included mystic incantations, lacking in earlier versions, which were important to followers of esoteric Buddhist traditions in the Tendai and Shingon schools. It was often recited at major court festivals. In Japan, major commentaries were written on it, including ones by Saichō and Kukai.

16. In Sanskrit, *Karunika-raja-sūtra*. Because the original is no longer extant, it is widely considered to be a composition conceived in China; see Kamata Shigeo, ed., *Chūgoku bukkyōshi jiten* (Tokyo, 1981): 307a. Two Chinese "translations" are extant, one by Kumārajīva in 401 (T 8, no. 245), the other by Amoghavajra (C. Pu-k'ung), c. 765 (T 8, no. 246).

17. Numerous commentaries were written on these scriptures by Chinese and Japanese Buddhist masters. The scriptures also provided the basis for numerous court rituals in Japan. On these points, see Inoue Mitsusada, *Nihon kodai no kokka to bukkyō* (*Buddhism and the State in Ancient Japan*) (Tokyo: Iwanami shoten, 1971), and M. W. de Visser, *Ancient Buddhism in Japan*, vol. 2 (Leiden: E. J. Brill, 1935).

18. Regarding the role of the *Ninnō kyō* (C. *Jen-wang ching*) in the Chinese context, see Charles Orzech, *Politics and Transcendent Wisdom: The Scripture for Humane*

Kings in the Creation of Chinese Buddhism (Pittsburgh: Pennsylvania University Press, 1998).

19. All references to the *Kōzen gokokuron* are to Yanagida's edition and translation in *Chūsei zenka no shisō* (see note 3), hereafter abbreviated as Yanagida, ed., and Yanagida, trans. I have also consulted the translation of Furuta Shōkin in *Eisai, Nihon no zen goroku* 1 (Tokyo: Kodansha, 1977), and the *Taishō* edition of the text, T 80, no. 2543.

20. Aside from the Preface, the *Ninnō kyō* is referred to in sections 1, 2, 3, and 8 of the *Kōzen gokokuron*.

21. All references to the *Ninnō kyō* in the *Kōzen gokokuron* are drawn from sections 7 and 8 of Kumarajiva's version. The following references are to Kumārajīva's version (T 8, no. 245) unless noted otherwise.

22. T 8: 832c23–26.

23. The *Ninnō kyō* closes with chapter 8, "[The Buddha] Entrusts [the *Ninnō kyō* and the Three Treasures] to the [Benevolent] Kings," and a warning reinforcing the responsibility incumbent upon kings for maintaining Buddhism. In particular, it states that at such times when the Buddha, Dharma, and Saṅgha, as well as the Buddhist faithful, are absent from the world, the *Ninnō kyō* and the three treasures will be entrusted to kings. It is the responsibility of the kings to initiate the path of wisdom (i.e., *prajñā*-teaching) by having members of the Buddhist assembly recite and explain the *Ninnō kyō* to sentient beings. In other words, the kings are responsible for reconstituting Buddhist teaching in the world; the *Ninnō kyō*, being representative of *prajñā*-teaching, serves as the basis.

24. In China and other ancient cultures, one frequently encounters the belief that unusual celestial phenomena presage natural disaster. Emperors in particular were concerned about the supposed effects of these phenomena over the fate of their regimes. The alleged effectiveness of ritual recitation of the *Ninnō kyō* greatly enhanced its reputation among secular rulers.

25. In Amoghavajra's version (T. 8: 843b7–11), the Buddha provides the kings with reasons why these calamities occur. Two of the reasons are distinctly Confucian in tone: lack of filial piety, and lack of respect for teachers and elders. A third is Buddhist: the fact that *sramanas* and *brahmans*, kings and ministers of state, fail to practice the True Law (*shōbō*).

26. T. 8: 832c26–833a4. The kings are instructed to make banners, arrange flowers, and light lamps to adorn the *Ninnō kyō*, and to construct boxes and covers made of jade in which to place copies of the text, and a table made of valuable materials on which to place the (evidently nine) boxed and covered copies. When the royal procession travels between locations, the table bearing the copies of the *Ninnō kyō* goes a hundred paces ahead of the procession (to guard against misfortune). After the manner of a Buddha himself, the *Ninnō kyō* is claimed to constantly emit rays of light, protecting the surrounding area for a thousand *li* from calamities and transgressions. While the king is residing at a particular location, he is instructed to place the copies of the *Ninnō kyō* on an elevated dais and to make offerings, scatter flowers, and burn incense, as if he were serving his parents or the god Śakra. Amoghavajra's version also includes a list of mystical incantations, or *dhāraṇī*, to be recited for protection, giving it an esoteric emphasis common to Tantrism.

27. Amoghavajra adds, "who are to establish Buddhism and protect it."

28. As an example, there are the well-known tracts by Mou-tzu, "Disposing of Error," and by Hui-yuan, "A Monk Does Not Bow Before a King," excerpts of which are translated in William Theodore de Bary and Irene Bloom, eds., *Sources of Chinese Tradition* 1 (New York: Columbia University Press, 1999), pp. 420–429.

29. See Harry D. Harootunian, *Things Seen and Unseen: Discourse and Ideology in Tokugawa Nativism* (Chicago: University of Chicago Press, 1988).

30. This phrase, reflecting a common opinion among the Japanese ruling elite, is taken from the "Gorakuji Letter" of Hōjō Shigetoki, translated in Carl Steenstrup, *Hōjō Shigetoki (1198–1261) and His Role in the History of Political and Ethical Ideas in Japan*, Scandinavian Institute of Asian Studies Monograph Series, No. 41 (London: Curzon Press, 1979), p. 178.

31. This is illustrated in the founding of the Tendai tradition in Japan. One of the principal issues surrounding the foundation of the Tendai school on Mount Hiei was ordination. In the *Sange gakushoshiki* (T 74, nos. 623–625), Saichō (767–822) argued on the basis of doctrine that Tendai monks be exempted form Hīnayāna ordination rites in favor of Mahāyāna ones. Saichō's real motivation, however, was highly political. The purpose was to establish the independence of the Tendai school from the control exerted over it by the Buddhist establishment based in Nara. To this end, Saichō sought, and eventually won, the right to ordain monks on Mount Hiei on the doctrinal pretext that Tendai monks follow the Mahāyāna ordination rites. A central proposition in Saichō's request was that Tendai teaching serve in the capacity of state ideology. One of the means of support for the state that Tendai monks were to provide was daily recitation of scriptures for protecting the country, namely the *Hokke kyō*, the *Konkōmyō kyō*, the *Ninnō kyō*, and the *Shugo-kokkai shu kyō* (T 19, no. 997). The promotion of Tendai Buddhist teaching as the central ideology of the Japanese state was furthered by Saichō in another work, the *Shugo kokkaisho* (*Treatise on Protecting the Country*) (T 74, no. 2362:135–145), and through his designation of Mount Hiei as the "Chief Seat of the Buddhist Religion for Ensuring the Security of the Country (*chingo-kokka no dōjō*)." Eventually the Tendai school became the leading ideological arm of the Japanese state during the Heian period.

32. Dōgen, for example, though usually depicted as shunning anything to do with politics, purportedly wrote an essay entitled *Gokoku shōbōgi* (*Principles of the True Dharma for the Defense of the Country*). Unfortunately, it has not survived, leading some to question whether it ever existed. See William Bodiford, *Sōtō Zen in Medieval Japan* (Honolulu: University of Hawaii Press, 1993), p. 28. This tendency is reflected most prominently in the chauvinism of Nichiren (1222–1282) and his *Risshō ankoku ron* (*Establishment of the Legitimate Teaching for the Protection of the Country*) (T 84, no.2688:203–208); translated by Burton Watson et al. in Philip B. Yampolsky, ed., *Selected Writings of Nichiren* (New York: Columbia University Press, 1990), pp. 11–49.

33. The first was a brief trip in 1168 at the age of 28, while he was still a committed Tendai monk. This trip coincides with his original interest in the tradition of Tendai esotericism. The second trip was taken nearly two decades later, from 1187 to 1191. Eisai's aspirations at this time were closely connected with his belief that Buddhist teaching was still flourishing in India. On this, see comments in section 9 (Yanagida, ed., p. 119a–b; trans., pp. 86–87).

34. These events are related specifically in section 5 of the *Kōzen gokokuron* text (Yanagida, ed., p. 111b; trans., p. 54), where Eisai states: "I wanted to go on a pilgrimage to India, to the eight sacred sights of the Buddha. . . . At first I went to Lin-an [Hang-chou] and paid a visit to the Military Commissioner to make a request for permission to travel to India . . . the Commissioner did not grant my request." This occurred in the fourteenth year of *ch'un-hsi* (1187), during the Southern Sung dynasty (1127–1279), when the north of China and the trade routes between China and India were controlled by the Jurchen (Chin dynasty) and Toba Turks (Hsi-hsia).

35. Throughout the *Kōzen gokokuron*, Zen is presented as both the culmination and essence of Buddhist teaching transmitted through Sung Ch'an masters. In the preface, Eisai states: "By studying [Zen], one discovers the key for understanding all forms of Buddhism. By practicing it, one attains enlightenment in the span of this life" (Yanagida, ed., p. 99a; trans., p. 9).

36. Eisai's description of this transmission lineage, as well as his claim to be an authentic recipient, are presented in section 5 (Yanagida, ed., pp. 110a–112a; trans., pp. 50–56),and treated in more detail later in this chapter.

37. T 8: 832c23–24.

38. Yanagida, ed., p. 99a. For my translation of the term *furitsu*, I rely on Yanagida's note, (trans., p. 13) and on Nakamura Hajime, *Bukkyōgo daijiten*: 1176d. According to Yanagida, the meaning of the term derives from the teaching of T'ien-t'ai master Chih-i. Nakamura traces it to the *T'ien-t'ai ssu-chiao i* (T 46:775c).

39. In the discussion of this *Nirvāṇa-sūtra* teaching in section 3 of the *Kōzen gokokuron*, Eisai quotes words attributed to Chih-i in the *T'ien-t'ai* (C. *mo-ho*) *chih-kuan* (T 46:4b17–18): "The destruction of evil depends on the purification of wisdom. The purification of wisdom depends on the purification of *zen* (C. *ch'an*) meditation. The purification of *zen* meditation depends on the purification of the precepts" (Yanagida, ed., p. 106b). It is also cited in Yen-shou's *Tsung-ching lu* (T 48:433b20–21).

40. For Eisai's identification of *prajñā*-teaching with the Zen school, see the beginning of section 2 (Yanagida, ed., p. 100b).

41. Yanagida, ed., p. 100a. According to Yanagida (trans., p. 10), the quote is from T 8:868c.

42. This concern is noted specifically in the title to the opening section of the *Kōzen gokokuron*, "Ensuring the Lasting Presence of Buddhist Teaching" (*ryōbō kujū*). The opening quote from the *Sūtra on the Six Perfections* leaves no doubt regarding how the preservation of Buddhism is to be accomplished.

43. Yanagida, ed., p. 100a; Yanagida, trans., p. 11.

44. Yanagida, ed., p. 99a.

45. According to the *Mahā-prajñāpāramitā sūtra* (J. *Dai-hannya kyō*), cited in section 1 of the *Kōzen gokokuron* (Yanagida, ed., p. 100b; trans., pp. 12–13):

[The Buddha said]:
    Śāriputra, five-hundred years after my passing into *nirvāṇa*, at the beginning of the age when Buddhist teaching has begun to degenerate, this *sūtra* on the most profound teaching of Buddhist wisdom (*prajñā*) will be found in a land to the northeast, where it will greatly enhance the practice of Buddhism. How is it so? All the Buddhas, the Thus Come Ones, together cherish this land and regard it as important; together they concentrate on

protecting it. They ensure that Buddhist teaching will always endure in that land and will not perish.

The passage is from Hsüan-tsang's translation, T 6:539a29–b6.

46. This is clear from Eisai's comments in section 3 (Yanagida, ed., p. 102a; trans., p. 19).

47. In this context, Eisai cites (at the beginning of section 2: "Protecting the Country [with the Teachings of the Zen School]") a passage from the *Ninnō kyō*: "The Buddha has entrusted the Buddhist teaching on wisdom [i.e., the teaching of the Zen School] to all present and future rulers of petty kingdoms; it is considered the treasure for protecting their countries" Yanagida, ed., p. 100b; trans., p. 13. The *Ninnō kyō* passage is found in T 8:832b22–25.

48. Yanagida, ed., p. 100a–b; trans., p. 12 (T 8:833b29-3c). A prominent reflection of the declining political situation at the end of the Heian era that speaks directly to the passage cited here is the incident involving the Tendai Abbot Meiun recorded in *Heike monogatari*. In response to the role played by Tendai warrior-monks in the burning of the imperial palace, retired emperor Go-Shirakawa revoked the status and privileges held by Meiun, imprisoning him and sending him into exile. The incident involves both excesses on the part of the Buddhist clergy (indicating their moral depravity) and illicit behavior on the part of the government toward Buddhist monks (indicating disrespect for Buddhist law). This is but one of many examples from this period typifying the breach of trust between the government and the Buddhist establishment (see Helen Craig McCullough, trans., *The Tale of Heike* [Palo Alto, Cal.: Stanford University Press, 1988], pp. 54ff).

49. Yanagida, ed., p. 100b; trans., p. 13 (T 8:689a11–14).

50. Yanagida, ed., pp. 117b–119a; trans., pp. 80–86.

51. Regarding the development of Ch'an monastic codes in China, see T. Griffith Foulk, "The 'Ch'an School' and Its Place in the Buddhist Monastic Tradition" (Ph.D. diss., University of Michigan, 1987); and Yifa, *The Origins of Monastic Codes in China: An Annotated Translation and Study of the* Chanyuan qinggui (Honolulu: University of Hawaii Press, 2002).

52. Two emphases of Eisai in this regard are "Receiving the Precepts [ordination]" (*jukai*) and "Guarding [or upholding] the Precepts" (*gokai*), which directly parallel the first two topics treated in the *Ch'an-yuan ch'ing-kuei*.

53. Following Yanagida's reading, trans., p. 81 note on *kōjō*.

54. Reading *hō* "treasure" for *hō* "law," as suggested by Yanagida, trans., p. 82.

55. Yanagida, ed., p. 118a; trans., p. 82.

56. A critique of the place Pai-chang's rules have traditionally been accorded in the Zen tradition is in Foulk, "The 'Ch'an School' and Its Place in the Buddhist Monastic Tradition."

57. T 8, no. 223.

58. See above and notes 13, 14, and 15.

59. Accompanying these aims are the propagation of Buddhist teaching, benefiting sentient beings, and repaying the kindness of donors.

60. T. Griffith Foulk, "The Ch'an Tsung in Medieval China: School, Lineage, or What?" *The Pacific World: Journal of the Institute of Buddhist Studies* 8 (1992): 18–31.

61. Some may argue that Lin-chi orthodoxy in the Sung context was predomi-

nant, and there is no disputing the sway it held, exhibited in the numerous Ch'an works edited and promoted by members of the Lin-chi lineage during this period. Yet it is instructive that transmitters of Zen to Japan such as Eisai and Dōgen brought back an understanding that defies Lin-chi Ch'an orthodoxy. The process of planting Zen in Japan was, of course, filled with complexities attributable to the Japanese Buddhist context, and it is not clear the extent to which these exigencies determined the type of Zen interpretation proffered. Some facets of these complexities will be introduced later in the chapter.

62. Philip Yampolsky, trans., *The Platform Sūtra of the Sixth Patriarch* (New York: Columbia University Press, 1967), pp. 155–156.

63. Ruth F. Sasaki, trans., *The Record of Lin-chi* (New York: Random House, 1969), p. 33.

64. Sasaki, *The Record of Lin-chi*, p. 45.

65. The Wu-yüeh kingdom was the most successful of the de facto independent regimes that flourished in China, especially in the south, with the demise of T'ang authority. The hallmark of Wu-yueh culture was its support for Buddhism. See Hatanaka Jōen, "Goetsu no bukkyō—toku ni tendai tokushō to sono shi eimei enju ni tsuite," *Otani daigaku kenkyū nenpō* 7 (1954): 305–365.

66. Abe Chōichi, *Chūgoku zenshūshi no kenkyū* (Tokyo: Kenbun shuppan, rpt., 1986), pp. 123–210.

67. T 51, no. 2076.

68. T 48, no. 2016, and T 48, no. 2017.

69. T 50, no. 2061; and T 54, no. 2126.

70. The fact that Eisai's interpretation of Zen is closely tied to Wu-yüeh is also reflected in the importance that Buddhist centers in Wu-yüeh played during Eisai's pilgrimages to China, a point considered in more detail later.

71. Jan Yun-hua, "Buddhist Historiography in Sung China," *Zeitschrift der Deutschen Morgandlischen Gesellschaft* 64 (1964): 360–381, and Ishii Shūdō, *Sodai zenshūshi no kenkyū*, ch. 1, "*Keitoku dentōroku* no rekishiteki seikaku" (Tokyo: Daitō shuppansha, 1987): 1–122.

72. The ten categories for attaining eminence in the *Sung kao-seng chuan* are: Translators (*i-ching*), Exegetes (*i-chieh*), Ch'an Practitioners (*hsi-Ch'an*), Vinaya Experts (*ming-lu*), Dharma Protectors (*hu-fa*), Miracle Workers (*kan-t'ung*), Self-Immolators (*i-shen*), Cantors (*tu-ching*), Promoters of Blessings (*hsing-fu*), and Various Categories of Invokers of Virtue (*tsa-k'o sheng-te*). These categories are the same as the ones used in the *Hsü kao-seng chuan* (T 50, no. 2060) and vary only somewhat with those used in the *Kao-seng chuan* (T 50, no. 2059).

73. Although the *Ching-te ch'uan-teng lu* records the biographies of Ch'an masters beginning with the seven Buddhas of the past and including each of the "Five Houses" of Ch'an, it culminates with the lineage of the Fa-yen faction: the biographies of Fa-yen Wen-i, T'ien-t'ai Te-shao, Yung-ming Yen-shou, and their respective disciples (see chs. 24–26).

In theory, the different criteria for assessing a monk's essential worth could (and usually did) exist side-by-side without tension. Most of the famous monks of the Ch'an tradition who were awarded eminence were recognized as "Ch'an Practitioners" (*hsi-Ch'an*) in the *Sung kao-seng chuan*, so the two sets of criteria were by no means mutually exclusive. In practice, however, there was also room for fundamental disagreement. This is apparent in two ways: in the exclusion of prominent Ch'an masters from any category of eminence, and in the inclusion of Ch'an masters in categories of eminence other than "Ch'an Practitioners." In the T'ang, where Ch'an was but one part of a multifactional Buddhist world, such discrepancies would have been inconsequential. As the situation changed after the T'ang and Ch'an came to assert its dominance over Sung Buddhism, such discrepancies became increasingly intolerable.

Two prominent examples are Yün-men Wen-yuan (864–949) and Yung-ming Yen-shou (904–975). Yün-men, the founder of one of the "Five Houses" of Ch'an, is not mentioned in the *Sung kao-seng chuan*. Yen-shou's biography was recorded in both the *Ching-te ch'uan-teng lu* and the *Sung kao-seng chuan*, but in ways that are not consistent. In the former, Yen-shou is regarded as a Ch'an patriarch in the lineage of the Fa-yen faction, but in the latter his biography was included under the category of "Promoters of Blessings" (*hsing-fu*). Yen-shou was well known to both Tao-yüan and Tsan-ning, so that neither was ignorant of the circumstances surrounding his career. The disagreement exhibited in the case of Yen-shou reflected an underlying tension between the sectarian-based definition of Ch'an adopted by the Ch'an school and the nonsectarian approach adopted by Tsan-ning. This later prompted Hui-hung to openly criticize Tsan-ning in the *Lin-chien lu*: "Tsan-ning compiled the extensive *Sung kao-seng chuan*, utilizing ten categories for the purpose of classification. He placed Exegetes at the top [of the list]. This is laughable. Moreover, he presented Ch'an master Yen-tou Huo as a Practitioner of Asceticism and Ch'an master Chih-chueh [J. Yen-shou] as a Promoter of Blessings. The great teacher Yün-men is chief among monks . . . but surprisingly, [Tsan-ning] does not even mention him" (Taipei ed. of *Zoku zōkyō*; HTC 148:294b).

74. Yanagida, ed., pp. 110a–112a; trans., pp. 50–56.

75. See Yampolsky, *The Platform Sūtra of the Sixth Patriarch*: 9, and pp. 47–49. The *Pao-lin chuan* is contained in Yanagida Seizan, ed., *Sōzō ichin Horinden, Dentō gyokuei shū* (Kyoto: Chūbun shuppansha, 1975).

76. T 51, no. 2076:204a–216b, chs. 1–2; T 48, no. 2016:937c–939c ch. 97.

77. On this, see Bernard Faure, "The Daruma-shū, Dōgen and Sōtō Zen," *Monumenta Nipponica* 42/1 (1987): 25–55.

78. Nishi Giyu and Fujimoto Chito, trans., *Honchō kōsōden*; *Kokuyaku issaikyō*, vol. 89 (Tokyo: Daitō shuppansha, 1961), pp. 272–273, cited from Philip Yampolsky, "The Development of Japanese Zen," in Kenneth Kraft, ed., *Zen: Tradition and Transition* (New York: Grove Press, 1988), p. 142.

79. Yanagida, ed., p. 112a; trans., p. 56.

80. Faure, "The Daruma-shū, Dōgen and Sōtō Zen," pp. 56–57.

81. See Yanagida, ed., pp. 104b–105a and 108b; trans., pp. 29–30 and 43.

82. T 54:254c14–15.

83. This is most evident in section 56 of the *Seng shih-lüeh* (T 54:253c21–254a21), "Leading the Imperial Carriage with [*Jen-wang ching* Scripture] Desks" (*chia-t'ou ch'uang-tzu*), but it is also evident in section 39 (p. 247b7–c13), "Buddhist Chapels in the Imperial Palace" (*nei tao-Ch'ang*), and section 57 (p. 254a22–b16), "[Placing] Guardian Deities over the Main Gates of City Walls" (*ch'eng-tu t'ien-wang*).

84. See Tsan-ning's comments regarding *Ch'an* in the *hsi-Ch'an* commentary to the *Sung kao-seng chuan*, ch. 13 (T 50:789b11–790a21), the *Ch'uan Ch'an-kuan fa* and *Pieh-li Ch'an-chu* sections of the *Seng shih-lüeh* (T 54:240a21–b5). The discussion here is based on the author's study, "Zanning and Chan: The Changing Nature of Buddhism in Early Song China," *Journal of Chinese Religions* 23 (1995): 105–140.

85. Eisai cites the *Isshin kai* (T 74:645c18–19) to claim, "In the Chen Dynasty, Ch'an master Nan-yüeh Hui-ssu met the great master Bodhidharma and received instruction from him." He also cites a postscript to Chih-i's *Kuan-hsin lun* (T 46, no. 1920; postscript no longer extant): "The great master of Shao-lin Temple on Mount Sung [i.e., Bodhidharma] transmitted Ch'an teaching to Ch'an master Hui-ssu. The Ch'an master Hui-ssu transmitted this Ch'an teaching to T'ien-t'ai Ch'an master Chih-i."

86. The remainder of Eisai's discussion in section 4 of the *Kōzen gokokuron* affirms historical links between Chinese Ch'an and Japanese Tendai masters, the most important being the claim that Dengyō Daishi (i.e., Saichō) was inducted into the Niu-t'ou (J. Gozu) Ch'an lineage. These links further support Eisai's attempt to join the Zen and Tendai traditions on the basis of supposed connections between masters of both schools. The culminating point in Eisai's discussion is the validation of Sung Ch'an practice as the legitimate form of *Ch'an* practiced by virtuous masters of old. The blueprint for this practice, according to Eisai, is the Sung Ch'an monastic code, the *Ch'an-yüanū ch'ing-kuei* (*Zen'en shingi*). This code, as we have seen, played an important role in Eisai's reform plan. The subject of monastic discipline will be treated in more detail later.

87. *Hsü-tsang ching*, vol. III:438–471; see also Kagamishima Genryū et al., eds., *Yakuch zen'en shingi* (Tokyo: Sōtōshū shūmuchō, 1972).

88. Yanagida, ed., p. 110a; trans., p. 50.

89. According to the T'ien-t'ai school, the Buddha's teaching may be divided into five periods: *Hua-yen* (after the scripture most highly regarded in the Hua-yen school), *A-han* (early Buddhist scriptures), *Fang-teng* (elementary Mahāyāna), *Ta p'an-jo* (perfection of wisdom), and *Fa-hua nieh-p'an* (after the scriptures most highly regarded in the T'ien-t'ai school).

90. See Reihō Masunaga, trans., *A Primer of Sōtō Zen*, pp. 13–14. (Dōgen refers to Yen-shou by his honorific name, Chih-hsueh.)

91. See Ishii Shūdō, *Dōgen Zen no seiritsu shiteki kenkyū* (Tokyo: Daizō shuppan-sha, 1991), p. 692.

92. Yanagida, ed., p. 107b; trans., pp. 39–40.

93. Yanagida, ed., p. 108a–b; trans., pp. 41–43.

94. Yanagida, ed., p. 113a; trans., p. 62.

95. T 48, no. 2017. I focus on this work because of my familiarity with it and the manageability of its size. Comments here are based on my study, *The Meaning of Myriad Good Deeds: A Study of Yung-ming Yen-shou and the Wan-shan t'ung-kuei chi* (New York: Peter Lang, 1993).

96. Self-immolation (either *wang-shen* or *i-shen*) is a criterion for inclusion as an "eminent monk" in the *Sung kao-seng chuan* tradition of Buddhist biography.

97. T 48: 417a22–25.

98. See section 7, "An Outline of the Principal Methods for Practicing Zen":

This method [i.e., encouraging the practice of Zen through conventional Buddhist teaching] is that of the *Tsung-ching lu*, in which the important teachings of the three schools [T'ien-t'ai, Hua-yen, and Fa-hsiang] have been collected by citing from sixty scriptures, and the main teachings of the Zen school have been explained by referring to the comments of over three hundred masters. (Yanagida, ed., p. 113a; trans., p. 62)

99. In this regard, note Eisai's comments in the preface of the *Kōzen gokokuron*:

[T]here are those who malign Zen teaching, calling it "the Zen of obscure realization," and those who harbor doubts about it, calling it "the false view of emptiness." Still others claim that it is ill suited to this degenerate age, or that it is not what our country needs . . . These people, while ostensibly upholding the Buddhist Law, are actually destroying the treasure that this Law contains. They reject my position outright, without knowing what I have in mind. Not only are they blocking the entryway to Zen teaching, they are also ruining the work of our great forbear at Mount Hiei, the Tendai master Saichō. It is sad and distressing that my position be so dismissed before ascertaining whether it is correct or not. (Yanagida, ed., p. 99b; trans., p. 9)

100. On this, also note Eisai's comments in the preface to the *Kōzen gokokuron*:

As a result, I have gathered here representative materials from the three branches of Buddhist learning [scriptures, monastic rules, and treatises] to inform those of our age with penetrating minds about Zen teaching, and to record the essential teachings of the one true school of Buddhism for posterity. (ibid.)

101. Ishii Shūdō, *Dōgen Zen no seiritsu shiteki kenkyū* (Daizō shuppan, Shohan edition, 1991), pp. 649ff.

102. Ishii Shūdō, *Dōgen Zen no seiritsu shiteki kenkyū.*, pp. 689–693.

103. Appended to the *Kōzen gokokuron*, see Yanagida, ed., p. 122a.

104. Yanagida, op. cit., pp. 470–471.; cited in Ishii, *Dōgen Zen*, p. 689. Eisai's rejection of Kakua and Nōnin follows implicitly from the suggestion that he attributes to Fo-hai (1103–1176) and Fo-chao (1121–1203), Sung Ch'an masters from whom Kakua and Nōnin reputedly received the transmission, that Zen will flourish in Japan only fifty years henceforth. There is some question, however, regarding Eisai's authorship of the *Mirai ki*.

105. Yanagida, op. cit., p. 471; Ishii, *Dōgen Zen*, p. 690.

106. Ishii, *Dōgen Zen*, p. 331.

107. This is based on Eisai's direct criticism of the Daruma faction in section 3 of the *Kōzen gokokuron* (Yanagida, ed., p. 108a; trans., p. 41); the question is translated by Yampolsky, "The Development of Japanese Zen," in Kenneth Kraft, ed., *Zen: Tradition and Transition* (New York: Grove Press, 1988), p. 143:

Some people recklessly refer to the Daruma faction as the Zen school. But these [Daruma adherents] say, "There are no precepts to follow, no practices to engage in. From the outset, there are no passions; from the beginning we are enlightened. Therefore we do not practice, do not follow precepts. We eat when we are hungry, rest when we are tired. Why recite the Buddha's name, why make offerings, why give vegetarian feasts, why curtail eating?" How can this be?

108. Ishii, *Dōgen Zen*, p. 693.

109. The first documented appearance of the four slogans is in the *Tsu-t'ing shih-yüan* (HTC 113:66c), dated 1108.

110. Yanagida, ed., p. 113b; trans., p. 62.

111. Tsan-ning's acceptance of these verses as representative of the Ch'an school is apparent from his discussion in the *Sung kao-seng chuan* (T 50:789b24-c7). Here he concludes, "Bodhidharma was the first to proclaim, directly point to the human mind; see one's nature and become a Buddha; do not establish words and letters," the acceptance of which is implicit in Yen-shou's writings as well.

112. Yanagida, ed., pp. 113a–117b; trans., pp. 62–80.

113. Following Nakamura Hajime (*Bukkyōgo daijiten*: 1375b), the term is associated with T'ien-t'ai school works such as the *Fa-hua wen-chu* (T 34, no. 1718) and the *T'ien-t'ai ssu-chiao i* (T 46, no. 1931). Does this indicate a tendency on Eisai's part to interpret Yen-shou in terms of T'ien-t'ai *Ch'an* as opposed to the *Ch'an* of the Ch'an school?

114. This term appears frequently in works associated with the Hua-yen school (see Nakamura, 877c–d), but it may be more instructive in the case of Eisai and his interpretation of Zen in terms of *prajñā*-teaching to think of it in reference to its appearance in Nagarjuna's *Chung-lun* (T 30:19b27) and *Ta chih-tu lun* (T 25, no. 1509). In the latter (ch. 31), it is stipulated as one of the aspects that characterize all created existence, namely that all things are impermanent (C. *wu-Ch'ang*; J. *mujō*) and are devoid of substantial identifying qualities (C. *wu-wo*; J. *muga*). This is most immediately contrasted with the individuating features that also characterize all created existence, exemplified by "firmness" in the case of earth and "wetness" in the case of water. Moreover, the *Ta chih-tu lun* is quoted directly later on in section 7 of the *Kōzen gokok-uron*, according to the great sage Nagarjuna: "Existence also is nonexistent. Nonexistence is also existent. Both existence and nonexistence are nonexistent. Neither existence nor nonexistence are nonexistent. Statements such as this are also nonexistent." And also: "To be free of idle talk; to be free of words and letters—if one is able to contemplate in this manner, this is what is meant as seeing the Buddha."

115. Based on the *Ch'i-hsin lun* (T 32:576a11–12). Remember that for Eisai, the reputed author, Ma-ming (Skt. Aśvaghoṣa), was a Zen patriarch.

116. Based on the *Chin-kang p'an-jo ching* (Diamond *Sūtra*); T 8:751c27–28.

117. Based on the *Chin-kang p'an-jo ching* (Diamond *Sūtra*); T 8:751c27–28.

118. Yanagida, ed., p. 113a–b; trans., pp. 62–63.

119. *See The Meaning of Myriad Good Deeds*, ch. 5, section 3 (pp. 121–127), "Major Influences: Sources Cited or Referred to in the *WSTKC*." The total number of references to T'ien-t'ai, Hua-yen, and *Prajñāpāramiāt* sources are 87, 66, and 48, respectively.

120. These tabulations are based on figures provided by Takagi Yutaka, *Kamakura bukkyōshi kenkyū*, pp. 78–80. By my accounting, 63 citations are associated with the Tendai tradition, 39 with the *Prajñā* tradition, and 21 with the *Vinaya* tradition. Eleven sources relate to Mikkyō, and only 2 to Kegon (C. Hua-yen).

121. HTC 111:460c–461a.

122. Yanagida, ed., p. 114a–b; trans., pp. 65–67.

123. Yanagida, ed., p. 114b; trans., p. 68.

124. Cited in Ishii, *Dōgen Zen*, p. 708.

125. Cited in Ishii, *Dōgen Zen*, p. 709.

126. Yen-shou's affinity with T'ien-t'ai tradition, described earlier, is beyond dispute. T'ien-t'ai teaching and practice were major components of his syncretism. His affinity to Mi-chiao (J. Mikkyō), however, is problematic. There is little evidence that it constituted a major source of his teaching, in terms of either doctrines mentioned or sources cited. Esoteric practices, however, do figure prominently in the *Tzu-hsing lu* (HTC 111:77–84), a work purporting to list the 108 activities that constituted Yen-shou's regular routine.

127. In this regard, one strong influence on Eisai from the post-Yen-shou Sung tradition that can be affirmed with certainty is the model of Buddhist monastic practice provided in the *Ch'an-yuan ch'ing-kuei (Zen'en shingi)*. Yen-shou is also associated with a model for Buddhist practice, namely the 108 activities in the *Tzu-hsing lu*, a record of the practices that Yen-shou is said to have regularly engaged in. The *Tzu-hsing lu* was undoubtedly inspirational to the individual practitioner but offered little guidance for organizing Buddhist practices at an institutional level. The *Ch'an-yuan ch'ing-kuei*, in contrast, provided a concrete plan for the institutional function of Buddhism that played an important part in substantiating Eisai's reform program.

128. The comments of Heinrich Dumoulin, *Zen Buddhism: A History*, vol. II (New York: Macmillan, 1990), pp. 310–311, regarding D. T. Suzuki are well worth citing here:

> In D. T Suzuki's efforts to make Zen known in the west, the principal bearers of his new message were, historically speaking, the Chinese patriarchs and masters of the T'ang period. Readers of his early English works were introduced to Hui-neng and the circles of Ma-tsu, Shih-t'ou, and Pai-Ch'ang up to Huang-po and Lin-chi. Suzuki's pioneering on behalf of Japanese Zen is not as well known. Yet even before World War II, his Japanese writings were drawing attention to the extraordinary creativity of Bankei. . . . In the introduction to his English translation of Bankei's sermons, Norman Waddell observes that Suzuki's studies "revealed for the first time in concrete terms the true significance of Bankei's Zen and its high place in the history of Zen thought". Waddell quotes a lengthy passage from Suzuki's Japanese writings that culminates in the recognition that "slightly before Hakuin's time was Bankei, whose 'Unborn Zen' advocated a new and original thought for the first time since Bodhidharma." To be sure, the place that Bankei holds in the history of Zen is an eminent one.

Recall also that D. T Suzuki was a disciple of Shaku Soen, a Rinzai master of the Hakuin line.

129. Bernard Faure, *The Rhetoric of Immediacy: A Cultural Critique of Chan/Zen Buddhism* (Princeton, N.J.: Princeton University Press, rpt., 1994), p. 21, seems to contradict this with his statement: "In Japan,. . . . Zen tried to present itself as an ideological instrument that could serve the interests of the country. Although scholars

usually look toward the Kamakura figure Eisai (1141–1215) as an example of this development . . . , the work of the Tokugawa Zen master Suzuki Shōsan (1579–1655) is more significant in this respect," but there is no contradiction in fact. Shōsan's attempt to reestablish the political and ethical role of Zen in the early Tokugawa was made in a changing ideological environment. Regardless of who is deemed most significant, the works of both Eisai and Shōzan are equally examples of "Zen [trying] to present itself as an ideological instrument that could serve the interests of the country," but in different historical contexts.

130. Yen-shou's influence was restricted in the later Chinese Buddhist tradition to a more narrowly conceived Ch'an-Pure Land synthesis, a view still held in modern scholarship. On the inadequacy of this view, see my study on Yen-shou and the *Wan-shan t'ung-kuei chi*, cited previously. Generally speaking, the nature of Yen-shou's influence over East Asian Buddhism needs to be more carefully addressed.

131. Dumoulin, *Zen Buddhism: A History*, p. 24.

132. Regarding Korean Sŏn, see Robert E. Buswell, *Tracing Back the Radiance: Chinul's Way of Korean Zen* (Honolulu: University of Hawaii Press, 1991), and *The Zen Monastic Experience: Buddhist Practice in Contemporary Korea* (Princeton, N.J.: Princeton University Press, 1992). Regarding Vietnamese Thin, see Cuong Tu Nguyen, "Tran Thai Tong and the *Khoa Hu Luc* [Instructions on Emptiness]: A Model of Syncretic Ch'an in 13th-Century Vietnam," paper presented at the conference "Medieval Chan/Zen in Cross-Cultural Perspective," Hsi Lai Temple, Los Angeles (1992).

133. Yanagida, ed., p. 106b; trans., p. 36; cited from the *Mo-ho chih-kuan* (T 46: 4b) via the *Tsung-ching lu* (T 48: 433b).

134. Yanagida, ed., p. 120b; trans., p. 92; based on the *Shih-teng kung-te ching* (T 16:803c23–804a3).

4

An Analysis of Dōgen's *Eihei Goroku*: Distillation or Distortion?

Steven Heine

The Role of Abbreviation in Dōgen Zen

The two main works by Dōgen are the *Shōbōgenzō* and the *Eihei Kō-roku* (hereafter occasionally referred to as EK). The *Shōbōgenzō* consists mainly of informal *jishu*-style sermons delivered in Japanese vernacular during the first half of Dōgen's career at Kōshōji temple and collected into various editions. The *Eihei Kōroku* consists mainly of formal *jōdō*-style sermons recorded in *kanbun* or Sino-Japanese sermons that were delivered during the second half of Dōgen's career at Eiheiji temple and included in the first seven of ten volumes. The remainder of the *Eihei Kōroku* contains miscellaneous materials containing other kinds of sermons, verse commentaries on kōans, and poetry composed in Chinese.

However, these monumental texts, which are so crucial for understanding Dōgen's life and thought, have generally been less known and less studied than abbreviated versions constructed by later editors. The main abbreviated version of the *Shōbōgenzō* is the *Sōtō Kyōkai Shushōgi* (*The Meaning of Practice-Realization in the Sōtō Zen Fellowship*). Also known as the *Shushōgi*, this is a compact, five-section, 31-paragraph text that consists of selections of brief passages extracted from the 95-fascicle edition of the *Shōbōgenzō*. This text was created over a period of several years in the late 1880s by several contributors, especially the lay leader Ōuchi Seiran, and was published in 1890 by the Sōtō sect.[1]

The primary abbreviated version of the *Eihei Kōroku* is the *Eihei Dōgen Zenji Goroku* (*Recorded Sayings of Dōgen, Founder of Eiheiji*

Temple), a one-volume edition that consists of sermons, lectures, kōan commentaries, and lyrical verse culled from the ten volumes of the original text.[2] The *Eihei Goroku* (hereafter occasionally referred to as EG) was compiled in China by Dōgen's Dharma-brother I-yüan (J. Gion) in the 1260s, about ten years after Dōgen's death. It was published in 1358 by Donki, who was the main disciple of fifth Eiheiji patriarch Giun and later became the sixth patriarch, as the very first publication of the still fledgling Sōtō sect.[3] Dōgen's approach to Ch'an/Zen literature and practice in the records included in this abbreviated text reflects mainly the impact of Chinese Ts'ao-tung (J. Sōtō) patriarchs, particularly twelfth-century master Hung-chih, who was a major influence on many of Dōgen's sermons and general attitudes toward Zen theory and practice, especially during the later period of his career, when he was at Eiheiji temple.

Indeed, it is fair to say that throughout most of the history of Dōgen Zen, the role of the abbreviated texts has eclipsed the much more substantive writings on which they are based. Dōgen has generally been known in medieval and modern times, not primarily for the *Eihei Kōroku* or *Shōbōgenzō*, which were largely lost, misunderstood, or limited in distribution to a highly specialized faction, but for the *Eihei Goroku* and the *Shushōgi*, which are short and readily accessible.[4] The aim of this chapter is to examine the origins, structure, and function of the *Eihei Goroku*, but this first section also comments on the role of abbreviation in the *Shushōgi*.[5] The phrase "Dōgen Zen" refers not just to Dōgen (1200–1253) or to the sum total of his life and works, but to the continuing impact and legacy of Dōgen's writings reverberating through the history of the Sōtō sect as well as Japanese intellectual history. This legacy encompasses monks and lay believers, the sectarian elite and secular thinkers, each of whom has interpreted Dōgen's writings for different purposes. There is often a fundamental distinction and discrepancy between the writings attributed to Dōgen and the way they have been recorded, edited, and appropriated, or between Dōgen the founder and the history of the sectarian tradition, which has been characterized by long periods of neglecting his major writings.

During the Muromachi era, for example, the Sōtō sect produced voluminous esoteric commentaries on classical Ch'an/Zen writings, including kōan collections such as the *Hekiganroku*, *Mumonkan* and *Shōyōroku*. In these works, which are known by the generic term *shōmono*, the *Eihei Goroku* received far more mention from sectarian commentators than did both the frequently ignored or suppressed *Eihei Kōroku* and *Shōbōgenzō*.[6] In the twentieth century it was the brief, user-friendly *Shushōgi*, expressing a view of repentance based in part on a response to the challenge of Christianity during the Westernization process of the Meiji era, that was memorized or chanted by Sōtō followers. The demanding *Shōbōgenzō* remains largely unread, even in various modern Japanese renderings (*gendaigoyaku*) that try to make the opaque original comprehensible to the average reader. The effective use of the *Shushōgi* is often given credit for much of the popularity of the Sōtō sect in modern Japan.

Table 4.1 shows the periods in the history of Dōgen Zen, divided into several stages lasting approximately 200 years each. Following Dōgen's life, the next stage (1253–1450) covers the early post-Dōgen period, when new editions of the *Shōbōgenzō* were debated and the *Eihei Goroku* was published, although the *Eihei Kōroku* was not yet studied seriously. The succeeding stage (1450–1650) is the period when the standard edition of the *Eihei Kōroku* was published, in 1598, but the main activity of Sōtō intellectual life was the creation of *shōmono* commentaries, including those dealing with the *Eihei Goroku*. During this stage there was minimal attention paid to the *Shōbōgenzō*, at least as far as we can tell from the *shōmono* records.

The third stage (1650–1850) saw a revival of studies of the *Shōbōgenzō* and the *Eihei Kōroku* by the scholarly elite, in addition to the publication of the popular edition of the latter text. However, despite considerable advances that continue to influence today's scholarship in a positive way, there were many limitations in the studies of this period due to lost texts, arbitrary emendations by overly eager editors such as Menzan Zuihō, and a general lack of critical apparatus or objective judgment. In the current period (1850–) there has been a boom in *Shōbōgenzō* translations into modern Japanese and English, particularly since World War II, as well as more moderate advances in studies of the *Eihei Kōroku*. Several other texts were discovered, including Dōgen's collection of 300 kōans, the *Mana Shōbōgenzō* (or *Shōbōgenzō Sanbyakusoku*), his Japanese

TABLE 4.1. Major Developments in the Unfolding of Dōgen Zen vis-à-vis the Time of Dōgen's Writings

Year	Dōgen	Dōgen Zen
1200–1253		
1233–1246	*Shōbōgenzō*	Role of continuous editing by Ejō, Senne, Gien, and others
1236–1252	*Eihei Kōroku*	
1253–1450		Various editions of *Shōbōgenzō* (75-, 60-, 28-, 12-fascicles) collected; *Eihei Goroku* created in 1264 and published in 1358, but *Eihei Kōroku* receives little attention
1450–1650		*Eihei Goroku* used in *shōmono* commentaries, and first *Eihei Kōroku* edition published (1598); little attention paid to *Shōbōgenzō*
1650–1850		Revival of Sōtō *Shōbōgenzō* and *Eihei Kōroku* studies, but with methodological shortcomings
1850–		Creation, publication, edict on *Shushōgi* (1890); postwar boom in *Shōbōgenzō* scholarship, with moderate interest in *Eihei Kōroku*

poetry (*waka*) collection, and the 12-fascicle *Shōbōgenzō*. But the most important development in Dōgen Zen, particularly in the area of religious practice, has been the *Shushōgi*.

This situation raises a key question pertaining to the authenticity and value of the abbreviated texts. To what extent can the *Eihei Goroku* and the *Shushōgi* be considered a distillation or a condensed yet essential expression of Dōgen's thought? Or, to the contrary, are they each an arbitrary and rather misleading summative digest that bears only a surface resemblance to the sources? Should the relative popularity of the texts that compress the source material into a nutshell version be attributed to the "replica culture" (*migawari no bunka*) of Japan, for which surrogates, doubles, and replacements regularly substitute for the original or genuine source?[7] In the Japanese Buddhist style of imitative expression (*nazoraeru*), for example, chanting a *sūtra* substitutes for reading it, reciting the title replaces the entire text, and gazing at the *sūtra* replicates chanting it. A concern about the *Shushōgi* is that it does not even mention the word *zazen* and it puts an emphasis on repentance that is uncharacteristic of much of the *Shōbōgenzō*.

There are similar concerns about the *Eihei Goroku*, which a translator refers to as "a distillation of *Eihei Kōroku*" that is based on what was "considered the creme."[8] The passages selected for the *Eihei Goroku* present a view of Dōgen as a Zen master who behaved very much in the mold of his Chinese predecessors; particularly Hung-chih and Dōgen's mentor Ju-ching, as a preceptor of monastic rituals and transmitter of the Ts'ao-tung lineage. But are these passages an adequate reflection or distillation of the entire *Eihei Kōroku* that was composed primarily during the later period of Dōgen's career after his move to Eiheiji? The picture that emerges from a variety of writings stemming from this period, especially the 12-fascicle edition of the *Shōbōgenzō*, is that the late Dōgen emphasized the doctrine of "true belief in causality" (*jinshin inga*) in a way that seems to diverge from the Chinese models that are based more on original enlightenment thought (*hongaku shisō*). Also, Dōgen's criticisms found in the *Eihei Kōroku* of syncretism and indigenous religiosity, as well as the exclusivism that characterized the Ch'an/Zen school, are missing from the *Eihei Goroku* selections. Nevertheless, a reciprocal relation exists in that studies of the *Eihei Goroku* may lead to a reexamination of the source text.

Distillation/Abbreviation in Zen Literature

To evaluate the origin and function of the *Eihei Goroku* as a major element of Dōgen Zen, it is necessary first to situate Dōgen's view of the role of abbreviation in relation to textuality in the context of the development of Ch'an/Zen literature. It has become increasingly well documented that despite espousing the rhetoric of "a special transmission outside the scriptures/without reliance on words and letters" (*kyōge betsuden/furyū monji*), classical Ch'an/Zen Buddhism is perhaps known primarily for its achievements as a literary tradition that generated voluminous texts in several genres.[9] The texts were produced during the Sung dynasty, especially the eleventh and twelfth centuries, and further developed in medieval (Kamakura/Muromachi) Japan.[10]

The Sung era genres include "transmission of the lamp" hagiographical texts depicting a multibranched lineal genealogy (*dentō-roku*); recorded sayings of the teachings of individual masters in the form of sermons, poems, and biographical anecdotes (*goroku*) (the *Eihei Kōroku* is part of this category); kōan collections which offer prose and verse commentaries on selected encounter dialogues and other epigrammatic anecdotes (*kōan-roku*) (vol. 9 of the *Eihei Kōroku*, none of which is included in the *Eihei Goroku*, is included in this category); and monastic rules texts detailing the guidelines and requirements for every aspect of temple life (*shingi*).[11] In medieval Japan, Zen writers expanded the variety of genres to produce a wide range of materials, including Dōgen's *Shōbōgenzō* in *kana* (Japanese vernacular) that comments on numerous kōan cases; Daitō's "capping phrase" (*jakugo*) commentaries on the *Hekiganroku*; the *kanbun* (Chinese script) poetry of the masters of *gozan bungaku* (literature of the "Five Mountains" monastic system), such as Ikkyū, Musō Sōseki, and others; and *shōmono* commentaries on Sung and Kamakura era kōan collections, including the *Eihei Goroku*, created by a broad range of Sōtō sect masters.

However, at the same time that Ch'an/Zen exhibited a tendency toward refined literature, many masters, in pursuit of the espoused goal of a silent transmission, emphasized various types of minimalist expression that use a highly compressed or abbreviated form of language in a deliberately self-deconstructive method of pointing beyond the need for words and toward a realm of experience unbound by speech and thought. For example, Yün-men's "one-word barrier," Lin-chi's "turning words," Tung-shan Shou-ch'u's "living words," the "*Mu!*" kōan in case 1 of the *Wu-men kuan* (J. *Mumonkan*), and Ta-hui's "critical phrase" (C. *hua-t'ou*, J. *watō*) are all examples of Ch'an/Zen developing an abbreviated, shortcut method for reaching and expressing enlightenment. In each case, the syllables, words, and phrases, brief yet allusive, are considered to have no abiding meaning of their own other than their function as pointers that must not be confused with the object (true reality, often symbolized by the moon) they indicate.[12]

The remarkable degree of tension, at times genuinely creative and at other times primarily partisan and polemical, involving the standpoints of *kyōge betsuden* and *kyōzen itchi* (unity of scriptures and meditation) can be traced back to classical T'ang dynasty debates between the Northern school, which took the side of letters, and the Southern school, which emphasized silence.[13] The tension continued to characterize the Lin-chi/Ts'ao-tung school debates during the so-called golden age of Ch'an in Sung China and Kamakura Japan, which produced voluminous kōan collections and hagiographical texts as well as a backlash that rebutted and negated those very writings. The most prominent exemplar of the tension was Ta-hui, who collected and commented on hundreds of kōan cases but who was also said to have burned the plates for the *Pi-yen lu* edited by his mentor, Yüan-wu, in support of the ideal that it is necessary to study only the critical phrases of kōans. Although the account of Ta-hui destroying his teacher's magnum opus is likely legend, it symbolizes the fact that he considered much of the commentary to be excessive or counterproductive if wrongly appropriated. The dual emphases on speech and silence may be considered an inner contradiction of Ch'an/Zen discourse or, conversely, an appropriate reflection of the doctrine of Two Truths encompassing a wordless absolute truth and a relative truth that remains bound by the rules of language. From the latter perspective, the shortcut method is understood as a skillful means to bridge the gap between the relative and absolute levels of truth or to lead one from being trapped by entangled vines to an experience of the realm of disentanglement.

The writings of Dōgen seem to epitomize the *kyōzen itchi* approach and to be antithetical to the abbreviation method for several reasons. A primary reason is simply that Dōgen was one of the most prolific Zen authors, composing the 75-fascicle *Shōbōgenzō* collection of *jishu*-style sermons in Japanese vernacular as well as the *Eihei Kōroku* collection of *jōdō*-style sermons in *kanbun* script. The 75-fascicle *Shōbōgenzō* was composed over a period of twenty years, but the majority of the fascicles were actually written over a six-year period from 1238 to 1244. This was during the time that Dōgen was first at Kōshōji temple outside Kyoto and then in the process of moving to Echizen Province, where he established Eiheiji temple.[14] The 75-fascicle *Sōbōgenō* was the main text of the period when Dōgen was undergoing a major mid-career transition from the capital to the provinces. The *Eihei Kōroku* was written over a period of fifteen years, but especially from the time Dōgen was ensconced in Eiheiji, beginning in 1245 and extending to 1252 (there were no sermons from the final year of his life). It was the major text of the last ten years of Dōgen's career.

Another reason for placing Dōgen on the side of *kyōzen itchi* is that he consistently praised and cited the *Lotus Sūtra*, articulating a philosophy of the identity of the *sūtras* and *zazen* meditation in a number of *Shōbōgenzō* fascicles, especially "Sansuikyō," "Nyorai zenshin," and "Hokke ten hokke." This outlook is expressed in the following *kanbun* verse composed while he was staying at a hermitage at Eiheiji:

> Joyful in this mountain retreat yet still feeling melancholy,
> Studying the *Lotus Sūtra* every day,
> Practicing *zazen* single-mindedly;
> What do love and hate matter

When I'm here alone,
Listening to the sound of the rain late in this autumn evening.[15]

In addition, Dōgen explicitly ridiculed exponents of the minimalist approach. For example, in the *Shōbōgenzō* "Sansuikyō" fascicle, Dōgen labeled as "pseudo-Buddhists" and "scatterbrains" speaking "sheer nonsense" those who concentrated on the critical phrases of kōans, such as "the East Mountain walks on water," or the "sticks and shouts" of Te-shan and Lin-chi. He was highly critical of those who viewed kōans only as "incomprehensible utterances" or viewed them in a manner that is devoid of thought, cognition, or conceptualization, the sole aim of which is to eliminate thinking at its root and to subvert and suppress the need for any use of language. "It is a pity that they do not know that thought is discourse, or that discourse releases [or breaks through] thought," Dōgen writes. In particular, he was at times harshly critical of Lin-chi master Ta-hui, the prime exponent of using the critical phrase as a shortcut method.[16]

However, there was also a tendency toward abbreviation throughout Dōgen's career. In an early *Eihei Kōroku* (vol. 1, no. 9, or EK.1.9) passage also included in the *Eihei Goroku* (no. 22, or EG.22), Dōgen comments on the role of abbreviation as a means of indirectly communicating the meaning of silence:

> One phrase causes the ice to melt and the tiles to crumble, and another phrase fills in the cracks and crevices. Tell me, which of the manifold phrases of the buddhas of past, present, and future, or of the six generations of patriarchs, is more effective in instructing people? Here . . . I will use a phrase that has never been uttered by the buddhas or expressed by the patriarchs. Now, listen: [after a pause] That's it![17]

Furthermore, toward the end of his life, Dōgen continued editing and revising *Shōbōgenzō* fascicles. There is an indication based on Ejō's postscript (*okugaki*) to the last sermon, "Hachidainingaku," that he was hoping to complete a 100-fascicle edition.[18] Because of his untimely death, this project was never completed. However, Dōgen did finish a revised version of the *Shōbōgenzō* known today as the 12-fascicle *Shōbōgenzō*, some of which consists of reworked versions of earlier fascicles. Yet it is unclear whether he intended the new, shorter text to be seen as a replacement for, an addendum to, or a abbreviation of the *Shōbōgenzō*. Nevertheless, on balance, Dōgen stands as an adamant opponent of minimalism in favor of an expansive view of language and the role of hermeneutics. He resisted abbreviation as an essentialist tendency that betrayed the goal of a continually renewed experience of a dynamic realization of impermanent existence. How and why, then, does abbreviation come to play such a prominent role in Dōgen Zen?

Background and Formation of the Text

The *Eihei Goroku*, also known as the *Eihei Gen Ryaku Roku* (*Abridged Record of the Founder of Eiheiji*), was created when Giin, one of Dōgen's most important followers, brought the *Eihei Kōroku* to China in 1264 to show to the heirs of Ju-ching at T'ien-tung-ssu temple, especially I-yüan, who had been a monk in training along with Dōgen in the 1220s and was then abbot of the monastery. Later, after the death of Ju-ching in 1228, I-yüan edited the text of his recorded sayings. This text reached Dōgen in 1242, although he was said to have expressed disappointment that the result was not representative of his mentor's teaching. Apparently Giin, on behalf of Eiheiji, felt that the *Eihei Kōroku*, largely a collection of Chinese *jōdō*-style sermons recorded in *kanbun*, was the representative text for the occasion of his visit rather than the vernacular *Shōbōgenzō*, and at the same time he wanted I-yüan to verify the authenticity of the contents of the *Eihei Kōroku*. I-yüan selected the passages he considered appropriate and wrote a brief postscript for the one-volume *Eihei Goroku* compilation, which Giin then showed to two leading Lin-chi (J. Rinzai) masters, Yüan-ning, whom Dōgen had once visited in China, and Hsü-t'ang, the teacher of Japanese Rinzai master Daiō Kokushi. Yüan-ning and Hsü-t'ang both wrote laudatory postscripts, although these are not always included in editions of the *Eihei Goroku*.

Unfortunately, there is no record of the edition of the *Eihei Kōroku* text Giin took with him to China. This absence has fueled a controversy concerning the relation between the *Eihei Goroku* and the *Eihei Kōroku* and jeopardizes any interpretation of the former as a distillation of the latter. We now have two main versions of the *Eihei Kōroku*, all from a century or more after Giin's journey. The first is the Monkaku edition of 1598 (named for the twentieth Eiheiji patriarch in the Jakuen lineage and also known as the Rinnōji edition), which seems to be identical to the Sozan manuscript discovered at Eiheiji in 1937; this manuscript is considered to stem from the early Muromachi period (or late fourteenth century)—the terms Monkaku text and Sozan text are often used interchangeably. The second version is the edition produced in 1672 by the important Sōtō scholastic, Manzan Dōhaku; it is also known as the *rūfū-bon* or popular edition.

The controversial relation between the *Eihei Goroku* and the two main *Eihei Kōroku* editions will be examined here in detail. The main point for now is that there is an affinity in sequence and wording between the *Eihei Goroku* and the Manzan edition, as well as some key differences between both of these texts and the older Monkaku/Sozan edition. This comparison has led several scholars to question the authenticity of the *Eihei Goroku* and to consider it more of an aberration than an abbreviation of the *Eihei Kōroku*: a text that shows more about the context in which it was created, or about Dōgen Zen, than about Dōgen himself. The main debate is between Sugawara Yūki, who supports the notion of continuity and consistency between the *Eihei Goroku* and both versions of the *Eihei Kōroku*, and Ishii Shūdō, who refutes that position with a careful comparative analysis of the texts.

Despite numerous and at times significant discrepancies between the Monkaku/Sozan and Manzan editions, the contents of all *Eihei Kōroku* editions follow the same basic structure (table 4.2). According to this list, the *Eihei Kōroku* contains four types of materials: the first seven volumes consist of 531 formal sermons (*jōdō*), beginning at Kōshōji but mostly from the time of Dōgen's abbacy at Daibutsuji/Eiheiji; the eighth volume contains 34 informal, vernacular sermons delivered at Eiheiji and Kōshōji temples (including both *shōsan* and *hōgo* styles, which are similar to yet somewhat different from the *jishu*-style of the *Shōbōgenzō*), plus the brief meditation manual, the *Fukanzanzengi*; the ninth volume contains verse comments (J. *juko*; C. *sung-ku*) on 90 kōans composed in 1236, a year after the compiling of the *Mana Shōbōgenzō* collection of 300 kōans (which have no commentary); and the tenth volume contains 150 lyrical poems in Chinese (*geju* and *jisan* styles), which were written throughout Dōgen's career beginning with his travels to China from 1223 to 1227—the Chinese verses are the only known writings from this very early period.

The first seven volumes of the *Eihei Kōroku* can be further subdivided in two ways: (1) by the three locations for the sermons, including Kōshōji (vol. 1); Daibutsuji, the original name of Eiheiji until it was changed in 1246 (vol. 2); and Eiheiji (vols. 3–7); and (2) by the three editors, including Senne, also the primary early commentator on the *Shōbōgenzō* (vol. 1, in addition to vols. 8–10); Ejō, also the primary editor of the *Shōbōgenzō* (vols. 2–4); and Gien, an Ejō disciple who became the fourth Eiheiji patriarch (vols. 5–7). The transition from Ejō's editorship to Gien's, which occurred around the ninth month/first day of 1249, is a significant turning point for some scholars because this period

TABLE 4.2. A List of the Contents and Dates of Composition of the *Eihei Kōroku* (10 vols.)

1. Kōshōji goroku (*jōdō* sermons, nos. 1–126 from 1236–1243, rec. Senne)
2. Daibutsuji goroku (nos. 127–184, 1245–1246, rec. Ejō)
3. Eiheiji goroku (nos. 185–257, 1246–1248, rec. Ejō)
4. Eiheiji goroku (nos. 258–345, 1248–1249, rec. Ejō)
5. Eiheiji goroku (nos. 346–413, 1249–1251, rec. Gien)
6. Eiheiji goroku (nos. 414–470, 1251, rec. Gien)
7. Eiheiji goroku (nos. 471–531, 1251–1252, rec. Gien)
8. Miscellaneous (20 *shōsan* at Daibutsuji/Eiheiji, 14 *hōgo* mainly at Kōshōji, *Fukanzazengi*, rec. Ejō and others)
9. Kōshōji collection (90 *juko* comments on kōans from 1236, ed. Senne and others)
10. Kanbun poetry collections, 1223–1253 (5 *shinsan*, 20 *jisan*, 125 *geju*; ed. Senne and others)

The first seven volumes are collections of *jōdō* from Kōshōji, Daibutsuji and Eiheiji, and the last three volumes collect various kinds of lectures, kōan commentary, and poetry.

also marks an important shift for Dōgen, who had completed work on the 75-fascicle *Shōbōgenzō* several years before and now began collecting the 12-fascicle *Shōbōgenzō*.

The *Eihei Goroku* was the product of Giin's second trip to China. Giin was one of the former followers of the defunct Daruma-shū sect, a group that included Ejō, Gien, and Gikai, among others. Ejō joined Dōgen in 1234 after the death of his teacher, Kakuan, and the others, most of whose names begin with the *kanji* "Gi," joined Dōgen at Kōshōji temple in Kyoto in 1241 and later made up the core of the Eiheiji community. Of these, Giin alone traveled to China, first in 1253, although he apparently returned promptly upon learning of Dōgen's death in the autumn of that year. It is not clear whether he took the *Eihei Kōroku* at Dōgen's own suggestion, but we do know that Giin brought only this text on his 1264 trip, so I-yüan apparently did not see and may not have been aware of the *Shōbōgenzō* in either the 75-fascicle or 12-fascicle edition. Figure 4.1 shows how the production of the *Eihei Goroku* by Gien (lineage D) and the first commentary by Giun (lineage B) emerged in relation to the role of three other main Dōgen lineages (A, C, and E).

After the formation of the text, the *Eihei Goroku* eventually passed into the hands of Giun, a disciple of Jakuen, another Dharma-brother of Dōgen in China who came to train with him in Japan after Ju-ching's death. Following the death of Dōgen, Jakuen left Eiheiji and set up Hōkyōki temple. Giun was not one of the original groups of former Daruma-shū followers who gravitated to Dōgen, but his name indicates that there likely was a connection or affinity with this community. The Jakuen-Giun lineage was known for its adherence to Dōgen's strict, nonsyncretic style of practice in opposition to the Gikai-Keizan faction, which advocated assimilative and esoteric tendencies. At this juncture in the history of Dōgen Zen, the *Eihei Kōroku* received little attention. Giun edited a version of the *Shōbōgenzō* in 60 fascicles (rather than the 75 fascicles edited by Senne and his disciple Kyōgō, which seems to have been

---

FIGURE 4.1. Five Sōtō Zen lineages and production of the *Eihei Goroku*; roles of Giin (D) and Giun (B) regarding *Eihei Goroku*, seen in relation to other Dōgen lineages. See also the lineage chart in William M. Bodiford, *Sōtō Zen in Medieval Japan* (Honolulu: University of Hawaii Press, 1993), p. 33. A: Although it was not long lasting, the Senne-Kyōgō lineage is known for an important commentary on the 75-fascicle *Shōbōgenzō*, the *Gokikigakishō* (or *Goshō*), the first such work and the only one until the revival of *Shōbōgenzō* studies in the Tokugawa era. They left Eiheiji before 1263 for Yōkōan near Kenninji in Kyoto. B: The Jakuen-Giun lineage was based in Hōkyōji temple, founded by Jakuen, who had been Dōgen's Dharma-brother in China and came to join him in Japan; he left Eiheiji in 1261, although Giun later returned to become the fifth abbot. Giun is known for his recorded sayings (*Giun Goroku*) and his edition of the 60-

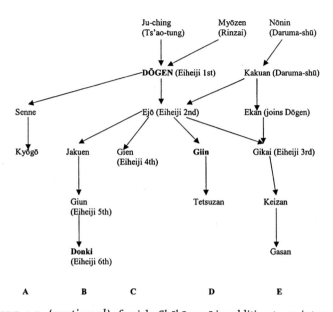

Ju-ching (Ts'ao-tung) Myōzen (Rinzai) Nōnin (Daruma-shū)

DŌGEN (Eiheiji 1st) Kakuan (Daruma-shū)

Senne Ejō (Eiheiji 2nd) Ekan (joins Dōgen)

Kyōgō Jakuen Gien (Eiheiji 4th) Giin Gikai (Eiheiji 3rd)

Giun (Eiheiji 5th) Tetsuzan Keizan

Donki (Eiheiji 6th) Gasan

A   B   C   D   E

FIGURE 4.1. *(continued)* fascicle *Shōbōgenzō* in addition to an interest in Dōgen's record (*Eihei Goroku*) published by Donki. C: The Ejō-Gien lineage was aligned with Jakuen in opposition to the attempt by Gikai, the third patriarch of Eiheiji, to introduce esoteric rituals and chants into Zen practice. In the 1270s Gikai abdicated and Gien became the fourth patriarch. D: The Ejō-Giin lineage led to the founding of Sōtō Zen in Kyushu, based on the efforts of Giin, who built on inroads made there by Eisai. Giin made a second trip to China in 1264 that resulted in the editing of Dōgen's *Eihei Goroku* by Wu-wai I-yüan, who had been one of Ju-ching's major disciples and who also compiled his teacher's recorded sayings that reached Dōgen in 1242. I-yüan wrote a eulogy for Dōgen, and Giin also got eulogies from Hsü-t'ang and Yüan-ning, prominent monks in the Five Mountains system. The text, an abbreviated, one-volume version of the voluminous ten-volume *Eihei Kōroku*, was the first Sōtō sect publication released in 1358 by Donki, and it was quickly followed by Dōgen's one-volume *Gakudōyōjinshū* and Giun's one-volume *goroku* (some sources date these as 1357) (see B). E: The Gikai lineage's syncretic religiosity became the most successful by far in converting Shingon and Tendai temples and gaining multitudes of followers for the Sōtō sect, especially through the missionary efforts of the Keizan-Gasan sublineage based in Sōjiji in the Noto peninsula. This sublineage was aligned with mountain worship of Mount Sekidōzan, which was part of the sacred network of Mount Hakusan. *Note:* (1) Dual lineages affecting Dōgen (from Ju-ching and Myōzen), Ejō (from Dōgen and Kakuan), and Gikai (from Ejō and Ekan); (2) the affinities between both Gien and Giin and the Jakuen-Giun line, in contrast to Gikai's independence, which perhaps stemmed from continued Daruma-shū influence; all the third-generation disciples studied with Dōgen, including Kyōgō, and Keizan also studied with Jakuen, Ejō, and Gien.

the main version of the *Shōbōgenzō* during the early medieval period). Giun's approach to editing Dōgen seemed to stress a sense of continuity with Chinese Ch'an through the process of leaving out of the 60-fascicle *Shōbōgenzō* those passages expressing a contentious attitude and a harsh critique of the Lin-chi school, especially fascicles, such as "Sansuikyō" and "Jishō zanmai," that target Ta-hui's critical phrase method. Giun was also known for producing his own collection of recorded sayings, the *Giun Goroku*, an important early Sōtō work, as well as for editing the *Gakudōyōjinsū*, a short Dōgen text from 1234; in that year Ejō joined Dōgen, and shortly thereafter he began compiling the *Shōbōgenzō Zuimonki*.[19] The *Gakudōyōjinsū* and the *Giun Goroku* were both published in 1358, right after the publication of the *Eihei Goroku* by Giun's disciple Donki, who became the sixth abbot of Eiheiji.

Structure of the Text

In order to clarify where the *Eihei Goroku* stands in relation to the issue of Dōgen versus Dōgen Zen, it is necessary to take a closer look at how the *Eihei Goroku* was selected from the *Eihei Kōroku*. As was indicated, the *Eihei Goroku* appears to be much closer in content to the Manzan edition than to the earlier Monkaku/Sozan version. Some scholars, particularly Ishii Shūdō and Kagamishima Genryū, argue that the Manzan text is a corruption of the text Giin carried to China and they view the *Eihei Goroku* as an aberration of the *Eihei Kōroku* that was probably mistakenly used by Manzan as a primary source. Ishii maintains that the Giin text(?) (the question mark is used here to highlight the fact that such a text is not extant and thus hypothetical) was a precursor to the Monkaku/Sozan edition. But the *Eihei Goroku* strayed from this text yet was used as a model for the Manzan edition. A key example is a discrepancy in the opening selection of the *Eihei Goroku*. This is the famous passage in which Dōgen announces during a sermon in the Dharma Hall at Kōshōji in 1236 that he had returned (some years earlier) to Japan from his travels in China "empty-handed" (*kūshū genkyō*). This passage is also the opening *jōdō* in the Manzan editon, but it appears as *jōdō* no. 48 (EK.1.48 in the Monkaku/ Sozan edition with wording that is somewhat variant). In addition, the *Eihei Goroku* and the Manzan edition both include the verse "Zazenshin" along with the *Fukanzazengi* (these are two meditation texts), but the "Zazenshin" does not appear in the Monkaku/Sozan edition.

There are dozens of other instances in which sequence and wording suggest that Manzan was influenced by the *Eihei Goroku* and failed to use the authentic *Eihei Kōroku* model, or chose to divert from it because of what Ishii considers an unwarranted acceptance of the authority of the *Eihei Goroku*.[20] However, since the Giin text(?) is not available (and will likely never be, save for the unlikely discovery of a lost manuscript), it is admittedly speculation that there must have been a consistency between this hypothetical text and the Monkaku/Sozan edition, as well as a divergence with the Manzan edition. This situation opens up another school of thought, led by Sugawara Yūki, which argues that there is a fundamental, underlying affinity between all the versions involved, and no serious discontinuity or inconsistency between the Giin text(?), the *Eihei Goroku*, the Monkaku/Sozan version, and the Manzan edition.[21] Figure 4.2 outlines the two approaches to textual history, with Ishii's (and Kagamishima's) view reflecting an "inconsistency" or "two-text" theory and Sugawara's view a "consistency" or "single-text" theory.

Ishii's argument is based on a careful examination of the structure of the *Eihei Goroku* in terms of its affinities and disparities with the *Eihei Kōroku*. Through this analysis he demonstrates not only discrepancies in wording and sequence but, more significantly, patterns of inclusion and exclusion which reveal the priorities and proclivities of I-yüan in Sung China that caused the *Eihei Goroku* to vary from the image of Dōgen as a Japanese master as displayed in the *Eihei Kōroku*. Ishii is critical of Sugawara for supporting the Manzan text that, he feels, based its edition of the *Eihei Kōroku* on a retrospective reading of the *Eihei Goroku* rather than seeing Manzan as a distortion of the source.

A reconstruction of Ishii's approach indicates a three-part analysis: (1) the structure of the *Eihei Goroku* text and discrepancies with the *Eihei Kōroku*; (2) patterns of inclusion/selection and exclusion/absence; and (3) a philosophical comparison of both the *Eihei Goroku* and *Eihei Kōroku* with other texts from

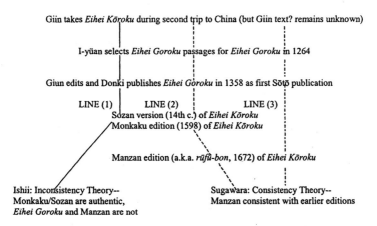

FIGURE 4.2. Two theories about the textual history of the *Eihei Goroku* and its relation to the three extant editions of the *Eihei Kōroku*. The solid line (1) traces Ishii's theory that bypasses the Manzan text, the dotted line (2) traces Sugawara's theory that includes Manzan, and the segmented line (3) traces Ishii's view of Sugawara's theory that, according to Ishii, sees the *Eihei Goroku* through the filter of the Manzan text without any role for the Monkaku text.

the later period of Dōgen, especially the 12-fascicle *Shōbōgenzō*. Ishii concludes that the *Eihei Goroku* neither expresses the real intentions of Dōgen nor reflects the uniqueness of his thought as expressed in the works of the later period, including the *Eihei Kōroku* and 12-fascicle *Shōbōgenzō*. He argues that the *Eihei Goroku* offers an inappropriate view of the late Dōgen as well as of the theoretical/philosophical issues that preoccupied this period of Dōgen's career, as suggested especially in vols. 5–7 of the *Eihei Kōroku* (the volumes edited by Gien) and the 12-fascicle *Shōbōgenzō*. Rather, the dominant motif of the *Eihei Goroku* is I-yüan's overriding concern with establishing continuity between Dōgen and Chinese masters as well as Sung-style monastic ritualism.

Table 4.3, which is derived from studies by Kagamishima Genryū and Ishii Shūdō, outlines the general structure of the *Eihei Goroku* and shows exactly what was selected from the *Eihei Kōroku*. According to these scholars, while the structure of the *Eihei Goroku* closely resembles the source text, the content reflects I-yüan's motive of overemphasizing the links between Dōgen and Chinese Ch'an rituals and patriarchs, thereby overlooking the Japanese influences apparent on Dōgen's post-1249 approach to religiosity.

TABLE 4.3. Comparison of the Structure of *Eihei Kōroku* (EK) and *Eihei Goroku* (EG)

	EK	EG	Correct list from EK
Jōdō (EK.1-7 total)	531	75 (74)	73 = 8.shōsan.7
From Kōshōji (EK.1)	126	22 (18)	2 = 2.129 19 = 2.176
			3 = 2.133 4 = 3.358
From Daibutsuji (EK.2)	58	n/a (12)	25 = 2.128 57 = 2.14 62 = 2.184
			26 = 2.127 58 = 2.156 [+2, 3, 19]
			27 = 2.140 59 = 2.172
			28 = 2.143 61 = 2.179
From Eiheiji (EK.3-7)	347	53 (44)	(25, 26, 27, 28, 57, 58, 59, 61, 62 incorrectly listed as Eiheiji)
Shōsan (EK.8)	20	4 (5)	73
Hōgo (EK.8)	14	2	
Fukanzazengi (EK.8)	1	1	
Zazenshin	—	1	(not included in EK)
Juko (EK.9)	90	none	
Verses (EK.10 total)	145	20	
Shinsan	5	none	
Jisan	20	3	
Geju	125	17	
Totals	713	103	

The numbers in parenthesis reflect the accurate count, and the items in the column "Correct List" indicate the authentic listing. The table is based primarily on Kagamishima, *Dōgen Zenji Goroku*, pp. 216–217, and Ishii Shūdō, "*Eihei Ryaku Roku Kangae*," pp. 80–86.

The general structure of the *Eihei Goroku* as a collection of lectures and verses is based on the *Eihei Kōroku*, but there are some fundamental differences, including several discrepancies between the way the *jōdō* are listed in the *Eihei Goroku* and their actual appearance in the *Eihei Kōroku*. The Daibutsuji record (EK.2) is not cited as a separate category in the *Eihei Goroku*, which makes no distinction between passages selected from the Kōshōji record (EK.1) of *jōdō* and the Daibutsuji record instead of grouping them together as one section of *jōdō* sermons. But, to follow the *Eihei Kōroku* accurately, the *Eihei Goroku* should have an independent section of Daibutsuji records with twelve listings in the *Eihei Goroku*, including three that are listed in the Kōshōji record (EK.1) and nine that are in the Eiheiji record (EK.3–7), as indicated in table 4.3 under the column "Correct List." This absence in the *Eihei Goroku* may give a misimpression about the proportions or sense of balance between the subcategories of the *Eihei Goroku*. Another difference is that the *Eihei Goroku* includes none of the *juko* in EK.9 or the *shinsan* in EK.10, and it also adds the poem "Zazenshin" to the *Fukanzazengi* that is cited from EK.8.

Ishii's analysis continues with a more detailed investigation of additional differences between the two texts. There are four main areas of texual discrepancies. First, there are two *Eihei Goroku* passages that do not exist in the *Eihei Kōroku*, although some similarity can be detected: *jōdō* no. 29 (EG.29, which is similar to EK.5.367) and no. 71 (similar to EK.4.320). Second, there are five examples of variation in wording between the *Eihei Goroku* passage and the *Eihei Kōroku* source: *jōdō* no. 44 (based on EK.6.422), no. 58 (based on EK.2.156), no. 72 (based on EK.5.375), *geju* no. 2 (based on EK.10.64), and *geju* no. 9 (based on EK.10.93/94). Third, two *Eihei Goroku* entries reflect an alteration of the *Eihei Kōroku* source: *jōdō* no. 16 (which is a combination of EK.1.57 and EK.7.471) and *shōsan* no. 4 (which seems to be a shortened version of EK.8.*shōsan*.9 combined with *shōsan*.10). Fourth, there are four other passages in the *Eihei Goroku* that represent a condensed form of the original: *jōdō* no. 2 (which consists of the final portion of EK.2.129, no. 4 (the final portion of EK.5.358), no. 48 (the second half of EK.7.513), and *shōsan* no. 3 (the first portion of EK.8.*shōsan*.13). The cumulative effect of Ishii's analysis thus far is to show that 13 of 103 selections in the *Eihei Goroku* (or 13%) have some major difference with the *Eihei Kōroku* source, in addition to over twenty-five divergences in the sequence of passages.

Patterns of Inclusion and Exclusion

The next and more significant stage of investigation deals with examining what types of passages were included in the *Eihei Goroku* and, just as important, what types were excluded. There are several patterns that emerge through a study of the selections: an emphasis on consistency with Sung Ch'an patriarchy, especially as expressed in the recorded sayings texts of Ts'ao-tung masters Hung-chih and Ju-ching and a variety of transmission of the lamp histories such as the *Ching-te ch'uan-teng lu*; an emphasis on the role of monastic rituals (*girei*), including memorials and anniversaries as well as ceremonies marking seasonal transitions; and a deemphasis on the refutation of syncretism and spiritism that seems to characterize other writings of the late period.

Table 4.4 shows the sources for the citations of passages in the *Eihei Kōroku* and the *Eihei Goroku*. The first five items on the list refer to recorded sayings (*lu* or *roku*) texts (plus *sung-ku* or *juko*, verse comments on kōans in the case of Yüan-wu in item no. 3), and the last six items are "transmission of the lamp" histories. Several interesting points become clear about the construction of the *Eihei Goroku*. First, in the *Eihei Kōroku* only 28 percent of the passages are based on citations from prominent Chinese recorded sayings and transmission texts, but in the *Eihei Goroku* collection of *jōdō* and other sermons this number nearly doubles to a sizable 54 percent. If one takes a closer look at the use of sources, the records of Ts'ao-tung patriarchs Hung-chih and Ju-ching *combined* (16 percent) are the major source for the *Eihei Goroku*, although the major source for the *Eihei Kōroku* is the *Ching-te ch'uan-teng lu*, which remains a close second among *Eihei Goroku* sources.

Compared with the priorities reflected in the *Eihei Kōroku*, the fact that the *Eihei Goroku* favors the *Hung-chih lu* and the *Ju-ching lu* indicates I-yüan's concern, perhaps more than Dōgen's, with following the model of the Chinese masters rather than relying on the transmission of the lamp hagiographies. Of the two Ts'ao-tung patriarchs, Ju-ching with nine citations (11%) plays a far greater role in the *Eihei Goroku* than in the *Eihei Kōroku* (where he has a total of ten citations, or under 2 percent), while Hung-chih's role, though still important, is somewhat reduced (from forty-three to seven citations). I-yüan's primary loyalty was to his and Dōgen's teacher. Of the transmission histories, the second main one cited in the *Eihei Goroku* is the *Chia-t'ai p'u-teng lu* rather than the *Tsung-men t'ung-yao chi*, as in the *Eihei Kōroku*. Although the *Tsung-men t'ung-yao chi* had a tremendous influence on Dōgen, as is seen in the number of citations that appear in the *Shōbōgenzō* and the *Mana Shōbōgenzō*, it was a relatively obscure text that was apparently not well known for most Chinese Ch'an masters and it was likely to have been unrecognized and somewhat overlooked in I-yüan's selection process.[22]

Another important aspect of the kinds of passages contained in the *Eihei Goroku* is highlight the role of ceremonialism. Ishii notes I-yüan's inclusion of fourteen out of seventy-five *jōdō* sermons (or nearly 20 percent) dealing with the ritual aspect of monastic life. These include three *jōdō* sermons that provide memorials for the Buddha: no. 7, on the anniversary of Buddha's enlightenment (or *jōdō-e*); no. 29, on the anniversary of Buddha's parinirvāṇa (or *nehan-e*), and no. 55, on *rohatsu*. In addition, no. 71 celebrates a ceremony for the bathing of the Buddha. There are also five sermons for other kinds of me-

TABLE 4.4. Comparison of Sources for the EK and EG

Text	EK	EG	EG listing (with corresponding EK no. in parenthesis)
1. *Hung-chih lu*	43	7	10 (1.20), 28 (2.143), 33 (6.465), 36 (4266), 38 (4.330), 41 (5.400), s.3 (8.s.13, half passage)
2. *Ju-ching lu*	10	9	1 (1.48), 16 (1.57)*, 23 (4.316), 40 (5.391), 43 (5.405), 47 (6.456) 55 (2.213), 61 (2.179)*, 66 (3.194), 69 (7.520)
3. *Yüan-wu lu/sung-ku*	9	4	27 (2,140), 61 (2.179)*, 67 (3.218), s.4 (8.s.10, wording altered)
4. *Ta-hui lu*	2	2	3 (2.133), 50 (5.365)
5. *Huang-po lu*	2	2	24 (4.282), 31 (4.281)
6. *Ching-te ch'uan-teng lu*	68	14	8 (1.53), 18 (1.55), 19 (2.176), 21 (1.40), 32 (3.208), 44 (6.422, wording altered), 46 (7.511), 48 (7.513, incomplete), 49 (7.524), 53 (2.212), 58(2.156, wording altered), 64 (3.191), 74 (3.192), h.2 (8.h.12)
7. *Chia-t'ai p'u-teng lu*	7	7	6 (1.43), 11 (1.23), 25 (2.128), 56 (3.201), 61 (2.179)*, 65 (3.199), h.1 (8.h.10)*
8. *Tsung-men lien-t'ung hui-yao*	24	6	2 (2.129), 12 (1.27), 35 (3.250), 57 (2.141), 63 (3.188), s.1 (8.s.16)
9. *T'ien-sheng kuang-teng lu*	9	2	15 (1.4)*, 70 (5.378)
10. *Hsü ch'uan-teng lu*	2	2	15 (1.4)*, 16 (1.57, mixed with 7.471)*
11. *Tsung-men t'ung-yao chi*	25	1	52 (6.433)
Totals	201	52 (4 duplications)	

The list of sources for passages is *not* the same as a list of citations or allusions. Other sources include the *Record of Layman P'ang* for EG.22 (EK 1.9), *Diamond Sūtra* for EG.54 (EK.3.202), *Chao-chou lu* for EG.59 (EK.2.172), and *Yün-men lu* for EG.h.1. (EK.8.h.10)*. In this list, s. is *shōsan*, h. is *hōgo*, and * indicates that there seems to be more than one source for the passage. In addition, sources cannot be identified for the following entries: Among EG 4 (EK 5.358, incomplete), 5 (1.47), 7 (1.37), 9 (1.14), 13 (1.49), 14 (1.2), 17 (1.72), 20 (1.11), 26 (2.127), 29 (5.367?), 30 (3.218), 37 (4.271), 39 (4.333), 45 (6.448), 51 (5.359), 60 (5.407), 62 (1.184), 68 (7.481), 71 (4.320?), 72 (5.375, wording altered), 73 (8.s.7).

morials: no. 20, when senior monk Sōkai is about to die; no 30, on the anniversary of the death of the founder of Japanese Rinzai, Eisai; no. 40, when a bikuni named Egi asks for an expounding of the Dharma on the occasion of the death of her mother; no. 49, on the anniversary of Dōgen's grandfather's death; and no. 62, on the anniversary of the death of Ju-ching. Furthermore, there are three sermons celebrating important occasions in monastery life: no.

9, on opening the hearth at Kōshōji; no. 42, on thanking the new and outgoing rectors of the temple; and no. 65, on opening the hearth at Eiheiji. Finally, there are two sermons on seasonal changes: no. 45, on the harvest moon, and no. 68, on the fifteenth day of the first month.

Actually, the *Eihei Kōroku* is filled with many other sermons dealing with these kinds of monastic rituals that were not selected for the *Eihei Goroku*. On the other hand, all of the *shōsan* in the *Eihei Goroku* are seasonal (although this is generally also true for the *Eihei Kōroku*). Therefore, the emphasis on memorial and seasonal ceremonies, like the emphasis on citations of the sayings of Ju-ching and other Ch'an records, highlights I-yüan's concern with establishing continuity with Sung-style Ch'an as well as an implicit criticism of T'ang era Ch'an practice, which had a style that was more irreverent and without such a clearly structured and regulated monastic routine.

Ishii's argument about the failure of the *Eihei Goroku* to reflect adequately the *Eihei Kōroku* deals largely with what has been excluded in the condensed text. The *Eihei Goroku*, he argues, does not convey the sense of transition or transmission of Zen to Japan, because it does not include passages that express Dōgen's criticisms about what he considers the problematic side of the Ch'an/Zen approach in both Sung China and the early stages of Kamakura Japan. According to Ishii, the fifth volume of the *Eihei Goroku* marks a significant though generally overlooked transition in the collection of *jōdō* sermons, reflecting a change in Dōgen's attitude toward a number of key issues, such as the ideological relation between Zen and syncretism with non-Buddhist religions, as well as the notions of naturalism and dualism. This shift in emphasis, which is also evident in the 12-fascicle *Shōbōgenzō* of the same late period, is not expressed in the makeup of the *Eihei Goroku*, which relies primarily on passages from an earlier stage in his career. Although the *Eihei Goroku* as a condensation of the *Eihei Kōroku* must in general terms be considered a text from the period of the late, post-75-fascicle *Shōbōgenzō*, according to Ishii it reflects only the earlier segment of this stage of Dōgen's career and not what he considers the more authentic stage of the late Dōgen, or what can more accurately be referred to as the "late late Dōgen," beginning in 1249.

Ishii stresses the importance of two key turning points for understanding the relation between the *Eihei Goroku* and the *Eihei Kōroku*. The first is the time of *Eihei Kōroku* 3.196 (around 9/15, 1246), which is about when Dōgen completed the last fascicle of the 75-fascicle *Shōbōgenzō*, "Shukke." Ishii points out that 37 percent of the *Eihei Kōroku* is from the period before no. 196, and 63 percent is from the period after this juncture, or a nearly 2 to 1 ratio favoring the later stage. But the *Eihei Goroku* contains 49 percent (or thirty-five sermons) from the period before no. 196, and 51 percent (or thirty-seven sermons, with two sermons of unclear dating and one *shōsan* mistakenly included among the *jōdō*) after this. The second turning point is the time of the fifth volume of the *Eihei Kōroku*, when editing was placed in the hands of Gien, who completed the task of working on the *jōdō* sermons, rather than those of Ejō, who was known primarily as the editor of the 75-fascicle *Shōbōgenzō*. The date of this transition was 9/1, 1249 (EK.5.346), about three years after the first turning point, which was also when Dōgen began to work in earnest on the 12-fascicle *Shōbōgenzō*, with its emphasis on the doctrines of karmic causality, the need for repentance, and criticism of indigenous religiosity.[23] Ishii shows that the *Eihei Kōroku* contains 185 sermons (or 35 percent) after no. 346, but the *Eihei Goroku* contains only twenty-one sermons (or 28 percent) from this period. Furthermore, while Hung-chih was a major influence on many of Dōgen's sermons before the second turning point, he is cited only rarely after this.[24] Yet the *Eihei Goroku* includes two of twenty-one sermons (nos. 33 and 41) citing Hung-chih from the post-no. 346 period.[25]

While these figures and percentages in and of themselves may not seem overwhelming, the more significant point is that there are a number of ideological standpoints Dōgen criticizes in *Eihei Kōroku* sermons from the period beginning after no. 346 that are not included in the *Eihei Goroku*. These include a critique of "the identity of the three doctrines, Buddhism, Confucianism, Taoism" (*sankyō ittō*) in nos. 383 and 412; of the notion of syncretism (*setchū-shugi*) in EK.5.390; spiritism (*shinga* and *reichi*) in nos.5.402, 6.447, and 7.509; of the naturalism heresy (*shizen gedō*) in no. 7.472; and of the assertion of exclusivity of the Zen sect (or *Zen-shū*) in no. 7.491. All of the refuted standpoints, according to Ishii, represent views that bypass or overlook the principle of karmic causality in the name of a false sense of transcendence, either by combining Buddhism with other doctrines (identity, syncretism, spiritism) or by asserting a single truth that does not require constant training (naturalism, exclusivism) based on understanding cause-and-effect. Another important perspective of the later stages of the *Eihei Kōroku* that is absent in the *Eihei Goroku* are sermons that emphasize the significance of karmic retribution (*sanjigo*), as expressed in nos. 7.516 and 7.517.

Sugawara is the main opponent of Ishii's inconsistency or two-text theory in arguing for the underlying consistency between the *Eihei Goroku* and the *Eihei Kōroku* editions. In a critical edition comparing the *Eihei Goroku* with the Manzan and Monkaku editions, he shows that there are numerous instances where the *Eihei Goroku* is actually more similar to the Monkaku edition than to the Manzan, or where the Monkaku edition is more similar to the Manzan than either of these is to the *Eihei Goroku*. However, Sugawara's criticism, which sticks mainly to this aspect of the textual debate, is muted by two factors. First, he acknowledges and does not dispute (though he interprets the significance differently) the textual discrepancies that Ishii demonstrates in the construction and sequence of the *Eihei Goroku*. Also, he does not question the broader ideological concerns Ishii raises in terms of the patterns of exclusion and inclusion in the *Eihei Goroku*, especially regarding the issues of causality as also expressed in the 12-fascicle *Shōbōgenzō* of Dōgen's late period.

Therefore, Ishii's argument, which is based on a comprehensive textual and theoretical analysis suggesting that the *Eihei Goroku* should not be considered the creme or essence of the *Eihei Kōroku*, prevails over the challenge of Sugawara.

Issues Concerning the Late Late Dōgen

Is the *Eihei Goroku* genuinely representative as a distillation of Dōgen, or is it a corruption of the source text that reflects Dōgen Zen? There are two main issues involved in analyzing this question: hermeneutic and historical. The first issue is whether Dōgen's *Eihei Kōroku* is distillable, and the second issue is, if so, would or could this quality result in the production of the *Eihei Goroku*? The first issue raises the question of whether the notion of distillation is in keeping with or in violation of the spirit of Dōgen's teaching. Although Dōgen seems to be a proponent of speech over silence, or of expressing the Dharma through discourse, his writings suggest a flexible standpoint that does not prohibit abbreviation. In principle, the abbreviation of the *Eihei Goroku* into the *Eihei Goroku* does not stand in opposition to Dōgen.

But the issue of whether or not this abbreviated text represents either a distillation/essence of Dōgen himself or a kind of condensation that skews the message toward Dōgen Zen cannot be dealt with in abstract theoretical terms. That is, the historical issue immediately transmutes into the hermeneutic issue because the text was the creation of Dōgen's followers, who were not fully aware of or were perhaps somewhat oblivious (in their preoccupation with other agendas) to the priorities of Dōgen's thought. Thus the issue of interpreting the abbreviated text is a matter of historical contextualization—to see how, when, and why the abbreviation was created as well as the function it serves. It seems clear that the creator undertook objectives that were characteristic primarily of Dōgen Zen rather than Dōgen. I-yüan wanted the *Eihei Goroku* to highlight the continuity between Dōgen and Chinese Ts'ao-tung influences including Hung-chih and Ju-ching (just as Ōuchi Seiran and other Meiji lay leaders created a view of repentance in *Shushōgi* based in part on the challenge of Christianity during the Westernization process). However, "Dōgen" and "Dōgen Zen" are by no means mutually exclusive or separable categories but are interconnected on both historical and hermeneutic levels. The abbreviated text as exemplary of Dōgen Zen is significant largely because it can lead us back to an understanding and appropriation of Dōgen.

Thus the historical level of significance reflects the fact that the *Eihei Goroku* demonstrates the importance of, and sharpens our focus on, the later Dōgen, an area of inquiry that has generally been much overlooked in studies of Sōtō Zen. The period of the late Dōgen generally refers to the time that begins around 1246, when he was fully settled into Eiheiji and had completed writing the 75-fascicle *Shōbōgenzō* and turned to the *Eihei Kōroku* and, eventually, the 12-fascicle *Shōbōgenzō*. But a study of the *Eihei Goroku* shows that the late Dōgen is complex—it is not a single period, but a multifaceted sequence of subperiods. There are several key turning points in the late Dōgen: (1) the beginning of the late period around 9/15, 1246, which is crucial for understanding the construction of the *Eihei Goroku*; (2) Dōgen's return from Kamakura in the third month of 1248, after which he focused on the doctrines of causality and monastic discipline (though not necessarily repentance); and (3) the period beginning around 9/1, 1249, when Gien started editing the *Eihei Kōroku* and Dōgen dedicated himself to the 12-fascicle *Shōbōgenzō*. Therefore, the *Eihei Goroku*, by its absence of material due to the fact that it is more a product of Dōgen Zen than of Dōgen, may be pointing to the most significant stage in Dōgen's career, though through a broken lens.

As Martin Heidegger repeatedly argues on the basis of Greek and Germanic sources, the remembrance of a text necessarily involves a forgetting, and in some instances the more profound the forgetting the greater the enhancement of the memory of what is lapsed. Heidegger asks whether we can ever truly know the origins or must "make appeal to a cultivated acquaintance with the past," and he cites the following brief verse by the German poet Hölderlin: ·

Reluctantly
that which dwells near its origin, departs.[26]

Thus the hermeneutic issue refers to the way this abbreviated text cannot help but lead back to an appropriation of Dōgen. Although not a pure distillation that provides an ideal introduction to the *Eihei Kōroku*, as some commentators or translations claim, the *Eihei Goroku* is also not merely arbitrary but is an extension that at once preserves yet distorts the source. Dōgen and Dōgen Zen are entangled in an ongoing process of creative misunderstanding and creative hermeneutics, a fact that illustrates that "Dōgen" is not a static entity that can exist apart from how he is perceived and received (heard, understood, interpreted, translated, commented on, transmitted—and distilled, even in a culture of convenience and simulation). The relative lack of focus on the third subperiod in the passages selected for inclusion in the *Eihei Goroku*, which Ishii shows goes against the grain of the *Eihei Kōroku* and the 12-fascicle *Shōbōgenzō*, ironically highlights the importance of the late late Dōgen, as well as the reasons it has been overlooked.

NOTES

1. The *Shushōgi* outlines the Zen religious life, which is based on the following principles (paraphrasing the titles of the five sections): understanding the problem of life and death (*shōji*) and the universality of karmic retribution, penitence leading to the eradication of evil karma (*zange metsuzai*), receiving the sixteen precepts (*jukai*

nyūi), benefiting others through a vow of benevolence (*hotsugan rishō*), and expressing gratitude by means of constant practice (*gyōji hōon*). The *Shushōgi* was declared the sect's manual for lay devotion as well as for monastic ritual, by a joint edict issued in 1892 by the abbots of Eiheiji (Takitani Takashū) and Sōjiji (Azegami Baisen), the two head temples (*honzan*) of Sōtō Zen.

2. A complete annotated text with modern Japanese translation of the *Eihei Goroku* is found in Kagamishima Genryū, *Dōgen Zenji Goroku* (Tokyo: Kodansha, 1990). The *Eihei Goroku* is based on the *Eihei Kōroku*, in Kagamishima Genryū, et. al., *Dōgen Zenji zenshū* (Tokyo: Shunjūsha, 1991–1993), vols. 3 and 4 (of 7); and it also appears in the *Dōgen Zenji zenshū* (1989), vol. 5, pp. 54–123.

3. The oldest extant version seems to be the Shōhō edition at Tōzenji temple in Aichi prefecture, apparently published not later than 1649.

4. This may seem somewhat surprising to those who have witnessed a boom in translations and studies of the *Shōbōgenzō* in recent years, both in Japanese and in English, but it is an accurate portrayal of the history of Dōgen Zen. On the other hand, the neglect of the *Shōbōgenzō* as well as of the *Eihei Kōroku* during the medieval period does not necessarily indicate an absence of intellectual life or the persistence of a sectarian "dark ages," as is often interpreted, because the vigorous activity of commentaries on the *Eihei Goroku* and other Zen texts, including Dōgen's kōan collection in Chinese, the *Mana Shōbōgenzō*, belies that argument.

5. This is the topic of another essay of mine, "Abbreviation or Aberration: The Role of the *Shushōgi* in Modern Sōtō Zen Buddhism," in *Buddhism and the Modern World: Adaptations of an Ancient Tradition*, ed. Steven Heine and Charles S. Prebish (New York: Oxford University Press, 2003), pp. 169–192.

6. On the role of the *shōmono* texts, see, for example, Kaneda Hiroshi, *Tōmon Shōmono to Kokugo Kenkyū* (Tokyo: Ōfusha, 1986), and Ishikawa Rikizan, "Chūsei Zen--shū Shi Kenkyū to Zenseki Shōmono Shiryō," *Dōgen Zenji to Sōtō-shū*, ed. Kawamura Kōdō and Ishikawa Rikizan (Tokyo: Yoshikawa kobunkan, 1985), pp. 76–98.

7. See Marilyn Ivy, *Discourses of the Vanishing: Modernity Phantasm Japan* (Chicago: University of Chicago Press, 1985).

8. Thomas Cleary, trans., "Eihei Goroku," unpublished translation (held at San Francisco Zen Center Library, n.d.), p. 1.

9. See T. Griffith Foulk, "The Form and Function of Koan Literature," *The Kōan: Texts and Contexts in Zen Buddhism*, ed. Steven Heine and Dale S. Wright (New York: Oxford University Press, 2000); and Steven Heine, *Dōgen and the Kōan Tradition: A Tale of Two Shōbōgenzō Texts* (Albany, N.Y.: SUNY Press, 1994).

10. Dale S. Wright, *Philosophical Meditations on Zen Buddhism* (Cambridge, Mass.: Cambridge University Press, 1998).

11. According to Heinrich Dumoulin, *Zen Buddhism: A History* I (New York: Macmillan, 1990), pp. 181, 249, of all the genres, the kōan collections are the most prominent examples of Zen literature. Dumoulin refers to the *Hekiganroku* (J. *Pi-yen lu*) as the "epitome of poetic composition in Zen literature . . . [and] one of the foremost examples of religious world literature." Robert E. Buswell maintains that "a more complex genre of literature can hardly be imagined, rivaling any of the exegetical commentaries of the doctrinal [Buddhist] schools," in "The 'Short-Cut' Approach of K'an-hua Meditation: The Evolution of a Practical Subitism in Chinese Ch'an Bud-

dhism," in *Sudden and Gradual: Approaches to Enlightenment in Chinese Thought*, ed. Peter N. Gregory (Honolulu: University of Hawaii Press, 1987), p. 345.

12. An example is a technique known as "calling the maid," used by Ta-hui and Musō Sōseki, among others. This sense of abbreviation implying an essential, unmediated wordless word may appear to be quite different from the sense of abbreviation previously mentioned in characterizing the *Eihei Goroku* and *Shushōgi* as abridgements or digests, trying to reduce a text that is too long to make it readable in a nutshell version. But it is necessary to explore the issue of whether the uses of the term are really distinct, or to what extent the abridged texts express a distilled essence of the sources, as some suggest.

13. See Bernard Faure, *The Will to Orthodoxy* (Stanford, Cal.: Stanford University Press, 1997).

14. Note that twenty-three of the seventy-five fascicles were composed in the compressed period of fall 1243 through spring 1244.

15. Steven Heine, trans., *The Zen Poetry of Dōgen: Verses from the Mountain of Eternal Peace* (Boston: Charles E. Tuttle, 1997), p. 137.

16. Dōgen also at times praised Ta-hui, and his criticisms may have been aimed more at Ta-hui's Daruma-shū followers in Japan than at Ta-hui's own doctrines.

17. In Kagamishima, *Dōgen Zenji Goroku*, p. 54.

18. A version of this fascicle discovered in 1930 confirmed the existence of the 12-*Shōbōgenzō* as a separate edition and also suggested that this text formed the basis of a projected 100-fascicle version of the *Shōbōgenzō*; see Heine, "Critical Buddhism and Dōgen's *Shōbōgenzō*: The Debate over the 75-Fascicle and 12-Fascicle Texts," *Pruning the Bodhi Tree: The Storm Over Critical Buddhism*, ed. Jamie Hubbard and Paul L. Swanson (Honolulu: University of Hawaii Press, 1997), pp. 251–285.

19. In *Taishō* vol. 82, which also includes the 2-volume *Giun Goroku* in addition to several works by Dōgen (*Fukanzanzengi, Gakudōyōjinshū*, the 95-*Shōbōgenzō, Eihei Juko* or the ninth volume of the *Eihei Kōroku*, and the *Eihei Shingi*), plus works by Keizan and subsequent leaders of the Sōtō sect.

20. Ishii Shūdō, "*Eihei Ryaku Roku* kangae: Jūnikanbon *Shōbōgenzō* to Kanren shite," *Matsugaoka Bunko kenkyū nempō* 11 (1997): 73–128. In other words, Ishii's argument is that other scholars tend to view the *Eihei Kōroku* retrospectively, through lenses inappropriately shaded by their view of the *Eihei Goroku* as an authentic digest.

21. Sugawara Yūki, "*Eihei Ryaku Roku* to *Eihei Kōroku*: Honbun taishō kō-i," part I, *Zen kenkyū kiyō* 25 (1996): 253–282, and part II, *Zen kenkyū kiyō* 26 (1997): 151–186. Nagahisa Gakusui is another proponent of this thesis.

22. The role of the *Tsung-men T'ung-yao Chi* (J. *Shūmon tōyōshū*) and its influence on Dōgen are discussed in Ishii Shūdō, *Cūgoku Zenshū shi hanasu: Mana Shōbōgenzō ni manabu* (Kyoto: Zen Bunka Kenkyūjō, 1988). See also Ishii, "Kung-an Ch'an and the *Tsung-men t'ung-yao chi*," *The Kōan*, pp. 110–136.

23. Some of the fascicles of the 12-fascicle *Shōbōgenzō* date from as early as 1240, and other fascicles are difficult to date because the colophons indicate they were edited by Ejō in 1255.

24. According to one count, Hung-chih is cited at least thirty times in EK vols. 2–4 but only four times in vols. 5–7; see Kagamishima Genryū et. al., eds., *Dōgen in'yō goroku no kenkyū* (Tokyo: Shunjūsha, 1995), pp. 123–125.

25. Ishii points out numerous examples in which the wording of passages in the *Eihei Kōroku* is nearly identical to that in Hung-chih's records.

26. Martin Heidegger cites this from "The Journey," verses 18–19, in "The Origin of the Work of Art," in *Basic Writings*, ed. David Farrell Krell (New York: Harper & Row, 1976), p. 187.

5

"Rules of Purity" in Japanese Zen

T. Griffith Foulk

The so-called transmission of Zen from China to Japan in the Kamakura period (1185–1333) was a complex event, but it is convenient to analyze it as having two distinct aspects: (1) the communication to Japan of Chan mythology, ideology, and teaching styles; and (2) the establishment in Japan of monastic institutions modeled after the great public Buddhist monasteries of Southern Song China. The first aspect of the transmission of Zen was accomplished largely through three genres of texts that contained the lore of the Chan lineage (C. *chanzong*; J. *zenshū*): histories of the transmission of the flame (C. *chuandenglu*; J. *dentōroku*), discourse records (C. *yulu*; J. *goroku*), and kōan (C. *gongan*; J. *kōan*) collections.[1] It was also facilitated by means of ritual performances in which the rhetorical and pedagogical methods of Chan (as represented in the aforementioned literature) were reenacted, the two most important being the rites of "ascending the hall" (C. *shangtang*; J. *jōdō*) and "entering the room" (C. *rushi*; J. *nisshitsu*).[2] The establishment of Song-style monasteries in Japan, on the other hand, was facilitated by various collections of monastic regulations, known generically as "rules of purity" (C. *qinggui*; J. *shingi*), that were brought from China at the same time.

This chapter outlines the history of the Japanese Zen appropriation and adaptation of Chinese "rules of purity" from the Kamakura period down to the present. It is the continuation of a piece previously published under the title "*Chanyuan qinggui* and Other 'Rules of Purity' in Chinese Buddhism."[3]

As is detailed in that essay, medieval Chinese "rules of purity" actually constituted a rather diverse body of literature. Several texts

belonging to this nominal genre were compiled in order to standardize bureaucratic structures and ritual procedures in a large group of monasteries;
others were written to address the unique circumstances of a single institution.
Some were aimed at individual monks in training, providing them with norms
of personal etiquette and behavior for ordinary activities such as meals, sleep-
ing, and bathing; others established guidelines for communal activities, including convocations for worship of the Buddha, sermons by the abbot, memorial services for patriarchs, prayers on behalf of lay patrons, and the like.
Still others addressed duties and concerns specific to particular monastic officers, such as the controller, rector, labor steward, and cook. Some "rules of
purity" also contained daily, monthly, and annual calendars of activities and
observations, liturgical texts, such as prayers and formulae for dedications of
merit, and meditation manuals. A few texts that are styled "rules of purity" are
comprehensive and lengthy enough to include most of the aforementioned
kinds of rules and regulations, but the great majority have a narrower focus
on one or another aspect of monastic discipline.

The history of the "rules of purity" in Japanese Zen is marked by periodic
borrowing from China, where the genre continued to develop from the Song
through the Yuan and Ming dynasties, and by the adaptation of Chinese Buddhist institutional and ritual forms to meet the needs of Japanese Zen monastic
communities.

Pioneers of Japanese Zen

All aspects of the transmission of Zen to Japan (mythological, ideological, pedagogical, and institutional) were the work of monks who had trained in major
Chinese monasteries in Zhejiang Province and become the dharma heirs of
Chan masters there, then returned to Japan armed not only with the aforementioned texts but with a great deal of personal experience as well. The pioneers were Japanese monks such as Myōan Eisai (1141–1215), Enni Ben'en
(1202–1280), and Dōgen Kigen (1200–1253), who had traveled to China in
search of the dharma and wished to introduce the new Buddhism they had
learned to their native land. They were followed by émigré Chinese monks,
such as Lanqi Daolong (1213–1278), Wuan Puning (1197–1276), Daxiu Zhengnian (1214–1288), and Wuxue Zuyuan (1226–1286), who hailed from the same
group of leading public monasteries in Zhejiang and also worked to establish
the Chan dharma and Chinese-style monastic institutions on Japanese soil.

All of the monks involved in the initial establishment of Zen in Japan were
well versed in the *Chanyuan qinggui* (*Rules of Purity for Chan Monasteries*),[4]
compiled in 1103 by Changlu Zongze (?–1107?). They were also familiar with
the kinds of behavioral guidelines, monastic calendars, ritual manuals, and
liturgical texts found in other Song Chinese rulebooks, such as: *Riyong qinggui*

(*Rules of Purity for Daily Life*); *Ruzhong xuzhi* (*Necessary Information for Entering the Assembly*); and *Jiaoding qinggui* (*Revised Rules of Purity*), and they used these materials to regulate the new Song-style monasteries they founded in Japan. During the Yuan (1280–1368) dynasty, the production of rules of purity continued unabated in China with a tendency toward ever more comprehensive collections. Some of them, we shall see, played an important role in the ongoing evolution of the Japanese Zen institution. Before considering those later developments, however, let us see how the pioneers of Japanese Zen made use of the aforementioned Song rules of purity.

The monk Myōan Eisai (1141–1215) is regarded as the first to establish a branch of the Linji (J. Rinzai) Chan lineage in his native Japan. Eisai visited a number of the leading monasteries in Zhejiang on two separate trips to China, the first in 1168 and the second from 1187 to 1191. He trained under Chan master Xuan Huaichang when the latter was abbot at the Wannian Monastery on Tiantai Mountain in Taizhou, and then abbot at the Jingde Chan Monastery on Tiantong Mountain in Mingzhou. In the decade following his return to Japan in 1191, Eisai founded Song-style monasteries in Kyushu (Shōfukuji), Kamakura (Jufukuji), and Kyoto (Kenninji). In doing so, he clearly relied on the *Chanyuan qinggui*, citing it several times in his *Kōzen gokokuron* (*Treatise on Promoting Zen for the Protection of the Nation*).[5] This work, completed in 1198, summarized the organization and operation of monasteries in China.

Enni Ben'en (1202–1280), founder of another major branch of the Linji lineage in Japan, entered Song China in 1235 and stayed until 1241, training at the Xingsheng Wanshou Chan Monastery on Jing Mountain, where he received dharma transmission from the eminent Chan master Wuzhun Shifan (1177–1249). Upon his return to Japan, Enni put the monastic rules that he had learned from Wuzhun into effect at a series of Song–style Zen monasteries in Kyushu (Jutenji, Sūfukuji, and Manjuji) and Kyoto (Tōfukuji).[6] Presumably, he also made use of the *Chanyuan qinggui*, the title of which is found in a catalogue of the works he brought back from China.[7]

Following in the footsteps of Eisai, Dōgen (1200–1253) spent the years 1223 to 1227 in Zhejiang visiting and training at such major centers as the Guangli Chan Monastery on Aśoka Mountain in Mingzhou, Tiantong Mountain, Tiantai Mountain, and Jing Mountain near Hangzhou. Upon his return to Japan, he devoted his life to replicating the Song Chinese system of monastic training, first at Kōshōji in Uji and then at Eiheiji (originally named Daibutsuji) in Echizen.

Dōgen is widely regarded today as an author of Zen monastic rules, but he never claimed to be one. He presented himself, rather, as a transmitter and authoritative interpreter of sacred rules, principles, and procedures that he had read, been instructed about, and/or witnessed in actual practice in the great monasteries of Song China. He promoted those rules on the grounds that they had been promulgated by Śākyamuni Buddha (in the case of *vinaya* texts) and by the Chan patriarch Baizhang (in the case of *shingi*). Virtually all the texts by Dōgen that scholars regard as his monastic rules are actually commentaries on the *Chanyuan qinggui* and works deriving from the *vinaya* tradition.

In his *Tenzokyōkun* (*Admonitions for the Cook*), for example, Dōgen asserted that "One should carefully read the *Chanyuan qinggui*." He then proceeded to quote that text six times as he explained the duties and proper attitude of the head cook.[8] More than 75 percent of the text of Dōgen's *Fushukuhanpō* (*Procedures for Taking Meals*) is taken verbatim from the *Chanyuan qinggui*.[9] His *Chiji shingi* (*Rules of Purity for Stewards*) too draws heavily on the sections of the *Chanyuan qinggui* entitled "Controller," "Rector," "Cook," and "Labor Steward."[10] All of these works were evidently produced by Dōgen as a means of introducing certain parts of the *Chanyuan qinggui* to his followers and elaborating on the significance of the rules and procedures in question.

The following chapters of Dōgen's *Shōbōgenzō* (*Collection of the Eye of the True Dharma*) also contain direct quotations of the *Chanyuan qinggui*: *Shukke* (*Leaving Home*),[11] *Jukai* (*Receiving the Precepts*),[12] *Shukke kudoku* (*Merit of Leaving Home*),[13] *Senmen* (*Face Washing*),[14] *Ango* (*Retreats*),[15] *Senjō* (*Purifications [for the Toilet]*),[16] *Hotsu bodaishin* (*Producing the Thought of Enlightenment*),[17] *Kie buppōsō* (*Taking Refuge in the Three Jewels*),[18] and *Fukanzazengi* (*Universal Instructions for Zazen*).[19] These texts too are representative of Dōgen's efforts to explain to his Japanese followers the letter and spirit of rules and procedures found in the *Chanyuan qinggui*.

Dōgen was basically a transmitter, not an innovator, of monastic rules. His style of commenting on the *Chanyuan qinggui* was highly creative, however, for it drew on the Chan discourse records and kōan collections, which previously had never been connected in any way with rules of purity. In Song China it was taken for granted that monastic rules, whether they derived from Śākyamuni or Baizhang, pertained to the entire Buddhist *saṅgha*. The Chan lineage records, on the other hand, comprised a distinctive body of literature that was of concern primarily to followers of the Chan School. It was only in Japan that Song-style monastic institutions came to be identified as uniquely "Zen" in their architectural layout, bureaucratic organization, and ritual function. In Dōgen's day that identification had not yet become firmly established, but he himself was keen to read the spirit of the Chan patriarchs into the rules of purity. In *Tenzokyōkun*, for example, he interspersed direct quotations from the *Chanyuan qinggui* with famous kōans and personal recollections of his own conversations with two cooks he met in China.[20] That mixing of genres served Dōgen's purpose well, for it helped to bring otherwise dry prescriptions of monastic etiquette to life and bestow them with spiritual significance. By the same token, it familiarized his Japanese followers with the rhetorical conventions of the Zen "question and answer" (*mondō*) literature, rendering that difficult material more accessible by placing it in a concrete, practical context. In my view, Dōgen's real genius as a pioneer of Japanese Zen consisted in this brilliant juxtaposition and elucidation of Chinese Buddhist monastic rules and Chan teachings, two types of literature that had been treated quite separately in China.

Several modern Japanese scholars have argued that Eisai's Kenninji and Enni's Tōfukuji were "syncretic" institutions that did not represent "pure" Song-style Zen but rather were an admixture of Zen with elements of indigenous Tendai and Shingon esotericism (*mikkyōi*). They point out that both monasteries had facilities for the practice of Tiantai meditation routines and esoteric rites. Kenninji, for example, had a "calming and insight hall" (*shikan–in*) which was used for practice of the four *samādhis*.[21] Tōfukuji had an "Amida hall" (*Amidadō*) and a "Kannon hall" (*Kannondō*), which may have been used for the same purposes.[22] Kenninji also had a "Shingon hall" (*Shingon–in*) that was used for "land and water offerings" (*suiriku gu*) to hungry ghosts,[23] consecrations (*kanjō*), and other esoteric rites. Tōfukuji also had a consecration hall (*kanjōdō*) that may have served the same functions. Takeuchi Dōyū regards even the prayer ceremonies (*kitō*) and *sūtra* chanting services (*fugin*) that Eisai and Enni incorporated into their monastic practice as "esoteric" observances borrowed from the "old Buddhism" of Japan.[24]

All the elements of "syncretic" practice that Eisai and Enni are supposed to have adopted from Japanese Tendai, however, were commonly found in the public monasteries of the Southern Song, including those that bore the Chan name. Song-period ground plans survive for three of the leading monasteries in Zhejiang that were visited by Eisai, Dōgen, and Enni: Tiantong Mountain, Tiantai Mountain, and Bei Mountain.[25] The plans reveal monastery layouts that were actually quite eclectic, with facilities to accommodate a wide range of Buddhist practices. In addition to saṅgha halls (C. *sengtang*; J. *sōdō*), common quarters (C. *zhongliao*; J. *shuryō*), and dharma halls (C. *fatang*; J. *hattō*), there were buildings for offering services dedicated to the buddhas (C. *fodian*; J. *butsuden*), patriarchs (C. *zushitang*; J. *soshidō*), arhats (C. *luohantang*; J. *rakandō*), Guanyin (C. *kuanyintang*; J. *kannondō*), and various local deities (C. *tuditang*; J. *dojidō*). There were also "quarters for illuminating the mind" (C. *zhaoxinliao*; J. *shōjinryō*) through *sūtra* study; *sūtra* libraries with revolving stacks (C. *luncang*; J. *rinzō*); *sūtra* reading halls (C. *kanjingtang*; J. *kankindō*), where prayer services for patrons were performed; *nirvāṇa* halls (C. *niepantang*; J. *nehandō*), where sick and dying monks were tended and prayed for with recitations of the buddhas' names (C. *nianfo*; J. *nembutsu*), and "water and land halls" (*shuilutang*), used for the esoteric rites of feeding famished spirits (*shieguihu*). It is likely that Eisai got the idea for the "Shingon hall" he built at Kenninji from the Chinese model, for he stated that it was used for "land and water offerings." The "calming and insight hall" at Kenninji too may well have been based on one that Eisai encountered on Tiantai Mountain; there is no need to assume that it was a concession to Japanese Tendai influences. The prayer ceremonies and *sūtra* chanting services that Eisai and Enni incorporated into their monastic practice, similarly, are all found in the rules of purity of Song China. Both Kenninji and Tōfukuji were, in fact, excellent replicas of the public monasteries in Zhejiang Province that were most often visited by Japanese monks in the thirteenth century.

Modern Japanese scholars, just as they have worked to depict the Zen of Eisai and Enni as "syncretic," have been at pains to portray Dōgen's Zen as especially "pure." One champion of this view, Kagamishima Genryū, has argued that Song Chan was already syncretic and degenerate compared with the "pure Chan" (*junsui zen*) that had existed in the golden age of the Tang.[26] According to him, virtually all of the Zen transmitted to Japan, whether by Eisai, Enni, or the Chinese monks who followed, was at its very source overly ritualized and beholden to the religious and political needs of the court and aristocracy. Dōgen alone, Kagamishima argues, spurned the syncretic doctrines he encountered among the Chan schools in Song China, criticized the worldly tendencies of continental Chan with its aristocratic patronage, rejected the syncretism of early Japanese Zen, and insisted on an "unadulterated" form of Zen. Thus, he concludes, what Dōgen transmitted to Japan was not the Zen that he actually encountered in Song China but rather the pure Zen of Baizhang that had flourished in China during the Tang dynasty.[27]

Dōgen's writings on monastic rules were rather typical in that they focused on some aspects of monastery organization and operation and took others for granted. The fact that he did not leave writings that dealt with every aspect of the "rules of purity" literature does not mean that he rejected or neglected the practices that were prescribed in them. I stress this point because scholars have too often taken Dōgen's silence on a particular feature of monastic practice as evidence that he was a purist who rejected it. If one pays attention to the many passing references to multifarious rituals and bureaucratic procedures that occur in his writings, however, there is ample evidence that Dōgen embraced the model of the Song Chan monastery in its entirety, including most of the ostensibly "syncretic" and "popular" ceremonies and rituals that were later treated explicitly in the *Keizan shingi* (*Keizan's Rules of Purity*).

Scholars associate the "purity" of Dōgen's Zen with his putative rejection of ritual and his emphasis on seated meditation (*zazen*). A passage from Dōgen's *Bendōwa* (*A Talk on Cultivating the Way*) is frequently cited in support of this interpretation:

> From the start of your training under a wise master [*chishiki*], have
> no recourse to incense offerings [*shōkō*], prostrations [*raihai*], recita-
> tion of buddha names [*nembutsu*], repentances [*shūsan*], or *sūtra*
> reading [*kankin*]. Just sit in meditation [*taza*] and attain the dropping
> off of mind and body [*shinjin datsuraku*].[28]

In this passage Dōgen gives advice to the beginning Zen trainee, stressing that sitting in meditation is the one practice essential for attaining enlightenment and thereby inheriting the true transmission of the buddha-dharma. Although Dōgen clearly did extol seated meditation as the *sine qua non* of Buddhism, scholars who seize on just this passage (and a few others like it) to characterize his approach to monastic practice badly misrepresent the historical record.

The specific rituals that seem to be disavowed in the *Bendōwa* passage are all prescribed for Zen monks, often in great detail, in Dōgen's other writings. In *Kuyō shobutsu* (*Making Offerings to All Buddhas*), Dōgen recommends the practice of offering incense and making worshipful prostrations before buddha images and *stūpas*, as prescribed in the *sūtras* and *vinaya* texts.[29] In *Raihaitokuzui* (*Making Prostrations and Attaining the Marrow*) he urges trainees to venerate enlightened teachers and to make offerings and prostrations to them, describing this practice as one that helps pave the way to one's own awakening.[30] In *Chiji shingi*, Dōgen stipulates that the vegetable garden manager in a monastery should participate together with the main body of monks in *sūtra* chanting services, recitation services (*nenju*) in which the buddhas' names are chanted (a form of *nembutsu* practice), and other major ceremonies; he should burn incense and make prostrations (*shōkō raihai*) and recite the buddhas' names in prayer morning and evening when at work in the garden.[31] The practice of repentances (*sange*) is encouraged in Dōgen's *Kesa kudoku* (*Merit of the Kesa*),[32] *Sanjigō* (*Karma of the Three Times*),[33] and *Keiseisanshiki* (*Valley Sounds, Mountain Forms*).[34] Finally, in *Kankin* (*Sūtra Chanting*), Dōgen gives detailed directions for *sūtra* reading services in which, as he explains, texts could be read either silently or aloud as a means of producing merit to be dedicated to any number of ends, including the satisfaction of wishes made by lay donors, or prayers on behalf of the emperor.[35] *Kankin*, as Dōgen uses the term, can also refer to "turning" (without actually reading) through the pages of *sūtra* books, or turning rotating *sūtra* library stacks (*rinzō*), to produce merit. He occasionally uses *kankin* to mean "*sūtra* study," but the *Bendōwa* passage most likely refers to *sūtra* reading as a merit-producing device in ceremonial settings.

In short, Dōgen embraced Song Chinese Buddhist monastic practice in its entirety, in a manner that was scarcely distinguishable from that of Eisai or Enni. It is true that he occasionally engaged in polemical criticism of certain members of the Linji lineage in China, but the disgust with and rejection of Song monastic forms that Kagamishima and other scholars ascribe to him is almost entirely missing from his lengthy, generally laudatory writings on the subject. Indeed, Dōgen had far more complaints about his Japanese compatriots who were ignorant in the proper way of doing things—that is, the way they were done in Song China.

The first of the émigré Chinese monks who helped transmit the Chan dharma and Song-style monastic forms to Japan was Lanqi Daolong (1213–1278). Shortly after his arrival in 1246, Lanqi was made abbot of Jōrakuji, which was converted into a "Zen" monastery and reorganized in accordance with Chinese monastic rules.[36] In 1252 he was installed by the shogun Hōjō Tokiyori as the founding abbot of Kenchōji, a large monastery constructed in Kamakura on the model of Jing Mountain in Zhejiang. The "Rules for Kenchōji" (*Kenchō kushiki*) that Lanqi established do not survive,[37] and his extant writings do not mention the *Chanyuan qinggui* by name, but there is little doubt that when he urged the strict observation of rules of purity, he had that text (or something very similar) in mind.

After Lanqi, a series of Chinese monks came to Japan and worked to spread the Chan dharma. Wuan Puning (1197–1276) arrived in 1260 and became the second abbot of Kenchōji. Daxiu Zhengnian (1214–1288), who had been invited to Japan by Tokiyori, came in 1269 and served as abbot at several Zen monasteries in Kamakura. When Lanqi died in 1278, Hōjō Tokimune (Tokiyori's son) invited Wuxue Zuyuan (1226–1286), an eminent monk who was at the time serving as head seat (*shouzuo*) at Tiantong Mountain. Upon his arrival in Japan in 1279, Wuxue became the abbot of Kenchōji; in 1282 he was installed as the founding abbot of yet another newly built Song-style monastery, Engakuji. Yishan Yining (1247–1317) came to Japan in 1299 and served as abbot at Kenchōji, Engakuji, and Nanzenji in Kyoto. None of those émigré Chinese monks left any monastic rules to posterity, but all of them have extensive discourse records, from which we may readily ascertain that the monasteries they presided over were organized and run in accordance with the *Chanyuan qinggui* and other Chinese rules of purity.

The vast majority of monks who led the way in establishing Song-style monasteries in Japan in the thirteenth century were dharma heirs in the Chan lineage. There were a few, however, who transmitted essentially the same institutional forms from China without also stressing the Chan teachings that were predominant there. The most striking example of such a monk is Shunjō (1166–1227), who spent twelve years in Song China studying the Chan, Tiantai, and especially Nanshan *vinaya* traditions. After returning to Japan in 1211, Shunjō became the abbot of a monastery in Kyoto that he turned into a Song-style institution, renaming it Sennyūji. Sennyūji was not identified as a Zen monastery, and Shunjō himself was known in his day as a *vinaya* master (*risshi*). A ground plan of Sennyūji, however, shows that its basic layout was the same as that of the Zen monasteries, such as Tōfukuji in Kyoto and Kenchōji in Kamakura, that were built a few decades later: all of them adhered closely to the same Song Chinese model.[38] A comparison of Shunjō's rules for Sennyūji with the monastic rules that Zen masters Eisai, Dōgen, and Enni prescribed, moreover, leaves no doubt that the monasteries founded by all of them were nearly identical in organization and operation.[39]

The case of Sennyūji is significant because it confirms that neither the arrangement of the public monasteries in Song China nor the rules of purity that regulated them were actually the invention or exclusive domain of the

Chan School. Despite the official designation of many important monasteries in China as "Chan" establishments, the attachment of the "Chan" name to the most influential rules of purity, and the promotion of Baizhang as the "founder" of those, opposition from the Tiantai and Nanshan Lü schools prevented the Chan school from gaining exclusive control of the Buddhist institution at large. Moreover, because so-called Teachings (Tiantai lineage) monasteries and *Vinaya* (Nanshan Lü lineage) monasteries featured the same facilities, bureaucratic structures, and ceremonial calendars as their Chan counterparts, it was difficult to see the designation "Chan monastery" as indicating anything more than the fact that the abbacy was reserved for monks in the Chan lineage, and that followers of the Chan school tended to congregate there. Thus, a monk such as Shunjō could train in China and promote Song-style Buddhist monastic practices in Japan, including the practice of seated meditation in a saṅgha hall,[40] without being a proponent of Chan.

Another aspect of the transmission of Zen to Japan that has not received sufficient attention from modern scholars is the extent to which the pioneers of Zen were part of a broader movement to revive strict monastic practice based on the Hīnayāna *vinaya*, which had been discarded by Saichō some three centuries earlier. Disaffection with the lack of monkish discipline in the dominant Tendai and Shingon schools, together with the belief that the world had entered the period of the decay and final demise of the buddha-dharma (*mappō*), had set the stage for two opposite developments in Japanese Buddhism in the Kamakura period. One was the Pure Land movement led by figures such as Hōnen (1133–1212) and Shinran (1173–1262), who tended to further deemphasize the strictures of the *vinaya* or abandon them altogether on the grounds that they were "difficult" or "sagely" practices that were no longer feasible in a degenerate age. The other approach, which appealed to some reform-minded monks within the established schools of Japanese Buddhism and to the newly empowered Kamakura shoguns, was a return to stricter observance of the *vinaya*. Leaders of this conservative approach included monks who tried to revive the *vinaya* tradition of the old Nara schools, such as Jōkei (1155–1213) of the Hossō School and Kakujō (1194–1249) of the *Vinaya* School. There were also monks with backgrounds in the Shingon School, such as Eison (1201–1290) and Ninshō (1217–1303), who actively promoted the upholding of "Hīnayāna" monkish and lay precepts (*kairitsu*). For the most part, however, the movement to restore strict monastic practice looked for inspiration to China, where, as is clearly reflected in the *Chanyuan qinggui*, the Buddhist institution had preserved the tradition of strict monastic practice based on the *vinaya* to a far greater degree than had the Buddhist schools of the Heian period in Japan. It should not be surprising, then, that most of the Japanese and Chinese monks whom history remembers as the first transmitters of the Zen to Japan were also known in their own day as promoters of the *vinaya*, especially the practice of receiving and upholding Hīnayāna as well as Mahāyāna precepts.

Eisai, for example, wrote in his *Kōzen gokokuron* that his teacher, Chan master Hsuan, had given him the precepts of the Hīnayāna Prātimokṣa (*shibunkai*) as contained in the *Sifenlu* (J. *Shibunritsu, Four Part Vinaya*) as well as the Mahayāna bodhisattva precepts.[41] In the same text he stated that "at present the Zen lineage holds the precepts to be essential"[42] and further remarked that outwardly one maintains the forms of the *vinaya* and guards against wrongdoing; inwardly one is compassionate and wishes to benefit others: that is what is called the principle of Zen and what is called the teachings of Buddha.[43]

Dōgen, too, relied on Hīnayāna *vinaya* texts that were commonly used in Song monasteries. For example, he quoted the *Sifenlu* and related commentaries in his *Kesa kudoku* and *Fushukuhanpō*, and he cited the *Sanqian weiiqing* (*Sūtra on Three Thousand Points of Monkish Decorum*), another *vinaya* text, no less than eighteen times in his *Senjō, Gyōji* (*Observances*), *Senmen*, and *Chiji shingi*.[44] Dōgen's *Taitaiko gogejari hō* (*Procedures for Relating to Monks Five Retreats Senior to Oneself*), moreover, is basically a commentary on the "Procedures for Relating to Teachers and Procedures for Entering the Assembly" (*shihshih fa juchung fa*) section of the *Chiao-chiai hsin-hsüeh-pi-ch'iu hsing-hu lü-i* (*Instructions on the Ritual Restraints to be Observed by New Monks in Training*) by Tao-hsüan.[45] In the opening lines of his *Shuryō shingi* (*Admonitions for the Common Quarters*), Dōgen recommended studying *vinaya* texts and stated that behavior in the common quarters (*shuryō*) should be in respectful compliance with the precepts laid down by the buddhas and patriarchs (*busso no kairitsu*), should follow in accord with the deportment for monks established in both the Hīnayāna and Mahayāna [*vinaya*] (*daishōjō no igi*), and should agree entirely with Baizhang's rules of purity (*Hyakujō shingi*).[46] The stance that both Eisai and Dōgen took on this issue, of course, was based directly on the *Chanyuan qinggui* and on what they had witnessed firsthand in the great monasteries of the Song.

The Importation and Production of the "Rules of Purity" in Medieval Japan

The fall of the Song dynasty to the Mongols in 1278 was, at first, reason for considerable trepidation within the Chinese Buddhist *sangha*, and a number of eminent Chan masters (Wuxue Zuyuan among them) did in fact flee to Japan. It soon became apparent, however, that the new rulers of China were more interested in patronizing and regulating the monastic order than in destroying it, and life in the great public monasteries continued much as before. Some of the monastic rules produced during the Yuan dynasty (1280–1368), most notably the *Beiyong qinggui* (*Auxiliary Rules of Purity*) and *Chixiu baizhang qingqui* (*Imperial Edition of Baizhang's Rules of Purity*), represented attempts to collate and systematize all previous rules of purity. Others, such as the *Huanzhu an qinggu* (*Rules of Purity for the Huan-chu Hermitage*), were pared-down documents intended to regulate a single, small monastery.⁴⁷ All of these rules found their way to Japan within a short time of their publication in China, where they had a significant impact on the ongoing development of Zen monastic institutions.

Throughout the thirteenth century, the *Chanyuan qinggui* remained the basic reference work for all Japanese and Chinese monks concerned with establishing Song-style monastic practices in Japan. By the first decades of the fourteenth century, however, one begins to find evidence of the production of rules of purity within Japan itself. The new texts composed from that time were no doubt conceived in response to the needs of the growing Zen institution and attuned to local conditions. They were, moreover, clearly influenced by the various rules produced in China after the *Chanyuan qinggui*.

Perhaps the oldest extant example of a set of monastic rules composed in Japan is a text entitled *Eizan koki* (*Old Rules of E[nichi] Mountain*).⁴⁸ E'nichi is the mountain name (*sangō*) for Tōfukuji, and these "old rules" are attributed to Enni. The text as we have it today, however, bears a colophon that dates its composition to 1318. It contains an annual schedule of rituals that is very similar to those found in the *Beiyong qinggui*, issued in 1311, and the *Huanzhu an qinggui* (*Rules of Purity for the Huanzhu Hermitage*), written in 1317. There is no way of knowing for certain if the *Eizan koki* was based on either of those Chinese texts, but its date of composition strongly suggests that it was at least influenced by similar materials arriving from China.

The next of the fourteenth-century texts worthy of note is the *Nōshū tōko-kuzan yōkōzenji gyōji shidai* (*Ritual Procedures for Tōkoku Mountain Yōkō Zen Monastery in Nō Province*),⁴⁹ written by Keizan Jōkin (1268–1325) in 1324. The text subsequently became known as the *Keizan oshō shingi* (*Preceptor Keizan's Rules of Purity*) and took on the role of a standard reference work in Sōtō Zen monasteries, but it seems likely to have originated as a handbook of ritual events and liturgical texts for use in the single monastery named in its title. The original *Keizan shingi* was similar in this respect to the *Huanzhu an qinggui*, written in China some seven years earlier. Another feature that the *Keizan shingi* shares with the *Huanzhu an qinggui* is a detailed daily, monthly, and annual calendar of rituals. Given the fact that the Chinese text is the oldest extant rules of purity to display that feature, it seems likely that it had a direct influence upon Keizan's work.

Another text worth mentioning in this connection is the *Daikan shingi* (*Daikan's Rules of Purity*),⁵⁰ compiled by the émigré Chinese monk Qingzhuo Zhengcheng (1274–1339) in 1332. Qingzhuo had been invited to Kamakura by Hōjō Takatoki and was working to spread Zen in provincial centers when he composed his rules of purity. The text is very similar in organization and content to the *Jiaoding qinggui*, compiled in 1274, which Qingzhuo mentions as a source. He also refers to the *Beiyong qinggui* (1311) as a source, so it seems that by this time, at least, those two Chinese codes were becoming known in Japan.

The *Daikan shingi*, it may be said, represented an effort to simplify those Chinese rules of purity and render them easier to use in smaller monasteries of the sort that Qingzhuo encountered in Japan.

Eventually the *Chixiu baizhang qingqui*, completed in 1338, became the standard set of rules for large Zen monasteries in Japan. Smaller monasteries, however, continued to rely on works such as the *Daikan shingi* and the *Rinsen Kakun* (*House Rules for Rinsenji*) that Musō (1275–1351) wrote in 1339 for his monastery in Kyoto.[51]

The Muromachi period (1333–1573) saw the rise of the "Five Mountains" (*gozan*) network of Zen monasteries, which were officially ranked by the Ashikaga shogunate. At its peak, prior to the outbreak of the Ōnin War in 1467, this network encompassed some 300 monasteries ranked in three tiers, with eleven Kyoto and Kamakura monastic centers at the top and several thousand affiliated branch temples throughout the country.[52] The single most important rules of purity text used within the Five Mountains system was the *Chixiu baizhang qingqui*. The first Japanese printing of the *Chixiu baizhang qingqui* was the "Five Mountains edition" (*gozan ban*), issued in 1356. The text was reprinted in 1458, and a Japanese language commentary on it entitled *Hyakujō shingi shō* (*Summary of Baizhang's Rules of Purity*) was produced, based on lectures on the text given by various abbots of major Zen monasteries in Kyoto between 1459 and 1462. Subsequent reprinting of the *Chixiu baizhang qingqui* took place during the Tokugawa period (1603–1868), in 1629, 1661, 1720, and 1768.[53]

During the fifteenth and sixteenth centuries, Japanese Zen institutions spread and evolved in ways that were relatively independent of developments on the continent. There was a tendency for Zen lineages to splinter as "brother" and "cousin" dharma heirs competed for the abbacies of monasteries in the generations succeeding a founding patriarch. That development, together with new patterns of patronage that linked individual Zen masters and their lineal descendants with particular lay clans among the wealthy and powerful, led to the proliferation of mortuary subtemples at the major metropolitan Zen monasteries and the eventual demise of their central facilities. The subtemples, called *stūpa* sites (*tatchū*), began as walled compounds that contained a worship hall (*shōdō*), where the memorial portrait (*chinzō*) of a former abbot and mortuary tablets (*ihai*) for the ancestors of the patron clan were enshrined; an abbot's quarters (*hōjō*) for the *stūpa* chief (*tassu*) or monk in charge of memorial services and his attendants (*jisha*); and a kitchen-cum-office building (*kuri*). As time went on, this layout was simplified with the worship hall moved into the abbot's quarters, which then became known as the "main hall" (*hondō*), and with the kitchen-cum-office building used as the residence of the monks who performed the services there.

The abbot's quarters of the memorial subtemples were often fine pieces of architecture that were lavishly appointed with secular as well as religious works of art, rock gardens, and adjacent teahouses, all provided by patrons, basically to enhance their own enjoyment and the prestige of their clans. The styles of gardens, tea utensils, calligraphy, and ink painting found in Japanese Zen subtemples had their origins in the elite literati culture of Song and Yuan China. They were brought to Japan in the thirteenth and fourteenth centuries in connection with the establishment of Chinese-style monasteries and the transmission of Chan lineages, but in their native China they were never known as "Chan" (or even as Buddhist) arts. The notion of "Zen" arts is strictly a Japanese conceit, and the idea that rock gardens were built as aids to meditation (or as artistic representations of meditative states) is a modern myth.

In any case, with the proliferation of subtemples,[54] the main monastery (*hongaran*) facilities—the great saṅgha halls, dharma halls, buddha halls (*butsuden*), administration cloisters (*kuin*), and other buildings designed to support large-scale communal training—emptied out and fell into ruin, or burned down and were not rebuilt. The type of Zen monastic institution that had originally been imported from China and regulated by the *Chanyuan qingui* and *Chixiu baizhang qingqui* had virtually disappeared by the latter half of the sixteenth century.

Under the circumstances, the old rules of purity were no longer of much interest in Japanese Zen, but some new sets of guidelines were written to meet the changing needs of the Zen institution. One such work was the *Shoekō shingi* (*Rules of Purity with Various Dedications of Merit*),[55] composed by the Rinzai monk Tenrin Fuin (n.d.) in 1566. The text contains verses for dedicating merit (*ekōmon*) to be used in conjunction with daily, monthly, annual, and occasional *sūtra*-chanting services, which were the main ritual activities in the mortuary subtemples. Those verses were based on ones found in earlier rules of purity such as the *Chixiu baizhang qingqui*, but they were adapted and expanded to include more prayers for the ancestral spirits of patron families. The *Shoekō shingi* also includes procedures for funerals, rites of repentance (*sanbō*), and receiving precepts (*jukai*), all of which were basic ways of involving lay followers in the practice of Buddhism.

The Revival of the "Rules of Purity" in the Tokugawa Period

The Tokugawa period (1603–1868) was a time of major institutional changes in Japanese Zen, and indeed in all the schools of Japanese Buddhism. Many of the changes were instigated by the Tokugawa shogunate, which ruled a newly unified Japan from its capital in Edo (Tokyo) and exercised strict control over all religious organizations in the country. Three policies implemented by the shogunate that had a great impact on Budhism were: (1) the banning of Christianity; (2) the establishment of a parish system (*danka seidō*), whereby every household in the country was compelled to register as a patron (*danka*, literally "donor house") of a Buddhist monastery in its locale; and (3) the organization of Buddhist monasteries and temples into a head/branch system (*honmatsu seidō*) in which all of the Buddhist monasteries in the country were linked, in accordance with traditional denominations and lineages, into hierarchical networks controllable from the top by the shogunate. The aims of these policies were: to seal Japan off from foreign influences associated with Christian missionary activity, which had flourished in the late sixteenth century; to curb the Christian *daimyō* who had fought against the Tokugawa; to prevent the spontaneous rise of popular, potentially seditious religious movements; and to provide the shogunate with a bureaucratic network capable of organizing and controlling the population and furthering the centralization of power in Edo.

Buddhist monasteries thus, in addition to whatever religious functions they served, became instruments of the state and charged with keeping birth, death, and residency records at the local level and with communicating government directives to the people. The demands of the parish system resulted in a huge increase in the number of Buddhist monasteries of all denominations in Japan, but the Zen schools in particular flourished. One reason was the intimate involvement of Zen monks in the formulation of the shogunate's policies.[56]

The typical Zen branch monastery of the Tokugawa period was a small facility occupied by an abbot (*jūshoku*) and a handful of monk disciples who had been recruited locally. Both the architectural layout and the ritual calendar of such ordinary monasteries were based on those of the mortuary subtemples (*stūpa* sites) that flourished on the grounds of the head monasteries of the various Zen orders. The main difference was that the *stūpa* sites at head monasteries such as Myōshinji and Daitokuji in Kyoto were all the mortuary temples (*bodaiji*) of a single wealthy family, whereas most of the Zen temples that came into existence under the parish system had dozens or even hundreds of ordinary households affiliated with them as patrons. The typical Zen temple thus became a place where a resident priest or abbot and a few assistant monks performed funerals and memorial services for their lay parishioners (*danka*) and perhaps engaged them in other Buddhist practices as well, such as receiving the precepts or repentances or celebrating the Buddha's birthday (*gotan e*) or his *nirvāṇa* (*nehan e*). The only rules of purity needed at the great majority of ordinary Zen temples were liturgical manuals, such as Tenrin Fuin's *Shoekō shingi*. That text, which had initially been written in 1566 and was handed down as an in-house document, was published in 1657 and widely circulated thereafter.

Even as those developments took place, however, the complacency of the established Rinzai and Sōtō schools of Zen was shaken by a new wave of Chinese Buddhism that entered Japan and threatened to lure away their brightest and most serious monks. The Ōbaku school of Zen, as the newcomer came to be called, represented a style of Ming-dynasty (1368–1644) Chinese Buddhist

monastic practice that had evolved directly from the public monasteries of the
Song and Yuan. The Ōbaku movement began about 1620, when Chinese trad-
ers, permitted by the shogunate to do business in Nagasaki, began inviting
monks from China to serve the religious needs of their community and build
monasteries in the late-Ming style with which they were familiar. The movement got a big boost when Yinyuan Longqi (1592–1673), a prominent Chan
master glad to leave war-torn China, arrived in Nagasaki in 1654. Yinyuan
gained the patronage of the fourth Tokugawa shogun, Ietsuna, who supported
the building of a large Ming-style monastery in Uji (south of Kyoto) in 1660.
Yinyuan was installed as founding abbot of the monastery, called Manpukuji,
and compiled a set of regulations for it entitled *Ōbaku shingi* (*Ōbaku Rules of
Purity*),[57] subsequently published in 1672. The text reflected a few evolutionary
changes that had taken place in Chinese monasteries since the Yuan, but it
was squarely in the tradition of classical rules of purity such as the *Chanyuan
qingui* and *Chixiu baizhang qingqui*.

From the perspective of Japanese Zen Buddhists, the most striking features
of Ōbaku Zen were: large-scale communal practice based on central monastery
facilities, such as a buddha hall, dharma hall, meditation hall (*zendō*), refectory
(*saidō*), and the like; the aforementioned rules of purity used to regulate that
practice; an emphasis on receiving precepts at all levels of participation in the
Buddhist *saṅgha*, including the full precepts (*gusoku kai*) of the Hīnayāna *vinaya*; a concern with copying and printing Buddhist *sūtras*, both as an encour-
agement to study and as a meritorious work; and the practice of *nembutsu kōan*,
common in Ming Buddhism, which entailed using *nembutsu*—recitation of
the Buddha Amitabha's (C. Amituo; J. Amida) name—as the basis for an introspection of one's own mind with the existential question (*kōan*), "Who is
reciting?"

In Japan, where the various Pure Land and Zen orders had existed (and
competed for patronage) in entirely separate institutional settings for the previous three centuries, the "combination" of *nembutsu* with *zazen* and kōan
practice struck some people as odd or objectionable. Reciting "Namu Amida
Butsu" had been touted by Japanese Pure Land teachers as an easy way to
salvation and as an expression of faith in the "other power" (*tariki*) or saving
grace of Amida. In the Japanese Zen tradition, on the other hand, "seeing one's
own buddha-nature" (*kenshō*) and inheriting the dharma (*shihō*) were considered difficult things that only a few exceptional monks could attain through
their own assiduous efforts. In Chinese Buddhism, however, there was no
history of institutional separation between followers of the Chan School and
devotees of Amitabha, and a person could be both at the same time without
feeling any conflict, as indeed was the case with Zongze, the compiler of the
Chanyuan qingui. And, regardless of its inclusion of Pure Land elements, the
fact remained that the Ōbaku school, with its group practice of *zazen* on the
platforms in a meditation hall and its emphasis on keeping the precepts, rep-

resented a type of communal monastic discipline far more rigorous than anything that existed at the time in Japanese Buddhism.

A number of Rinzai and Sōtō monks gravitated to Ōbaku teachers and monasteries, but there were also those who, while impressed with the newly imported Chinese institutions, remained loyal to their own lineages and strived to reform their own monasteries along the lines of the Ōbaku model. An early example is the Rinzai Zen master Ungo Kiyō (1582–1659), who in 1636 assumed the abbacy of Zuiganji, the family mortuary temple of the Date clan (*daimyō* of Sendai) and converted it into a training monastery where the precepts were strictly observed and a regular schedule of twice daily meditation (*niji no zazen*), three daily *sūtra*-chanting services (*sanji no fugin*), and manual labor (*fushin samu*) was implemented.[58] At the same time, he convinced the *daimyō* to ban hunting and fishing in the region and began teaching a form of *nembutsu* Zen to laypeople, including a group of samurai women. Although Ungo did not study under Ōbaku masters, it is clear that he was greatly influenced by the main currents of Ming Buddhism.

In 1645 Ungo became abbot of Myōshinji, where he was criticized by some monks for taking a syncretic approach that was alien to the so-called Ōtōkan branch of the Rinzai lineage deriving from the founding abbot, Kanzan Egen (1277–1360). Even so, when Yinyuan arrived in Japan, there were some other monks at Myōshinji who wished to invite the Chinese prelate to become abbot. The move was blocked by Gudō Tōshoku (1579–1661), 137th abbot and champion of the Ōtōkan line, but even Gudō was sufficiently impressed by the new Ming-style Zen monasteries to set about rebuilding some of Myōshinji's central facilities (the main gate, buddha hall, and dharma hall, but not the saṅgha hall) in the Chinese manner.

The revival of rigorous communal training in Rinzai Zen during the Tokugawa period was stimulated by the appearance of Ōbaku school monastic institutions, but it did not result in the building of any new Rinzai monasteries on the large scale of Manpukuji, let alone the vast Zen edifices (such as Tōfukuji or Kenchōji) that were originally erected in Kyoto and Kamakura during the thirteenth and fourteenth centuries. Rather, what usually occurred was something along the lines of Ungo's conversion of Zuiganji: the transformation of a relatively small Zen monastery, often a family mortuary temple with a single powerful patron (such as a *daimyō* or wealthy merchant), into a somewhat larger facility for communal training called a "saṅgha hall."[59] The typical Tokugawa-period Zen monastery, as was noted earlier, was a mortuary temple consisting of a main worship hall (*hondō*, also known as *hōjō* or abbot's quarters) and a residence building with a kitchen and offices. The key elements in the transformation to saṅgha hall status were the installation as abbot of an eminent Zen master who could attract students, and the construction of a communal meditation hall, modeled after the ones found at Ōbaku monasteries. The technical term for this process was "opening a meditation platform" (*kaitan*) as opposed to "opening a mountain" (*kaisan*), which meant founding a new monastery.

Most Rinzai saṅgha halls retained the character of the clan mortuary temple that they had had prior to "opening a meditation platform." The increase in the number of resident monks, of course, meant considerably greater expense for the patron. On the other hand, the merit produced and available for dedication to ancestors was also understood to be much greater, since it resulted from the sponsorship of an entire community of monks who were keeping the precepts and engaging in rigorous Buddhist practice; a saṅgha hall, in short, was a more fertile "field of merit" than an ordinary mortuary temple. The establishment of saṅgha halls was a significant phenomenon that changed the face of Rinzai Zen in the Tokugawa period, but it affected less than one percent of the Rinzai monasteries, the vast majority being simply local branch temples in the parishioner system.

Mujaku Dōchū (1653–1744) was a leading Rinzai reformer of the Tokugawa period who twice served as abbot of Myōshinji. Familiar with both the *Ōbaku shingi* and Dōgen's writings on monastic discipline, Mujaku set out to produce a Rinzai alternative. Carefully studying all of the earlier Chinese rules of purity that were available to him, including the *Chanyuan qingui* and *Chixiu baizhang qingqui*, he wrote the *Shōsōrin ryaku shingi* (*Abbreviated Rules of Purity for Small Monasteries*).[60] Published in 1684, the work became a standard reference for Rinzai monks who converted ordinary temples into saṅgha halls during the Tokugawa period, and it remains the basis for various sets of rules presently in use in Rinzai monasteries. Mujaku was a prolific scholar who left a huge collection of writings on many aspects of Zen history and literature, but his lifelong work on Chan and Zen rules of purity was particularly thorough and remains useful to scholars even today. Two outstanding products of his research are the *Chokushū hyakujō shingi sakei* (*Commentary on the Imperial Edition of Baizhang's Rules of Purity*),[61] which he worked on from 1699 until 1718, and his *Zenrin shōkisen* (*Encyclopedia of Zen Monasticism*),[62] whose preface is dated 1741.

Historically, the most influential of the Rinzai masters who made use of elements of Ōbaku Zen was Kogetsu Zenzai (1667–1751). Kogetsu received the full 250 precepts and bodhisattva precepts (*bosatsukai*) from an Ōbaku monk and emphasized keeping the precepts in his teachings. He also shared the Ōbaku concern with promoting Buddhist *sūtras*. Kogetsu engaged in copying the *Great Perfection of Wisdom Sūtra* (*Dai hannya kyō*) and strived to obtain a copy of the Buddhist canon (*issai kyō*) from China. Monks in the lineage of Kogetsu were initially in the forefront of the movement to convert ordinary monasteries into saṅgha halls. For example, Seisetsu Shūcho (1745–1820), a "grandson" dharma heir of Kogetsu, became the abbot of Engakuji in Kamakura and converted the founding abbot's *stūpa* subtemple into a saṅgha hall. Later, Seisetsu moved to Kyoto and was instrumental in establishing subtemple sangha halls at Tenryūji and Shōkokuji, two other high-ranking monasteries in the shogunate's head/branch system. His dharma heir, Sengai Gibon (1750–1837), opened a sangha hall at Shōfukuji in Fukuoka.

The efforts of monks in Kogetsu's lineage, however, were eventually overshadowed and co-opted by dharma heirs of Hakuin Ekaku (1685–1768). Hakuin is honored in Rinzai Zen circles today as *the* reformer of the Tokugawa period, a hero who acted virtually single-handedly to fight off the Ōbaku threat and maintain the integrity of the Rinzai tradition. Hakuin was adamantly opposed to the Ming style of "mixing" Pure Land and Zen. Scorning *nembutsu kōan*, he championed a "pure" form of Rinzai Zen practice based on *zazen*, contemplating the "old cases" (*kosoku*) of the Tang and Song patriarchs, and manual labor. He did not oppose the Ōbaku concerns with precepts and *sūtra* copying, but neither did he view them as vital matters.

Hakuin converted the Shōinji (in present-day Shizuoka) into a sangha hall where he promoted his own vision of Rinzai monastic practice, and later he founded the Ryūtakuji sangha hall. Insofar as those monasteries featured Ōbaku-style meditation halls and rigorous communal discipline, Hakuin was not as free from the influence of Ming Buddhism as he liked to profess. In his approach to lay followers, moreover, he took an eclectic and tolerant approach that owed much to Ōbaku Zen. His well-known *Zazen wasan* (*Vernacular Hymn in Praise of Zazen*), for example, belongs to the genre made popular by Ungo Kiyō's *Ōjō yōka* (*Song of Rebirth in the Pure Land*) and even contains some lines that are almost identical to the latter work. For lay followers, Hakuin also recommended recitation of the *Enmei jukku kannongyō* (*Life Prolonging Ten-Clause Kannon Sūtra*) as a form of practice similar to the *nembutsu* recitation of the Pure Land schools.[63] Dharma heirs of Hakuin opened many new sangha halls and eventually, in the nineteenth century, succeeded in taking over those that had been established earlier by monks in the Kogetsu line.

In the Sōtō Zen school, an early example of a reformer influenced by Ōbaku practices is Gesshū Sōko (1618–1696), who trained with Yinyuan and other Chinese monks in the middle of his career and then went on to become the abbot of Daijōji, an important Sōtō monastery. Inspired by the *Ōbaku shingi* and desirous of producing a Sōtō counterpart that could be used to facilitate communal sangha-hall training and hold formal retreats (*kessei*) at Daijōji, Gesshū consulted Dōgen's commentaries on the *Chanyuan qingui* and Keizan's *Nōshū Tōkokuzan Yōkō zenji gyōji shidai*, then compiled the *Shōjurin shinanki* (*Record of Guidelines for Shōju Grove [Daijōji]*), also known as *Shōjurin shingi* (*Rules of Purity for Shōju Grove*), in 1674.[64] In 1678 Gesshū and his disciple Manzan Dōhaku (1636–1715) took the aforementioned set of rules that Keizan had written for Yōkōji and published them for the first time under the title of *Keizan oshō shingi*.

The need that Sōtō lineage monks felt to have proprietary rules of purity to counter the *Ōbaku shingi* can also be seen in the actions of the thirtieth abbot of the Sōtō head monastery Eiheiji, Kōshō Chidō (?–1670), who pieced together such a text from six separate commentaries that Dōgen had written on different aspects of the *Chanyuan qingui*. Kōshō's compilation, styled *Nichiiki Sōtō shoso Dōgen zenji shingi* (*Rules of Purity by Zen Master Dōgen, First Patriarch of Sōtō in Japan*), was published in 1667. The text later became known as the *Eihei shingi* (*Eihei Rules of Purity*). Dōgen's various writings on monastic discipline were also the basis of the *Tōjō kijō* (*Sōtō Standards*),[65] compiled by Jakudō Donkō (Donkō, n.d.) and published in 1733. The title of that work echoed the references to "Baizhang's standards" (*Hyakujō kijō*) found in the *Chanyuan qingui* and Dōgen's own writings.

The single most influential reformer of Sōtō Zen in the Tokugawa period was Menzan Zuihō (1683–1769), whose work continues to serve as a standard for the modern Sōtō school. Continuing the movement started by Gesshū and Manzan, Menzan produced the *Sōdō shingi* (*Rules of Purity for Saṅgha Halls*), which was published in 1753.[66] Written in Japanese (as opposed to classical Chinese, which had previously been the norm for monastic rules), the text was intended to establish the definitive Sōtō approach to various ritual procedures on the basis of historical study. To that end, Menzan compared the *Nichiiki Sōtō shoso Dōgen zenji shingi* and *Keizan oshō shingi* to all of the various Song and Yuan Chinese rules of purity to which he had access. He explained the decisions he had made and presented his research findings in a companion volume entitled *Tōjō sōdō shingi kōtei betsuroku* (*Separate Volume of Notes on the Sōtō Rules of Purity for Saṅgha Halls*),[67] published in 1755. Menzan also researched the arrangement of Zen monastery buildings and sacred images used in Dōgen's and Keizan's day, publishing his findings in 1759 in his *Tōjō garan shodō anzōki* (*Record of Images Placed in the Various Halls of Sōtō Monasteries*).[68] Menzan was not the only one interested in countering the Ming style of monastery layout with an older Song-style layout sanctified by the Sōtō founding patriarchs: the Sōtō monk Futaku (n.d.) compiled a similar work entitled *Tōjō garan zakki* (*Miscellaneous Records of Sōtō Monasteries*),[69] which was published in 1755.

Gentō Sokuchū (1729–1807) was heir to the movement (starting with Gesshū and Manzan and continuing with Menzan) to oppose the *Ōbaku shingi* and revive the "old rules of purity" of Dōgen and Keizan. In 1794, a year before he became the fiftieth abbot of Eiheiji, Gentō edited the *Nichiiki Sōtō shoso Dōgen zenji shingi* and published it with the title *Kōtei kanchū Eihei shingi* (*Revised and Captioned Eihei Rules of Purity*).[70] His new edition was widely distributed and subsequently became known simply as the *Eihei shingi*. With its attribution to Dōgen (who did, in fact, write each of the six essays contained in the work), it helped to cement the erroneous but convenient notion that Dōgen himself had compiled a set of rules of purity. The text is also referred to today as the *Eihei dai shingi* (*Large Eihei Rules of Purity*), to distinguish it from a set of regulations by Gentō entitled *Eihei shō shingi* (*Small Eihei Rules of Purity*),[71] published in 1805. Written to regulate training at Eiheiji while Gentō was abbot, the latter text is similar in many respects to Menzan's *Sōdō shingi*. That is to say, it makes reference to various Song and Yuan rules of purity such as the *Chanyuan qingui*, *Huanzhu an qinggui*, and *Chixiu baizhang qingqui*, favoring the first on the grounds that it was closest to Baizhang and relied on by Dōgen.

In general, the movement of the Tokugawa-period Sōtō Zen to "restore the old" (*fukko*) ways of monastic training associated with Dōgen and Keizan was centered in a few relatively large and important monasteries in the head/branch system, such as Daijōji, Eiheiji, and Sōjiji. Despite the efforts of Sōtō purists such as Menzan to promote ground plans and sacred images that were in keeping with ones originally established by Dōgen, those places were rebuilt in what was basically a Ming Chinese style, with main gates (*sanmon*), meditation halls, buddha halls, and refectories similar to those found at Manpukuji (the Ōbaku head monastery). There were also a few examples of "opening a meditation platform" at smaller Sōtō monasteries, as was the norm in Rinzai Zen.

Zen Monastic Rules in the Meiji Era

Tokugawa rule ended in 1867 with the restoration of the Meiji emperor, and Japan embarked on a course of rapid modernization and industrialization that was inspired by the model of the leading Western colonial powers. Because Buddhism was closely associated with the old feudal regime and regarded as a backward, superstitious religion by many leaders of the new government, it was subjected to very harsh treatment in the early years of the Meiji era (1868–1912). A movement to "discard the buddhas and destroy [the followers of] Śākyamuni" (*haibutsu kishaku*) wreaked havoc (with degrees of severity that varied according to the locale) by destroying temples, confiscating their lands, and forcing priests to return to lay life.[72] By 1876 the number of Buddhist temples in Japan had dropped to 71,962, which by one estimate was a reduction of more than 80 percent from the Tokugawa period.[73] Government policies dictated a clear separation of Shinto and Buddhism (*shinbutsu bunri*) and established the former as the official ("ancient" and "pure") religion of the Japanese nation. The associations of households with temples, mandatory under the Tokugawa parishioner system, were rendered voluntary, and many of the Zen saṅgha halls that had been mortuary temples for *daimyō* clans found themselves deprived of support when their patrons lost power. The Meiji government also passed a number of laws designed to laicize what remained of the Buddhist priesthood and turn it into an ordinary profession. Thus, for example, an ordinance of 1872 permitted "eating meat, marriage, and wearing hair" (*nikujiki saitai chikuhatsu*) for monks. Other laws required Buddhist monks to keep their lay family names (as opposed to their traditional dharma names) for purposes of the national census, and subjected them to conscription into the military.

The Meiji government did, however, retain the principle of state control of Buddhism that had informed the old head/branch monastery system. In 1872 it decreed the administrative unification of each of the main Buddhist traditions: Tendai, Shingon, Jōdo, Jōdo Shin, Nichiren, Ji, and Zen. A new bureaucratic entity called the Zen Denomination (*Zenshū*) thus came into existence, forcibly uniting all the diverse lineages and temple groupings of the Rinzai, Sōtō, and Ōbaku traditions under the control of a single state–appointed superintendent priest (*kanchō*). That heavy–handed policy proved unworkable, however, and in 1874 the various historical groupings of Rinzai and Sōtō temples were permitted to form into two separate religious corporations. Government controls were further relaxed in 1876, allowing a group of temples formerly affiliated with Manpukuji to regain an independent identity as the Ōbaku school and the newly formed Rinzai school to dissolve into nine distinct corporations, each with its own head monastery and network of affiliated branch temples that closely resembled the late-Tokugawa head/branch system.[74] The newly created Sōtō school remained a single religious corporation, albeit one with two head monasteries, Eiheiji and Sōjiji.

The attacks on Buddhist institutions and ideas that occurred early in the Meiji era must be understood within the broader context of the vast project of modernization (Westernization) and nation building. James Ketelaar, in his examination of the persecution of Buddhism in Meiji Japan, identifies three main thrusts to the anti–Buddhist critique:

(1) the socio–economic uselessness of its priests and temples, which detracted from the nation's entrance into the "realm of civilization";
(2) the foreign character of its teachings, which promoted disunity and was incompatible with the directives of the Imperial Nation; and
(3) its mythological—that is, "unscientific"—history.[75]

The first two of these arguments, while couched in terms of the detrimental effect that Buddhism supposedly had on the effort to modernize and unify Japan under the imperial banner, were actually clichés of anti-Buddhist rhetoric that had already seen more than a millennium of use in China; nevertheless, they seemed relevant enough to be repeated frequently by opponents of Buddhism and to elicit responses from its supporters. The third argument—that Buddhism was a superstitious religion with a false (mythological as opposed to scientific) cosmology and history—was the most potent, for it derived from the same rationalist and historicist mindset of "civilization and enlightenment" (*bunmei kaika*) that was inspired by the West and promoted by Japan's new Westernizers.

Given the aforementioned policies and criticisms, it is remarkable that any aspects of the Zen reforms of the Tokugawa period were able to survive the Meiji Restoration. After all, those reforms had been characterized by stricter adherence to the precepts of the Indian *vinaya* and the study and reimplementation of monkish rules of purity originally formulated in China. The main thrust of Meiji government policies, however, was in exactly the opposite direction—toward the relaxation of precepts, the laicization of the Buddhist institution, and the promotion of a "pure Japanese" national religion styled "Shinto." The traditional history of the Zen lineage (*zenshūshi*), with its stories of the twin patriarchs Bodhidharma and Hyakujō (Baizhang) and the subsequent transmission of the formless buddha-mind to Japan, was particularly vulnerable to the charge of being mere mythology. Proponents of Zen, however, did not shrink from their past as they struggled for survival and relevance in the new world of the Meiji regime. Rather, they seized on saṅgha-hall training and the rules of purity that regulated it as potent symbols of everything that was positive about the Zen tradition and used them to forge a new identity adapted to the needs of the time.

That process of self-reinvention was highly complex, but key elements in it may be singled out as follows. In the first place, proponents of Zen stressed the communal, hierarchical, ascetic, and highly disciplined nature of traditional monastic training—all characteristics of social structure that were, clearly enough, also desirable in the new world of corporations, factories, and military units that the Meiji oligarchs were building. Recalling that the initial establishment of Zen monasteries in Japan in the thirteenth century had taken place with the patronage of the Kamakura *bakufu*, they also emphasized the putative link between Zen and Bushidō (*bushidō*), the "way of the warrior," promoting both as traditional values ideally suited to modern Japan. Remarkably, this polemic was even shared with the English-speaking world by Nukariya Kaiten (1867–1934), a leading Sōtō Zen scholar, in a 1913 book entitled *The Religion of the Samurai*. Nukariya wrote:

> As regards Japan, it [Zen] was first introduced into the island as the faith first for the Samurai or the military class, and molded the characters of many distinguished soldiers. . . . After the Restoration of the Mei-ji (1867) the popularity of Zen began to wane, and for some thirty years remained in inactivity; but since the Russo-Japanese war its revival has taken place. And now it is looked upon as an ideal faith, both for a nation full of hope and energy, and for a person who has to fight his own way in the strife of life. Bushidō, the code of chivalry, should be observed not only by the soldier in the battle-field, but by every citizen in the struggle for existence. If a person be a person and not a beast, then he must be a Samurai—brave, generous, upright, faithful, and manly, full of self-respect and self-confidence, at the same time full of the spirit of self-sacrifice. We

can find the incarnation of Bushidō in the late General Nogi, the
hero of Port Arthur, who, after the sacrifice of his two sons for the
country in the Russo-Japanese war, gave up his own and his wife's
life for the sake of the deceased Emperor.[76]

Nogi (1849–1912) made an excellent case in point for Nukariya because
the general had, in fact, taken up the practice of Zen as a relatively young, up-
and-coming officer in the 1880s, training at the Kaisei Sangha Hall (*Kaisei
sōdō*) in Nishinomiya City under the famous Nantenbō Rōshi (1839–1925).
Later, before his ritual suicide upon the death of the Meiji emperor, he had
also served as schoolmaster to the emperor's grandson (the future Shōwa emperor) Hirohito, incorporating some elements of sangha-hall training into the
young prince's daily routine.

Apologists such as Nukariya nurtured the mythical ideal of the warrior
who, through the practice of Zen, was ostensibly able to face combat and the
prospect of death with complete equanimity, thereby gaining a decisive advantage over his opponents. They even claimed that the samurai who repelled the
Mongol invasions of the thirteenth century (with the aid of the famous *kami-
kaze* or "winds of the kami") had been steeled in their resolve by their Zen
training. In point of fact, there is little historical evidence for the notion that
the Kamakura samurai actually practiced *zazen* or meditated on kōans; as Martin Collcutt has pointed out, most were Pure Land devotees who patronized
Zen for very different reasons: its tradition (inherited from China) of docile
cooperation with the state; its rules of purity which forbade weapons in monasteries (an undesirable feature of some Tendai and Shingon school monasteries in the preceding Heian period); and its function as a conduit for trade
with China and the desirable trappings of elite Song culture.[77] Moreover, it was
more than a little ironic that Bushidō should be celebrated during the Meiji
era, a time of great social upheaval that saw the dissolution of the samurai
class and formerly unthinkable conscription of masses of peasants into the
military. Nevertheless, the myth of "warrior Zen" did appeal to elements of the
Meiji elite as Japan went through its successful wars with China and Russia
and geared up for future conflicts as a colonial power. By focusing attention
on the rigorous training that took place in the sangha halls or "special training
centers" (*senmon dōjō*) that retained the rigorous communal Zen practice implemented by Tokugawa-period reformers on the basis of Chinese rules of
purity, Meiji Zen Buddhists were able to counter the charge of the social uselessness of its priests and temples. The figure of Hyakujō (Baizhang) and his
ancient rules of purity were also invoked in this connection, to argue that Zen
monasteries instilled the values of hard work and economic self-sufficiency.

Although Buddhism in general came under attack early in the Meiji era
as a "foreign" creed, after two or three decades of rapid modernization and
wrenching social change such criticisms rang hollow. Indeed, it was now West-

ern "materialistic" culture that was increasingly characterized as spiritually bankrupt and alien to Japan's traditional values. Viewed in that nostalgic light, Buddhism seemed rather familiar and attractive. Zen Buddhists were quick to remind their countrymen that many domestic arts and cultural refinements that were considered traditionally Japanese, such as rock gardens, tea ceremonies, and calligraphy, had originally been developed in the context of Zen monasticism.

Buddhism, of course, had originally been imported from China, but apologists for the tradition argued that Japan was now the leading representative and guardian of this profound "Eastern" (tōyōteki) tradition of philosophy and spirituality. Zen Buddhists, in particular, used their story of the transmission of the dharma from India to China to Japan to argue that the flame of enlightenment still burned brightly in their saṅgha halls, whereas it had entirely died out in the "syncretic" and "degenerate" monastic institutions of Ming and Qing dynasty Chan. As keeper of the flame of oriental culture, that argument seemed to imply, Japan had a right and a duty to bring not only China but perhaps even India under its protection.

Toward the end of the nineteenth century it became fashionable and prestigious not only for military officers such as Nogi but also for leaders of banking and industry to associate with and patronize Zen masters just as samurai rulers and wealthy merchants had in the past. Moreover, a number of saṅgha halls were opened up for lay men and women (called koji and daishi, respectively) to join with monks in zazen and kōan practice under a master (rōshi). Suzuki Daisetsu (1870–1966), influential author of numerous books on Zen in English as well as Japanese, got his start as a lay practitioner under Sōen Rōshi (1859–1919) in the Shōzokuin Saṅgha Hall at Engakuji in Kamakura.[78] Being close to Tokyo, the latter was a convenient place for many of the Meiji elites to get a taste of Zen monastic practice.

Finally, Japanese Buddhists countered the charge that their religion was irrational and mythological, as opposed to scientific, by opening numerous Western-style schools and universities and taking a critical, historical approach to the study of their own traditions.[79] The Myōshinji branch of Rinzai Zen opened the Hanazono Academy (Hanazono gakuin, later called Hanazono University) in Kyoto, and the Sōtō School University (Sōtōshū daigaku, later renamed Komazawa University) was founded in Tokyo. Those became centers for the academic study of the history of Zen, which lent weight to the aforementioned apologetics. Modern Japanese scholarship on the "rules of purity" literature got its start at that time and was instrumental in idealizing Dōgen's monastic rules as "pristine" and close to the original spirit of Baizhang, while portraying Yuan, Ming, and later Chinese monastic institutions as "degenerate" and "spiritually dead."

The government-induced unification of the two main branches of Sōtō Zen (the Eiheiji and Sōjiji factions) under the nominal control of a single administrative headquarters (*Sōtō shūmukyoku*) in Tokyo necessitated the production of a single, authoritative manual that could be used when Sōtō monks from different lineages got together for joint ritual performances. Such a manual was first published in Meiji 22 (1889) under the title of *Tōjō gyōji kihan* (*Standard Rites of the Sōtō Tradition*). According to the preface, it was based primarily on three sources: Gesshū Sōko's *Shōjurin shinanki*, compiled in 1674; Menzan Zuihō's *Sōdō shingi*, published in 1753; and Gentō Sokuchū's *Eihei shō shingi*, published in 1805. Those Tokugawa-period works were themselves modeled after the *Keizan oshō shingi*, with its schedule of daily, monthly, annual, and occasional observances, and they incorporated many elements of Dōgen's various commentaries on the *Chanyuan qinggui*, as those were found in the collections entitled *Eihei shingi* and *Shōbōgenzō*. While taking the three aforementioned Tokugawa-period texts as a starting point, the editors of the Meiji-era *Tōjō gyōji kihan* also stated in their preface that they had consulted a wide range of earlier Chinese and Japanese rules of purity: the *Chanyuan qinggui*, *Eihei dai shingi*, *Keizan shingi*, *Jiaoding qinggui*, *Beiyong qinggui*, *Riyong qinggui*, *Huanzhu an qinggui*, *Chixiu baizhang qinggui*, *Ōbaku shingi*, and various other related works.

The academic study of all the extant rules of purity that took place in the Meiji era, influenced by Western methods of text criticism and historical criticism as well as the research of earlier scholar monks such as Menzan and Mujaku, fueled a movement at Eiheiji to return to the original, "authentic" modes of Zen monastic practice that had first been established in Japan by Dōgen. What that meant, in practical terms, was to purge Eiheiji of various buildings and procedures that had been adopted during the Tokugawa period under the influence of Ming-style Ōbaku Zen, replacing them with older Song-style facilities and ritual forms that the modern research had begun to reconstruct. Thus, for example, the Ming-style meditation hall that had served to revive the practice of communal *zazen* at Eiheiji in the eighteenth century was replaced by a "proper" Song-style saṅgha hall. Later, Sōjiji (after moving to Yokohama in Meiji 44, 1911) and a few other Sōtō training monasteries also strived to embody Song-style ground plans and ritual procedures, to whatever degree was practicable.

Because the various branches of the Rinzai lineage broke apart into institutionally independent entities as soon as the relaxation of Meiji government controls allowed them to, they did not form a single Rinzai denomination comparable to that of the Sōtō school and had no need to craft a common set of monastic rules or ritual procedures. Nevertheless, a group of abbots from leading Rinzai training monasteries (*sōdō*) formed an association toward the end of the Meiji era in order to standardize admission formalities and various other aspects of monastic practice, establishing uniform procedures that have held down to the present. This association, originally called the "League of Monasteries" (*sōrin dōmeikai*), was founded in 1900 with twenty-two Rinzai

monasteries participating, including those at the headquarters temples Myōshinji, Daitokuji, Nanzenji, Kenninji, Tōfukuji, Tenryūji, Engakuji, and Kenchōji.
Later the name was changed to the "League of Rinzai School Special Training
Centers" (*Rinzaishū senmon dōjō dōmeikai*), and the number of participating
saṅgha halls increased to about thirty. The standard procedures it agreed on
and revised over the years (the latest revision being in 1938) were distributed
to the various saṅgha halls in manuscript copies.[80]

The Legacy of the "Rules of Purity" in Contemporary Japan

The legacy of Song, Yuan, and Ming Chinese rules of purity is still very much
alive in contemporary Japanese Zen, both as a major topic of academic study
at Zen universities and in the ritual manuals and liturgical texts currently in
use in Zen monasteries and temples. There are at present only about sixty
training monasteries (called *senmon sōdō* in the Sōtō school and *senmon dōjō*
in the various branches of Rinzai Zen) in all of Japan where anything akin to
the old rules of purity are actually put into systematic practice. The vast majority
of Zen "monasteries" (*jiin*), more than 20,000 in number, are simply parish
temples dedicated mainly to performing funerals and memorial services for
their lay parishioners.[81] Nevertheless, all Zen temple priests (nominally *jūshoku*
or "abbots") are graduates of one of the training monasteries, and the rigorous
communal training that goes on in them is universally heralded as the true
"essence" of Zen.

A number of texts that derive more or less directly from Sung and Yuan
Chinese and medieval Japanese rules of purity are in use today. The *Sōtōshū
gyōji kihan* (*Standard Rites of the Sōtō Zen School*), published by the Sōtōshū
shūmuchō (Administrative Headquarters of Sōtō Zen) in Tokyo, is an updated
version of the *Tōjō gyōji kihan* first compiled in 1889. It was first published
with its present title in Taisho 7 (1918) and was subsequently revised in Showa
25 (1950), Showa 41 (1966), and Showa 63 (1988). Major Sōtō training monasteries such as Eiheiji, Sōjiji, and Zuiōji all follow their own calendars of daily,
monthly, annual, and occasional observances (*gyōji*) and make use of their own
slightly different versions of various liturgical texts, but none of those proprietary texts vary in any significant way from materials found in the *Sōtōshū gyōji
kihan*, which is distributed to all Sōtō temples nationwide. The Sōtō school,
like every organization registered with the Japanese government as a tax-
exempt religious corporation or "juridical person" (*shūkyō hōjin*), is required
by law to have a set of "Denominational Regulations" (*shūsei*) in which it declares its basic teachings, objects of worship, ritual observances, bureaucratic
structure, and so on.[82]

The fifteen branches of Rinzai Zen in Japan today have no single set of shared monastic rules comparable to the *Sōtōshū gyōji kihan,* because they are independent religious corporations each with its own "Denominational Regulations" traditional ritual manuals. Training monasteries and ordinary temples belonging to the Myōshinji branch (Myōshinji-ha) of Rinzai Zen, for example, makes use of a manual entitled *Gōko hosshiki bonbai shō (Summary of Ritual Forms and Melodic Chanting for Communal Services),* which was compiled by the Center for Research on Ritual (Hōgi Kenkyūshitsu) at Hanazono University in 1956 and subsequently updated in 1964 and 1967. According to its preface, the *Gōko hosshiki bonbai shō* is based on several sources: the Yuan *Chixiu baizhang qingqui,* Mujaku Dōchū's Tokugawa-period *Shōsōrin ryaku shingi,* the *Hōzan shoshiki (Various Rites for Myōshinji),*[83] and Myōshinji's "Denominational Regulations."[84]

Every one of the training monasteries affiliated with Rinzai Zen has its own set of ritual procedures and ceremonial calendars that derive from earlier rules of purity literature. In the early 1980s, for example, the Daitoku Sōdō was using a *Nyūsei kokuhō (Admonitions for Retreats),* which consisted of two parts: "rules for the [officers of the] administrative branch" (*jōjū kitei*) and "standards for daily life" (*nichiyō kikan*). Both were manuscripts that had been edited and copied within the past twenty years, but they were attached to and based on two similar manuscripts dated Taisho 2 (1913) and Meiji 40 (1907), respectively. Daitoku Sōdō also had a *Kaisei kokuhō (Admonitions for Between Retreats)* and a frequently updated manuscript entitled *Nenju gyōji (Annual Observances).*[85]

In visits to a number of Rinzai training monasteries in the 1980s, I obtained copies of various rules and ritual manuals that were actually in use on the premises. This is not the place to list all the manuscripts in question, still less to give a detailed account of their contents, but I can confirm that, on the whole, they derive directly from the various Sung and Yuan Chinese and medieval Japanese rules of purity discussed earlier.

A book entitled *Rinzaishū nōto (Rinzai School Notes),* compiled by Itō Kōkan and published by the Kichūdō Bookstore in Kyoto in 1980, gives a good account of the actual practices that go on in Rinzai training monasteries today. Itō's intention in producing the *Rinzaishū nōto,* in fact, was to provide a standard handbook for Rinzai monasteries. He based the work on: Mujaku Dōchū's *Shōsōrin ryaku shingi;* the *Hosshiki bonbai shishin (Manual of Ritual Forms and Melodic Chanting);* and the *Gōko hosshiki bonbai shō.* In contents, the *Rinzaishū nōto* deals with: (1) basic ritual forms (*gyōji kihon*), such as *gasshō, sanpai,* and *kekka fuza;* (2) daily observances (*nikka gyōji*), such as *sūtra*-chanting services, *zazen,* and meals; (3) monthly observances, including *sūtra*-chanting memorial services, head shaving, and bathing; (4) annual observances, such as new year's rites, opening and closing retreats, memorial services, and Buddha's birthday, enlightenment, and *nirvāṇa;* and occasional observances (*rinji gyōji*), such as funerals, special prayer services, installing new images, and so on. In its organization as well as its specific contents, the *Rinzaishū nōto* harks back to many earlier rules of purity.

There is no way to sum up all of the historical and textual data presented in this chapter in a meaningful conclusion, except to note the remarkable resilience of ritual forms over long periods of time. Many of the basic procedures outlined in the Song rules of purity are clearly recognizable today in Japanese Zen training monasteries and in North American and European Zen centers modeled after them. The social, political, and religious meanings given to those ritual forms, however, have changed greatly over time, for they have frequently been subjected to "revivals" and reinterpretations in different historical periods and cultural settings.

ABBREVIATIONS

DZZ   *Dōgen zenji zenshū*, ed., Ōkubo Dōshū 7 vols. 1970 and 1971, Tokyo: Chikuma shobō.

YZS   *Yakuchū Zen'en shingi*, eds., Kagamishima Genryū, Satō Tatsugen, and Kosaka Kiyū Tokyo: Sōtōshū shūmuchō, 1972.

ZGDJ   *Zengaku daijiten*, ed., Zengaku daijiten hensanjo. Tokyo: Taishūkan, 1985.

SZ   *Sōtōshū zensho*, ed., Sōtōshū zensho kankōkai 1970–73. rev. and enlarged ed. 18 vols. Tokyo: Sōtōshū shūmuchō.

NOTES

1. For a detailed discussion of kōan collections, see T. Griffith Foulk, "The Form and Function of Kung-an Literature: A Historical Overview," in Steven Heine and Dale S. Wright, eds., *The Kōan: Text and Context in Zen Buddhism* (New York: Oxford University Press, 2000), pp. 15–45.

2. For a description of these and other rituals characteristic of Song Chan, see T. Griffith Foulk, "Myth, Ritual, and Monastic Practice in Sung Ch'an Buddhism," in Patricia Buckley Ebrey and Peter N. Gregory, eds., *Religion and Society in T'ang and Sung China* (Honolulu: University of Hawaii Press, 1993), pp. 147–208.

3. T. Griffith Foulk, "*Chanyuan qingui* and Other 'Rules of Purity' in Chinese Buddhism," in Steven Heine and Dale S. Wright, eds., *The Zen Canon* (New York: Oxford University Press, 2004), pp. 275–312.

4. ZZ 2–16–5; SZ, *Shingi*, pp. 867–934; *Kanazawa bunkoshi zensho, Zenseki hen*; and for a critical edition and annotated Japanese translation see YZS.

5. T 80:9b, 14b–15b.

6. In his *Tōfukuji jojogoto* (*Articles for Tōfukuji*), written in 1280, Enni stated that "the monastic rules [*sōrin kishiki*] of Zen Master Bukkan [Bukkan zenji] [Wu-chun Shih-fan] should be put into practice and never changed" (cited in Imaeda Aishin, *Chūsei zenshūshi no kenkyū* [Tōkyō Daigaku shuppankai, rpt., 1970], 1961).

7. Imaeda Aishin, *Chūsei zenshūshi no kenkyū*, p. 61, note 5.

8. Passages in DZZ 2:295 correspond to passages in YZS 116 and 269; DZZ 2:

296 = YZS 273; and DZZ 2:300 = YZS 276. For these and the following references in this paragraph, I am indebted to Yifa, "The Rules of Purity for the Chan Monastery: An Annotated Translation and Study of the *Chanyuan qinggui*" (Ph.D. diss., Yale University, 1996), pp. 88–90. See also Yifa, *The Origins of Buddhist Monastic Codes in China: An Annotated Translation of the Chanyuan Qinggui* (Honolulu: University of Hawaii Press, 2002).

9. DZZ 2:348–9 = YZS 42–43; DZZ 2:350 = YZS 50; DZZ 2:351–352 = YZS 46–48; DZZ 2:352–353 = YZS 52–53; DZZ 2:353–354 = YZS 54–55 DZZ 2: 355–356 = YZS 55–56; and DZZ 2: 356–357 = YZS 58.

10. DZZ 2:331–333 = YZS 105–109; DZZ 2:339–340 = YZS 110–115; DZZ 2:340–341 = YZS 116; DZZ 2:345 = YZS 119; DZZ 2:341 = YZS 269; DZZ 2:341 = YZS 270; DZZ 2:342 = YZS 116; DZZ 2:342 = YZS 273; DZZ 2:343 = YZS 116; DZZ 2: 345 = YZS 119; DZZ 2:345 = YZS 269; DZZ 2:345 = YZS 270; and DZZ 2:345 = YZS 275.

11. DZZ 1:597 = YZS 13.

12. DZZ 1:619 = YZS 13.

13. DZZ 1:617 = YZS 13.

14. DZZ 1:431 = YZS 16.

15. DZZ 1:571 = YZS 85; DZZ 1:574–576 = YZS 86–88; and DZZ 1:580–581 = YZS 91.

16. DZZ 1:470 = YZS 233; DZZ 1:472 = YZS 153; and DZZ 1:473 = YZS 235.

17. DZZ 1:649 = YZS 285.

18. DZZ 1:667 = YZS 285.

19. DZZ 2:3–4 = Carl Bielefeldt, *Dōgen's Manuals of Zen Meditation* (Berkeley, Cal.: University of California Press, 1988), pp. 279–283.

20. For an annotated translation, see T. Griffith Foulk, "Instructions for the Cook," in *Nothing Is Hidden: Essays on Zen Master Dōgen's Instructions for the Cook*, ed. Jisho Warner, Shōhaku Okumura, John McRae, and Taigen Dan Leighton (New York: Weatherhill, 2001), pp. 21–40.

21. Eisai states that the hall was used for the *Lotus samādhi* (*hokke–zanmai*), Amitabha samādhi (*mida–zanmai*), Guanyin samādhi (*Kannon–zanmai*), and so on (T 80: 15a); and for details of these practices see Daniel Stevenson, "The Four Kinds of Samadhi in Early T'ien–t'ai Buddhism," in Peter N. Gregory, ed., *Traditions of Meditation in Chinese Buddhism* (Honolulu: University of Hawaii Press, 1987), pp. 45–97.

22. Furuta Shōkin, "Nihon Zenshūshi: Rinzaishū," in Nishitani Keiji, ed., *Zen no rekishi: Nihon, Kōza zen* no. 4 (Tokyo: Chikuma shobō, 1967), p. 22.

23. T 80:15a; and Ishida Jūshi, ed., *Kamakura bukkyō seiritsu no kenkyū: Shunjō risshi* (Kyoto: Hōzōkan, 1972), p. 395.

24. Takeuchi Michio, *Nihon no Zen* (Tokyo: Shunjūsha, 1976), p. 186.

25. The plans are preserved in the *Gozan jissatsu zu*; see ZGDJ 3:12–13.

26. See, for example, Kagamishima, *Dōgen zenji to sono monryū* (Tokyo: Seishin shobō, 1961), pp. 8–27.

27. Kagamishima, *Dōgen Zenji to sono monryū*, pp. 30–56; Takeuchi Dōyū, "Shoki sōdan no tenkai: kyōdan," in Kagamishima Genryū and Tamaki Kōshirō, eds., *Dōgen zen no rekishi, Kōza Dōgen*, vol. 2 (Tokyo: Shunjūsha, 1980), pp. 2–5.

28. Nakamura Sōichi, *Zenyaku Shōbōgenzō* (Tokyo: Seishin shobō, 1972) 4:286 (my translation).

29. Nakamura, *Zenyaku Shōbōgenzō* 4:110–143; and Yuhō Yokoi, *Zen Master Dōgen: An Introduction with Selected Writings* (New York: Weatherhill, 1976), pp. 113–127.

30. Nakamura, *Zenyaku Shōbōgenzō* 2:30–52; and Kosen Nishiyama and John Stevens, *Shōbōgenzō: The Eye and Treasury of the True Law*, vol. 2 (Tokyo: Nakayama shobō, 1977), pp. 158–162.

31. DZZ 6:96–167.

32. Nakamura, *Zenyaku Shōbōgenzō* 4:61; and Yokoi, *Zen Master Dōgen*, p. 93.

33. Nakamura, *Zenyaku Shōbōgenzō* 4:199; and Yokoi, *Zen Master Dōgen*, p. 150.

34. Nakamura, *Zenyaku Shōbōgenzō* 1:452–453; and Nishiyama and Stevens, *Shōbōgenzō*, vol. 1 (Tokyo: Nakayama shobō, 1975), pp. 98–99.

35. Nakamura, *Zenyaku Shōbōgenzō* 2:72–94; and Nishiyama and Stevens, *Shōbōgenzō*, vol. 1, pp. 8–16.

36. The "Regulations for Jōraku Zen Monastery" (*Jōraku zenji kitei*) that Lanqi left are included in the *Daikaku zenji goroku* (*Discourse Records of Zen Master Daikaku*), *Dainippon Bukkyō zensho*, 112a–b; also quoted in Imaeda Aishin, *Chūsei zenshū-shi no kenkyū*, pp. 62–63.

37. They are mentioned in his final admonitions (*yuikai*): *Daikaku zenji goroku*, in *Dainippon Bukkyō zensho*, 112b.

38. For a ground plan of the monastery as it was in Shunjō's day, see plate 9 in Ishida Jūshi, ed., *Kamakura Bukkyō seiritsu no kenkyū: Shunjō risshi* (Kyoto: Hōzōkan, 1972).

39. For Shunjō's "rules for the pure assembly" (*shinshū kishiki*), "catalogue of the halls and quarters at Sennyūji" (*Sennyūji dendōbōryō shokumoku*), and various other manuscripts that prove this point see, Ishida, *Kamakura Bukkyō seiritsu no kenkyū*, pp. 391–407.

40. Like Dōgen, Shunjō wrote a short *Principles of Seated Meditation* (*Zazengi*); see Ishida, *Kamakura Bukkyō seiritsu no kenkyū*, p. 407.

41. T 80:10b.

42. T 80:7a.

43. T 80:7b.

44. Suganuma Akira, ed., *Dōgen jiten* (Tokyo: Tōkyōdō, 1977).

45. T 45:869a–874a; see ZGDJ 2:805b, s.v. *taitaikohō*.

46. DZZ 2:363.

47. All of these Chinese rules of purity are discussed in detail in Heine and Wright, eds., *The Zen Canon*, pp. 275–312.

48. The text is preserved in the Naikaku Bunko (no. 17873, box 193, shelf 11).

49. T 82:423c–451c.

50. Part of this text appears in T 80:619b–624b under the title *Daikan zenji shō shingi* (*Zen Master Daikan's Small Rules of Purity*). A manuscript copy of the full text, dated Meiji 37, is held at the Chōshōin, a subtemple of Nanzenji in Kyoto; a photocopy of that is held at the Tokyō Daigaku Shiryō Hensansho.

51. Martin Collcutt, *Five Mountains: The Rinzai Zen Monastic Institution in Medieval Japan* (Cambridge, Mass.: Harvard University Press, 1981), pp. 149–165.

52. Collcutt, *Five Mountains*, pp. 109–115.

53. ZGDJ 1050b–c.

54. At the height of this trend, the number of subtemples reached 66 at Kenninji, 76 at Shōkokuji, 95 at Tenryūji, 101 at Nanzenji, and 120 at Tōfukuji, all of which had been important monastic centers under the old "Five Mountains" system. Myōshinji and Daitokuji, two monasteries that had not been favored with "five mountain" status but had emerged after the Ōnin War as powerful new centers, had as many as 165 and 104 subtemples, respectively (Ōta Hirotarō, Matsushita Ryōshō, and Tanaka Seidai, *Zendera to sekitei, Genshoku Nihon no bijutsu*, vol. 10 [Tokyo: Shōgakkan, 1967], pp. 184–185).

55. T 81:624b–687c.

56. One of the chief architects of the shogunate's control of the civil court aristocracy (*kūge*) and samurai (*buke*) as well as Buddhist institutions was a Rinzai monk named Sūden (1569–1633), who served as an advisor to the first shogun, Tokugawa Ieyasu, on a wide range of domestic and foreign affairs. Another Rinzai monk, Takuan Sōhō (1573–1645), also served as an influential advisor to the shogunate.

57. T 82:766a–785c.

58. Ogisu Jundō, *Myōshinji, Jisha shiriizu*, vol. 2 (Kyoto: Tōyō bunkasha, 1977), pp. 71–87. Ungo's observation of the precepts included the strict prohibition of alcohol in his monastery and a personal refusal to handle money.

59. The term "sangha hall" originally referred to a single, large building in the layout of Song Chinese and medieval Japanese monasteries, where monks sat in meditation, took formal meals, performed various religious services (e.g., chanting *sūtras* to make merit at the request of patrons), and slept at night, all at their "single places" (*tan*) on long raised platforms. In the arrangement of Ming-style Chinese monasteries such as Manpukuji, however, the sangha halls of old had given way to smaller meditation halls which still had platforms but were no longer used for meals. In the Tokugawa period any Zen temple that had a meditation hall and a community of monks in training came to be called, in its entirety, a "sangha hall."

60. T 81:688a–723c.

61. The Tokugawa-period manuscript is held at Ryūkoku University library. Reprint edition: Yanagida Seizan, ed., *Chokushū hyakujō shingi sakei, Zengaku sōsho*, vol. 8A–B (Kyoto: Chūbun shuppansha, 1979).

62. The original manuscript in Dōchū's hand is held at Myōshinji in Kyoto. Reprint edition: Yanagida Seizan, ed., *Zenrin shōkisen, Zengaku sōsho*, vol. 9 (Kyoto: Chūbun shuppansha, 1979); originally published as *Zenrin shōkisen* (Kyoto: Kaiba shoin, 1909). Tokyo: Seishin shobō, 1963 (ZGDJ 709b).

63. Philip B. Yampolsky, *The Zen Master Hakuin: Selected Writings* (New York: Columbia University Press, 1971), pp. 185–187, 229. Many of his vernacular treatises (*kana hōgo*) aimed at lay audiences, Hakuin held that any form of Buddhist practice could be fruitful provided one engaged in it with single-minded intensity; this belief was similar to the idea that even *nembutsu* recitations could function as a kind of kōan practice.

64. SZ, *Shingi*, pp. 439–548. The full title of the text is *Shōjurin daijō gokoku zenji shingi shinanbo* (*Rules of Purity Handbook for Shōju Grove Daijō Nation-Protecting Zen Monastery*). Gesshū's disciple, Manzan Dōhaku, assisted to such a degree in the compilation that he should be considered a co-author.

65. SZ, *Shingi*, pp. 1–12.

66. SZ, *Shingi*, pp. 29–207. The original full title of the text is: *Tōjō sōdō shingi gyōhōshō* (*Summary of Procedures in Rules of Purity for Sōtō Saṅgha Halls*). The colophon has the date 1741, so the text may have been completed then, but Menzan's preface to its publication is dated 1753.

67. SZ, *Shingi*, pp. 209–330.

68. SZ, *Shingi*, pp. 815–836.

69. SZ, *Shingi*, pp. 837–866.

70. T 82:319a–342b.

71. SZ, *Shingi*, pp. 331–416. The original full title is *Kichijōzan Eiheiji shōshingi* (*Small Rules of Purity for Kichijō Mountain Eihei Monastery*). Note that the title *Eihei dai shingi* is a nickname for the *Kōtei kanchū Eihei shingi*, which in turn is a revision of the *Nichiiki Sōtō shoso Dōgen zenji shingi* (*Rules of Purity by Zen Master Dōgen, First Patriarch of Sōtō in Japan*); the word "Eihei" in *Eihei dai shingi* thus refers to Eihei Dōgen ("Dōgen of Eihei[ji]"). The word "Eihei" in *Eihei shō shingi*, on the other hand, refers not to Dōgen but to the monastery Eiheiji.

72. In Satsuma, for example, Buddhist institutions and practices were almost entirely eradicated between 1866 and 1870; see James Edward Ketelaar, *Of Heretics and Martyrs in Meiji Japan* (Princeton, N.J.: Princeton University Press, 1990), pp. 54–65. Major attacks against Buddhism also occurred in other domains (Ketelaar, *Of Heretics and Martyrs in Meiji Japan*, p. 78), but in many areas the depredations were less; see Kishimoto Hideo, ed., *Japanese Religion in the Meiji Era*, trans. John F. Howes (Tokyo: ōbunsha, 1956), pp. 114–120.

73. Martin Collcutt, "Buddhism: The Threat of Eradication," in Marius B. Jansen and Gilbert Rozman, eds., *Japan in Transition: From Tokugawa to Meiji* (Princeton, N.J.: Princeton University Press), p. 162.

74. The nine head monasteries were: Myōshinji, Daitokuji, Tenryūji, Shōkokuji, Kenninji, Nanzenji, Tōfukuji, Kenchōji, and Engakuji. Subsequently, other monasteries that had served as headquarters in the Tokugawa head/branch system broke off from those nine, taking their branch temples with them. Eigenji, which had become a branch temple of Tōfukuji in 1876, declared its independence in 1880. In 1903 Hōkōji broke off from Nanzenji, with which it had been affiliated since just after the Meiji Restoration. In 1905 Buttsūji split off from Tenryūji, its parent temple since 1873, and Kokutaiji declared its independence from Shōkokuji. Finally, Kōgakuji, which had been a branch temple of Nanzenji since Tokugawa times, received permission from the government to split from the parent temple in 1890 and actually took that step in 1908. With this change, the Rinzai school was divided into fourteen independent branches (*ha*). This number remained steady until 1941, when wartime constraints again resulted in the enforced administrative unification of the Rinzai school. Following the war, the fourteen branches again declared their independence, and Kōshōji split off from Shōkokuji, bringing the number of Rinzai administrative branches to the present fifteen.

75. Ketelaar, *Of Heretics and Martyrs in Meiji Japan*, p. 132.

76. Kaiten Nukariya, *The Religion of the Samurai: A Study of Zen Philosophy and Discipline in China and Japan* (London: Luzac, 1913), pp. 50–51.

77. Martin Collcutt, *Five Mountains*, pp. 87, 99.

78. Suzuki later idealized the saṅgha hall at the Shōzokuin in his book *The Training of the Zen Buddhist Monk* (Kyoto: The Eastern Buddhist Society, 1934), using quotations from the discourse records of Tang dynasty Chan patriarchs to explain the monastic routine that took place there, as if the twentieth-century Japanese saṅgha hall were the perfect embodiment of the ancient spirit of Zen, and an ideally "democratic" society to boot!

79. By Meiji 37 (1904) the various Buddhist denominations were operating some 110 schools with a total of 7,293 male and 72 female students (Kanaoka, Kasahara, and Nakamura, eds., *Ajia bukkyōshi, Nihon hen 8: Kindai bukkyō*, 268–269).

80. A photocopy of this document is in my possession.

81. See T. Griffith Foulk, "The Zen Institution in Modern Japan," in Kenneth Kraft, ed., *Zen: Tradition and Transition* (New York: Grove Press, 1988), pp. 157–177.

82. Sōtōshū Shūmuchō ed., *Sōtōshū shūsei* (Tokyo: Sōtōshū shūmuchō, Heisei 11).

83. Shōbōzan is the mountain name for Myōshinji.

84. Myōshinjiha Shūmuhonsho, ed., *Rinzaishū Myōshinjiha shūsei* (Kyoto: Rinzaishū Myōshinjiha Shūmuhonsho, 1981).

85. I obtained photocopies of the aforementioned manuscripts at Daitokuji in 1982 and 1983.

6

Zen Kōan Capping Phrase Books: Literary Study and the Insight "Not Founded on Words or Letters"

G. Victor Sōgen Hori

Along with kōan collections, monk biographies, and records of the patriarchs, Zen phrase books comprise a subgenre within Japanese Zen literature. In the broad sense of the term, Zen phrase books include several kinds of texts: books of proverbs or wise sayings, Chinese poetry composition handbooks compiled by early Zen monks, dictionaries of Chinese dialect or colloquial language, and guidebooks for reading tea ceremony scrolls. In the narrow sense of the term, the Zen phrase book is the handbook that Japanese Rinzai Zen monks use for the "capping phrase" exercise in the Zen kōan practice. These special collections of kōan capping phrases are called by the generic title, *Zenrin kushū* (*Zen Sangha Phrase Collection*).

In China, the service of appending capping phrases was the practice of masters. From the Sung period on (tenth to thirteenth century), Chinese Ch'an masters appended capping phrases to kōans, sometimes to a kōan as a whole, sometimes to each line of a kōan. Much later in Japan, probably around the sixteenth and seventeenth centuries, the capping phrase exercise became a required practice for even ordinary monks in training. Presently in the Japanese Rinzai kōan practice, when a monk has passed a kōan or part of a kōan, the master will ask him to append a verse or phrase.[1] The capping phrase, called *jakugo* or *agyo*, expresses the insight the monk has had while meditating on the kōan. It is usually a line or two of Chinese verse. (Sometimes, but rarely, a Japanese vernacular verse, called *sego*, is requested.) The monk searches for the capping phrase in one of the handbooks of collected capping phrases for kōans. Though these handbooks have been compiled in Japan, they consist entirely of Chinese verses and phrases and are drawn from every branch of Chinese literature, including the following: the records of Zen patriarchs, Buddhist *sūtras*, Confucian classics, Taoist texts, Chinese dynastic histories, Chinese poetry, and sometimes even children's street songs. Although there are, of course, Chinese collections of Zen verses and phrases, only in Japan are these collections of Chinese verses used as an integral part of kōan practice.

The capping phrase book deserves a much closer study for at least two reasons. First, the practice of appending capping phrases to a kōan raises an interesting philosophical problem: it is manifestly a literary exercise. How can Zen, supposedly "not founded on words and letters," have a practice in which words are used to express Zen insight? Some critics may immediately jump to the conclusion that in the *jakugo* exercise, the kōan practice, originally directed to the attainment of an enlightenment experience beyond language, has degenerated into the rote repetition of wooden phrases. Although there is some justice to the claim that the Rinzai kōan practice has deteriorated into a pro forma exercise, I do not think we can fully understand the problem of relating literary study to the insight "not founded on words and letters" until we investigate the second reason for studying the capping phrase book: the paradigm underlying the kōan.

Writers in the Zen tradition often begin a discussion about the kōan by explaining that the characters for the word "kōan" mean "public case," a case before a magistrate in a court of law. In this legal paradigm, just as a magistrate pronounces the judgment of the law, which both settles the present case and sets a precedent for subsequent cases, the kōan also pronounces the Dharma and sets a standard for later judgments. More recently, Steven Heine has argued that the "Hyakujō and the Fox" kōan is structured on the paradigm of a folktale. Folktales about foxes were usually morality tales with several standard features: a fox in disguise, a confession, exorcism in which the fox was returned to its original form, and a pronouncement of the moral of the story. Although most Zen kōans are not based on folktales, at least not the very important kōans, "Hyakujō and the Fox," the second case in the *Mumonkan* collection, clearly uses the structure of a morality folktale (Heine 1999). However, though the legal paradigm and the folktale paradigm account for some features of the kōan, they do not account for the most important features. First of all, in the root case of the kōan and in the commentaries to the kōan, the language is often perplexing and mysterious. Neither the legal paradigm nor the folktale paradigm explains the perplexing language. Furthermore, the partners in kōan dialogue are in competition and engage in a back-and-forth repartee in which either can win. This is an element not frequently found in either court cases or folklore morality tales. There is also a sense of fun and play, not found in a solemn court. Other important elements of a kōan are wordless communication and, of course, spontaneous insight. Is there another paradigm that in-cludes these other characteristic features of a kōan: perplexing language, com-petition in repartee, the sense of fun, wordless communication, insight? I believe it is the paradigm of the Chinese literary game.

In Chinese culture long before the rise of Ch'an in the T'ang and Sung, there was a very old and widespread custom of literary games. The most im-portant was the game of capping poetic verses.[2] In old poetry capping verse games, two or more persons, highly trained in poetry, would test each other's powers of memory and poetic composition. One person would present a verse, the first line of a couplet, and challenge the other person to recall the second line or to compose an appropriate couplet verse on the spot. The verses would use the highly allusive language of Chinese poetry in which one spoke of something without ever mentioning it directly. Part of the fun of capping phrase games was to speak in such allusive language that the other person missed the connotation. Another part of the skill of a good player was the ability to recognize the hidden meaning of the other person's allusions and, by "turn-ing the spear around," thrusting back using a similar allusion with some other hidden meaning. These are general features of the capping verse game: the use of highly allusive language in which people communicated something without directly saying it (a kind of "mind to mind transmission"); two players jousting with each other; the fact that either player could win; the elements of fun, deception, and insight; the fact that the best win "turns the spear around." They are all features of the Zen kōan dialogue as well. In fact, the resemblance is so strong that we can say a Zen kōan is a kind of Chinese capping verse game, where the two players test and apply not merely their training in poetry but the clarity of their awakened eye.

The Zen kōan thus derives from two sources. One source is the wordless insight of Zen, the insight "not founded on words and letters." The other source is the Chinese literary game. To speak about the insight that language could not describe, Chinese Zen monks in the T'ang and Sung periods adapted the capping phrase game. For centuries, literati played a highly sophisticated game of speaking about something without naming it directly. Thus the much later Japanese monastic practice wherein Rinzai Zen monks append a capping phrase to a kōan signifies not a degeneration of the Zen kōan tradition but a return to one of its origins. The very existence of the capping phrase exercise challenges us to investigate how such a literary exercise can be part of the practice for developing an insight, which is "not founded on words and letters."

Topics of interest will be discussed in three parts: (1) describing the capping phrase exercise in modern Japanese Rinzai kōan practice; (2) describing the capping phrase collections in the genre of texts called *Zenrin kushū;* and (3) arguing that the kōan is built on the paradigm of the Chinese literary game. In particular, the "beyond language" features that are so often associated with Zen, the fact that it is not "not founded on words and letters," its "mind-to-mind transmission," its sudden insight expressed, and so on are all adaptations from the Chinese literary game. Toward the end, a word of caution is stated because people might leap to the mistaken conclusion that the insight in the kōan is merely a literary flourish.

The Capping Phrase Practice in Japanese Rinzai Zen

The Masters' Commentaries

The ZGDJT (468) gives a useful definition of the *jakugo* or capping phrase:

> *Jakugo*, also *agyo, kengo*. A short commentary appended to a phrase from either the main case or the verse in a Zen text. Though it is clearly a commentary, in it one uses one's own eye-for-the-essential, either to assess and praise the words or actions of the ancients in support of their point or to substitute one's own rendering of their essential core, freely manipulating the dynamic of life and death. Forms an essential element of certain Zen texts like the *Hekiganroku* and *Shōyōroku*.

Kenneth Kraft has aptly described the capping phrase as a "cross between a kōan and a footnote" (Kraft 1992, 5). Although the capping phrase may appear in a text, like a kind of footnote, it does not function like a footnote, which usually cites a source, supplies a gloss to clarify a difficult passage, or provides more detailed information. (That is why they should not be called "Notes," as is done in Cleary and Cleary 1977.) Instead, a monk who offers a *jakugo* uses it to assess the Zen core or point (*shūshi*) of the words or actions of the ancients and gives appropriate praise or criticism. His *jakugo* displays his own eye-for-the-essential (*shūjōgan*) and his own way of manipulating life and death. The usual literary footnote comments on the text of a Zen text, but a *jakugo* comments on the Zen of a Zen text.

The practice of appending capping phrases to kōans began in the Sung period (960–1126 C.E.), when Ch'an masters started appending their own commentaries to stories of earlier masters. Their commentaries sometimes took the form of a prose essay attached to the story of the previous master; sometimes the form of poetic verse. Collections of these stories and commentaries became the kōan texts. This practice of appending capping phrases is so important that it has shaped the structure of basic kōan texts, such as the *Hekiganroku* and *Mumonkan* (two of the main kōan collections used for the Rinzai kōan practice).

In the *Hekiganroku*, Ch'an master Setchō Juken (C. Hsüeh-tou Ch'ung, 980–1052) compiled 100 kōan cases and added a verse (called a *ju*) to each. This verse is itself a *jakugo*, a capping verse expressing Setchō's insight into the matter of the kōan. In addition to this *jakugo* to the kōan as a whole, Setchō also appended *jakugo* to individual lines of the kōan in fifteen cases (cases 4, 18, 23, 31, 33, 36, 42, 48, 55, 61, 74, 82, 84, 85, 91). The *Hekiganroku* is a double-layered *jakugo* text, since its second editor, Engo Kokugon (C. Yüan-wo K'o-ch'in 1063–1135), created another layer of commentary on top of Setchō's commentary. Engo added an introduction to each case and also lengthy prose commentaries both to the main case of the kōan and to Setchō's verse. Then he added more line-by-line *jakugo* to both the main case and even to Setchō's *jakugo*. Thus the cases of the *Hekiganroku* are quite complicated in structure, consisting of eight identifiable parts representing three layers of text editing, as is diagrammed in table 6.1.

Although kōan prose commentaries resemble most scholarly prose commentary in being sober and discursive, a *jakugo* does not comment on the kōan dialogue but actually attempts to enter into the rough and tumble of the dialogue. The opponents in a kōan dialogue are depicted as being in competition; they are always making strategic moves against each other—probing, defending, feigning, attacking, and so on. The interlinear *jakugo* of Setchō Zenji, who was the first editor of the *Hekiganroku*, corresponds to the cheering and jeering of the bystander to the match. In case 4, hearing Isan's unnecessary praise of Tokusan, Setchō declares with resignation, "He adds frost on top of snow." In case 55 he is ironically aghast at the dialogue in the kōan: "Oh Lord! Oh Lord!" Sometimes bystanders think they themselves can do better than the competitors. For example, in case 42 Setchō boasts, "When Puang first asked, I would have made a snowball and hit him," and in case 48 the self-appointed expert claims, "At that time I would have just kicked over the tea stove." The *jakugo* of Engo Zenji, the second editor, resembles Setchō's *jakugo* with similar boos

TABLE 6.1.

Original case	Setchō Juken Zenji	Engo Kokugon Zenji
		1 *Suiji*, Introduction (called "Pointer" in Cleary and Cleary 1977) by Engo
2 *Honsoku*, the main case of the kōan	3 *Jakugo*, Setchō's interlinear capping phrases to main case in 15 cases	4 *Agyo*, Engo's interlinear capping phrases to both main case and Setchō's capping phrases
		5 *Hyōshō*, Engo's commentary to the main case
	6 *Ju*, Setchō's verse in response to the main case	7 *Jakugo*, Engo's capping phrases to Setchō's verse
		8 *Hyōshō*, Engo's commentary to Setchō's verse

and hurrahs from bystanders at a game. Since Engo's *jakugo* are responses to Setchō's *jakugo*, Engo is like the bystander who boos and hurrahs not only the players but also the other bystanders.

It is worthwhile to look at an example, such as case 23 of the *Hekiganroku*. Text in italics indicate either Setchō's *jakugo* or Engo's *jakugo*.

MAIN CASE AND SETCHŌ ZENJI'S JAKUGO	ENGO ZENJI'S *JAKUGO*
1. Once when Hofuku and Chōkei were wandering in the mountains,	*These two guys have fallen into the weeds.*
2. Hofuku pointed with his hand, "This right here is Mystic Peak."	*He's made a pile of bones where there's level ground. You mustn't speak about it. Dig up the earth and bury it deep.*
3. Chōkei said, "That may be so but it's a pity."	*If you lack iron eyes and copper pupils, you will be lost. Two people sick with the same disease are consoling each other. Bury them both in the same hole.*
4. *Setchō's jakugo: When you wander in the mountains with these guys, you can't tell what they will do.*	*Though [Setchō] has nicely reduced their net worth, still they're worth something. They're on both sides of you with their hands on their swords.*
5. *Another [Setchō jakugo]: A hundred thousand years from now, I'm not saying there won't be anyone, just that there will be few.*	*Pompous salesman! Here's another holy man up in the clouds!*
6. *Later this story was related to Kyōshō,*	*There's good, there's bad.*
7. *Who said, "If it weren't for Mr. Son [Chōkei], then you would have seen skulls filling the field.*	*Only someone on the same path knows. The great earth is so vast, it makes people utterly sad. When a slave meets a bondsmaid, they are mutually courteous. If Rinzai and Tokusan had appeared, for sure they would have given them a taste of the stick.*

The original story of this kōan is quite simple. One day while walking with Chōkei, Hofuku pointed with his hand and said, "This right here is Mystic

Peak," to which Chōkei said, "That may be so but it's a pity [that you had to say it]." Everything else is *jakugo*. In his *jakugo* at line 4 Setchō, the first editor of the text, expresses his amusement at the clumsy Zen antics of Hofuku and Chōkei, each trying to display his enlightenment; in line 5 he laments that in the future there will be few left who have even this level of Zen. Engo Zenji not only reverberates Setchō's condescending superior tone, but he trumps Setchō. In his *jakugo* at line 2 Engo decries the clumsiness of Hofuku, whose unnecessary words destroy the very mysticism they describe. He even finds Chōkei is just as bad as Hofuku ("Bury them both in the same hole"). Then in his *jakugo* to Setchō's *jakugo*, he agrees with Setchō that Hofuku and Chōkei are not completely worthless (line 4), but he also lambastes Setchō for his high self-opinion (line 5).

Line 7 is open to different interpretations. Cleary and Cleary (1977, 154) identify Mr. Son (C. Sun) as Hofuku (C. Pao Fu). However, the majority of other commentators identify Son as the informal name for Chōkei (Iriya et al., 1992, vol. 1, 306; Ōmori 1994, vol. 1, 187; Asahina 1937, vol. 1, 280). Thus taken, the line "If it weren't for Mr. Son [Chōkei], then you would have seen skulls filling the field" means, if it were not for Chōkei, Hofuku would have gotten away with his atrocious display of Zen. But Engo's *jakugo*, "When a slave meets a bondsmaid, they are mutually courteous," means "It takes one to know one," implying both parties are mutually Zen clowns. The greater part of this kōan consists of *jakugo*. And though they look like footnotes, none of them supplies the information one expects in a footnote; they are all thrusts and parries in the jousting of Zen.

The *Mumonkan*, another important kōan collection used in the Rinzai kōan curriculum, is a less complex text, yet it too would not have its present structure were it not for the practice of *jakugo*. The *Mumonkan* is a collection of forty-eight cases edited by Mumon Ekai (C. Wu-men Hui-k'ai, 1183–1260). After each of the forty-eight cases, Mumon Ekai appends both a commentary and a short four-line verse that expresses his Zen insight into the matter of the kōan. The four-line verse is his *jakugo*. Each case of the *Mumonkan* contains some moment of Zen insight. But Mumon's *jakugo* in which he expresses his insight into the kōan can be just as profound as the insight presented in the main case. In case 2, "Hyakujō and the Fox," an old man reveals that once long ago he wrongly claimed that a person of great awakening does not fall into karmic causation; for that mistake he was punished, and his punishment was to be reborn for 500 lives as a fox. Although he did not realize it at the time, the old man's answer of "not fall" was based on a false dichotomy between falling into karma and not falling into karma. Hyakujō releases the fox from punishment by saying that a person of great awakening is not blind to karmic causation, thus avoiding entirely the dichotomy of falling and not falling. But Mumon's verse on this kōan begins, "Not falling, not being blind, two sides of the same die." Thus Mumon goes even further than the main case of the kōan and shows that even Hyakujō's answer, "not blind," sets up another false dichotomy between "not falling" and "not being blind." Mumon's comment even goes so far as to claim that the fox enjoyed his 500 lives.[3]

The Monk's Practice

Kenneth Kraft's study of Daitō Kokushi's capping phrase records provides ample evidence that the practice of appending *jakugo* was transmitted from China directly into Rinzai Zen in Japan in the thirteenth century (Kraft 1992). Though there is no systematic evidence yet to document how quickly and how broadly it spread, the practice of appending *jakugo* did become an integral part of Rinzai training practices. Ikkyū Sojun, in his *Jikaishū* (*Self Precept Collection*), records that in 1455, a little more than a century after Daitō (1282–1337), as part of the opening ceremonies for a new training hall, he conducted several training activities including *suiji jakugo*, "Introducing a kōan" and "Appending a verse" (cited in Sanae 1996, 603). It seems to me inevitable that the practice of *jakugo* should take root within Japanese Zen, not merely because Japanese Zen monks attempted to replicate the practices of their Chinese teachers, but also because much of the literary ambience of Chinese elite culture was also transplanted to Japan, an ambience in which poetry was the vehicle of official document, in which poetic skill was considered the mark of education and intelligence. Not surprisingly in the Gozan ("Five Mountains") culture of the Kamakura and Muromachi periods the writing of poetry in general was widely thought to be a form of Buddhist practice.[4]

Although it is unclear when the capping phrase component was first incorporated into the kōan practice, the appending of a verse or phrase to a kōan is now a quite standard part of the Rinzai kōan practice. A variety of terms are now used for capping phrases. The common term *jakugo* is written with characters that mean "to append a phrase" (*go o tsukeru*) in Japanese. A common synonym is *agyo* whose characters also mean "to append a phrase." The term *kengo* encountered in the ZGDJT aforementioned definition simply means "selected phrase." Some *jakugo* assignments may ask for a front phrase, back phrase, and combined phrase (*zengo, gogo and sōgo*); this is a request for a *jakugo* that expresses *hen'i*, the Crooked, one that expresses *sho'i*, the Straight, and one that combines both. Sometimes *jakugo* and *teigo* are used as a pair, *jakugo* to mean the *sho'i* or Straight verse and *teigo* to mean the *hen'i* or Crooked verse. Instead of the traditional *jakugo* to a kōan, a monk may offer a *betsugo*, "alternate phrase," or *daigo*, "substitute phrase."

All these terms refer to phrases and verses in Chinese. There are also capping phrases in Japanese called *sego*, "vernacular phrases," with lines taken from Japanese *tanka, haiku,* and other Japanese verses. A collection of Japanese verses suitable for use as capping phrases has been created for Zen monks, the *Zenrin segoshū* (*Zen Sangha Vernacular Phrase Collection*) (Tsuchiya

1957).[5] *Sego* assignments are comparatively few in comparison with *jakugo* assignments.

In a slightly different class are *heigo*, a "colloquial phrase" created from ordinary Japanese colloquial language, and *nenrō*, a verse of "deft play." These phrases or verses must be composed by the monk himself; they cannot be found in the published capping phrase collections.

The *jakugo* assignment serves several purposes. First, a *jakugo* assignment is a kind of checking question (*sassho*) through which the Zen master confirms the monk's insight. It can also trigger new insight. As the monk pages through the Zen phrase book, he reads each phrase in light of the kōan. Suddenly he will read an old verse and see it in a new way. When I got the *jakugo* assignment for the kōan "Mu," the first case in the *Mumonkan*, try as I might, I could not find a capping phrase that summed up "Mu." Weeks went by. I lost count of the number of times I read the *Zen Phrase Book* from cover to cover. I could not find a verse that expressed the kōan "Mu." For me there was no such verse in the *Phrase Book*. Finally the Rōshi master, in disgust and impatience, gave me a hint. And then suddenly in an avalanche of phrases, I found numerous verses that expressed "Mu," all of which I had read many times before. The *Zen Phrase Book* was full of them.

Beyond confirming and deepening insight, the *jakugo* assignment functions also as a spur to practice. As Akizuki Ryōmin explains, when the monk offers a phrase he has selected and the Rōshi accepts it, the Rōshi will often discuss some of the other phrases that are accepted as *jakugo* for that kōan. By constantly seeing the classic *jakugo* for that kōan set side by side with the phrase that he has himself selected, the monk realizes the modesty of his own ability and is impressed with the depth of insight of the ancients. Thus he is spurred on to further practice (Akizuki 1987, 75–76).

Investigation of the kōan through the *jakugo* can get quite complicated. A long kōan may be divided into many subsections, each of which may require a *jakugo*. Following is an example of an advanced kōan, Rinzai's Four Discernments (*Rinzai shiryōken*), with its many divisions and *jakugo* assignments. Not every Rōshi uses this structure, but this is an actual example of one Rōshi's teaching style.

RINZAI'S FOUR DISCERNMENTS (*RINZAI SHIRYŌKEN RINZAI ROKU* §10, *KATTŌ SHŪ* CASE 218)

1. Remove the person, not the surroundings (Standpoint of principle and fact).[6]
2. Remove the person, not the surroundings (Standpoint of dynamic action).
3. *Jakugo.*
4. *Jakugo.*

5. *Nenrō* verse.
6. Remove the surroundings, not the person (Standpoint of principle and fact).
7. Remove the surroundings, not the person (Standpoint of dynamic action).
8. *Jakugo.*
9. *Nenrō* verse.
10. *Nenrō* verse.
11. Remove both person and surroundings (Standpoint of principle and fact).
12. Remove both person and surroundings (Standpoint of dynamic action).
13. *Jakugo.*
14. *Jakugo.*
15. *Nenrō* verse.
16. *Nenrō* verse.
17. Do not remove either person or surroundings (Standpoint of principle and fact).
18. Do not remove either person or surroundings (Standpoint of dynamic action).
19. *Jakugo.*
20. *Jakugo.*
21. *Nenrō* verse.
22. *Heigo* (colloquial phrase) for "Remove the person, do not remove surroundings."
23. Another same as above.
24. *Heigo* (colloquial phrase) for "Remove the surroundings, do not remove the person."
25. *Heigo* (colloquial phrase) for "Remove both person and surroundings."
26. *Heigo* (colloquial phrase) for "Do not remove either person or surroundings."
27. How do you handle the entire Buddhist canon on the basis of the Four Discernments?

The kōan, Tōzan's Five Ranks (*Tōzan goi*) can divide into 47 parts with numerous *jakugo*. Even an early kōan like "The Cypress Tree in the Garden" divides into 17 parts. In fact, once past the beginning stages, most kōans divide into at least two parts (*shō'i* and *hen'i*, the Straight and the Crooked), often with accompanying *jakugo* for each part.

Zen Phrase Books

Because *jakugo* is such an integral part of kōan practice, handbooks of collected Zen phrases and poetic verses are now among the standard possessions of all practicing Rinzai monks. Zen phrase books constitute a genre of text which deserves to be recognized as part of the overall Zen canon. This section gives a short account of the several kinds of Zen phrase books and their historical evolution; they did not start out as capping phrase collections. It describes the main capping phrase texts and also speculates on how and when the capping phrase exercise got incorporated into the kōan practice.

Early Zen Phrase Collections

GOLDEN PHRASE COLLECTIONS: *KINKUSHŪ*. From ancient times in both China and Japan, collections were made of proverbs, wise sayings, pithy phrases drawn from Chinese literature, maxims for everyday actions, and "golden phrases." Several of the Chinese literature classics are basically collections of such sayings, the Confucian *Analects* and the *Tao te ching* being probably the best-known examples. Such books had two uses. For the wider public, they were handy collections of memorable phrases to be consulted by the educated person in moments of reflection on life. During the Muromachi period many kinds of Golden Phrase Collections were compiled. Because Zen monks, buoyed by the literary culture of the Gozan, were assuming the social role of teachers, the Golden Phrase Collections that they compiled began to include more and more phrases from Buddhist sources (Iriya 1996, 566).

For the Western reader, the *Amakusaban kinkushū* is a particularly interesting example of a Golden Phrase Collection. In the late 1500s the Jesuit Mission at Amakusa in Hizen in Western Japan (the area straddling the present-day Saga and Nagasaki prefectural border) published several works to help the Jesuit brothers learn the language and culture of Japan and to assist them in propagating Christianity in Japan. One of these was entitled *Qincuxu*, or in modern English romanization, *Kinkushū*. It was 47 pages long and contained 282 maxims, which were meant to be used by the Jesuit missionaries in their sermons to the Japanese. This text is especially valuable for Japanese philological research, since each maxim is followed by a short Japanese commentary written not in Japanese *kana* but in Portuguese romanization. Because it is unclear exactly how some of the Japanese *kana* were meant to be pronounced at that time, this Portuguese romanization is especially valuable to Japanese linguists, since it gives a more accurate indication of actual pronunciation. The maxims were taken from a variety of both Chinese sources, such as the Confucian *Analects*, Chinese poetry, and so on, and Japanese sources, such as the *Seventeen Article Constitution* of Shōtoku Taishi. About a quarter of the total, 77 maxims, coincide with phrases in the *Kuzōshi*, the Zen phrase book that had been compiled by Tōyō Eichō Zenji about a century earlier (Sanae 1996, 602–603). Zen phrases are particularly prominent in this collection, probably because one of the Jesuit brothers who edited the text was a former follower of Zen (Yoshida 1938, 7).

ZEN POETRY COMPOSITION HANDBOOKS. Monasteries in medieval Japan were often built to house émigré Chinese masters who ran their monasteries according to Sung-period Chinese monastery rules and used Chinese language in their teaching (Collcutt 1981, 57–90). Under the direction of these émigré monks, and also of Japanese monks who had returned to Japan after training in China, early Japanese Zen monks had to become skilled in literary Chinese (Pollack 1986, 111–157). The monks used classical Chinese to compose verse for ritual occasions, record Dharma talks, write monastery documents, and carve inscriptions of icons and images. The monks did not actually read the Chinese script as Chinese, however, but rather learned to read classical Chinese writing, called *kanbun*, and give it a reading in Japanese, called *kundoku*. With this reading into classical Japanese, they attempted to approximate the Chinese pronunciation of the Chinese characters while reading them according to the order required by Japanese grammar. Although *kundoku* managed to preserve some of the terseness of the Chinese original and some approximation of the sounds of Chinese pronunciation, the elements of tone and rhyme, so important for Chinese poetry, were lost. Nevertheless, a skilled Japanese writer in *kanbun* was expected to compose Chinese prose and poetry according to the Chinese rules of tone and rhyme. Since nothing in the Japanese pronunciation corresponded to tone and rhyme in the Chinese original, the Japanese needed guidebooks to tell them what characters rhymed with what. In fact, by the end of the T'ang Dynasty, most Chinese themselves needed handbooks of rhyme and tone in order to write poetry correctly, because the language had changed so much since the time when rhyme and tone were codified.[7]

Chinese poetry is allusive and allegorical. To become proficient in it, one has to be constantly studying the vast corpus of past Chinese literature, always tracking down the source of an allusion for its original meaning as well as the subsequent history of any usage that colored the nuance it later came to carry. Because of the importance of allusion to such poetry, early on in China, handbooks were compiled of words and allusions sanctioned by classical precedent. For use in Zen verse, the early Japanese Zen monks also made their own, such as *Jōwashū* (*Collection of the Jōwa Era*, 1347), in which the Zen poet-monk Gidō Shūshin (1325–1388) collected some 3,000 poems by Chinese monks (Dainippon Bukkyō Zensho, 1953). The handbook, which was the most useful for the composition of poetry, was the *Shūbun inryaku* (*Classified Rhymes*) compiled in 5 fascicles by Kokan Shiren in 1306 (Kimura 1995). In this text, approximately 8,000 *kanji* were categorized according to rhyme-tone class and then within each class the *kanji* were further divided according to meaning under such categories as Heaven and Earth, Season, Plants, Food and Clothing, Artifacts, and others. For each *kanji* there was attached a short explanation and some example compounds. For looking up the flat/oblique tone and rhyme class of *kanji* when they were composing poetry, this dictionary proved to be so useful that apparently the *Shūbun inryaku* was the equivalent of a best-seller in its time; it was widely circulated in several sizes including a small portable edition and a larger edition with a wide margin at the top for notes (Sanae 1996, 582).

A great many such poetry handbooks were produced in the time from the Kamakura period through the early Edo period, early ones handwritten and later versions printed, some with identifiable authors, others whose authors are anonymous, some with nothing but the Chinese characters and others with varying degrees of annotative information. Noteworthy among these books is the *Tentetsushū* (reprinted in Yanagida 2000), which was clearly a predecessor to the *Zenrin kushū*, the Zen capping phrase book. The *Tentetsushū*, 25 Fascicles in ten volumes, compiled by Gyakuō Sōjun (1433–88) in 1485, was a huge compilation of 4-character, 5-character and 7-character couplets from both Buddhist and non-Buddhist sources. In this, the largest of the poetry composition books, approximately 43,000 verses were categorized in rhyme classes with headnotes citing original sources (Sanae 1996, 583; Iriya 1996, 572).

DIALECT BOOKS, *HŌGO*. Among early Zen phrase books were a class called *hōgo*, a term that literally means "local speech." The Zen kōan collections and the records of the Zen patriarchs contain numerous examples of Chinese vulgar, colloquial, or dialect language which the Japanese monks did not understand and for which they required an explanation. Numerous phrases in the *Zenrin kushū* cite *hōgo* in the headnote followed by an explanation. Phrase 4.122 is *Mimi o ōte suzu o nusumu*, "He covers his ears to steal the bell." The headnote explains it as *hōgo* for *Donzoku*, "A clumsy thief." Phrase 4.192 is *Reiki o o hiku*, "The spirit turtle sweeps its tail." The headnote identifies it as *hōgo* for *Ato o haratte ato o shōzu*, "Erasing traces creates traces." Phrase 4.230 is *Jisa jiju*, "Make it yourself, receive it yourself." The *hōgo* headnote gives the nuance: *Shōnin kase o tsukuru*, "The master carpenter makes his own fetters." Inevitably dictionary-like collections were made listing such vulgar, dialectic, and colloquial phrases with accompanying explanations. Two kinds of *hōgo* text were compiled in Japan: those based on the Chinese and learned by the Japanese monks who had gone to China during the Sung and Yüan periods, and those compiled during the Ming and Ching periods, when Ōbaku sect monks from China arrived in Japan (Sanae 1996, 586).

Whereas poetry composition guidebooks helped the Japanese Zen monks learn the classical high culture of T'ang and Sung China, the *hōgo* colloquial language guidebooks helped them learn the language of low culture. The Japanese scholar of the T'ang-period colloquial Chinese, Iriya Yoshitaka, charges that although the first generation of monks who compiled *hōgo* guidebooks knew they were dealing with colloquial language, in succeeding generations most Japanese Zen monks were probably incapable of distinguishing between classical literary language and vulgar colloquial language. He says that not only did Japanese Zen monks mistakenly take Chinese colloquialisms as Zen technical terminology, they also used the strange-sounding Japanified Chinese as their house trademark in an elitist attempt to distinguish themselves from other schools of Buddhism (Iriya 1996, 567).

The First Capping Phrase Collections: Daitō Kokushi's Record, Kuzōshi (Phrase Notebook), and Zenrin kushū (Zen Sangha Phrase Collection)

At some point in the evolution of Rinzai kōan practice, the practice of appending capping phrases became a formal part of the kōan curriculum. Exactly when this happened and under what circumstances is unclear. In any case, at some point in the history of kōan training every monk in his individual practice was expected to emulate the great T'ang and Sung Chinese masters in appending a capping phrase that expressed his insight into a particular kōan. At this point, a capping phrase book became necessary. In Zen monasteries it is often said that in the past (*mukashi*, whenever that was), Zen monks were well educated and could compose their own Chinese verse capping phrases. By contrast, modern-day monks, bereft of classical learning, are said to be incapable of composing poetry and need a handbook from which they merely choose an appropriate verse.

However, it is also possible to think that the cause-and-effect relation was reversed and the very availability of a Zen phrase book made possible the incorporation of the capping phrase exercise into the Rinzai kōan practice. If so, then the capping phrase exercise probably became incorporated into Rinzai kōan practice, first, when the number of phrases in Zen phrase books grew large enough to support *jakugo* practice, and second, when it became technically possible to publish Zen phrase books cheaply and in large numbers. Whatever the case, the incorporation of the *jakugo* exercise into Rinzai kōan practice and the development of Zen phrase books containing the *jakugo* in all likelihood were two parts of the same process.

DAITŌ KOKUSHI'S RECORD. The *Record of Daitō* contains Daitō Kokushi's commentaries to kōan in which he expresses his responses through more than 2,000 capping phrases spread throughout the *Record*. In his capping phrases he both quotes traditional Zen phrases, applying them to new situations, and composes new *jakugo* of his own. In a text entitled simply *Hyakunijussoku* (*One*

Hundred and Twenty Cases), Daitō selected this number of kōans and appended interlinear *jakugo*. In another text, entitled *Hekigan agyo* (*Hekigan Capping Phrases*), he has substituted his own for the *jakugo* appended by both Setchō and Engo to the 100 cases of the *Hekiganroku*. Significant for a history of the Zen phrase book, an untitled, undated, and unsigned manuscript containing a collection of about 900 capping phrases has been attributed to Daitō. If this manuscript was indeed compiled by Daitō Kokushi, it would rank as the first capping phrase collection in Japan, predating Tōyō Eichō's *Kuzōshi* by approximately 150 years (Kraft 1992, 210–212; Hirano 1988).

TŌYŌ EICHŌ'S *KUZŌSHI*. The document attributed to Daitō Kokushi exists only as a single unidentified and fragmented text; it does not appear to be a handbook used by monks appending phrases to kōans as a regular assignment in kōan practice. The first collection of Zen phrases to be used for appending *jakugo* were probably the *Kuzōshi* compiled at the end of the 1400s by Tōyō Eichō Zenji (1426–1504) and the *Zenrin kushū* compiled in 1688 by Ijūshi (n.d.). These two texts need to be discussed together even though they were created more than 150 years apart. There is quite a bit of looseness in the use of titles and in attribution of authorship in both these texts. Both the terms *Kuzōshi* and *Zenrin kushū* have been used as general titles for all monastic capping phrase books. Tōyō Eichō, who lived in the 1400s, is often said to be the editor of the *Zenrin kushū*, which was compiled in the 1600s.[8]

Tōyō Eichō Zenji (1426–1504), who received *inka* from Sekkō Sōshin and was abbot at both Daitokuji and Myōshinji temples, founded the temple Shōtakuji and established the Shōtaku sublineage within the Myōshinji line. He compiled his collection of Zen phrases originally under the title *Kuzōshi*, but the exact date is uncertain. It is hard to identify an event that corresponds to its "publication" in either the sense of the completion of a printed copy or the making of it into a public document. Kawase estimates that the *Kuzōshi* was probably completed after Bunmei, that is, after 1486 (Kawase 1942, 120). Before the *Kuzōshi*, however, Tōyō Eichō compiled some earlier collections, called the *Zensen* (*First Arrow*) and the *Gosen* (*Later Arrow*),[9] a fact indicating that for Tōyō Eichō the compiling of Zen phrases was a continuing project, one perhaps without a clearly defined end. All of these versions were written by hand and most likely were shown originally only to a small number of disciples.[10]

By the time of Tōyō Eichō, the Rinzai kōan curriculum may have evolved to the point where monks were being required to append *jakugo* to kōans. However, his *Kuzōshi* contains only a few more than 1,200 phrases. If the *Kuzōshi* was being used as a handbook to support a *jakugo* practice, the small number of phrases itself is evidence that the *jakugo* practice could not have been very detailed or developed.

The *Kuzōshi* was compiled more than 500 years ago, and in the centuries that immediately followed its appearance it served as the model for numerous other versions, which copied it, expanded upon it, or otherwise imitated it in some fashion (including the Portuguese *Amakusaban Qincuxu*, mentioned earlier). Many generations of copies and variations of the original text were made, frequently entitled *Kuzōshi* or *Kuzōshishō* (*Annotated Kuzōshi*). The variant *Kuzōshi* texts display a great many differences. Some versions provide full readings, usually in *katakana* along with margin symbols to indicate the order of reading of characters. Others provide only margin symbols and the *katakana* for a few verb endings and difficult *kanji*.[11]

ZENRIN KUSHŪ (ZEN SANGHA PHRASE COLLECTION). The *Zenrin kushū*, a much larger collection of Zen phrases, may be considered "the revised standard version" of Zen capping phrase books. In 1688, almost 200 years after Tōyō Eichō compiled the *Kuzōshi*, a scholar-monk who identified himself only as Ijūshi created a greatly expanded Zen phrase collection consisting of approximately 4,380 phrases (I say "approximately" because some phrases occur twice, some couplets are simply the same as other couplets but in reverse order, some phrases are simply slight one-character variants of others, etc.). He appended commentary that supplied both original sources and explanations of meaning for many of the phrases, and he changed the title of the collection to *Zenrin kushū*. The annotation and headnotes cite kōan cases in the *Hekiganroku* and *Mumonkan* where that particular phrase is used as an *agyo*, thus showing that at that time the *Zenrin kushū* must have been used in conjunction with kōan practice. The large number of phrases and the sheer volume of detailed information in the annotations are evidence that the Rinzai kōan practice in the mid-1600s was organized into some sort of curriculum and that the appending of *jakugo* was part of that practice. Even now it is still used as one of the main capping phrase collections although more than 300 years have elapsed since the time of Ijūshi.

Ijūshi, the editor of the *Zenrin kushū*, attached a postscript, which gives us a little idea of the provenance of this text.

> This collection of material from previous sources was compiled by Tōyō Eichō Zenji, seventh-generation descendant of Kanzan Kokushi, the founder of the [Myōshinji temple] in Hanazono. Eichō made meritorious contribution to the [Zen] school and created an independent line. He may be deemed a master teacher of the profound truth who had the one eye in his forehead and with it illuminated the world, who raised high the single horn of the *ch'i-lin* and extended the claws and teeth of a lion. Consequently the circulation of this collection in the world has been met with great appreciation.
>
> The entirety of this material is what is first learned by those who study in the Zen forest. It is like entering the Elementary Learning in Confucian study. If one has read it in its entirety, will

not one have a ladder for viewing all texts? Nonetheless if one wants to use them in composing literary works, one is often frustrated at not being able to find the original source of these phrases.

I first studied the Confucian classics and in midlife donned the black robes, seeking instruction in the courtyard of the Patriarchs. But now, as the years have been unlucky and the times untoward, I have once again returned to Confucian studies. In order to repay my debt for having received instruction from many fine Zen teachers, I have noted the original sources [for the phrases] and at the end of the phrases have added another five hundred. In its entirety, there are six thousand phrases. I call it *The Zen Phrase Miscellany*. I have also made a separate collection in five fascicles which I call *Gold Chips from the Dense Forest, Arranged According to Rhyme*. Selected prose and poetry from numerous authors, outstanding phrases from all works of world-class reputation, single phrases and couplets used as common Zen sayings, all have been selected and compiled here for the benefit of later generations of students.

In the *Zen Phrase Miscellany* mentioned above, there are passages from Buddhist *sūtras*, records of the Patriarchs, Taoist texts, Confucian canon, prose and poetry of numerous authors. Though I have noted their original source, in most cases the phrase compiled here is from a later text. Where the original has been abbreviated and a later version recorded, I have avoided variant characters. In the *Huai-nan tzu*, it says, "That there was a beginning implies there was also a time when there was not 'There was a beginning.'" I have recklessly insisted on adding addition to addition the way this phrase does and, without restraining my runaway tongue, appended my own opinions. Nevertheless the elbow does not bend outward. So far, phrases whose original source still remains unclear number five or six out of a hundred, so I await future scholars of great wisdom. Those who pretend more than they know will not escape punishment for their sins. But for students of Zen who study its many records, my work may not be lacking in usefulness.

1688 Feast Day of the New Year
At Sengu Sanpu in Rakuhashi
Respectfully
Ijūshi[12]

Ijūshi's postscript clearly identifies the two elements that kōan training brings together: the direct insight of awakening ("the one eye in his forehead [which] illuminated the world") and the literary study of texts. Although Ijūshi says the literary study required of entrants to the Zen *sangha* is comparable to the elementary learning in Confucian studies, there is nothing elementary about such study if the contents of the *Zenrin kushū* provide any standard. To learn how to read with the eyes of Zen, understanding the thousands of phrases culled from hundreds of original sources, must have required years, perhaps decades, of both meditation practice and literary study. Through the ritual flowery humility of his language, one can see that monastic training in Ijūshi's time must have been conducted at a quite rigorous level.

What conclusions can we draw from the internal evidence presented here? First, Ijūshi set himself a task, the identification of the original sources from which *jakugo* phrases were taken. The texts that he used did not contain that information. Second, both the *Kuzōshi* and the *Zenrin kushū* use the same ordering system. The phrases are ordered according to number of characters as follows: 1-character, 2-character, 3-character, 4-character, 5-character single verses, 5-character couplets, 6-character, 6-character couplets, 7-character, 7-character couplets, 8-character single verses, and 8-character couplets. Third, although the earlier *Kuzōshi* contains only about 1,200 phrases and the later *Zenrin kushū* contains about 4,380, almost all the phrases of the *Kuzōshi* reappear in the *Zenrin kushū* and—interestingly—in much the same order but separated by interjected phrases. Finally, in the later and larger *Zenrin kushū*, verses and phrases of a similar topic tend to be clustered together. For example, in the 4-character phrase section, phrases 70–83 deal with sin, guilt, law and judgment; phrases 133–144 deal with thieves; phrases 286–289 all contain repeated characters; phrases 290–304 are about doing things twice unnecessarily; phrases 347–351 are about the perfect harmony of matching actions, and so on. What accounts for this crude clustering of phrases? What picture can we draw about the development of Zen phrase books here?

Here is a scenario. In the early period of Rinzai kōan practice, probably only a very few advanced monks were engaged in kōan *jakugo* practice while the great majority did just meditation. These advanced monks most likely kept a *sanzen* record of their meetings with the Zen master, a handwritten private notebook strictly for their own personal use, and when they were asked for *jakugo*, they kept a private record of these as well. Not being scholars, they were not meticulous in recording the original sources for the phrases; since they were monks in practice, their interest was in the meaning of the phrase itself as a lens to view a kōan. Each monk kept his own collection of *jakugo* a secret, showing it, if at all, only to a younger brother disciple from the same temple. The younger monk would copy the senior monk's collection of *jakugo* to use as the basis for his own *jakugo* practice. If he learned a new phrase on the theme of thieves, he would most likely note the new phrase in the margin next to an already present phrase about thieves; if he learned a new phrase on the theme of doing things twice unnecessarily, he would most likely note that in the margin next to an already existent phrase on the same theme. When the next generation of younger monks hand-copied this notebook with all its margin notes and paper inserts, the copier would incorporate the margin phrases directly into the body of his new text. In this way the original phrases of the *Kuzōshi* would retain their original order but become separated as more and more phrases were inserted between them, and so in some places a rough clustering of phrases around topics would naturally result.

With repeated copying, another kind of change took place as well. Originally each monk's collection of *jakugo* was a personal record and kept secret. As the book got copied by successive generations, the originally secret handbook evolved into a public reference book. Printers got hold of some of these books and sold copies of the *jakugo* collection, making it easily available to anyone. About the same time, Zen masters recognized the value of a sourcebook of capping phrases and made the *jakugo* exercise a requirement not just for the advanced few but for all monks in kōan practice. This is how the *jakugo* exercise got incorporated into kōan practice. At least, this is the scenario as I imagine it. This is all speculation until some enterprising scholar finally uncovers the history of the *jakugo* practice in Japanese Rinzai Zen. But I fully expect two events will be seen as linked together as two parts of the same process: the incorporation of the *jakugo* exercise into kōan practice, and the development of Zen phrase books.

Since the *Zenrin kushū* is still consulted by present-day monks in training, several versions are presently available. For the practicing Zen monk, a pocketbook-size Meiji 27 (1894) reprint is available from Baiyō shoin, the Buddhist text printer in Kyoto. For academic study, the Zen bunka kenkyūjo (Research Institute for Zen Culture) at Hanazono University has published a Meiji 19 (1886) reprinting with character index. Many more Zen phrase collections were made in the centuries after Ijūshi, but his *Zenrin kushū* was considered the authoritative edition and it continued to be reprinted. Used bookstores still turn up copies of old handbound woodblock print editions whose pages are made of thin mulberry paper folded in half.

Twentieth-Century Capping Phrase Collections

Three Zen phrase books meant for *jakugo* practice have been compiled in the twentieth century. It is inevitable that such new *jakugo* collections would appear, for at least two reasons. First, there is gradual change. Zen masters in every generation add a new phrase or two and drop an old phrase or two from the corpus. Thus the *Zenrin kushū* by Ijūshi, which may have been appropriate for the Rinzai kōan system at the end of the 1600s, is no longer adequate for the Rinzai kōan system in the twenty-first century. In addition to such gradual change, there is also radical systematic change. Hakuin is said to have revised the entire traditional kōan practice in the eighteenth century and forged it into the present system. The new systematized kōan responses, which Hakuin accepted as correct, must surely have caused all teaching rōshi to revise their lists of correct *jakugo*. There is also a third factor which I am in no position to judge at present. The Hakuin lineage divided into two sublineages, the Inzan and the Takujū. Though they both teach the Zen of Hakuin, they have developed slightly different sets of responses for their kōan, and consequently slightly different sets of *jakugo*.

ZUDOKKO KUSHŪ (*POISON PAINTED DRUM* PHRASE COLLECTION). The *Zudokko* (*Poison Painted Drum*) is a two-volume Zen monk's handbook compiled by Fujita Genro (1880–1935), a layman who trained under Takeda Mokurai Rōshi of the Kenninji monastery in Kyoto. Though a small-format handbook, the *Zudokko* is an enormous resource containing almost all the documents necessary for Rinzai practice: all the major kōan collections including the *Hekiganroku*, the *Mumonkan*, the *Kattōshū* (*Tangled Vine Collection*), and the *Chin'ushū* (*Collection of Poisonous Wings*); the entire *kanji* text of the *Rinzai roku* and the *Kidō Daibetsugo* (*The Alternate Phrases of Kidō Oshō*, an advanced kōan text); excerpts from the records of the Zen Patriarchs and from Hakuin's writings; and many other Zen documents. The *Zudokko* was originally published by Kenninji monastery. Fujita's Afterword to the second volume is dated Taishō 11 (1922), which will be taken here as its year of publication. The title—*Zudokko* (*Poison Painted Drum*)—symbolizes the effects on learners of these Zen teachings. The skin of the drum of Zen is painted with a virulent poison taken from the wing of the poison blackbird; when the drum is beaten, all who hear it die.

Fujita Genro was born Fujita Tokujirō in 1880 in Naniwa, Osaka Prefecture, and from an early age showed a strong interest in Buddhism. After graduating from high school, he made his way to Kyoto, where in 1900 he came into contact with Takeda Mokurai Rōshi. He left Japan in 1905 to study at New York University as a foreign student and returned to Japan in 1908 (ZGDJT 1073c; Obata 1938 624–626). He was part of a successful business family which is still active in commerce and arts today. His layman's name, Genro, conferred by Takeda Mokurai Rōshi, is probably taken from the line in the *Nandō benken jūmon* (*Nandō's Ten Examination Gates*), "You must go by the dark path [genro] of the flying bird," *Subekaraku chōdō no genro o yukubeshi* (in vol. 2 of *Zudokko*). The dark path is the path of one who leaves no traces, just as a bird leaves no traces in its path of flight. The two Afterwords which he wrote for the two volumes of the *Zudokko* are written in lines of 4-character verse in the so-called "horse-hoof style" (*bateikei*, because a galloping horse leaves hoofprints in series of four), probably in a deliberate imitation of the style of the opening preface to the *Rinzai roku*. They make numerous allusions to the Chinese classics and display the self-effacing ironic style of Zen writing. They show that Genro had progressed to quite an advanced stage of kōan practice and that he was also a serious scholar of the Chinese classics.

At the end of the second volume of the *Zudokko* is a section entitled simply *Kushū*, "Phrase Collection." This collection contains 2,397 phrases categorized according to the number of characters. Only the characters are printed. No *kanbun* margin symbols are provided; no readings are given; there is no commentary providing citation of source or explanation of meaning. As Takeda Mokurai says in the Foreword to the second volume, "Companion on the way, layman Genro is the author of the *Poison Painted Drum.* He has snatched up the many poisons of our school and flung them at the faces of people. He gives no reading for any character; he gives no annotation for any phrase. He does this out of the goodness of his grandmotherly heart." Some Zen priests argue that the *Zudokko kushū* is thus the best text to use in searching for *jakugo,* since one confronts the bare *kanji* without the interference of margin symbols and annotation. But practitioners consider the *Zudokko kushū* hard to use for the same reasons—it does not provide these aids to assist the reader.

ZENGOSHŪ (ZEN PHRASE COLLECTION). Layman Tsuchiya Etsudō compiled the *Shinsan Zengoshū* (*A New Compilation of the Zen Phrase Collection*) under the direction of Unkankutsu Shaka Taibi Rōshi (1973). This collection contains 3,040 phrases, categorized by number of characters in each phrase. Within each category, the verses or phrases are arranged according to the Japanese reading, not according to the Chinese character. That is, they are arranged in a-i-u-e-o order according to the *yomikudashi* reading, not according to the *on-yomi* reading of the first character of each phrase. Although the full *yomikudashi* reading is not given, the usual *kanbun* margin symbols indicate the order for reading the characters. There are no explanations of meanings and no citations of sources.

Tsuchiya Etsudō (1899–1978) was born Tsuchiya Kiichi in Tochigi Prefecture. He was a mathematics teacher and during his teaching career had been principal of several local schools. He probably first came into contact with Zen while teaching in the town of Nasu in Tochigi Prefecture, where one of the senior teachers at the same school was a teaching disciple of the well-known Zen monk Nantenbō. At about the beginning of the Shōwa period (late 1920s) Tsuchiya moved to the city of Ashikaga to teach at the Ashikaga Prefectural Middle School and joined the Ashikaga Zendōkai *zazen* group, where he became a disciple of its teacher, Unkankutsu Shaku Taibi Rōshi (1889–1970), a Dharma successor to the well-known Meiji-period rōshi, Shaku Sōen (1859–1919). Tsuchiya received the layman's name of Etsudō during a *sesshin* (intensive meditation) with Taibi Rōshi in November 1930.

Taibi Rōshi led the Suigetsu Dōjo of the Ashikaga Zendōkai from 1925 until his death in 1970, a remarkably long period of forty-five years. Since Tsuchiya Etsudō formally became a disciple to Taibi Rōshi in 1930, they were related as master to student for more than forty years. During this fortuitious coming together of a long-time student with a long-time teacher, Tsuchiya Etsudō had time to compile a Zen phrase book that would overcome what he considered the two faults of the *Zudokko kushū*—its lack of margin symbols and *kana* to indicate how the phrases were to be read into Japanese, and the fact that it contained only 2,397 phrases, a number insufficient for the *jakugo* practice he was doing with Taibi Rōshi. According to anecdotal evidence from Asanō Genjū, the leader of the Ashikaga Zendōkai in 1998, Tsuchiya combed the Chinese classical literature for phrases and verses suitable for use as *jakugo*. These he would take to Taibi Rōshi, who would either approve or disapprove. Over a period of many years Tsuchiya kept adding to his collection of phrases and verses. The final version of his *Zengoshū* contains 3,040 phrases, almost a one-quarter increase over the 2,397 phrases of the *Zudokko kushū*. It is the largest of the three *jakugo* phrase books compiled in the twentieth century.

KUNCHŪ ZENRIN KUSHŪ (ANNOTATED ZEN SANGHA PHRASE COLLECTION) EDITED AND REVISED BY SHIBAYAMA ZENKEI RŌSHI (KICHŪŌ 1972). Shibayama Zenkei Rōshi (1894–1974) began his long career in Buddhism when, under the influence of his devout mother, he entered a Buddhist temple at age fourteen. As he grew older, he grew critical of the Buddhist institution in Japan and for a while left Buddhism for Christianity. He also studied Esperanto and became one of the best Esperanto speakers in Japan at that time. Still on the spiritual search, he heard an inspiring lecture from a rōshi, which made him decide to enter a Zen monastery in 1916. After many years of monastery training at Nanzenji, he taught as a professor at Hanazono and Ōtani Universities in Kyoto. He was invited back to the Nanzenji monastery as its Rōshi in 1948 and was elected *kanchō* or chief abbot of the entire Nanzenji line in 1959. Shibayama Rōshi became known to the West in 1965, when he took the first of several visits to the United States to present special lectures and teach *zazen* at selected universities (Kudō 1975).

Shibayama's revised version of the *Zenrin kushū* is one of the standard handbooks that Japanese Rinzai monks consult when assigned *jakugo*. The first edition of the book appeared in 1952 and, although he probably intended it for monks doing kōan practice, it also became popular with people practicing the tea ceremony and calligraphy. Consequently Shibayama produced a revised second edition in 1972, increasing the number of phrases by 300 and simplifying the ordering system. The second edition contains 2,646 phrases and verses, arranged according to number of characters within each number division, according to the *on*-reading of the first Chinese character of the phrase (and not according to the Japanese reading, as is the case in the *Zengoshū*). In addition, each phrase or verse is accompanied by a full Japanese reading written in *kana* and a short annotation or explanation. Often a source is cited. This particular text is easily the most user friendly of the several *jakugo* texts but it is also the one that attracts criticism. Some critics say that the Shibayama collection encourages monks to read the explanations and not the original phrases themselves. Others say that the explanations tend to consist of stereotypical intellectual phrases which are irritating to the practitioner who is seeking words to capture a living experience. Some monasteries actively discourage their monks from using this text.

Other Buddhist Phrase Books

Throughout the Edo period, Zen phrase books continued to appear but most were reprints or modifications of Tōyō Eichō's *Kuzōshi* or Ijūshi's *Zenrin kushū*. Sōtō sect Zen monks made similar Zen phrase books; the *Zenrin meiku jiten* compiled by Iida Rigyō is a modern-day Sōtō example (Iida 1975). There was also apparently a Jōdo-shū (Pure Land Buddhist) *Kuzōshi* (Sanae 1996, 593), although I have never seen one.

In the twentieth century there continue to be numerous published books listing and explaining Zen verses and phrases. Many are general books for the average informed reader (Matsubara 1972, Akizuki 1981, Hirata 1969, 1982). Introductory popular books on Zen sometimes contain a short section explaining Zen verses and phrases (Takahashi 1988). Because scrolls with Zen verses are so important for the tea ceremony, several books have been published especially for this readership, often giving detailed information and interesting background to Zen verses. The *Zengokushō* (*Annotated Zen Phrases*, Hekian 1982) is a useful handbook of Zen verses which indexes both the top and bottom verses of every couplet. Nishibe Bunjō's *Zengo no ajiwaikata* (*How to Savor Zen Phrases*, Nishibe 1985) and the four-volume series *Ichigyōmono* (*Scrolls in Single Lines*) by Haga Kōshiro, the respected scholar of medieval Japanese Buddhism (Haga 1973, 1974, 1977, 1984), not only list Zen phrases but also provide short explanatory lectures.

The Chinese Buddhist publishing industry similarly produces many collections of Zen phrases. I have not been able to keep up with the Chinese publication in this area, but one recent publication is noteworthy as an interesting example of reverse cultural flow, the *Ch'anlin Huiyu* (*Zen Forest Words of Wisdom*, Ling Yun, n.d.). Though compiled by Chinese authors in Taipei, it is based partly on Japanese Zen phrase books. It cites as sources Gidō Shūshin's *Jōwashū*, Hakuin's *Kaian kokugo*, Dōgen's *Shōbōgenzō* and *Eihei kōroku*, and the *Collected Poems of Natsume Sōseki*.

In English, selected phrases from the *Zenrin kushū* were translated by several writers. The earliest was probably D. T. Suzuki, whose many translations of Zen phrases are scattered throughout his voluminous corpus. R. H. Blyth in *Haiku Volume 1: Eastern Culture* gives translations of seventy-three verses in a section devoted solely to *Zenrin kushū* translations and gives translations for several other verses throughout the rest of his book (Blyth 1981, 23–33 and *passim*). *Cat's Yawn*, the short-lived (July 1940–July 1941) monthly publication of the First Zen Institute of America under Sasaki Sōkei-an, had a regular feature, the "Zenrin Collection," which gave the romanized reading of a Zen verse, its English translation, and the context from which the verse was taken (First Zen Institute of America 1947). Sōkei-an died in 1945 but his work was continued by his wife, Ruth Fuller Sasaki, who went on to establish the First Zen Institute of America in Japan, a research institute and Zen practice center at Daitokuji in Kyoto. In March 1956 she published a short selection of poems from the *Zenrin kushū* in an article, "Anthology of Zen Poems," in the Japanese journal *Zen bunka*, (no. 4, 22–26).

Then Ruth Fuller Sasaki and Isshū Miura Rōshi, in *Zen Dust*, published a translation of 210 Zen verses with original *kanji*, *romaji* reading, English translation, and occasional notes (Miura and Sasaki 1966, 79–122). This set of translations continues to be available in the shorter *The Zen Kōan* (Miura and Sasaki 1965). At the time of her death in 1967, among the many documents left in her research center were a stack of notebooks with rough notes intended for a full translation of the *Zenrin kushū*.[13] In 1981 Shigematsu Sōiku published *A Zen Forest*, an English translation of 1,234 verses with *kanji* (Shigematsu 1981). Although this remains the longest version of the Zen phrase book in English, it is interesting primarily as a sampling of Zen phrases and verse; it does not contain enough phrases and verses to serve as a handbook for *jakugo* practice. Robert E. Lewis, who is associated with the New York Zendo-Shōbō-ji, has translated *The Book of the Zen Grove*, a translation of 631 phrases, based on the Shibayama *Zenrin kushū*, with *rōmaji* readings, a commentary, indices, and a bibliography (Lewis 1996). The Pure Land scholar Inagaki Hisao has published *A Glossary of Zen Terms*, a dictionary of 5,500 terms with *kanji* and explanations (Inagaki 1991). This dictionary focuses primarily on 2-character and 4-character *kanji* compounds and set phrases. Although many longer phrases are included, this dictionary is not suitable for use as a capping phrase handbook, but its content overlaps with the 1-character to 4-character phrases of the Zen phrase book.

The Chinese Literary Game and the Kōan

Why did Buddhist meditation practice in Ch'an/Zen take the form of kōan training? Why do kōans have the characteristics they have? Authors in the Zen tradition often quote Chung-feng Ming-pen (J. Chūhō Myōhon, 1263–1323), who may have been the first to draw an analogy between the kōan and legal court case:

> The word *kung*, or "public," means that the kōans put a stop to private understanding; the word *an*, or "case records," means that they are guaranteed to accord with the buddhas and patriarchs. When these kōans are understood and accepted, then there will be an end to feeling and discrimination; when there is an end to feeling and

discrimination, birth-and-death will become empty; when birth-and-death becomes empty, the Buddha-way will be ordered. (Miura and Sasaki 1965, 6)

Foulk has recently modified this basic paradigm slightly, first by claiming that the word *kung-an* more specifically signified a brief on a magistrate's table, and second by emphasizing the element of a magistrate making a judgment (Foulk 2000, 20). Foulk in fact defines a kōan as (1) a narrative about a Zen personality from a biography or discourse record, and (2) upon which there has been some commentary or judgment. This definition is considerably narrower than other possible definitions, such as that a kōan is (1) a narrative about a Zen personality from a biography or discourse record, and (2) that it is used as an object of meditation (Foulk 2000, 27). This new definition better fits "kōan commentary" than "kōan." In any case, the legal paradigm highlights primarily the judgmental or commentarial aspect, but it is an open question whether, in either the traditional version or Foulk's version, it is really helpful for understanding how kōans actually work.

Neither the legal paradigm nor the folktale paradigm suggested by Heine explains the more central features of a kōan, such as the perplexing language, the possibility that either side can win, sudden insight, "mind-to-mind transmission," and the constant presence of *jakugo*. The more central features of the kōan become much more understandable if it is seen against the context of Chinese poetry. I argue that the paradigm for the kōan is the Chinese literary game.[14]

Chinese Literary Games

The Chinese language, like many other languages, employs parallelism, two or more lines with the same structure, rhythm, imagery, and sometimes rhyme.[15] But the nature of the Chinese language, which consists of ideographic characters and lacks inflection, makes it particularly easy to construct and display parallel verses, with the consequence that the Chinese language has a huge stock of paired verses or couplets. This fact sets the stage for the Chinese literary game called "capping phrases" or "capping verses." In a simple version of this game, one person gives the first line of a well-known couplet and challenges the other to recall the second line. Or, one person composes a verse to which the other person must compose a matching verse with parallel structure, imagery, rhythm, and so on. to form a couplet. Or, four people can compose a quatrain, each person composing one line yet striving to create an integrated 4-line poem. Or, several people can compose extended linked verse, each person composing a line of verse playing upon the rhythm, imagery, and characters of the previous verse, and so on.

Players made up many rules, such as restricting images to one theme, or imposing a certain rhyme, or using a certain Chinese character. There was usually a time limit, often determined by the burning of a short stick of incense or fixed length of a candle. One person took on the role of host and judge, setting the rules and topic of that particular game and declaring the winner. Tallies, like poker chips, kept track of wins and losses. Losers paid forfeits, such as having to drink a round, or perhaps as much as "three pints of wine" (Owen 1977, 275). Such poetry games, with their emphasis on competition, humor, repartee, and erudite on-the-spot invention, provided the entertainment both high and low at imperial banquets, excursions into the countryside, parties hosted by influential officials, and informal gatherings of literati bureaucrats in local drinking places. Poetry competitions became a feature of annual festivals such as the Double Ninth Festival, a way of deciding disputes, a means of wooing a maiden, and so on. Poetry competitions could be elegant and refined court occasions or they could be as banal as a modern karaoke party, to which they have a family resemblance. The products of these poetry competitions were not considered serious poetry, partly because the verses were composed just for entertainment and did not contain any morally uplifting message, partly because the quality of verse used was much diluted by the wine consumed by the poets (Pollack 1979). However, in the *Platform Sūtra of the Sixth Patriarch*, the fifth patriarch decides who will be his successor through a poetry competition.

When the culture of literary games was transmitted to Japan, the Japanese extended the game to create "linked verse" (*renku* or *renga*). In Japanese "linked verse," a group of poets compose a 36-, 50- or 100-verse linked poem, each poet composing a verse which continues the imagery of the previous verse and yet turns it in a new direction.[16] Pollack comments that in China, creating linking verse never lost its character as game and informal amusement, but in Japan, it was invested with an element of high seriousness and elevated to formal ceremony (Pollack 1979, Owen 1975, 116). Another variation of the literary game is *Hyakunin isshū, which is* still played in Japan, usually at the New Year. Here 100 couplets, one each from 100 Japanese poets, have been selected. The second verse of each couplet is printed on cards and arrayed between two people, usually a young lady and a young man, dressed in their New Year's best. When the teacher intones the first verse of a couplet, the young lady and the young man compete to snatch the card with the matching verse. In former times, more influenced by Confucian practices, when young men and women led very separate lives, the game in which for just a brief instant one's hand might brush the hand of a member of the opposite sex must have been thrilling indeed.

Perplexing Language

The Chinese literary game and the Zen kōan share so many features that they must be relatives. Initially, the most prominent of these shared features is their perplexing language. The language of the Zen kōan is mysterious, but so also is the language of Chinese poetry in general, and for much the same reasons— they are both full of allusion and analogy. As Lattimore has pointed out, every allusion has the character of an inside joke; it is meant to be deliberately puzzling except to those who are insiders to the allusion (Lattimore 1973, 405). As the very word "allusion" shows, masking the object of reference is done with a ludic attitude, in the spirit of play. A good allusion masks but also reveals its object of reference in a clever way such that the dawning revelation brings pleasure to the reader or listener of the verse.

Allusion packs a poem with hidden meaning. In Chinese literature, a single name such as that of an ancient virtuous emperor like Yao or Shun, a tragic beauty like Yang Kuei, a valiant warrior like General Li Kuang, a vicious scoundrel like Chieh, the ruler who brought the Chou to downfall, could evoke a wealth of associations, since such personages were the heroes of many stories, legends, and poems. Also, common words that acquired set connotations and common images were invested with special conventional meanings. Bamboo connoted uprightness and integrity; pines connoted endurance and fortitude; plums connoted freshness, youth, and feminine beauty. A "nomad's flute" was always understood to be sad. A "monkey's cry" was an image for terrible loneliness. "Clouds and rain" referred to sexual intercourse. "Flowing sands" referred to the desolate desert frontier. Very ordinary words could evoke profound associations. For example, the phrase "three persons" reminded the literate reader of Confucius' famous saying, "Where three persons go, for certain there will be a teacher for me" (*Analects* VII, 21). In addition, the meaning of any term included not only its original meaning in its first use but also its use in allusion by later poets. The long custom of allusion in Chinese poetry worked like compound interest, multiplying allusions by allusions, all of which became part of the cloud of associations that clung to any term.

If the structure of analogy is "A1 is to A2 as B1 is to B2," then analogy can be said to run throughout Chinese thought and literature. The Chinese division of all phenomena into yin or yang works upon an analogy. As dark is to light, then so also are night to day, winter to summer, north to south, inside to outside, and so on. As female is to male, so also are softness to hardness, moisture to dryness, water to earth, moon to sun. Analogical thinking in the Chinese tradition is much more than seeing resemblances between different phenomena. Analogical connections were thought to give causal explanation. Why is it that the rivers overflow their banks and flood the earth? It is because the emperor dallies too much with his concubines. In both these phenomena, the yin element (waters of the river, the concubines) overpower the yang element (the earth, the emperor). Therefore to stop the flooding, the emperor must reduce the power of the yin element and he does so by evicting some concubines. The analogy between flooding and the emperor's behavior, at first mysterious, becomes immediately understandable once one sees that yin–yang thought establishes a resemblance between them.[17] Allusion and analogy are the general features of Chinese literature at work in the Zen kōan, making it an incomprehensible cipher to those not steeped in the literary world of Chinese symbol and metaphor, history and legend. Allusion refers to a subject without naming it. An early predecessor to the capping verse game was the making and guessing of riddles, a kind of charade in literary form. The practice used a verse form called *yung-wu*, "writing poetry about an object," or *fu-te*, "writing a poem on a topic received" (Pollack 1976, 38, 39) without mentioning its name. The host would give each person a slip of paper with a word, perhaps the name of a household object like "broom" or "bucket," perhaps the name of an animal like "dragon" or "tiger." One tried to compose a clever verse that referred to the object but stumped the others from guessing.

Some of the verses that have found their way into Zen phrase books resemble these riddle verses.

> *Tasukatte wa dankyō no mizu o sugi,*
> *Tomonatte mugetsu no mura ni kaeru.*

> Supported by it, I cross the water where the bridge is broken;
> Accompanied by it, I return to the village without moon. (ZS 10.317)

Here "it" is a traveler's staff, which is unnamed but which anyone steeped in Chinese literature would know, and, of course, the staff, an object much used in Zen kōans, is itself a symbol for a further unnamed object in Zen.

> *Himo kore yori e,*
> *Sabutsu mo mata ta ni shitagau.*

> Furred creatures are gotten from this,
> Making a Buddha depends on that. (ZRKS 10.65)

> *Ikitari matsu no kukkyoku,*
> *Hofutsutari ishi no ranpan.*

> Like the pine, it's crooked,
> As is the stone, it's mottled. (ZRKS 10.132)

In English translation, "this," "that," and "it" allude to an unmentioned object. In a Zen context, what would that unnamed object be?

In both Chinese literature and Zen circles, it was considered inelegant literary form to speak directly of important things. One spoke in the language of metaphors, which were always based on some analogy. Standard Chinese poetic images such as "pure wind" and "bright moon" take on another meaning

in Zen. One could say boldly, "Form is emptiness and emptiness is form," but
it is far more elegant to say:

Seifū meigetsu o harai,
Meigetsu seifū o harau.

The pure wind skims the bright moon,
The bright moon skims the pure wind. (ZS 10.279)

In philosophical explanation, one can say that in emptiness all duality is overcome and in form all duality is resurrected.[18] But one can avoid such tedious
technical language by saying:

Shunshoku ni kōge naku,
Kashi onozukara tancho.

In spring colors, there is neither high nor low,
The flowering branches are by nature some long, some short. (ZS 10.252)

In Chinese, a "wooden man" is a puppet, a "stone woman" is a barren woman
incapable of bearing children, but in Zen, these negative connotations are
made to connote something positive. One could say in plodding prose that in
the no-self of Zen the ups and downs of daily life are effortlessly accomplished.
But to avoid such clumsiness, one says:

Bokujin yahan ni kutsu o ugachisari,
Sekijo tenmei ni bō o itadaite kaeru.

Putting on his shoes, the wooden man went away at midnight,
Wearing her bonnet, the stone woman returned at dawn. (ZS 14.26)

Allusive language and analogical meaning in Chinese literature drew a
line between those who had inside knowledge and those who did not. The
skillful poet thus displayed his great knowledge of allusion and analogy while
simultaneously concealing his true intentions to anyone who knew only the
literal meaning of his words. If the listener did not understand all the allusions
and analogical implications in a verse, then he could not know if he was being
silently ridiculed. If the listener did understand, then he could compliment
himself on his own erudition.

In addition, for any group that reveres texts of the past, allusion to those
revered texts is like citation of authority. Any individual who makes such allusion implies that he is not voicing his own individual opinion but repeating
the wisdom of the ancients. At the same time, the entire group reinforces its
sense of "corporate legitimacy" by demonstrating its continued link with the
great textual authorities of the past (Lattimore 1973, 411).

These features are clearly at work in Zen texts. Kōan after kōan depicts
one Zen monk testing the clarity of another's eye through the skillful use of

such allusive language and analogical meaning in the language of "sound of one hand," "your original face before your mother and father were born," "coming from the West," "three pounds of flax," "wash your bowl," "the cypress tree in the front garden." Mastery of the allusive and analogical language of Zen is taken as one of the marks of an awakened one. By so speaking, he speaks not his personal opinions but the secret truth of enlightenment itself.

Competition between Equal Partners

Both the players in a literary game and the dialogue partners in a kōan think of themselves as equal combatants engaged in a competition, which they liken to military combat. They win, they lose. They engage in strategy, feigning, probing, using surprise, and so on. Engo Kokugon's *agyo* to the various kōans in the *Hekiganroku* clearly adopt the military metaphor. "He carries out his strategy from within his tent" (*Hekiganroku* case 4, Main Case *agyo*); "He gives up his first position and falls back to his second" (*Hekiganroku* case 10, Main Case *agyo*), "When you kill someone, make sure you see the blood" (*Hekiganroku* case 31, Main Case *agyo*), "The sword that kills people, the sword that gives life" (*Hekiganroku* case 34, Main Case *agyo*), "He captures the flag and steals the drum" (*Hekiganroku* case 38, Main Case *agyo*).

The partners in a kōan dialogue joust with each other knowing that they each have an equal chance of beating the other. They are not like judge and defendant in a court case, who are quite unequal in status and power, and where the judge always has the last word.

"Reversing the Other's Spear"

The criterion of a good win in both the literary game and the kōan are the same: surprise, deception, improvising on the spot, and "reversing the other's spear." Harada Kenyū comments on the poetry of Han Yü thus:

> The task in linked-verse poetry is to take the opponent unaware. In doing this the writer himself is compelled by unforeseen detours, overhangs, obstacles, and abrupt changes in rhythm. There is not time for either omissions or repetitions. Rather, by turning the tables on the handicaps brought by chance or the difficulties one's opponent has thrown at one, a veritable storm of associations is stirred up.[19]

In poetry composition, especially in the context of the imperial examinations, men's characters were judged and their careers were often determined on the basis of quick wit and ability to improvise on the spot (Pollack 1976, 100). The same abilities are highly valued in the Zen kōan. In a kōan dialogue, monk and master probe each other with disguised allusions, trick questions, and baited traps. To show skill in kōan dialogue is also to turn the tables against the opponent. An important phrase in the everyday vocabulary of a Zen monastery is *rinki ōhen*, "on the spot improvisation."

When a monk asks Baso, "Without getting involved in the 'four propositions and the hundred negations,' show me directly the point of Bodhidharma's coming from the West," Baso smoothly replies, "I'm tired today and can't explain for you" (*Hekiganroku* case 73 Main Case). The monk took this answer as a refusal to give an answer and did not recognize that this apparent refusal itself was a direct presentation of the point of coming from the West. The monk takes Baso's answer as if it were a descriptive when actually it is a performative. The case is much like replying to the question, "What is amnesia?" with the answer "I forget." The answer taken descriptively is a refusal to answer, but taken performatively it is an actual example of what the question asks for. In admiration for the fact that Baso has deceived the monk so skillfully, Engo comments in *agyo*, "The monk stumbled past without recognizing it" (*Hekiganroku* case 73, Main Case *agyo*). A truly skillful poet recognizes his opponent's strategy, turns it around, and uses it to deceive his opponent. When Zen monks do this, the feat is called "Taking the other's own spear and turning it around" (*Hekiganroku* case 35, Main Case *agyo*, *Hekiganroku* case 38, Main Case *agyo*, *Hekiganroku* case 46, Main Case *agyo*) or "mounting the bandit's horse to pursue him" (*Hekiganroku* case 59, Main Case *agyo*). When, for example, a monk says to Joshū, "As soon as there are words and speech, this is picking and choosing," Joshū asks, "Why don't you quote this saying in full," skillfully luring the monk into words and speech. Here Engo's *agyo* is "He mounts the bandit's horse and pursues the bandit" (*Hekiganroku* case 59, Main Case *agyo*).

"Mind-to-Mind Transmission"

The Chinese literary game and the Zen kōan share a similar conception of "mind-to-mind transmission" or *ishin denshin*. If Zen is "not founded on words and letters," then it cannot be transmitted from one person to another through verbal explanation or intellectual interpretation. Nevertheless the Zen tradition attaches great importance to the transmission of the Dharma from master to disciple. If that transmission is not done verbally, then it must be done "mind to mind." The story of Śākyamuni holding up a flower (*Hekiganroku* case 6) provides the archetype. Śākyamuni was surrounded by an assembly who gathered to hear a discourse on the Dharma. He merely held up a flower instead of speaking. No one reacted except his first disciple, Kāśyapa, who broke into a smile. Śākyamuni replied, "I have the all-pervading True Dharma, incomparable nirvāṇa, exquisite teaching of formless form. It does not rely on letters and is transmitted outside scriptures. I now hand it to Mahākāśyapa" (adapted from Shibayama 1974, 59). To most people this story emphasizes clearly that transmission in Zen has nothing to do with language, that realization in Zen is "not founded on words and letters." But the notion of a mind-to-mind transmission outside of language does not originate with Zen; Zen got it from Chinese literati culture, the culture founded on words and letters.

In Chinese literature in general, because of the heavy use of allusion and analogy, much language says one thing in words and another thing in meaning. In the Chinese literary game, if nothing is said directly and all is said indirectly through allusion and analogy, ultimately there is emotional satisfaction in the game only if one's opponent has the same skill and shares the same learned repertoire of literary knowledge. In such learned play, although the two game players are opponents, they are also partners in a very special way. The game is best played when the opponent partners are so well matched that each understands the other's use of images, allusions, and turns of phrase without requiring anything to be explained or deciphered.[20]

In the Confucian literati tradition, such an intimate friend was called a *chiin* (C. *chih-yin*), a term whose characters literally mean "knower of sound." The term refers to the story of Po Ya, who played the *ch'in*, a stringed musical instrument like a lute, and his intimate friend, Chung Tzu-ch'i. Po Ya was a good lute player and Chung Tzu-ch'i was a good listener:

> Po Ya strummed his lute, with his mind on climbing high moun
> tains and Chung Tzu-ch'i said: "Good. Lofty like Mount T'ai!" When
> his mind was on flowing waters, Chung Tzu-ch'i said: "Good!
> Boundless like the Yellow River and the Yangtse!" Whatever came
> into Po Ya's thoughts, Chung Tzu-ch'i always grasped it. (Graham
> 1986, 109–110; see also Dewoskin 1982, 105)

Although this story appears in the Lieh-tzu, usually considered a Taoist text, the story of Po Ya and Tzu-ch'i spread throughout Confucian literati culture because ritual and music were the last two of the six arts of Confucian self-cultivation, and the ability to play the *ch'in* was associated very closely with the Confucian cultivated person.[21] But it also spread so widely because it symbolized an ideal that was widely accepted by all schools of thought—whether Taoist, Confucian, or Buddhist—the notion of *wu wei* or nonaction.

The ideal of *wu wei* or nonaction is not merely the simple refusal to act or the not taking of action. This is the crude interpretation ("crude" is a bit of a technical term here; "crude" implies dualistic interpretation). Rather *wu wei* is a cluster of overlapping concepts that describe the truly accomplished person: such a person acts effortlessly without deliberation and conscious intention, acts without focusing on technique and means, acts without self-regard and self-consciousness. The true archer's skill transcends mere technique with a bow and arrow, the true swordsman's ability is more than just skillful slash and parry with a sword, the true *ch'in* player communicates something more than the sound of plucked strings. The notion of *wu wei* extended to speech implies a mind-to-mind transmission beyond the mere speaking of words. Not merely the Zen tradition but the entire educated world of China saw the epitome of learned discourse as one in which the partners were so learned in language that they communicated more in silence than in mere words. But accomplishment in *wu wei* always depended on accomplishment in action. First one mastered the technique of the bow and arrow or the sword or the *ch'in*, and then, beyond the mere mastery of technique, one accomplished one's end without relying on the material bow and arrow or the sword or the *ch'in*. For the literati, mind-to-mind transmission transcended language not by rejecting it—this is the crude interpretation—but only by being firmly based in language. Mind-to-mind transmission is the perfection of technique in language, not the rejection of language.

Against this larger context of Chinese literature, the Zen notion of mind-to-mind transmission appears to be merely a late and local transformation of an ideal already held for centuries by the class of men educated in literature. The story of Po Ya and Tzu-ch'i predates by many centuries the use of Zen phrases such as "mind-to-mind transmission." The *Lieh Tzu*, once thought to date from the Warring States period in China, (403–222 B.C.E.), is now dated at about the third or fourth century C.E.,[22] whereas the earliest known reference to the "Śākyamuni holds up a flower" story is thought to be found in the *T'ien-sheng kuang-teng lu* published in 1036 C.E., almost seven centuries later.[23] The story of Śākyamuni and Kāśyapa is now widely thought to imply that Zen experience is quite independent of words and letters, that one must unlearn language to attain it. This is the crude interpretation. But if the story is read against the background of the tradition from which it comes, then the lesson it teaches is that the ability to communicate mind to mind without language first depends on the mastery of language.

Given this prior established tradition, it is not surprising to find that unlabeled allusions to the story of Po Ya and Tzu-ch'I, and the term "hearer of sound" (J. *chiin*; C. *chih-yin*), occur frequently in Zen literature, where they are adapted to emphasize the ineffability of the Dharma in Zen.

> *Moshi kinchū no omomuki o shiraba,*
> *Nanzo genjō no koe ni rō sen.*
>
> When you appreciate the flavor of the lute,
> What need to use the sound from the strings?
> (ZRKS 10.235/ZS 10.495)
>
> *Kaigaku o kenpon shite chiin o motomu,*
> *Ko-ko mikitareba nitchū no tō.*
>
> I overturn the seas and mountains seeking an intimate,
> But it is like a one-by-one search for a star at noon.
> (ZRKS 14. 202/ZS 14.76)

Kinpū gyokkan o fuku,
Nako ka kore chiin.

The golden wind blows the jade flute,
Who can appreciate this sound? (ZRKS 10. 440)

Shi wa kaijin ni mukatte ginji,
Sake wa chiki ni aute nomu.

My songs I sing to one who enjoys them;
Wine I drink with the friend who knows me well.
    (ZRKS 10.78)

What is the significance of this story for understanding Rinzai kōan practice? In Zen writings, we are used to the idea that language distorts what
originally is, that language creates false dichotomies imposing artificial categories upon what naturally is, that language cannot transmit the real nature of
things as they are.[24] For antecedents of this idea in earlier Chinese literature,
one can go directly to the first chapter of the *Tao te ching* ("The Tao that can be
spoken of is not the constant Tao") or "The Equality of All Things" chapter in
the *Chuang Tzu.* But there was also in Chinese literature another paradigm of
language. In the "expressive-affective conception of poetry" (Saussy 1993, 84),
the feelings and emotions of the heart were said to express themselves naturally
in words, music, and dance. The classic expression of this notion is found in
the "Great Preface" to the *Book of Songs*:

> Feeling is moved inwardly and takes form in speech. It is not
> enough to speak, so one sighs [the words]; it is not enough to sigh,
> so one draws them out and sings them; it is not enough to draw
> them out and sing them, so without one's willing it, one's hands
> dance and one's feet stamp. (after Saussy 1993, 77)

Saussy has pointed out that this passage is in turn derived from the *Records
of Music* section of the *Record of Ritual* (*Li chi*). The fact that this conception of
language was associated with such important texts implies that it was widely
studied and accepted. Expression in language is depicted as being similar to
expression in music. Just as melody in the heart spontaneously expresses itself
in music, so the feelings and emotions spontaneously express themselves in
words, sighs, song, and dance. The result is poetry and language.[25]

If the writer's feelings and emotions spontaneously express themselves in
words, then it is possible for the reader to follow words back to the feelings
and emotions of the writer. Stephen Owen points out that there was a paradigm
of "linguistic adequacy" in which it was thought that language was capable of
expressing the minds and hearts of another. The chapter called "The Hearer
of Sounds" (*Chih-yin*) of the *Wen-hsin tiao-lung* by Liu Hsieh states:

In the case of composing literature, the emotions are stirred and the words come forth; but in the case of reading, one opens the literary text and enters the emotions [of the writer], goes up against the waves to find the source; and though it be [at first] hidden, it will certainly become manifest. None may see the actual faces of the far-away age, but by viewing their writing, one may immediately see their hearts/minds. (Quoted in Owen 1985, 59)

In reading, one moves upstream from the words to their very source and enters the emotions of the writer. This motion upstream merely reverses the organic and seamless process by which the written words originally flowed from the heart of the writer. For two people whose cultivation is equally refined, language is not a medium that prevents people from knowing each other's mind but the very vehicle for immediately seeing each other's heart and mind.

There are two conceptions of language, one in which language is depicted as imposing conceptual categories that falsify experience and prevent us from seeing things as they are, and one in which language is depicted as the means by which people immediately know each other's mind. They are both at work in the kōan. On the one hand, while the rhetoric of Zen constantly emphasizes that Zen is "not founded on words and letters," implying that language is always inadequate, the kōan practice promises to transport the practitioner to the enlightened mind of the patriarchs. As Dale Wright says, "Given that these sayings epitomize the mental state from which they have come forth, if the practitioner could trace back (*hui-fan*) the saying to its source, he or she would at that moment occupy a mental space identical to that of its original utterer" (Wright 2000, 201). Then, in the words of Mumon, one will "see with the same eye and hear with the same ear" as the patriarchs (*dōichigen ni mi, dōichini ni kiku, Mumonkan* case 1). If one presupposes that the Zen tradition has one fixed attitude to language, that Zen is not founded on words and letters, that language cannot express the awakened mind, then Rinzai literary practices will seem totally misguided. But if one acknowledges that Rinzai Zen, as the Chinese literary tradition from which it developed, worked with more than one paradigm of language, then literary study as part of kōan practice will be both natural and inevitable.

Two Kinds of Insight

The perplexing language of the Zen kōan is related to the perplexing language of Chinese poetry in general. But it would be a mistake to think that the incomprehensibility of a kōan consisted in nothing more than the inability to decode the allusions and analogies imbedded in its language.

A monk asked Ummon, "What is Buddha?" Ummon replied, "A lump of dried shit." (*Mumonkan* case 21)

A monk asked Tōzan, "What is Buddha?" Tōzan said, "Three pounds of flax." (*Mumonkan* case 18)

A monk asked Jōshū, "What is the point of the First Patriarch's coming from the West?" Jōshū said, "The cypress tree in the courtyard." (*Mumonkan* case 37)

One suspects that analogy is at work here and that if we only knew the principle of resemblance, we could make sense of the answer logically. Or we suspect there must be some hidden allusion behind "lump of dried shit" or "three pounds of flax" which will provide the missing information necessary to understand the kōan. Here is where allusion and analogy in the kōan differ from allusion and allegory in Chinese literature. Although explaining allusion and analogy can clarify individual terms, it cannot explain completely the kōan. The basic problem of the kōan is to "realize" the kōan not as a third-person description but as a first-person performance of the Fundamental.

It is possible to take the "one hand" in "Sound of One Hand" as a symbolic analogue for the nonduality of subject and object. Thus interpreted, "Two hands clap and make a sound. What is the sound of one hand?" means, "You know the duality of subject and object. What is the nonduality of subject and object?" But understanding allusion and analogy is still an intellectual fact; such understanding does not bring one closer to solving the kōan. The kōan is solved only when one first realizes (makes real) the nonduality of subject and object, only when one becomes an instance of that nonduality oneself. It is for this reason that Zen masters instruct their kōan students to become one with the kōan, to BE the sound of one hand.

The insight one has in seeing that "sound of one hand" means "nonduality of subject and object" I will call horizontal insight. It takes one sideways from one phrase in language, such as "What is your original face before your father and mother were born?" to another phrase in language, such as "What is original nonduality before duality got born?" This insight within language is utterly different from vertical insight, the insight that comes from the experience of realizing, making real, the nonduality of subject and object. Vertical insight takes one outside language to experience itself.

To elaborate further, the fundamental problem in solving a kōan is religious. It is not merely a literary matter of understanding allusion and analogy. It is not merely an epistemological matter of attaining a nondual state of consciousness. It is not merely a matter of training and drilling oneself to a level of spontaneous improvisation. The kōan is both the means for, and the realization of, a religious experience that finally consumes the self. That experience is the final referent for the symbolic language of "A lump of dried shit," "Three pounds of flax," or "Cypress tree in the courtyard."

The Zen tradition displayed the greatest genius in adapting the structure of the Chinese literary game to the Zen meditation practice. The player of the literary game was so learned in poetry that he could, through the skillful use of allusion and analogy, express a meaning without saying it in words. His opponent had to be equally learned to have the insight to understand that meaning which was not expressed in words. The kōan substitutes for this horizontal insight cultivated within language the vertical insight of direct experience outside language. In this way, the kōan and the *jakugo*, both constructed in language, become the literary expression of that which is "not founded on words and letters."

ABBREVIATIONS

ZGDJT   *Zengaku daijiten* [Great Dictionary of Zen Studies]. 1977. Komazawa Daigaku Zengaku Daijiten Hensanjo, ed. Tokyo: Taishūkan.

ZRKS   See Ijūshi in References. An entry like ZRKS 10.65 means 10-character verse number 65.

ZS   *Zen Sand: The Book of Capping Phrase for Kōan Practice* (Honolulu: University of Hawaii Press, 2003). An entry like ZS 14.461 means 14-character verse number 461.

NOTES

This chapter is an abbreviated version of the introductory chapters in Victor Hori's *Zen Sand: The Book of Capping Phrase for* Kōan *Practice* (Honolulu: University of Hawaii Press, 2003). I wish to thank the University of Hawaii Press for permission to publish this material.

    1. Although I use the term "monk" and masculine pronouns, I am not trying to ignore or belittle the fact that women practitioners engaged in kōan practice. However I wish to avoid the clumsy English that results when male nouns and pronouns are doubled with the addition of their feminine counterparts, such as "His or her *jakugo* displays his or her own eye-for-the-essential (*shūjōgan*) and his or her own way of manipulating life and death." Until the English language develops some gender-neutral nouns and pronouns, I opt to use "monk" and masculine pronouns in the interest of smoother language.

    2. For a survey study of Chinese literary games, see Pollack 1979.

    3. Heine 1999 is a thorough examination of this kōan, its various versions in Zen texts, and the influence that the folklore tradition has had upon the structure of the kōan.

    4. For more discussion of the cultural background of Japanese Zen Buddhism in the Kamakura and Muromachi periods, and especially of the arguments for and against poetry as a Buddhist practice, see Miner 1979, Pollack 1986, and Kraft 1992. For a discussion of the development of the *jakugo* practice as a part of monastic kōan practice, see the introductory chapters to Victor Sōgen Hori, *Zen Sand* (Honolulu: University of Hawaii Press, 2003).

5. Seven hundred seventy-three verses from this collection have been translated under the title, *A Zen Harvest*, by Shigematsu Soiku (San Francisco: North Point Press, 1988).

6. For an explanation of the terminology of "Straight and Crooked," "principle and fact," "dynamic action," and so on, see Hori 2000.

7. Pollack, personal communication.

8. For studies of the relation of *Kuzōshi*, its commentary texts, and the *Zenrin Kushū*, see Iriya 1996, Kawase 1942, Sanae 1996, Yanagida 1975, and Yoshida 1941.

9. "The first arrow was shallow, the later arrow went deep" (ZS 7.268).

10. For discussion of Tōyō Eichō Zenji and the texts that may have served as his model, see Kawase 1942; Yoshida 1941, 1174–1175; and Sanae 1996, 60–62.

11. For more detail on these early *kuzōshi* texts, see Iriya 1996, Kawase 1942, Kawase 1979, Kimura and Katayama 1984, Kita 1991, Sanae 1996, Yanagida Seiji 1975, and Yoshida 1941.

12. Some of Ijūshi's expressions in this postcript need to be explained. The one eye in the forehead is the Buddha's eye of awakening, which illuminates the world, depicted, for example, in chapter 1 of the *Lotus Sūtra*. The ch'i-lin is a fantastic animal with a single horn in Chinese mythology, whose rare appearance was considered an omen of good fortune. Here its single horn is symbolically equivalent to the single eye in the Buddha's forehead. Both are metaphors for the great awakening of Zen. The claws and teeth of the lion are a metaphor for the fierce but compassionate techniques of the skillful Zen teacher. The Zen forest is the Zen *sangha*. When Ijūshi says he first studied Confucianism and then in midlife donned the "black robes," he means he became a Buddhist monk. The "elbow does not bend outward" is a well-known Zen saying with many meanings, but here it means simply that there is a limit to how far one can push things.

13. I would like to thank Kobori Nanrei Oshō of Ryōkō-in, Daitoku-ji, who gave me permission to consult these notebooks.

14. For a survey study of Chinese literary games, see Pollack 1976. See also Miner 1979.

15. For studies of parallelism in the Chinese language, see Plaks 1988 and Hightower 1965. For parallelism in other cultures, refer to the Introduction to Fox 1988, 1–28.

16. For a historical account of *renku*, or *renga*, see Keene 1977; Miner 1979; and Ueda 1970/1982, 69–111.

17. Needham originally opened discussion on this topic in "Correlative Thinking and Its Significance" in *Science and Civilization in China*, vol 2 (Needham and Wing 1956, 279–303). For later discussion on correlative thinking, see Graham 1986, Graham 1992, and Henderson 1984.

18. On the topic of relating two particulars, Nitta Daisaku identifies the feature of "indicating a particular with a particular," *ji o motte ji o shimesu*, as one aspect of a kōan shared with the wider tradition of Chinese thought. This in turn matches the Confucian emphasis on ritual, an emphasis that gave priority to actual performance of concrete actions and less attention to philosophical explanations (Nitta 1967):

Confucius was capable of acting much like a Zen master. Someone asked
for an explanation of the Ancestral Sacrifice. The Master said, I do not

know. Anyone who knew the explanation could deal with all things under Heaven as easily as I lay this here; and he laid his finger upon the palm of his hand (*Analects* III, 11; adapted from Arthur Waley, trans., *The Analects of Confucius* [New York: Vintage Books, rpt. 1999])

The claim to ignorance, the equating of dealing with all under Heaven with moving a finger, and the enigmatic action are all elements also to be found in the Zen kōan.

19. Harada Kenyu, *Han yu, Kanshi taikei* 11, 2 quoted in Pollack 1976, xii.

20. Stephen Owen has a good study of the special intimacy between Meng Chiao and Han Yu as expressed in their linked verse (Owen 1975, esp. 116–136).

21. Dewoskin 1982 documents the role that music and ideas about music played in Confucian literati culture.

22. See A. C. Graham, *The Book of Lieh-tzu* (New York: Columbia University Press, 1960, rpt., 1990).

23. ZZ 8.4.306b–d.

24. For an interesting critical discussion of the notion of the transcendence of language in Zen, see Wright 1992.

25. The language skeptic, who is wont to claim that language distorts and falsifies the nature of things as they are in themselves, is usually working with the "reference" theory of language, which assumes that a word is just a sound that gets meaning by being arbitrarily associated with an object. Individual words are assumed to refer to, denote, or label the object; the sentence is said to describe or report it. Since the relation of the word to the object, of the proposition to the fact, is merely one of arbitrary convention, it is always possible to raise doubt about the veracity of linguistic expression. In contrast, the "expressive-affective" theory of language claims that language is the natural expression of emotion and not just its conventional sign. A cry of pain expresses pain and does not describe it. When an animal cries in pain, its cry expresses its pain, but not because it speaks a language in which the cry has been conventionally defined as the sign of pain.

REFERENCES

Akizuki Ryōmin 1972. *Rinza iroku* [*The Record of Rinzai*]. Tokyo: Chikuma shobō.

———. 1979. *Zen mondō* [*Zen Dialogue*]. Tokyo: San'ichi shobō.

———. 1981. *Zen no kotoba* [*Zen Words*]. Tokyo: Toppan insatsu.

———. 1987. *Kōan: jissenteki Zen nyūmon* [*Kōan: A Practical Introduction to Zen*]. Tokyo: Chikuma shobō.

Asahina Sōgen. 1935. *Rinzai roku* [*Record of Rinzai*]. Tokyo: Iwanami shoten.

———. 1937. *Hekiganroku* [*Blue Cliff Record*]. 3 vols. Tokyo: Iwanami shoten.

———. 1941. *Zen no kōan* [*The Zen Kōan*]. Tokyo: Yūzankaku.

Blyth, R. H. 1981. *Haiku, Vol. 1: Eastern Culture*. Tokyo: Hokuseido Press.

Cleary, Thomas, trans. 1990. *Book of Serenity*. Hudson, N.Y.: Lindisfarne Press.

———. 1993. *No Barrier: Unlocking the Zen Koan*. New York: Bantam Books.

———. 1998. *The Blue Cliff Record*. Berkeley, Cal.: Numata Center for Buddhist Translation and Research.

Cleary, Thomas, and J. C. Cleary, trans. 1977. *The Blue Cliff Record*. Boulder: Shambhala.

Collcutt, M. 1981. *Five Mountains: The Rinzai Zen Monastic Institution in Medieval Japan*. Cambridge, Mass.: Harvard University Press.

Daichūji. 1966. *Shaku Taibi Zenji Unkan-kutsu kōroku. [The Great Record of Shaku Taibi Zenji Unkan-kutsu]*. Numazu, Shizuoka: Daichūji.

Dainippon Bukkyō Zensho. 1953. Gidō Shūshin. *Jōwa ruijū soenrenpōshū* [The Jōwa Classified Collection of the Fragrant Cappings from the Garden of the Patriarchs], [The Jōwa Collection—New Selection]. Tokyo: Dai Nihon Bukkyō Zensho, vol. 143.

Dewoskin, Kenneth J. 1982. *A Song for One or Two: Music and the Concept of Art in Early China*. Ann Arbor, Mich.: Center for Chinese Studies, University of Michigan.

First Zen Institute of America. 1947. *Cat's Yawn* (13 numbers from 1940 to 1941). New York: First Zen Institute of America.

Foulk, T. Griffith. 1993. "Myth, Ritual and Monastic Practice in Sung Ch'an Buddhism." In Patricia B. Ebrey and Peter N. Gregory, eds., *Religion and Society in T'ang and Sung China*. Honolulu: University of Hawaii Press. pp. 147–208.

———. 2000. "The Form and Function of Kōan Literature: A Historical Overview." In Heine and Wright 2000, pp. 15–45.

Fox, James J. 1988. "Introduction." In James J. Fox, ed., *To Speak in Pairs: Essays on the Ritual Languages of Eastern Indonesia*. Cambridge: Cambridge University Press, pp. 1–28.

Fujita Genro, ed. Vol. 1, 1917; vol. 2, 1922. *Zudokko [The Poison Painted Drum]*. Kyoto: Kenninji Sōdō.

———. 1917 and 1922. *Zudokko Kushū (Poison Painted Drum Phrase Collection)*, contained in Fujita, *Zudokko [Poison Painted Drum]*.

Graham, A. C. 1986. "Yin-Yang and the Nature of Correlative Thinking." Singapore: Institute of East Asian Philosophies. Occasional Paper and Monograph Series No. 6 1986.

———. 1992. "Poetic and Mythic Varieties of Correlative Thinking." In A. C. Graham, *Unreason Within Reason: Essays on the Outskirts of Rationality*. LaSalle, Ill.: Open Court, pp. 207–223.

Haga Kōshirō. 1973. *Ichigyōmono [Scrolls]*. Kyoto: Tankōsha.

———. 1974. *Zoku ichigyōmono [More Scrolls]*. Kyoto: Tankōsha.

———. 1977. *Zokuzoku ichigyōmono [More and More Scrolls]*. Kyoto: Tankōsha.

———. 1984. *Mata zoku ichigyōmono [Even More Scrolls]*. Kyoto: Tankōsha.

Heine, Steven. 1999. *Shifting Shape, Shaping Text: Philosophy and Folklore in the Fox Kōan*. Honolulu: University of Hawaii Press.

Heine, Steven and Dale S. Wright, eds. 2000. *The Koan: Texts and Contexts in Zen Buddhism*. New York: Oxford University Press.

Hekian Shūdō, compiler. 1982. *Zenrin gokushō [Zen Sangha Words and Phrases]*. Tokyo: Nigensha.

Henderson, John B. 1984. *The Development and Decline of Chinese Cosmology*. New York: Columbia University Press.

Hightower, James Robert. 1965. "Some Characteristics of Parallel Prose." In John L. Bishop, ed., *Studies in Chinese Literature: Harvard-Yenching Institute Studies XXI*. Cambridge, Mass.: Harvard University Press, pp. 108–138.

Hirano Sōjō. 1983. *Daitō kokushi goroku*. Tokyo: Kōdansha.

―――. "*Den Daiō Senkushū (Hōshun-in Zō)*" ["Collection of Selected Zen Phrases Attributed to Daitō (Hōshun-in Archives)"]. *Zen Bunka Kenkyūjō Kiyō.* 15 (1988): 561–600.

Hirata Takashi. 1969. *Mumonkan.* Tokyo: Chikuma shobō.

―――. 1982. *Hekiganshū.* Tokyo: Daizō shuppan.

Hori, G. Victor Sōgen. 2000. "Kōan and Kenshō in the Rinzai Kōan Curriculum." In Heine and Wright 2000, pp. 280–315.

Iida Rigyō., ed. 1975. *Zenrin meiku jiten* [*Dictionary of Well-Known Zen Sangha Phrases*]. Tokyo: Kokusho Kankōkai.

―――. 1994. *Zenrin yōgo jiten* [*Dictionary of Zen Sangha Language*]. Tokyo: Kashiwa bijutsu shuppan.

Iida Tōin, ed. 1955. *Kaian kokugo teishōroku* [*Record of Lectures on the Kaiankokugo*]. Kyoto: Kichūdō.

Ijūshi, ed. 1688. *Zenrin kushū* [*The Zen Sangha Phrase Collection*]. Kyoto: Baiyo Shoin rpt.

Imai Fukuzan and Nakagawa Shūan, eds. 1935. *Zengo Jii* [*Zen Glossary*]. Tokyo: Haku-rinsha.

Inagaki, H. 1984. *A Dictionary of Japanese Buddhist Terms.* Kyoto: Nagata bunshodō.

―――. 1991. *A Glossary of Zen Terms.* Kyoto: Nagata bunshodō.

Iriya Yoshitaka. 1996. "Kuzōshi Kaisetsu" ["An Explanation of *Zen Phrase Books*"]. In Yamada, Iriya, and Sanae 1996, pp. 564–580.

Iriya Yoshitaka, Kajitani Sōnin, and Yanagida Seizan. 1981. *Setchō juko* [*Setchō's Old Cases with Verses*]. Zen no Goroku 15. Tokyo: Chikuma Shobō.

Iriya Yoshitaka and Koga Hidehiko, eds. 1991. *Zengo jiten* [*Zen Word Dictionary*]. Kyoto: Shibunkaku.

Iriya Yoshitaka, Mizoguchi Yūzō, Sueki Fumihiko, and Itō Fumio, trans.. and annot. 1992. *Hekigan-roku.* 3 vols. Tokyo: Iwanami shoten.

Kajitani Sōnin, ed. 1977. *Shūmon Kattō-shū* [*Tangled Vine Collection*]. Kyoto: Hōzōkan.

Kao, Yu-kung and Tsu-lin Mei. 1978. "Meaning, Metaphor and Allusion in T'ang Poetry." *Harvard Journal of Asiatic Studies* 38 (2): 281–356.

Kawase Kazuma. 1942. "Kuzōshiko" ["Thoughts on Kuzōshi"]. In Noguchi Shinji, ed., *Sekisui Sensei kakōju kinen ronsan* [*Memorial Volume to Sekisui Sensei on His Sixtieth Birthday*]. Tokyo: Ippan Insatsu, pp. 119–144.

―――. 1979. *Kuzōshi kanashō kaisetsu* [*An Explanation of the Kana Annotated Phrase Book*]. Tokyo: Kotenseki Fukusei Sōkan Kankōkai.

Keene, Donald. 1977. "The Comic Tradition in Renga." In J. W. Hall and Toyoda Takeshi, eds., *Japan in the Muromachi Age.* Berkeley, Cal.: University of California Press, pp. 241–77.

Kimura Akira, ed. 1995. Shūbun Inryaku repr. in Koji Kenkyū Shiryō Sōkan, vol. 1. Tokyo: Daikūsha.

Kimura Akira and Katayama Seiken. eds. 1984. *Zenrin Kuzōshi-shū* [*Collected Versions of the Zenrin Kuzōshi*]. Tokyo: Kobayashi insatsu.

Kita Takashi, ed. 1991 [Comprehensive Index to the Annotated Kuzōshi]. Osaka: Seibundō.

Kraft, Kenneth. 1992. *Eloquent Zen: Daitō and Early Japanese Zen.* Honolulu: University of Hawaii Press.

Kudō Sumiko. 1975. "Shibayama Zenkei, 1904–1974." *Eastern Buddhist*. New Series 8 (1): 149–154.

Kusumoto Bunyū. 1982. *Zengo nyūmon [Introduction to Zen Language]*. Tokyo: Daihōrinkaku.

Kuzōshi n.a., n.d. Hōsa Bunko. Manuscript number 123–15 Hōsa Bunko, Nagoya.

Lattimore, David. 1973. "Allusion and T'ang Poetry." In Arthur F. Wright and Denis Twitchett, eds., *Perspectives on the T'ang*. New Haven, Conn.: Yale University Press, pp. 405–439.

Lewis, Zenrin Chidō Robert E. 1996. *The Book of the Zen Grove*, 2nd ed. Jacksonville, Fla.: Zen Sangha Press.

Ling Yün, ed., Bai Mu, supervisor. n.d. *Ch'anlin Huiyu [Zen Sangha Words of Wisdom]*. Taipei: Ch'ang-ch'un shushufang.

Luo Zhu-feng, ed. 1990. *Hanyu dacudian [Great Dictionary of Chinese]*, 12 vols and index. n. p. Hanyu Dacudian Chubanshe.

Matsubara Taidō. 1972. *Zengo hyakusen [One Hundred Selected Zen Phrases]*. Tokyo: Shōgakkan/Non Book.

Miner, Earl. 1979. *Japanese Linked Poetry*. Princeton, N.J.: Princeton University Press.

Miura Isshū and Ruth Fuller Sasaki. 1965. *The Zen Kōan*. New York: Harcourt.

———. 1966. *Zen Dust: The History of the Koan and Koan Study in Rinzai [Lin-chi] Zen*. Kyoto: The First Zen Institute of America.

Mochizuki Shinkō, ed. 1958. *Mochizuki Bukkyo Daijiten zōteiban [Mochizuki Great Buddhist Dictionary, rev. ed.]*. Tokyo: Sekai Seiten Kankō Kyōkai.

Mohr, Michel. 1993. "Examining the Sources of Rinzai Zen." *Japanese Journal of Religious Studies* 20(4): 331–344.

Morohashi Tetsuji, compiler. 1960. *Dai kanwa jiten [Great Chinese-Japanese Dictionary]*, 13 vols. Tokyo: Daishūkan Shoten.

———. 1979. *Chūgoku Koten meigen jiten [Encyclopedia of Famous Sayings from the Chinese Classics]*. Tokyo: Kōdansha.

Needham, Joseph, and Wing Ling, eds. 1956. "Correlative Thinking and Its Significance." In *Science and Civilization in China*, vol. 2: *History of Scientific Thought*. Cambridge: Cambridge University Press, pp. 279–303.

Nishibe Bunjō. 1985. *Zengo no ajiwaikata [How to Savor Zen Phrases]*. Kyoto: Tankōsha.

Nitta Daisaku, 1967. "Zen to Chūgoku Shisō" [Zen and Chinese Thought]. In Nishitani Keiji, ed., *Kōza Zen daiikkan Zen no tachiba [Lectures on Zen]*, vol. 1: *The Standpoint of Zen*. Tokyo: Chikuma Shobō, pp. 85–111.

Obata Buntei. 1938. *Kinsei zenrin sōhōden [Modern Zen Monk Biographies]*, vol. 3. Kyoto: Shibunkaku.

Ōmori Sōgen. 1967. "Kōan no Zen" [Kōan Zen]. In Suzuki Daisetsu and Nishitani Keiji, eds. *Kōza Zen Dainikan Zen no Jissen [Lectures on Zen, vol. 2: The Practical Application of Zen]*. Tokyo: Chikuma Shobō.

———. 1994. *Hekiganroku*, vol. 2, Tachibana Kyōyō Bunko.

Otobe Kaihō, ed. 1918. *Zenmon kōan taisei [Zen School Koan Compilation]* Tokyo: Kōmeisha.

Owen, Stephen. 1975. *The Poetry of Meng Chiao and Han Yü*. New Haven, Conn: Yale University Press.

———. 1977. *The Poetry of the Early T'ang*. New Haven, Conn.: Yale University Press.

———. 1985. *Traditional Chinese Poetry and Poetics*. Madison: University of Wisconsin Press.

Plaks, Andrew H. 1988. "Where the Lines Meet: Parallelism in Chinese and Western Literatures." *Chinese Literature Essays Articles Reviews* 10: 43–60.

Pollack, David. 1976. *Linked Verse Poetry in China: A Study of Associative Linking in "Lien-chu" Poetry with Emphasis on the Poems of Han Yü and His Circle*. Ph. D. diss., University of California Berkeley.

———. 1979. "Literature as Game in the T'ang." In Sarah Allan and Alvin Cohen, eds., *Legend, Lore and Religion in China*. San Francisco: Chinese Materials Center, pp. 205–224.

———. 1986. *The Fracture of Meaning: Japan's Synthesis of China from the Eighth through Eighteenth Centuries*. Princeton, N.J.: Princeton University Press.

———. May 18, 1999. Personal correspondence.

Sanae Kensei. 1996. "Kuzōshi no Shohon to Seiritsu" [The Kuzōshi Texts and their Development], in Yamada et. al., pp. 581–606.

Sasaki, Ruth Fuller. 1956 (March). "Anthology of Zen Poems." *Zen bunka* 4:22–26.

———. 1975. *The Record of Lin-chi: The Recorded Sayings of Ch'an Master Lin-chi Hui-chao of Chen Prefecture*. Kyoto: The Institute for Zen Studies.

Saussy, Haun. 1993. *The Problem of a Chinese Aesthetic*. Stanford, Cal.: Stanford University Press.

Schloegl, Irmgard. 1975. *The Zen Teaching of Rinzai*. Berkeley, Cal.: Shambhala.

Shibayama Zenkei, compiler. 1972. *Kunchū Zenrin kushū* [Annotated Zen Sangha Phrase Collection]. Kyoto: Kichūdō.

———. 1974. *Zen Comments on the Mumonkan*, trans. Sumiko Kudo. New York: Mentor/New American Library.

———. 1984. *Mumonkan* [*The Gateless Gate*]. Kyoto: Kichūdō.

Shigematsu Sōiku 1981. *A Zen Forest*. New York: Weatherhill.

———1988. *A Zen Harvest*. San Francisco: North Point Press.

Shinmura Izuru. 1960. *Kōjien*. Tokyo: Iwanami Shoten.

Snyder, Gary. 1983. *Axe Handles*. San Francisco: North Point Press.

Suzuki Daisetsu, Ui Hakuju, and Inoue Tetsujirō, eds. 1952. Zen no Kōza Daisankan: *Zen no kōan to mondō* [*Lectures on Zen, No. 3: The Zen Kōan and Koan Dialogue*]. Tokyo: Shunyōdō.

Takahashi Hiroshi. 1988. *Zen no chie monoshiri jiten* [*The Know-It-All's Dictionary on Zen Wisdom*]. Tokyo: Daiwa shuppan.

Takasaki Jikishō, ed. 1934. *Shōyō roku* [*Book of Serenity*]. Tokyo: Kōmeisha.

Tsuchiya Etsudō, ed. 1957. *Zenrin segoshū* [*Zen Sangha Vernacular Phrase Collection*]. Kyoto: Kichūdō.

———, ed. 1973. *Shinsan zengoshū* [A New Compilation of the Zen Phrase Collection]. Compiled under the direction of Unkankutsu Shaku Taibi Rōshi. Kyoto: Kichūdō.

Ueda, Makoto. 1970/1982. *The Master Haiku Poet Matsu Basho*. Tokyo: Kodansha.

Wright, Dale S. 1992 (January). "Rethinking Transcendence: The Role of Language in Zen Experience." *Philosophy East and West* 42: 113–138.

———. 2000. "Kōan History: Transformative Language in Chinese Buddhist Thought." In Heine and Wright 2000, pp. 200–212.

Yamada Toshio, Iriya Yoshitaka, and Sanae Kensei. eds. 1996. *Teikun ōrai Kuzōshi* [*Teikunōrai* and *Kuzōshi*]. Tokyo: Iwanami Shoten.

Yamamoto Shungaku. 1920. *Wakun ryakkai zenrin kushū* [*Zen Sangha Phrase Collection with Japanese Readings and Concise Explanations*]. Tokyo: Kōyūkan.

Yanagida Seiji. 1975 (Oct.). "*Kuzōshishō no shohon to sono hōhō*" [The Varieties of "Annotated Phrasebooks" and Their Methods]. *Kokugo kokubun* 44: 1–22.

Yanagida Seizan. 1967. *Shoki zenshū shisho no kenkyū* [*Research into Historical Texts of the Early Zen School*]. Tokyo: Hōzōkan.

———. 1971, 1977. *Shoki no zenshi* [*Early Zen History*]. 2 vols. Tokyo: Chikuma Shobō.

———. 1972. *Rinzai-roku* [*The Record of Rinzai*]. Tokyo: Daizō shuppan.

———. 1983. "The 'Recorded Sayings' Texts of Chinese Ch'an Buddhism." In Whalen Lai and Lewis Lancaster, eds., *Early Ch'an in China and Tibet*. Berkeley, Cal.: Berkeley Buddhist Book Series, pp. 185–205.

———. 2000. *Tentetsushū, Kaidai*, in Yanagida Seizan and Tsuina Hirō, eds. *Zengaku tenseki sōkan*, vol. 10B. Tokyo: Rinsen shoten.

Yoshida Sumio. 1938. *Amakusaban kinkushū no kenkyū* [*Studies on the Amakusa Golden Phrase Collection*]. Tokyo: Tōyō bunko kankō.

———. 1941. "Kuzōshishō ni tsuite" [Regarding Kuzōshi Commentary Texts]. In Uematsu Yasushi, ed., *Andō Kyōju kanreki shukuga kinen ronbunshū* [*A Collection of Commemorative Essays for Professor Andō on His Sixtieth Birthday*]. Tokyo: Sanseidō, pp. 1171–1191.

Yoshizawa Katsuhiro, ed. 1999. *Shoroku zokugokai* [*Explanation of Colloquial Language in Several Texts*]. Kyoto: Zen bunka kenkyūjō.

Yü Chün-fang. 1979. "Ta-hui Tsung-kao and *Kung-an* Ch'an." *Journal of Chinese Philosophy* 6: 211–235.

Zen Bunka Kenkyūjō. 1991a. *Teihon Zenrin kushū Sakuin*. [*Index to the Standard Text of the Zenrin kushū*]. Kyoto: Zen bunka kenkyūjō. Based on a Meiji 19 (1886) rpt.

———. 1991b. *Zengo Jisho ruiju* [*Dictionary of Classified Zen Phrases*]. Kyoto: Zen Bunka Kenkyūjō.

———. 1992a. *Zengo Jisho ruiju: Ni* [*Dictionary of Classified Zen Phrases, vol. 2*] Mujaku Dōchū Cho Kattō Gosen [Mujaku Dōchū's *Tangled Vine Word Notes*]. Kyoto: Zen Bunka Kenkyūjō.

———. 1992b. *Tōshisen santaishi sōgō sakuin*. [*Joint Index for the Tōshisen and Santaishi*]. Kyoto: Zen bunka kenkyūjō.

———. 1993. *Zengo Jisho Ruiju: San* [*Dictionary of Classified Zen Phrases, vol. 3*]: Hekiganroku Funishō [*Nondual Commentary on the Hekiganroku*]. Kyoto: Zen Bunka Kenkyūjō.

7

Imagining Indian Zen: Tōrei's Commentary on the *Ta-mo-to-lo ch'an ching* and the Rediscovery of Early Meditation Techniques during the Tokugawa Era

Michel Mohr

The *Ta-mo-to-lo ch'an ching* (T 15 no. 618), the Chinese translation of a canonical text primarily concerned with essential Buddhist meditation techniques,[1] is a little-known sūtra that has nevertheless played an interesting role in the development of the Chinese and Japanese Buddhist traditions, particularly the Ch'an/Zen schools. At first glance, the story of this text seems relatively simple. We have an Indian meditation treatise that was translated into Chinese in the early fifth century C.E., which attracted renewed interest among Sung Ch'an people as a text associated with Bodhidharma, and that was transmitted to Japan and later "rediscovered" by the eighteenth-century Japanese Zen teacher Tōrei Enji (1721–1792). The result of this encounter is his voluminous commentary entitled *Darumatara zenkyō settsū kōsho*, first published in 1784.[2] Despite the importance of Tōrei in Rinzai Zen and the erudition of his commentary, there is no modern printed edition of the text[3] and, to the best of my knowledge, no in-depth study of it.[4]

Examining the reasons for this neglect is my first duty, for it immediately brings up some of the "hot topics" so harshly debated today. One such topic is the sectarian self-understanding and ideology of the present Japanese Zen schools, each of which claims the highest degree of authenticity as the true recipient of the historical Buddha's legacy, the famous "special transmission outside [scholastic] teachings" (*kyōge betsuden*).[5] In many respects, the eighteenth-century Japanese perception of Indian Buddhism, with its many mythicized images, remains the most prevalent view. Among these images is that of the supposed founder Bodhidharma, whose enigmatic character has served as a screen upon which the retrospective quest for legitimacy could make its projections. For those unable to satisfy themselves with popular legends, Bodhidharma has remained a source of frustration, causing scholarly monks to search for textual evidence that would better support the historicity of their founding patriarch.

Tōrei's commentary can be seen in precisely these terms: as a quest for Bodhidharma beyond the usual *Image d'Épinal*. His scholarship is not devoid of naive assumptions, of course, and as one is now perhaps a bit more aware, his "search for the real Bodhidharma" is meaningful chiefly as a legitimization of the Zen tradition.[6] Nevertheless, in view of some of the excesses of twentieth-century scholarship, such as the simplifications of so-called "Critical Buddhism," one cannot help being struck by the modesty of such Tokugawa monks as Tōrei, who were often sincerely trying to unravel the maze of remaining sources *before* presenting their own interpretations. Not only does Tōrei's mastery of Buddhist and non-Buddhist literature go beyond that of the average cleric, but his commentary builds on the meticulous philological approach seen in the work of Dokuan Genkō[7] and Mujaku Dōchū.[8] It is striking to encounter such scholarly endeavors in the Tokugawa period, prior to similar developments that emerged on the Chinese continent with the surge of textual exegesis known as *Hsün-ku hsüeh* (J. *Kunkogaku*).

Two main reasons may be inferred as to why Tōrei's *Darumatara zenkyō settsū kōsho* (abbreviated hereafter as the *Commentary*) has been so neglected by modern buddhologists. First, on a scholarly level, the fact is that Tōrei, who quotes from a wide range of sources (including obscure Shinto texts),[9] goes far beyond the usual borders of Japanese Buddhist studies. Academics have thus avoided any investigation of the *Commentary*, because it would mean venturing into unknown territory. Second, on a sectarian level, the qualified picture of Bodhidharma that emerges in Tōrei's account is less convenient for proselytical purposes than the image of Bodhidharma that already exists in the popular imagination.[10]

In this sense the *Commentary* offers new insights on the extent to which Tokugawa "scholar-monks" shaped our present understanding of the Zen tradition, particularly with regard to its avowedly Indian origins. Their presentation of the tradition was taken a step further in the post-Tokugawa philosophical development known as *Zen shisō* (Zen thought),[11] which relied heavily on such premises of Indian roots. The importance of the *Commentary* to Meiji-era Rinzai teachers is reflected in the fact that the Meiji reprint contains a preface by Kōgaku Sōen (Shaku; 1860–1919) and introductory material by several other high-ranking priests.[12] The text seems to have been especially valued as a counteragent to the distrust of traditional values brought by the collision with modernity.

Nevertheless, Tōrei's *Commentary* is only the most recent of the multifarious layers of interpretation that have been added onto the original text of the *Ta-mo-to-lo ch'an ching*. An examination of the various issues involved leads not only to matters of textual interpretation but also to a consideration of some of the questions that generations of Buddhist readers of this text have asked themselves, such as, "Which types of meditation did the historical Buddha practice?" "Which types of meditation did he teach?" and "How did Mahāyāna assert its specificity in regard to meditation?"

I obviously cannot answer these highly speculative issues here;[13] rather, I will attempt to clarify how Tōrei and his predecessors understood the *Ta-mo-to-lo ch'an ching* with these concerns in the back of their minds. We are, of course, not bound to their views; indeed, the task of reading the commentaries of Tōrei and his predecessors implies a questioning of the authors' hidden motivations. Let us first look at the *Ta-mo-to-lo ch'an ching* and at its place in Chinese and Japanese Buddhist history, then examine its contents, and finally try to assess the significance of Tōrei's *Commentary* today.

I have chosen to speak of the *Ta-mo-to-lo ch'an ching*—that is, to treat it as a Chinese document—rather than adopt the hypothetical reconstruction "The Sūtra of Dharmatrāta,"[14] because so little is visible beyond the horizon of Chinese sources; I will examine this issue further in the section entitled "The False Issue of the Title." For the same reason, the section following this one is cautiously entitled "The Pseudo-Indian Context."

The *Ta-mo-to-lo ch'an ching*: Translation and Context

The Pseudo-Indian Context

Our knowledge of the time and place when a lost Indian meditation treatise was translated or condensed into the *Ta-mo-to-lo ch'an ching* essentially derives from the preface of Hui-yüan (334–416 var. 415 or 417) of Mount Lu. The full text of this preface is also found in the *Ch'u san-tsang chi chi* by Seng-yu (445–518), albeit with a different title.[15] The same catalogue also contains another preface, ascribed to Hui-kuan (n.d.).[16]

The translation of the *Ta-mo-to-lo ch'an ching* is attributed to Buddhabhadra (359–429) and was completed about 413.[17] The title of the original text was, apparently, *Yogācārabhūmi*, one of many treatises bearing the same name.[18] From what can be inferred through its Chinese translation, the original *Yogā-*

cārabhūmi text belonged to a relatively early phase of Indian Buddhism. In content, it fits what Zürcher writes concerning the Buddhist meditation techniques transmitted to China:

> The system of mental exercises commonly called *dhyāna [ch'an]* in Chinese sources, but which is more adequately covered by the term 'Buddhist yoga,' comprises such practices as the preparatory technique of counting the respirations leading to mental concentration [*ānāpānasmṛti*]; the contemplation of the body as being perishable, composed of elements, impure and full of suffering; the visualization of internal and external images or various colours, etc.[19]

The *Ta-mo-to-lo ch'an ching* was either the Chinese translation of one of the meditation treatises brought from India or Central Asia, or a compilation from existing Indian sources. No Sanskrit original remains, unfortunately, so we must rely on the Chinese rendition. Despite this limitation, the comparative study of this and other such treatises remains a very promising field, one that throws much light on the development of Indian Buddhism. It shows in particular the coexistence of two different trends in the understanding of practice, which were later to develop into the Hīnayāna and Mahāyāna traditions.[20] Thus, despite the presence of the character *ch'an* in the title of the *Ta-mo-to-lo ch'an ching*, we are obviously dealing with a document belonging to a period when there was still nothing close to a "Ch'an tradition" in China, although the practice of meditation was central to many Buddhist teachers. When considering the circumstances surrounding the translation of the *Ta-mo-to-lo ch'an ching*, one should avoid being influenced by later Ch'an and Zen "filters," including Tōrei's *Commentary*.

It is not possible here to embark on a detailed study of these early meditation texts,[21] but to understand the significance of the *Ta-mo-to-lo ch'an ching* we need to have at least a general idea of the type of meditation treatises prevalent in China when Buddhabhadra's translation was made. Roughly speaking, it is possible to identify three main groups of closely related texts: (1) early Chinese translations by An Shih-kao and subsequent translations by Dharmarakṣa and Buddhabhadra; (2) similar texts translated by Kumārajīva; and (3) fundamental Yogācāra scriptures composed in Gandhāra.

These documents appear to represent different facets of a general movement aimed at systematizing Buddhist practice. The teachers and translators who contributed to their redaction not only were concerned with doctrinal matters but were themselves deeply involved in practice. This fact is becoming increasingly obvious thanks to the work of scholars such as Yamabe Nobuyoshi, who has discussed, for instance, the example of the fifth-century monks Dharmakṣema and his disciple Tao-chin. For Dharmakṣema, obtaining a personal vision of the Buddha was a necessary prerequisite for receiving the Bodhisattva precepts or realizing true repentance.[22] Let us further examine the outline of these three groups of "meditation sūtras" translated into Chinese.

Meditation Treatises Translated by An Shih-kao, Dharmarakṣa, and Buddhabhadra

The corpus of sūtras translated into Chinese during the Han Dynasty by the Parthian prince An Shih-kao and his team represents one of the earliest stages in the assimilation of Indian Buddhist texts. This occurred some time after the initial transmission of Buddhism from India; Zürcher notes that there was "a gap of about eight decades between the first unquestionable sign of Buddhism in China (65 A.D.) and the arrival of An Shigao in Luoyang (148 A.D.), [which] marks the beginning of regular translation activities."[23]

These early translations are now being reexamined from the viewpoint of their linguistic features. Although translations attributed to An Shih-kao have grown to 179 works, one of the conclusions of this reevaluation is that "the oldest and most primitive nucleus in our materials is formed by the sixteen short scriptures which may be regarded as genuine products of An Shih-kao and his collaborators. It is a very homogeneous group of texts, clearly recognizable by their linguistic and stylistic features."[24] What is relevant for this study is that among these sixteen scriptures is the *Tao-ti ching* (T 15 no. 607), one of the *Yogācārabhūmi* texts that later evolved into the *Ta-mo-to-lo ch'an ching*. The original *Yogācārabhūmi* treatise is attributed to Saṃgharakṣa, a teacher from Kashmir who is supposed to have taught the emperor Kaniṣka. This attribution suggests the strong connection of these meditation treatises with the Sarvāstivādin of Kashmir.[25] Tao-an (314–385) wrote a preface to the *Tao-ti ching* in which he asserts that the original *Yogācārabhūmi* text translated by An Shih-kao contained twenty-seven chapters, and that this was *summarized* by Shih-kao into seven chapters.[26]

This brings us to the second important translator, Dharmarakṣa, who attempted to provide a more complete Chinese version of the original *Yogācārabhūmi* treatise that included all twenty-seven chapters. The product of this translation work, dated 284 C.E., contains, in fact, thirty chapters, but the last three appear to be a later addition, which Demiéville identifies as the text's "Mahayanist appendix." Dharmarakṣa's translation may be regarded as an expanded version of An Shih-kao's pioneering work—indeed, some passages are so close that they can be compared line by line. Demiéville's partial translation and analysis still provides an excellent outline of the entire thirty-chapter sūtra.[27]

Buddhabhadra, the translator of the *Ta-mo-to-lo ch'an ching*, is one of the few Indian figures of that time whose dates are known and whose profile has some degree of reliability, thanks to the details provided in Hui-yüan's preface and in the *Biography of Eminent Monks* by Hui-chiao (497–554).[28] The pivotal place accorded to Buddhabhadra in Chinese historical records is not surprising, since he is credited also with translating the 60-fascicle *Flower Ornament Sūtra* (T 9 no. 278) and several other important scriptures. However, Buddhabhadra's biography recounts that before being recognized for these accomplishments, he had to leave northern China with his disciples[29]—the victim, apparently, of obscure dissensions with Kumārajīva's followers[30]—and subsequently moved to Mount Lu in the south. There Hui-yüan not only welcomed him but provided him with all facilities to engage in translating activities. "Hui-yüan then asked him to translate several sūtras [about] meditation and the Abhidharma" (C. *ch'an-shu chu ching; J. zenshu no shokyō*).[31] One of the results of this work was the *Ta-mo-to-lo ch'an ching*, which represents a blend of Indian Buddhism slightly different from the one introduced in northern China by Kumārajīva and his disciples. The redaction of the sūtra translated by Buddhabhadra is attributed to his teacher Buddhasena, but too little is known about this figure to speculate about this assertion.[32]

Meditation Treatises Translated by Kumārajīva

Kumārajīva (344–413),[33] probably the best-known translator of Buddhist texts into Chinese, is known for his elegant prose and verse, and his redactions have generally been preferred over all others in China and the rest of East Asia. The study of his prodigious output of translations is interesting in itself, but here I wish to focus on his translation of meditation treatises. There are several works belonging to this category of scriptures,[34] but the most important for this discussion of the *Ta-mo-to-lo ch'an ching* is the *Tsuo-ch'an san-mei fa-men ching* (*Sūtra on the Approach to Samadhi [through] Seated Meditation*; T 15 no. 614). Tōrei confesses in the introduction to his *Commentary* that upon first reading the *Ta-mo-to-lo ch'an ching* in 1762, "I couldn't understand its meaning" but that when "I finally obtained the *Tsuo-ch'an san-mei [fa-men] ching*, the meaning [of the *Ta-mo-to-lo ch'an ching*] became increasingly clear."[35]

Comparison of the *Tsuo-ch'an san-mei fa-men ching* and the *Ta-mo-to-lo ch'an ching*, translated respectively in 407 and in 413, reveals the different approaches to meditation transmitted by Kumārajīva, working under official patronage at Ch'ang-an in the north, and by Buddhabhadra, working under Hui-yüan on Mount Lu in the south. These two approaches to the Chinese reception and reinterpretation of the Indian tradition have been characterized by Satō Taishun as, respectively, "the meditation sūtra from the capital" (*kanchū no zenkyō*) and the "the meditation sūtra from Mount Lu" (*Rozan no zenkyō*).[36]

While both sūtras give meticulous descriptions of the various techniques for focusing the mind, it is interesting to note that the *Tsuo-ch'an san-mei fa-men ching* divides these techniques into five main rubrics: (1) the practice to cure greed (*chih t'an-yü fa-men*), which involves contemplation of foulness (*pu-ching kuan*);[37] (2) the practice to cure hate (*chih ch'en-hui fa-men*), which requires developing a compassionate mind (*tz'u-hsin*); (3) the practice to cure stupidity (*chih yü-ch'ih fa-men*), which amounts to examining dependent origination (*yin-yüan*); (4) the practice to cure [excessive] reasoning (*chih szu-chüeh fa-men*), which implies concentration on mindful breathing (*a-na pan-na san-mei*); and (5) the practice to cure [the sentient beings'] equal share [of delusion][38] (*chih teng-fen fa-men*), which uses concentration on the Buddha (*nien-fo san-mei*). These five types of practice later came to be known as the "five contemplations [for] stopping [the perverted] mind" (C. *wu t'ing-hsin kuan*; J. *gojōsh-inkan*).[39] The interesting point about these five approaches is that, despite minor variations, they appear to have also been core teachings of the *Yogācārabhūmi-śāstra* (T 30 no. 1579).

In contrast to the well-organized *Tsuo-ch'an san-mei fa-men ching*, the *Ta-mo-to-lo ch'an ching* seems more practical in orientation and goes into detail only on the practices of mindful breathing (*an-pan-nien*)[40] and on the contemplation of foulness; no mention is made of the remembrance of the Buddha.[41] In this point the two texts seem to fit Odani's argument for a development in three stages, from (1) diverging expressions of these five contemplations, to (2) their standardization, to (3) their simplification into the two main items of mindful breathing and the contemplation of foulness.[42] Yet this process doesn't seem to reflect a linear historical evolution. In any event, given the proximity in the dates of the two works, one would expect that Buddhabhadra knew of Kumārajīva's translation, or even that Buddhabhadra's text would have constituted a response to Kumārajīva's description of meditation techniques, but in fact there is no evidence of the *Ta-mo-to-lo ch'an ching* borrowing from or reacting to the former translation. Tōrei reached the conclusion that the father of the *Ch'an ching*, whom he supposed to be Bodhidharma, had known of the *Tsuo-ch'an san-mei fa-men ching*.

Conversely, Kumārajīva's translation seems to reflect more acutely the trends of his time. For example, after giving a first description of the five practices, Kumārajīva's text repeats them with different headings beginning with the word "bodhisattva." To emphasize that the meditation techniques described belong to the Mahāyāna, it would take the trouble to add the word "bodhisattva" whenever possible. For instance, in discussing contemplation of the "twelve links of dependent origination" the text explicitly says, "The bodhisattva contemplates the twelve links of dependent origination," to be sure that the practice won't be mistaken for a technique of the so-called "lesser vehicle" (T 15 no. 614 p. 283b15–b16). This approach is in striking contrast to the *Ta-mo-to-lo ch'an ching*, in which bodhisattvas are scarcely mentioned (one can find only two occurrences of this term in the whole text, in the very last chapter; T 15 no. 618 p. 324b07–b08).

Another element that deserves scrutiny is the apparent relationship between Buddhabhadra and the cult of Maitreya,[43] which was widespread in the Gandhāra or Kashmir areas and appears to have coincided with the emergence of Yogācāra as a distinctive school—indeed, Maitreya was regarded as Yogācāra's founding patriarch and the transmitter of its teachings.[44]

Early Yogācāra Texts

The origins of the Yogācāra school still remain shrouded in mist, especially because of the fuzzy hagiographical accounts of two of its cardinal proponents, Aśvaghoṣa and Asaṅga. The filiation between Yogācāra-school texts and various earlier Yogācārabhūmi scriptures is in little doubt, in view of the many common terms, concepts, and contents.[45] For example, with regard to the Yogācārabhūmi-śāstra (T 30 no. 1579) and the Mahāyānasaṃgrahabhāṣya (T 31 no. 1604), the central texts attributed to Asaṅga, Demiéville concludes that, "the Yogācārabhūmi of Saṃgharakṣa must have been the major Hinayanist prototype, and probably the oldest."[46] Another feature that suggests a close relation between the early Yogācāra practitioners and the translators of these meditation sūtras is the aforementioned connection with Maitreya. I cannot engage here in a detailed examination of these various links, but figure 7.1 might help summarize the complex relationships before we move to an examination of the Chinese context.

The Chinese Context

The False Issue of the Title

Let us now focus more closely on the Ta-mo-to-lo ch'an ching. The presence of the name "Ta-mo-to-lo" in the title has led to much speculation[47] about who this figure might be. The speculation has centered on whether Ta-mo-to-lo is the transliterated name of a certain Dharmatrāta, and whether this Dharmatrāta could be the same person as Fa-chiu, the author of the Tsa-a-p'i-t'an hsin-lun (T 28 no. 1552).[48] One recent suggestion is that there were, at different times, no less than three figures bearing the name Dharmatrāta.[49] Other scholars are skeptical of the attribution of the Ta-mo-to-lo ch'an ching to this highly hypothetical figure, regarding the creation of such an Indian lineage as a convenient way to justify the orthodoxy of early Ch'an. Yanagida Seizan takes this standpoint by arguing that "Shen-hui, relying on the main text of the Ch'an ching, changed Ta-mo-to-lo into P'u-t'i-ta-mo, clearly emphasizing the transmission of the flame by eight Indian patriarchs. His alteration in [presenting] six Chinese patriarchs is obvious, but accurately speaking one can also consider that the theory of a patriarchal lineage among Ch'an followers began at precisely that time."[50]

Nevertheless, the traditional Buddhist scholar-monks who studied the Ta-

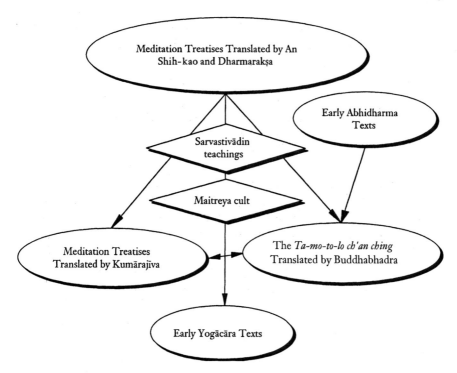

FIGURE 7.1. Relationships between early Yogācāra practitioners and translators of meditation sūtras.

mo-to-lo ch'an ching, particularly Fo-jih Ch'i-sung (1007–1072) and Tōrei, apparently had no doubt that Ta-mo-to-lo *was* Bodhidharma (P'u-t'i-ta-mo), and their understanding of the Ch'an tradition doesn't seem to have been simply a strategic device. Therefore, it appears safer to assume that they genuinely believed Bodhidharma to have been the source of this document, written by his fellow disciple Buddhasena and transmitted by Buddhabhadra. Tōrei, who borrows much of his information from Fo-jih Ch'i-sung, explains, for example, "in his childhood [the master's] name was P'u-t'i-to-lo. He then became a disciple of Po-je-to-lo. When the patriarch transmitted to him the seal of Dharma, the robe and the bowl, he said [to his disciple]: 'You should now take the name P'u-t'i-ta-mo.' " Tōrei explains that Ta-mo-to-lo results from the conjunction of the last two syllables of his newly attributed name, P'u-t'i-ta-mo, with the last two syllables of his childhood name, P'u-t'i-to-lo. Tōrei also specifies that since there were many meditation sūtras, the name of Ta-mo-to-lo was appended to differentiate it from similar treatises.[51]

In summary, polemics about the identity of a supposed "Dharmatrāta" do not appear entirely relevant here, because traditional accounts simply assume this figure to be another name for Bodhidharma. Consequently, should we translate the title of this text; it might as well be rendered *The Bodhidharma Sūtra*. Even if we could give credentials to Dharmatrāta as a historical figure (one among two or three different persons), it is highly probable that his name was borrowed at a certain stage to give more weight to the authority of this scripture. After taking these few precautions, let us now make a leap in time and have a closer look at the developments within the Chinese sphere during and after the Sung dynasty.

Rediscovery of the Ta-mo-to-lo ch'an ching during the Sung

Among peculiarities of the religious environment under the Sung dynasty, verbal attacks on the Buddhist clergy by Confucian teachers, or controversies between Ch'an and T'ien-t'ai monks, have already received considerable attention.[52] No doubt these external factors have contributed to reinforcing the need for orthodoxy and to producing various scholarly responses. One such reaction is embodied in the vast literary production of Fo-jih Ch'i-sung. Ch'i-sung, besides trying to show that the three teachings fundamentally didn't contradict each other, devoted remarkable energy to linking the Ch'an lineages to Indian patriarchs. He was neither the first nor the last monk to engage in this activity, but his originality was in going one step further than Shen-hui in systematically using the *Ta-mo-to-lo ch'an ching* as a central piece of evidence.

To condense Ch'i-sung's argument: like Shen-hui, he reasserted that there was no breach in the transmission of the Dharma from India to China. He maintained that the Ch'an teachings and practice represented the legitimate legacy of a lineage including twenty-eight Indian patriarchs, in contradistinction to his T'ien-t'ai opponents who maintained the existence of only twenty-four Indian patriarchs. For this claim, Ch'i-sung relied on the *Pao-lin Tradition* and on the *Ching-te Record of the Transmission of the Flame*, but he also quotes extensively from the *Ta-mo-to-lo ch'an ching* to support his claim. The authority conferred by Hui-yüan's venerable and cryptic Preface served to undermine the views of his T'ien-t'ai adversaries, even though the *Ta-mo-to-lo ch'an ching* mentions only nine of the Indian figures who are supposed to belong to this lineage.[53]

As Griffith Foulk puts it, "Ch'i-sung's polemical strategy would thus appear to be threefold: (1) to use historical arguments that could not be denied by T'ien-t'ai critics of the Ch'an lore, (2) to concede that certain aspects of the Ch'an transmission lore could not be substantiated historically, and (3) to evoke the special nature of dharma transmission in Ch'an in order to shield it from the very sort of historical criticism that he himself employed."[54]

What eventually contributed to Ch'i-sung's success in these polemics was his literary skill and the support he gained from the emperor,[55] but his work illustrates the extent of the Sung obsession with lineages. Nowhere in his writings do we see an analysis of the contents of the *Ta-mo-to-lo ch'an ching* and of its emphasis on meditative practice. In this regard, Tōrei's *Commentary*, because it follows the text paragraph by paragraph, gives a better idea of the purpose of Buddhabhadra's translation. As will be seen, Tōrei was, however, not the first Japanese monk to be impressed by the detailed descriptions found in this sūtra.

Japanese Developments

Myōe Shōnin

The *Genkō shakusho*, a collection of biographies of eminent Japanese priests compiled during the Genkō era (1321–1324), contains a perspicuous pronouncement by Myōe Kōben (1173–1232) about the state of Buddhism in his time:

> In our country, there are many wise and learned individuals [*egaku no mono*], but those who practice meditation [*jōshu no hito*] are extremely rare.[56] For some reason the approach of realization [*shōdō no mon*] is missing among practitioners; this is my great distress and the evil of this final period of the Law.[57]

The biography goes on to tell that "Myōe settled in a cave in the northern mountains [of Kyoto], building a temple where he would [absorb himself in] still meditation [*zen'en*] and thinking [*shiyui*], taking the *Wu-men ch'an-yao*[58] and the *Ta-mo-to-lo ch'an ching* as a means [to train his] mind [*shinjutsu*]."

This account does not allow us to infer the extent of Myōe's involvement in the study of the *Ta-mo-to-lo ch'an ching*, but it suggests that he used this text as a manual to deepen his own training. During his days as a young monk, Myōe seems to have been unable to find a human teacher who would match his expectations, and he recalls turning to the meditation sūtras, reading first the *Ch'an-fa yao-chieh* (T 15 no. 616) in 1191.[59] Myōe's case implies that some monks of the Kamakura period, whether or not affiliated with the Zen traditions,[60] were reading such sūtras and trying to put them into practice.

Tokugawa Zen Figures

If we now turn to the Tokugawa period, Dokuan Genkō (1630–1698) provides an illustration of how the contemplation of foulness (*fujōkan*) was still used for both proselytizing purposes and meditation. Among Dokuan's works, the *Kinzan Dokuansō gohōshū hannya kusōzu* ("The nine visualizations [taught in the] *Prajñā [-pāramitā-sūtra]*") deals specifically with this subject (fig. 7.2). This text, published in 1692, contains realistic black and white representations of the nine stages in the decomposition of a corpse, illustrated by the painter Terada Masanobu (n.d.).[61] According to Dokuan's own explanations, he decided

FIGURE 7.2. Pictures found in Dokuan's work. Dokuan Genkō (1630–1698) provides an illustration of how the contemplation of foulness (fujōkan) was still used for both proselytizing purposes and meditation. Among Dokuan's works, the *Kinzan Dokuansō gohōshū hannya kusōzu* ("The nine visualizations [taught in the] *Prajñā [-pāramitā-sūtra]*") deals specifically with this subject. This text, published in 1692, contains realistic black and white representations of the nine stages in the decomposition of a corpse, illustrated by the painter Terada Masanobu (n.d.). The nine stages are as follows: top row: left: (1) visualization (of the corpse) swelling (*chōsō*, Skt. *vyādhmātaka-sañjñā*); center: (2) visualization (of the corpse) breaking up (*kaisō*, Skt. *vipaśumaka-sañjñā*); right: (3) visualization of the blood spreading (on the ground) (*kettosō*, Skt. *vilohitaka-sañjñā*); middle row: left: (4) visualization of the (corpse) purulent and dislocating *nōransō*, Skt. *vipūyaka-sañjñā*); center: (5)

to write this manual for two of his young disciples who were in danger of infringing the precepts. At the beginning of his text, Dokuan mentions the passages of the *Large Prajñā pāramitā sūtra* describing these nine stages.[62] He further quotes the *Treatise of the Great Virtue of Wisdom*, which develops this method of contemplation.[63] One of the interesting features of Dokuan's text is that he confesses that he had tried to use the poems of Su Shih (1036–1101), *T'ung-p'o chiu- hsiang- shih* (J. *Tōba kusōshi*) but that they were too difficult for his young pupils.[64]

This work, including visual representations aimed at helping both monks and laypersons to become aware of impermanence, seems to be one of the last examples of this type of Buddhist painting. In Japanese art history there has been a long tradition of painted scrolls representing these nine successive aspects of the dead body (*kusōshi emaki*), at least since the Kamakura period,[65] but the traditional aversion toward death seems to have gradually contributed to its disappearance. Apparently, there is no trace of such artworks after the Tokugawa period, and to my knowledge no contemporary Japanese monk mentions it. My suspicion is that the fading of this practice may have been proportional to the rise of clerical marriage since the Meiji era.[66] One indication that supports this view is that in other East Asian countries some contemporary Buddhist orders emphasizing celibacy are still widely using the imagery of dead (female) bodies as an antidote to the monks' temptations.[67]

Tōrei's Commentary

The Autobiographical Dimension

By now Tōrei's prominent place among the successors of Hakuin Ekaku (1686–1769) might be known to some extent. Since my first inquiry concerning Tōrei's discovery of the *Ta-mo-to-lo ch'an ching*,[68] the circumstances of his encounter with this text have become increasingly clear. Tōrei's introduction to his *Commentary* provides the fullest account:

visualization of the (corpse) blue and soiled (*seiosō*, Skt. *vinīlaka sañjñā*); right: (6) visualization of the (corpse) being eaten (by animals) (*tansō*, Skt. *vikhāditaka-sañjñā*); bottom row: left: (7) visualization of the (corpse) being dispersed (*sansō*, Skt. *vikṣiptaka-sañjñā*); center: (8) visualization of the bones (*kossō*, Skt. *asthi-sañjñā*); right: (9) visualization of the cremation (*shōsō*, Skt. *vidagdhaka-sañjñā*). The Sanskrit equivalents follow Nakamura Hajime, ed. *Kōsetsu bukkyōgo daijiten* (Tokyo: Tōkyō shoseki, 2001), p. 336, where the nine stages are given in a different order. See also Tsukamoto Zenryū, ed., *Mochizuki bukkyō daijiten*, vol. 1 (Tokyo: Sekai seiten kankōkyōkai, 1973), pp. 678–679.

[Since] I left the house to become a monk at a young age, I have [always] had an especially [strong] faith in Bodhidharma [*daishi*], and for many years I have been searching for a sūtra [including] his teachings. When I incidentally read the biography of Saint Myōe in the *Genkō shakusho*, it included the title of this sūtra. I was deeply longing for it, but since nobody recommended or mentioned it, [I thought that] I couldn't trust [Myōe's story]. For a while I obtained the *Anthology of the Six Entrances by Bodhidharma* [C. *Shao-shih liu-men chi*; J. *Shōshitsu rokumonshū*][69] and [used it to] atone for my original intention.

However, there were people saying that this [anthology] didn't contain the teachings of Bodhidharma. While I got depressed by this for three or four years, I asked the painter Aoki to draw a picture of Bodhidharma [for me]. I always kept it in my pocket and made prostrations [in front of this image] for a thousand days. Additionally, I wrote a Eulogy [*raimon*] and prayed [to obtain his] inspiration [*kannō*]. When I later saw that the late master [Hakuin] quoted this [text] in his *Sokkōroku kaienfusetsu*, I asked [him] his opinion [concerning the anthology]. He said: "Even if it would not be the teachings of Bodhidharma, as long as [the author] was someone endowed with his insight, there is no point in arguing about it." This persuaded me to make up my mind, and I faithfully received [this text]. relishing [its contents].

In this connection, I received a small statue of Bodhidharma on the fifth day of the fifth month of 1746. While I was absorbed in seated meditation after having made prostrations [in front of the statue], I suddenly entered the ineffable melody of the flute without holes [*mukuteki no myōchō*].[70]

In the fall of 1762, I got for the first time [a copy] of the *Ch'an ching* but couldn't understand its meaning. Then, on the sixteenth day of the seventh month of 1765, I had a great insight [*ōini tokusho ari*]. From that time on, I kept reflecting [about this text] on every possible occasion. In the summer of 1774, I gave for the first time a lecture [on it] at Shōsen-ji in the country of Kōshū [present Shiga Prefecture]. Then [I lectured] once at Ryūtaku-ji [Entsū-zan] and once at Chōju-ji in Asakusa [Buryō]. After having eventually lectured three times [on this sūtra], I thought that I had done my best [with it]. In the winter of 1776, since the temple [where the *Commentary* was kept] suffered a fire and the text was burned into ashes,[71] I had to gather all my energy again and to renew my great vow. Forgetting tiredness for this research, I finally obtained [a copy of] the *Tsuo-ch'an san-mei ching*, and the meaning [of the *Ta-mo-to-lo ch'an ching*] became increasingly clear.[72]

In this account Tōrei discloses the main personal factors that led to his passionate study of the *Ch'an ching*. The way Hakuin eludes the issue of authorship is very instructive, but Tōrei's intellectual curiosity kept pushing him to gather any possible piece of evidence to clarify the origins of this text. Yet, since Tōrei used the same sources as Ch'i-sung, it is not surprising that most of his conclusions would closely follow those of his predecessor

Tōrei's Understanding of Bodhidharma Alias Dharmatrāta

Tōrei gives, for example, the following assessment concerning the Preface of the *Ch'an ching* by Hui-yüan:

> First, we have seen from the main text of Hui-yüan's Preface that this sūtra definitely has been taught [*toku tokoro*] by Bodhidharma and compiled [*amu tokoro*] by Buddhasena. Secondly, even if we consider this sūtra to have been taught by Bodhidharma before [the age of] twenty-seven, it is clear that it [represents a phase] posterior to his encounter with Prajñātāra and the [ensuing] transmission of the seal of the Buddha-mind. Otherwise, how would it have been possible for Hui-yüan to say that they were "the most talented [teachers] of the Western region, the founders of the meditation teachings" [*hsi-yü chih chün, ch'an-hsün chih tsung*]?[73]

According to this passage, Tōrei had a very precise idea of Bodhidharma/Dharmatrāta's lineage and of the timing for the transmission of the *Ch'an ching*. As will be seen, Tōrei's understanding of Bodhidharma/Dharmatrāta's characteristics was that of a master in the Abhidharma who had also become consummate in meditation and knowing human nature. It discloses a picture of Bodhidharma/Dharmatrāta much closer to that of an Indian scholar-monk than to the image of the silent thaumaturge that became widespread in the popular imagination. Tōrei gives this explanation for a passage in Ch'i-sung's work:

> In other words, at that time the great teacher [Bodhidharma] had personally received the essence of the *Tsuo-ch'an san-mei chin* [T 15 no. 614] written by Saint Saṃgharakṣa [*Sogyarasha sonja*]. Then after having met with Prajñātāra and transmitted the seal of the Buddha-mind, he again exposed the essentials of meditation [*zen'yō*] for his younger brothers in the Dharma including Buddhasena and Buddhabhadra, bringing [thus] to completion the purport [of the teachings he had received].[74]

From the criteria of today's scholarship, Tōrei's reconstruction of these Indian master–disciple relationships appears to be a nexus for legends, especially because there is so little firm ground concerning figures such as Prajñātāra or

Saṃgharakṣa. On the other hand, if we put ourselves in the position of a monk living in the eighteenth century, these stories may sound plausible. After all, research done after the twentieth century has fueled doubts about all these traditional accounts but has yet to propose a credible alternative. It may appear legitimate to discard all these figures as being pure fiction, but we then have to demonstrate that the contemporary prefaces by Hui-yüan and Huiguan were forgeries. Since careful research done by Kimura Eiichi and his team[75] tends to validate the materials attributed to Hui-yüan, the challenge remains intact.

Structure of the Text

Now that we have observed some of the factors related to the genesis of the *Ta-mo-to-lo ch'an ching* and its *Commentary*, it appears necessary to get an idea of the outline of the sūtra and of its two fascicles. The first striking mark of these seventeen chapters is that each of them begins with the word "practice" (*hsiu-hsing*). Concerning the distinction between the "expedient way" (*fang-pien tao*) and the "superior way" (*sheng tao*), it can be considered to express more or less advanced levels in the understanding of the same practice.

First fascicle:

1. Practice of the expedient way—backslide in mindful breathing
2. Practice of the superior way—backslide
3. Practice of the expedient way—stagnation[76] in mindful breathing
4. Practice of the superior way—stagnation
5. Practice of the expedient way—progress
6. Practice of the superior way—progress
7. Practice of the expedient way—decisive [stage] in mindful breathing
8. Practice of the superior way—decisive [stage]

Second fascicle:

9. Practice of the expedient way—backslide in the contemplation of foulness
10. Practice of the expedient way—stagnation in the contemplation of foulness
11. Practice of the expedient way—progress in the contemplation of foulness
12. Practice of the expedient way—decisive [stage] in the contemplation of foulness
13. Practice of contemplating the constituents (*dhātu*)
14. Practice of the samadhi of the four boundless [qualities] (*apramāṇa*)
15. Practice of contemplating the aggregates (*skandha*)
16. Practice of contemplating the sense-data (*āyatana*)
17. Practice of contemplating the twelve links of dependent origination (*pratītya-samutpāda*).

This table of contents shows a relatively simple structure, the most substantial part (the first eight chapters) being dedicated to presenting the different modalities and obstacles in mastering mindful breathing. In Tōrei's *Commentary*, three of the six volumes are thus devoted to examining this topic. The next four chapters describe the contemplation of foulness, with a similar progression from backslide (failure in practicing correctly) to the decisive stage, which represents mastery of that technique. Finally, the last five chapters focus on different doctrinal topics intended to develop further the wisdom (*prajñā*) of the practitioner. The sequence of these seventeen chapters is clearly intended to propose a progression, which culminates with the full understanding of the root of all dis-ease (*duhkha*): ignorance, and its manifold correlates.

Explicit and Implicit Purposes of Tōrei's Commentary

Given the present limits of speculations about the historicity of the various characters who appear on the stage of the *Ta-mo-to-lo ch'an ching* and its *Commentary*, I shall now concentrate on the significance of this text for Tōrei and his time.

In the autobiographical section translated earlier, it was seen that Tōrei had been attracted to the figure of Bodhidharma since he had become a monk. Even after meeting Hakuin at the age of twenty-three and after having received his certification at the age of twenty-nine, Tōrei's interest in Bodhidharma did not abate; it was indeed multiplied after he obtained the copy of the *Ch'an ching* at the age of forty-two. During his own training under the guidance of Hakuin, Tōrei was assigned kōans, and his biography tells how on several occasions he reached a deep insight into these old cases. Why then could he have been so fascinated by a text giving a rather down-to-earth description of mindful breathing, contemplation of foulness, or other topics of ancient Buddhist meditation?

Elsewhere I have mentioned Tōrei's propensity to emphasize the inseparability of Buddhist canonical teachings and the meditative approach.[77] Tōrei was not the first one to face this difficulty, but such a statement implies a dilemma: The postulate is that the teachings of early Buddhism are the closest to the historical Buddha and therefore should represent most faithfully his approach to practicing the way and realizing it. On the other hand, Ch'an teachers since the T'ang dynasty have claimed to be the only recipients of the essence of the original teachings, thus representing an antithesis to T'ien-t'ai and other scholastic schools. With the emergence of the Ch'an tradition as a distinctive group and its search for official support, this claim has evolved into the exclusive expression "Pure Ch'an of the Tathāgata" (*ju-lai ch'an*) used by Kui-feng Tsung-mi (780–841),[78] and then in its remolding as "Ch'an of the patriarchs" (*tsu-shih ch'an*). These hallmark slogans obviously imply uniqueness and superiority, or greater orthodoxy. However, reverence for the founder

(Śākyamuni Buddha) forbids contending that later generations have reached a deeper understanding. How did Tōrei resolve this apparent contradiction?

As a first measure, Tōrei espoused the classical view of the Buddha's teachings being divided into different periods and adapted to the capacities of his auditors. The innovation came when Tōrei resorted to no less than establishing his own classification of the teachings (hankyō), which comprises seven periods:[79]

1. The *Flower Ornament Sūtra* (*Avataṃsaka*)
2. The Deer Park (*Āgamas*)
3. The Developed sūtras (*vaipulya*)
4. The Perfection of Wisdom sūtras (*Prajñā-pāramitā*)
5. The *Lotus Sūtra* (*Saddharma-puṇḍarīka*) and the *Extinction Sūtra* (*Nirvāṇa*)
6. Shingon esoterism (Hidden splendor)
7. The Ch'an/Zen tradition (Going beyond).

We can easily recognize here the five periods (*goji*) taught in Tendai/T'ien-t'ai,[80] to which Tōrei added the categories 6 and 7.

One might ask whether Tōrei considered the *Ta-mo-to-lo ch'an ching* a classical sūtra belonging to one of the first five categories. Since he believed it to contain the teachings of Bodhidharma, the answer is negative. In his *Commentary*, Tōrei establishes detailed correspondences between the descriptions found in the *Ta-mo-to-lo ch'an ching* and the practice in his own Rinzai tradition, an indication of the fact that he considered this sūtra to belong to the seventh category of the Ch'an/Zen tradition. As an example, Tōrei would give this comment:

> The sixth chapter, "Practice of the superior way—progress," clarifies post-awakening [practice] [*gogo*], consultation [of a teacher] [*shin'eki*], passing the barriers [of kōans] [*tōkan*], and delving [*sensaku*]. It corresponds to what is described in the *Record of Lin-chi* by saying, "With further delving, when he becomes a great tree . . ." [81]

From our perspective, this type of exegesis appears to be a retrospective projection of Ch'an/Zen understanding and terminology onto the original text of the sūtra, but Tōrei seems completely comfortable with his interpretation. His explicit purpose is to unfold the meaning of a canonical text that would have already subsumed the whole curriculum assigned to Zen practitioners in the Tokugawa Rinzai school. We should also remember that the *Commentary* is the result of three rounds of oral teachings (*teishō*) given to the monastic community, with probably some lay audience. Tōrei's intention in using this sūtra was thus to spend time with his auditors pondering the fundamentals of meditation practice, with the greatest emphasis on mindful breathing and the contemplation on foulness. Since Tōrei was simultaneously instructing his disciples in using kōans, this return to the essentials of meditation must have been meant as a way to avoid one of the most frequent dangers of kōan practice: its falling into a mere literary exercise. He says in his other major work: "After having broken through the multiple solid barriers [of the kōans] [rōkan], when you return to the examination of the sūtras and treatises, it is as if you were yourself teaching [these texts]."[82]

If we go one step further in questioning some of the implicit agendas of Tōrei's Commentary, we can surmise his intention of using the prestige of the Ta-mo-to-lo ch'an ching to enhance the respectability of the tradition he represents. Much in the same way as Ch'i-sung did during the Sung period, Tōrei had to use scholarly skills to demonstrate that his school was the recipient of a tradition stemming directly from the historical Buddha. During Tōrei's abbacy, the Ryūtaku-ji was actually meant to become a central practice center for the whole country (konpon dōjō), fulfilling the role that Mount Hiei had played in the past.[83] In the Commentary as well as in Tōrei's other works, one sees a commitment to describe a religious path that would even go beyond the borders of Buddhism and encompass all the other religions of which he was aware:

> In the case of the teachings by Confucius or Lao-tzu, as well as in the Way of the kamis, they were all bodhisattvas [having attained] equal awakening [tōgakui]. Hiding their virtue and concealing their brightness, they [appeared] similar to human beings. They taught according to circumstances; inside, they spontaneously encouraged the approach by the unique vehicle of kenshō; outside, they gave to the world everlasting models.[84]

In this regard, the importance Tōrei gave to Shinto is a conspicuous dimension of his life, one that regularly surfaces in the Commentary.

Importance of the Shinto Dimension

Tōrei's biography reminds us that his interest in Shinto scriptures goes back to his days as a young monk, when he practiced in the community of Kogetsu Zenzai (1667–1751). Kogetsu had suggested that he study the Daiseikyō whenever he found some spare time. The biography adds that Tōrei later heard about this text, which Chōon Dōkai (1628–1695) of Kurotaki had received from Nagano Uneme (1616–1687), but that he could not procure it until 1764, when he met a man named Hakuō (n.d.), Nagano's descendent in the seventh generation.[85] Almost one century had elapsed since the publication of the Sendai kujihongi daiseikyō and its subsequent interdiction by the Bakufu, so it was perhaps less dangerous to study or quote this scripture.

In Tōrei's Commentary, the Introduction contains several quotations of the Sendai kujihongi daiseikyō, which are in particular related to the legend of Bodhidharma's being reborn in Japan. The whole story presupposes another tradition that considered Shōtoku Taishi to have been a reincarnation of the T'ien-t'ai patriarch Hui-szu (515–577).[86] The legend as recounted by Tōrei and his sources distinguishes four phases in Bodhidharma's Japanese manifestations.

First, he proceeded to the northeast of Japan, "concealing his brilliance and hiding his traces in Matsushima for thirty years."[87] Then, seeing that the birth of Shōtoku was imminent and that the time was ripe, Bodhidharma "came flying and instantly transformed into a swift horse, which was fostered by Tachibana no Toyohinomiya."[88] One day, "when [the pregnant mother of Shōtoku] Princess Hashibito[89] passed in front of the [Imperial] Mews, the horse bent its knees and gave three [loud] neighs. Upon [hearing] this, the Princess gave birth to [Shōtoku] Taishi without being aware of it. The horse immediately transformed into a maid, who took the baby in her arms and entered the main aisle of the palace."[90]

The fourth extraordinary event is related to the encounter with a beggarlike figure who was lying on the roadside: "On his way back [Shōtoku] made a detour and entered Kataokayama. On the road there was a starving man [uebito]. [The imperial train] had barely progressed three jō [about ten yards] when [Shōtoku's horse] Kurogoma approached [the man] and wouldn't move [an inch]."[91] Finally, Shōtoku alit from his horse, questioned the man about his whereabouts, and asked why he was lying there. The prince also took off his own attire to cover the starving man. They exchanged a few words, but although the attendants heard the conversation they did not understand its meaning. Eventually Shōtoku Taishi composed a poem, the man raised his head and offered his reply in verses. The following day, retainers sent to examine the site where the starving man was lying reported him to be dead. Shōtoku lamented and ordered his ministers to build a grave. Shōtoku's unusual solicitude for a man of such poor extraction provoked dissidence among members of the Court. To settle the matter, Shōtoku commanded the enraged ministers to go and inspect the grave. They found the grave to be perfectly sealed; although the coffin was intact, no corpse was found. Instead the coffin was filled with an extraordinary fragrance and they found Shōtoku's attire folded on the coffin.

The prototype of this story is already included in the Nihonshoki,[92] but one of the characteristics of the Sendai kujihongi daiseikyō is to associate this enigmatic figure with Bodhidharma:

One day, the Emperor [Shōtoku] asked his attendants, "What was the name of the starving man of Kataokayama?"

The attendants: "We ignore it, but [the diviner] Hitoatomi no Ichihi is the only person who might know it." The Emperor summoned him and asked [the same question]. Ichihi prostrated himself and said, "I have heard words whispered by a divine being [kanto no *hito*]. It may have been the Brahman-monk Bodhidharma [*Bara-monsō Bodaidaruma*][93] from the most remote Western [land]."[94]

Apparently annoyed by this evasive reply, Shōtoku inquires whether there is any deity in the palace. Thereupon, a kami materializes in the form of an aged duke who claims to be Sumiyoshi no kami. Shōtoku asks again for the confirmation of the identity of the starving man. The deity gives a hearty laugh and throws off an auspicious poem, giving a concluding verse to which he asks Shōtoku to append the first verse. This ending in the form of a literary pirouette contributes a further touch of mystery to the whole tale of the starving man, alias Bodhidharma.

These accounts conclude Tōrei's Introduction and are given without comments. They reveal a facet of Tōrei's fascination for Shinto teachings that is quite different from the more philosophical dimension, about which he provided original interpretations. In his comments on texts belonging to the Five Ise Scriptures of the Watarai school, Tōrei has in particular established a strict equivalence between primeval chaos (*konton*) and the realization of one's intrinsic nature (*kenshō*).[95]

One might therefore wonder to what extent Tōrei believed in such stories. In other words, his choice to include these legends in his *Commentary* suggests three main hypotheses: (1) He believed them and wanted to share them with his auditors; (2) he accepted them as belonging to the lore but mentioned them to make his teaching more accessible to his Japanese audience; (3) he understood that they represented sheer legend but chose to cite them to underline that the *Ta-mo-to-lo ch'an ching* does not represent purely foreign teachings but also comprises an indigenous dimension.

The lack of Tōrei's comments on these Shinto sources seems to denote his distance, and I would be inclined to adopt the third hypothesis, but in these subjective interpretations it is always safer to suppose the "worst," namely the first hypothesis. In any event, these Japanese narratives relating to Bodhidharma illustrate the indigenization process of Buddhist doctrines, practices, and symbols. They also demonstrate that during the Tokugawa period the propagation of teachings that suggest an alien or Indian dimension, such as mindful breathing or contemplation of foulness, had to be put into relation with anecdotic, "local" events, to make people feel that they were dealing with something "close at hand" and not with some exotic meditation practice. The whole equilibrium between "familiarity" and "strangeness" is precisely one of the parameters that was to change, at least on the surface, with the advent of the Meiji Reformation.

Conclusions

This limited journey back and forth between the eighteenth and the fifth centuries leaves little doubt about the fact that the *Ta-mo-to-lo ch'an ching* belongs to a relatively early stage in the development of Chinese Buddhism. It systematically presents some of the meditation techniques used around the beginning of the fifth century and before, allowing us to get a glimpse of Buddhist practice before the emergence of the T'ien-t'ai and Ch'an schools. Tōrei's fascination with that period and that peculiar text might be related to the assumption that it represents a stage of Chinese Buddhism before the most visible rise of sectarian rivalries. Although Tōrei's affiliation makes him fully endorse the legend of twenty-eight Indian patriarchs culminating with Bodhidharma, one can presume that his level of scholarship made him aware that it did not necessarily represent factual history. If the distinction between sacred history and factual history had a meaning at his time, he deliberately chose to tell sacred history to his auditors while digging out for himself what he could glean from remaining documents. What he tells about Bodhidharma does appear naïve, essentially because he cannot reassess the true character of the patriarch. Nevertheless, the figure of Bodhidharma is *useful* for conveying his own message to the public. In other words, the enigmatic figure of Bodhidharma alias Dharmatrāta is ideal for proposing reform of his school—that is, a return to the essentials of Buddhist practice—or even enlarging it in the direction of a pan-Buddhist movement as seen in the ambitious aim for Ryūtaku-ji.

At the level of practice, Tōrei's *Commentary* can be read as a quest for the roots of Zen in early meditation techniques. The original *Ta-mo-to-lo ch'an ching* itself already provides a testimony to the perception that meditation techniques do exist independently from doctrinal contents. Mindful breathing or contemplation on foulness was sometimes labeled Hīnayāna, sometimes Mahāyāna. Later they would be incorporated into the practice of Ch'an/Zen adepts, and now mindful breathing is still widely practiced in Theravāda circles or in many Zen congregations; the labels are changing, but for those immersed in such concentration exercises, the focus of the mind is identical. Since ancient times, meditative absorption (*dhyāna*) and wisdom (*prajñā*) have been depicted as complementary, like the two "wings of awakening" (*bodhipakṣa*).[96] The significance of Tōrei's *Commentary* today is related to the understanding of the place of meditation within the whole framework of Buddhist practice. At the end of his six volumes, Tōrei says, "Don't laugh [at me] for my careless commentaries: I have only opened the way, waiting for wise people to come in the future!"[97] A lot remains to be done to further pave the way.

NOTES

1. The word "meditation" will be used here as a generic term to indicate the different forms of cultivation (Skt. *bhāvanā*) taught in the texts examined in this chapter. Several titles of *sūtras* discussed here contain the Chinese characters *ch'an ching* or *san-mei ching*, which respectively correspond to *dhyāna-sūtra* or *samādhi-sūtra*. The Sanskrit *dhyāna* and its Pāli equivalent *jhāna* both refer to the *technique* of focusing the mind on one object and to the *state* of concentration obtained therefrom. There are, of course, further classifications such as the four *dhyānas* and the four *samapattis*, culminating in the "attainment of cessation" (*nirodhasamāpatti*). A useful introduction on the subject of Buddhist meditation, showing also distinctions from Christian "meditation," is found in Griffiths 1993, pp. 34–47.

2. The text was completed in 1780 (Tenmei 1). It was first published in 1784, and one of the few copies of this first edition is kept at the Jinbun Kagaku Kenkyūsho in Kyoto. However, the 1894 (Meiji 27) edition can be more easily found and scrupulously reproduces the original, with a slightly different pagination. Hereafter, all the quotes of Tōrei's *Commentary* will refer to the 1894 edition.

3. I conducted a research seminar on this text between November 1999 and February 2002. The whole work is made of six volumes in sixteen fascicles, and the first step in conducting a systematic study of this text must be its publication. The primary stages of this project having now been completed, I here present some initial results and working hypotheses.

4. There is only one article in Japanese dealing specifically with Tōrei's text: Kimura Jōyū (1963).

5. A good literal translation for this expression is "a separate transmission apart from the teachings," in Foulk 1999, p. 220. However, since this phrase already implies a critique of the "teachings" and challenges the reliance on mere written scriptures that are supposed to reflect the instructions of the historical Buddha, I prefer to add the adjective "scholastic."

6. Faure 1993, p. 128.

7. See Mohr 2002.

8. Concerning Mujaku in English, see App 1987.

9. Tōrei was an expert in Watarai Shinto, and in his *Commentary* he often quotes the *Sendai kujihongi daiseikyō*, a text that was forbidden at his time and that has only recently become available in Shintō taikei hensankai, ed. 1999. The relation between monks belonging to the Ōbaku school and this text is being reexamined. See Nogawa Hiroyuki 1999–2000, and Satō Shunkō 2002.

10. The importance of Bodhidharma, or rather its avatar as "Daruma," in Japanese popular religion and its deep links with various beliefs coming from the theory of the "five agents" (*gogyō*) have been thoroughly examined by Yoshino 1995.

11. The concept itself is attributed to Suzuki Daisetsu (1870–1966), who shared many of his ideas with his friend Nishida Kitarō (1870–1945). I have examined the story of the emergence of "Zen thought" (*Zen shisō*) during the Meiji period in the fall 2002 issue no. 943 of the journal *Shisō*.

12. The poem and the few words at the beginning of the book are signed by

Kyōdō Etan (Ashi 1809–1895), the Myōshin-ji chief-abbot, who was eighty-six years old at that time. It is followed by another foreword by Nan'in Zengu (Watanabe 1834–1904), a fellow teacher in the Rinzai school. The date of this reprint is also extremely interesting: it was the winter of 1893 (Meiji 26), a few months after the World's Parliament of Religions, where Kōgaku Sōen had for the first time represented his school abroad.

13. An interesting approach to these issues can be found in Bronkhorst 1993, 1998.

14. See McRae 1986, pp. 80–82. McRae focuses on the role of this sūtra in the theory of patriarchal lineages, saying that "Buddhabhadra's *Ta-mo-to-lo ch'an ching* and its prefaces by Hui-yuan and Hui-kuan constitute a very important source for the development of the Ch'an transmission theory," p. 80. The focus on this aspect of the text can also be found in Yanagida 1983, pp. 27–29.

15. T 55 no. 2145: 65b22–66a23. The pioneer studies of Kimura 1960 and 1962 remain important resources for the study of Hui-yüan, including his preface.

16. It bears the title *Hsiu-hsing-ti pu-ching hsü* (Preface to the Yogacarabhumi [on] the Contemplation of Foulness) but apparently refers to the same text (T 55 no. 2145: 66b03–67a13). See also Lin 1949, pp. 348–349, for a partial translation of this preface.

17. There is a whole section in Tōrei's *Commentary* entitled "Reflections about Dates" (*nenkō*) in the Introduction, pp. 34b–37a. Tōrei carefully avoids being too affirmative and says: "We can infer from [Ch'i-sung's] *Discussion of the True Lineage of Dharma Transmission [Ch'uan-fa chen-tsung lun]* that the time Hui-yüan wrote his Preface and circulated this sūtra corresponds to the seventh or eighth year of the I-hsi era (412–413), during the reign of the Emperor An of the Eastern Chin (317–420) dynasty." The capital was Chien-k'ang, present Nan-ching. Tōrei adds further references to show that this year 412 corresponds to that of the translation of the *Nirvāṇa-sūtra* and the *Laṅkāvatāra-sūtra* by T'an-wu-ch'en (Dharmakṣema), and he also mentions that the next year (413) saw the demise of Kumārajīva.

18. The Chinese phonetic equivalent of the Sanskrit title is mentioned by Hui-yüan in his Preface T 15 no.618: 301b22. For a recent state of the question concerning the different *Yogācārabhūmi* texts, see Odani Nobuchiyo 2000, p. 177. At least one other text translated by Buddhabhadra, the *Tathāgatagarbha-sūtra*, has been rendered into English, but I cannot help having serious reservations on some passages in Grosnick 1995.

19. Zürcher 1972, p. 33.

20. Since the pioneering works of Ui Hakuju and Paul Demiéville, some progress has been made in this area, with recent scholarship favoring Demiéville's interpretation of a gradual incorporation of Mahayanist concepts into basically Hinayanist techniques. Odani 2000, pp. 170–180.

21. One of the most comprehensive surveys to date is found in Yamabe 1999.

22. Yamabe 2000, pp. 208–216.

23. Zürcher 1991, p. 282.

24. Zürcher 1991, p. 283.

25. There were actually two different groups within the Sarvāstivādin school, with slight differences in their teachings. See Hirakawa and Groner 1990, p. 135.

26. T 55 no. 2145: 69b14–15 and b21. See the partial translation in Demiéville 1954, pp. 346–347.

27. Demiéville 1954, pp. 397–434.

28. T 50 no. 2059: 334b26–335c14.

29. T 50 no. 2059: 335b02–b15.

30. The *Biography of Eminent Monks* gives a rather positive account of the meeting between Buddhabhadra and Kumārajīva in Ch'ang-an, relating that "Kumārajīva was delighted [of this encounter]. They discussed together the Yogācāra (*fa-hsiang*) [doctrines], and [their] unveiling of the most subtle [aspects] brought many enlightening benefits" (T 50 no. 2059: 335a04–a05). The biography even hints at Buddhabhadra's superiority by saying that "whenever Kumārajīva had a doubt, he would unfailingly discuss it [with Buddhabhadra] and settle [the matter]" (ibid., p. 335a04–a07). Finally, the ruler took interest in these two Indian teachers, organizing a public debate between them, which met with great success. This apparently caused jealousy among the monks who had been residing in Ch'ang-an for longer, so that "they expressed their disagreement and deceived the people" (ibid., p. 335a22–a23). As a result of further maneuvers, Buddhabhadra was forced to leave Ch'ang-an with his disciple Hui-kuan and about forty followers (ibid., p. 335b03–b06). This episode is also summarized in the *Record of the True Lineage of Dharma Transmission* (*Ch'uan-fa chen-tsung chi*) by Fo-jih Ch'i-sung (1007–1072; T. 51 no. 2078: 767c09–c11). Tōrei incorporates Ch'i-sung's version in his own *Commentary* (fascicle 1, p. 1a). Later, Hui-yüan personally wrote a letter to the ruler Yao Hsing, asking him to revoke the verdict of the unjust expulsion of Buddhabhadra in 410 C.E. (T 50 no. 2059: 335b14–b15; Zürcher 1972, p. 212 and note 185, p. 397).

31. T 50 no. 2059: 335b16.

32. There are a few mentions of Buddhasena in the *Ch'u san-tsang chi chi* (T 55 no. 2145: 66a26, 66c25, 66c26, 67a03, 67a04, 106b29), three of them being from Hui-yüan's preface to the *Ta-mo-to-lo ch'an ching*. The name of Buddhasena also appears in the *Mochizuki bukkyō daijiten*, Tsukamoto 1973, vol. 5, pp. 4262b and 4467b, but only marginally in articles on other figures. See also Zürcher 1972, p. 223, and Akanuma 1979, p. 107b. In his dictionary, Saigusa Mitsuyoshi (1987, pp. 222b–223a) also mentions Buddhasiṁha, who might be related to Buddhasena.

33. See Watson 1993, pp. xxiv–xxv for a succinct biography of Kumārajīva. For the sake of simplification, I have adopted the dates given by Watson 1993, p. xxv. There are, however, many variants and no agreement has been reached yet. See Demiéville 1978, p. 267, and Kamata 1981, pp. 75–77.

34. In particular the *Ch'an mi-yao-fa ching* (T 15 no. 613), a translation that might have been wrongly attributed to Kumārajīva, and the *Ch'an fa-yao chieh* (T 15 no. 616).

35. *Commentary*, fascicle 1, p. 10a. The full passage is translated on page 228.

36. Satō 1984, pp. 348–349.

37. For the translation of *pu-ching kuan* (Skt. *aśubhabhāvanā*, Pāli-*asubhabhavana*), I have followed Buddhaghosa, Ñāṇamoli 1999, and Wilson 1996. The Indian words denote the negation of "beauty," "radiance" (Skt. *śubha*, Pāli *subha*), and evoke something "repulsive" or "horrible" in Wilson 1996, p. 103, while the Chinese expression is constructed with two characters indicating the negation of "purity."

38. This is a tentative translation for *teng-fen*, which is the equivalent of *t'ung-fen* and corresponds to the Sanskrit *sabhāga* in *Mochizuki bukkyō daijiten*, vol. 5 p. 4320a.

39. See Nakamura 2001, p. 486c. The first use of the term *wu t'ing-hsin kuan* is credited to the other Hui-yüan (523–592) in his *Ta-ch'eng i-chang* (T 44 no. 1851: 658a08, 668b16–b19, 755c07), but the techniques themselves had been employed before him. A discussion of these parallels is found in Odani 2000, pp. 137–142. There are unmistakable correspondences with the six kinds of temperament taught in the Pāli sources and summarized in the *Visuddhimagga*. They are "greedy temperament, hating temperament, deluded temperament, faithful temperament, intelligent temperament, and speculative temperament," according to Buddhaghosa,and Ñāṇamoli 1999, p. 101.

40. Among the meditation sūtras included in T 15, the *Ta-mo-to-lo ch'an ching* is the only text to use the term *an-pan-nien*, a phonetic rendering for mindful breathing that corresponds to the Sanskrit *ānāpānasmṛti*. The other texts sometimes use the longer form *a-na pan-na* but most often employ the Chinese translation *shu-hsi*, which literally indicates "counting the breath" but refers to the same technique.

41. T 15 no. 618: 301c02.

42. Odani 2000, pp. 138–139. However, Odani's contention that the *Ta-mo-to-lo ch'an ching*, although it focuses on mindful breathing and the contemplation of foulness, contains all five contemplations, is not entirely convincing (p. 185). The main reason is that concentration on the Buddha cannot be found in this text.

43. An anecdote in Buddhabhadra's biography recounts that his friend Datta was once absorbed in seated meditation within a closed room when he suddenly saw Buddhabhadra approaching. Datta asked how he came to be there, and Buddhabhadra replied that he had just been to the Tuṣita Heaven to pay his respects to Maitreya. As soon as he said these words, he vanished. *Kao-seng-chuan* 2, T 50 no. 2059: 334c09–c11.

44. See Takasaki 1982, pp. 2–42.

45. These features are well summarized by Odani 2000.

46. "De la grande somme mahāyānāniste d'Asaṅga, c'est donc la *Yogācārabhūmi* de Saṃgharakṣa qui devait être le prototype hīnayāniste le plus considérable et sans doute le plus ancien." Demiéville 1954, p. 396.

47. See in particular Lin 1949 and Demiéville 1978.

48. The common view on Fa-chiu is that he was the first patriarch of the Sarvāstivādin school in India and probably lived around the second century C.E. Charles Muller, ed. Digital Dictionary of Buddhism (http://www.acmuller.net/ddb/index.html). He is also considered the author of the *Wu-shih p'i-p'o-sha lun* (T 28 no. 1555).

49. Kodama. 1993, p. 168.

50. Yanagida 1999, p. 595; reprint of *Tōshi no keifu* 1954. Concerning the dates for Ho-tsê Shen-hui (684–758), see Faure 1988 and its English translation in Faure 1997.

51. *Commentary* fascicle 1, p. 1a.

52. One of the first scholars to spotlight the depths of the Ch'an-T'ient'ai polemics was Takao 1941. Takao largely accepts the T'ien-t'ai critique and acknowledges the "distortions" by Fo-jih Ch'i-sung, saying that "Ch'i-sung takes Ta-mo-to-lo for P'u-t'i-ta-mo, and the passage in the fifth fascicle of his *Record of the True Lineage of Dharma*

Transmission where he considers the *Ch'an-ching* as the work of P'u-t'i-ta-mo before the age of twenty-seven is rather comical" (ibid., p. 10). In English, two collective volumes provide a good overview of the Sung period and of its Buddhist and non-Buddhist dimensions: Ebrey and Gregory 1993, and Gregory and Getz 1999.

53. This criticism is in particular expressed by the T'ien-t'ai scholar Tzu-fang, one of Ch'i-sung's opponents who had been claiming that the use of the *Ta-mo-to-lo ch'an ching* was misleading. His position is summarized in the *Fo-tsu t'ung-chi*, T 49 no. 2035: 242a03–a23. More on these debates can be found in English in Huang 1986, pp. 182–183.

54. Foulk 1999, p. 259.

55. Huang 1999, pp. 314–316.

56. Paraphrase of the words "Those who understand the Way are many, those who practice it are few. Many explain the principle, few penetrate it," which are attributed to Bodhidharma. This sentence appears in the *Tzu-t'ang chi* (Chung-wen pp. 39b10–b11) and became "canonical" after its inclusion in the *Ching-tê Record of the Transmission of the Flame*, (T 51 no. 2076: 219c14–c15). Tōrei also quotes the first part of it in his *Commentary* (Introduction, pp. 2b and 13b) and in his *Shūmon mujintōron* (*Treatise on the Inexhaustible Lamp of our Lineage*), T 81 no. 2575: 594c11–c12.

57. *Dainihon bukkyō zensho*, vol. 101, p. 73a (Tokyo: Bussho kankōkai 1913). *Commentary*, Introduction, p. 9b.

58. The *Wu-men ch'an-ching yao-yung-fa* ("How to Use the Essentials of the Meditation Sūtra of the Five Gates," T 15 no. 619).

59. Girard 1990, pp. 74–75.

60. The affiliation of Myōe is somehow ambiguous in that regard, because although he is mainly regarded as a reviver of the Kegon school, some biographical accounts report that he received a certification from the Rinzai monk Myōan Yōsai (1141–1215). This is the case of Tōrei's *Commentary*, Introduction, p. 17b. Despite Yōsai's appearance in one of Myōe's dreams, Girard has serious reservations concerning a direct affiliation of Myōe with Yōsai. Girard 1990, pp. 255–256.

61. Yoshida Michioki 1996, p. 159.

62. T 7 no. 220: 7b24–b27 and 429c17–c19.

63. T 25 no. 1509: 217a–218d. Lamotte's French translation (1944–1981, vol. III, pp. 1311–1328).

64. *Sōtōshū zensho: Goroku* 1, p. 817b16 (Tokyo: Sōtōshū zensho kankōkai, 1931).

65. See Chin 1998.

66. This phenomenon is well depicted in Jaffe 2001.

67. See in particular the numerous figures from a contemporary illustrated edition of the *Dhammapada* printed in Taiwan, reproduced in Wilson 1996.

68. Mōru 1987.

69. See the translation and discussion of this text in Broughton 1999.

70. This metaphor also appears in Chinese sources. Like "a harp without strings," it refers to a musical instrument whose resources are limitless. See Koga Hidehiko 1991, p. 440. Here it is an allusion to Tōrei's state of *samādhi*.

71. This is the fire that burnt Ryūtaku-ji on the seventeenth day of the twelfth month of An'ei 5 (= January 26, 1777). The event is also recounted in Tōrei's biography, when he was fifty-six. See Nishimura Eshin 1982, p. 239.

72. *Commentary*, Introduction, pp. 9b–10a.

73. *Commentary*, Introduction, p. 31b. This passage corresponds to T 55 no. 2145 p. 66a11–a12 in Hui-yüan's Preface quoted in the *Ch'u-san-ts'ang chi-chi*. It is repeatedly mentioned by Ch'i-sung in his works (T 51 no. 2079: 772b28, no. 2080: 776c18, 777a23, 778a26, and 780c12). See also Kimura 1960, p. 447.

74. *Commentary*, fascicle 1, p. 32a.

75. Kimura 1960 and 1962.

76. I chose to translate *chu* as "stagnation" because there are two passages in the sūtra that explicitly speak of "getting rid of the two mistakes of backslide and stagnation" (*li t'ui-chu kuo*; T 15 no. 618: 301b26 and 314b06).

77. Mohr 2000, p. 263.

78. In his *Preface to the Collected Writings on the Source of Ch'an* (*Ch'an-yüan chu-ch'üan-chi tu-hsu*) Tsung-mi says after describing four inferior types of meditation: "If you immediately realize that your own mind is intrinsically pure, that since the beginning defilements never existed, that the nature of wisdom without misery has always been endowed by itself, that this mind is nothing else than Buddha, and that eventually there is no difference, and if you practice accordingly, then this is the meditation of the highest vehicle [*tsui-shang-ch'eng ch'an*]. It is also named Pure meditation of the Tathāgata [*ju-lai ch'an*] or One-practice samādhi [*i-hsing san-mei*]. The one developed and transmitted among the disciples of Bodhidharma is this type of meditation. It is only the one transmitted by Bodhidharma that is immediately identical to the essence of the Buddha (*fo-t'i*), and it differs completely from the other approaches" T 48 no. 2015: 399b16–b27. Peter Gregory mentions two dissertations containing English translations of this text, but I have not been able to consult them (1981, p. 316).

79. This classification scheme is developed in Tōrei's *Shūmon mujintōron* (*Treatise on the Inexhaustible Lamp of our Lineage*) T 81 no. 2575: 600b19–b29. Translation in Mohr 1997. A less elaborate version is found in Tōrei's *Commentary*, Introduction, pp. 12a–12b.

80. See, for instance, Chegwan and Masao 1983, pp. 31 and 57–69.

81. *Commentary*, fascicle 6, p. 1a. This corresponds to the *Record of Lin-chi* T 47 no. 1985: 504c12, containing an allusion to the future achievements of Lin-chi. The full sentence is: "In the future, with delving, he will become a great tree providing cool shade for the people of the world." In the compound *ch'uan-tso* both characters mean "piercing," and this expression literally indicates "digging up, deepening, searching [further]," often used with the nuance of a "useless search." Yanagida has the note, "Open a hole. Here it means training oneself and reach perfect maturity" (1972, p. 234), hence my translation "delving."

82. *Shūmon mujintōron* (*Treatise on the Inexhaustible Lamp of our Lineage*) T 81 no. 2575: 584a22–a23.

83. This argument is developed by Suzuki 1985.

84. *Shūmon mujintōron* T 81 no. 2575: 602b13–b16.

85. Tōrei's biography, age forty-four. See Nishimura 1982, p. 192.

86. See Durt 1985, pp. 18–19. One of the first attempts to connect the figure of Shōtoku Taishi with Hui-szu seems to be the work of the T'ien-t'ai Chinese missionary Szu-ch'a (n.d., around the eighth century), who came to Japan and wrote the *Jōgū kōtaishi bosatsu den* (included in *Dainihon bukkyō sho* vol. 112).

87. *Commentary*, Introduction, p. 39b. Here Tōrei quotes the *Daruma sanchōden*, a text attributed to Taisū (n.d.). I have recently obtained a copy of this rare book, kept at the library of Ritsumeikan University. The Preface, bearing the date 1791, specifies that it is the posthumous publication of a text left by Shikyō Eryō (1721–1787). The passage quoted here is found in the third fascicle of the *Daruma sanchōden*, pp. 1a and 5a. Tōrei must have seen an earlier version of the *Daruma sanchōden*, since his *Commentary* is dated 1780.

88. The future father of Shōtoku Taishi, who was the fourth son of Emperor Kinmei and later became Emperor Yōmei. Sanseidō henshūsho, 1988, p. 1178a.

89. Also known as Anahobe no Hashihito no himemiko. Sanseidō henshūsho, 1988, p. 36.

90. *Commentary*, Introduction, p. 39b. This quote from the *Daruma sanchōden* comes from the third fascicle p. 5a, which explicitly mentions Bodhidharma. In the second quote, except for "The horse immediately transformed into a maid," this text repeats almost textually the account found in *Sendai kujihongi daiseikyō* fascicle 35 in Shintō taikei hensankai 1999, vol. 2, pp. 336–337.

91. *Commentary*, Introduction, p. 41. Here Tōrei quotes from the *Sendai kujihongi daiseikyō* fascicle 38 in Shintō taikei hensankai 1999, vol. 2, pp. 389–390.

92. Fascicle 22 of the *Nihonshoki*. See Kojima Noriyuki 1998, vol. 3, pp. 569–571.

93. The *Sendai kujihongi daiseikyō* has *Barasō Bodaidaruma*, where *Barasō* apparently is a mistake for *Baramonsō*. I have followed Tōrei's correction in adding the missing character *mon*. Shintō taikei hensankai 1999, vol. 4, p. 172. *Commentary*, Introduction, p. 42a.

94. *Commentary*, Introduction, p. 42a, in Shintō taikei hensankai 1999, vol. 4, p. 172.

95. I have investigated this matter in Mōru 1995, pp. 207–238. Concerning Watarai Shinto, an excellent study is now available: Teeuwen 1996.

96. Bugault 1968, p. 56.

97. *Commentary*, fascicle 6, p. 38a.

REFERENCES

Akanuma Chizen. 1979. *Indo bukkyō jinmei jiten.* Kyoto: Hōzōkan.

App, Urs. 1987. "Chan/Zen's Greatest Encyclopaedist Mujaku Dōchū." *Cahiers d'Extrême-Asie* 3: 155–174.

Bronkhorst, Johannes. 1993. *The Two Traditions of Meditation in Ancient India.* Delhi: Motilal Banarsidass.

———. 1998. *The Two Sources of Indian Asceticism.* Delhi: Motilal Banarsidass.

Broughton, Jeffrey L. 1999. *The Bodhidharma Anthology: The Earliest Records of Zen.* Berkeley, Cal.: University of California Press.

Buddhaghosa, and Ñāṇamoli. 1999. *The Path of Purification: Visuddhimagga.* 1st BPE Pariyatti Ed. ed. Seattle, Wash.: BPE Pariyatti Editions.

Bugault, Guy. 1968. *La notion de "prajñā" ou de sapience selon les perspectives du "Mahāyāna": Part de la connaissance et de l'inconnaissance dans l'anagogie bouddhique.* Paris: E. de Boccard (repr. 1982).

Chegwan, David W., and Masao Ichishima. 1983. *T'ien-t'ai Buddhism: An Outline of The Fourfold Teachings*. Tokyo: Daiichi Shobō; distributed by University Press of Hawaii.

Chin, Gail. 1998. "The Gender of Buddhist Truth: The Female Corpse in a Group of Japanese Paintings." *Japanese Journal of Religious Studies* 25/3–4: 277–317.

Demiéville, Paul. 1954. "La Yogācārabhūmi de Saṅgharakṣa." *Bulletin de l'École Française d'Extrême-Orient* 44/2: 339–436.

———. 1978. "Appendice sur 'Ta-mo-to-lo' (Dharmatrāta)." In *Peintures Monochromes de Dunhuang (Dunhuang baihua)*. Paris: Adrien-Maisonneuve.

———, Hubert Durt, and Anna Seidel, eds. 1978. *Répertoire du Canon Bouddhique Sino-japonais: Edition de Taishō (Taishō shinshū daizōkyō), Fascicule annexe du Hōbōgirin*. Paris: Adrien-Maisonneuve.

Durt, Hubert. 1985. "Clichés canoniques bouddhiques dans les légendes sur les débuts du bouddhisme au Japon." *Cahiers d'Extrême-Asie* 1: 11–20.

Ebrey, Patricia Buckley, and Peter N. Gregory, eds. 1993. *Religion and Society in T'ang and Sung China*. Honolulu: University of Hawaii Press.

Faure, Bernard. 1993. *Chan Insights and Oversights: An Epistemological Critique of the Chan Tradition*. Princeton, N.J.: Princeton University Press.

———. 1997. The Will to Orthodoxy: A Critical Genealogy of Northern Chan Buddhism. Stanford, Calif.: Stanford University Press.

———. 1998. La Volonté d'orthodoxie dans le bouddhisme chinois. Paris: Editions du Centre National de la Recherche Scientifique.

Foulk, T. Griffith. 1999. "Sung Controversies Concerning the 'Separate Transmission' of Ch'an." In *Buddhism in the Sung*, ed. P. N. Gregory and D. A. G. J. Getz. Honolulu: University of Hawaii Press.

Girard, Frédéric. 1990. *Un Moine de la Secte Kegon à l'époque de Kamakura, Myōe (1173–1232) et le "Journal de ses rêves."* Vol. 160, *Publications de l'École Française d'Extrême-Orient*. Paris: Adrien-Maisonneuve.

Gregory, Peter N. 1981. "Tsung-mi's Inquiry into the Origins of Man: A Study of Chinese Buddhist Hermeneutics." PhD. diss., Harvard University.

——— and Daniel A. Getz, Jr., eds. 1999. *Buddhism in the Sung*. Honolulu: University of Hawaiii Press.

Griffiths, Paul J. 1993. "Indian Buddhist Meditation." In *Buddhist Spirituality: Indian, Southeast Asian, Tibetan, and Early Chinese*, ed. Y. Takeuchi and J. V. Bragt. New York: Crossroad.

Grosnick, William H. 1995. "The Tathāgatagarbha Sūtra." In *Buddhism in Practice*, ed. D. S. J. Lopez. Princeton, N.J.: Princeton University Press.

Hirakawa, Akira, and Paul Groner. 1990. *A History of Indian Buddhism: From Śākyamuni to early Mahāyāna, Asian Studies at Hawaii No. 36*. Honolulu: University of Hawaii Press.

Huang, Chi-chiang. 1986. "Experiment in Syncretism: Ch'i-sung (1007–1072) and Eleventh-Century Chinese Buddhism." Ph.D. diss., University of Arizona, Tucson.

———. 1999. "Elite and Clergy in Northern Sung Hang-chou: A Convergence of Interest." In *Buddhism in the Sung*, ed. Peter N. Gregory and Daniel A. G. J. Getz. Honolulu: University of Hawaii Press.

Jaffe, Richard M. 2001. *Neither Monk nor Layman: Clerical Marriage in Modern Japanese Buddhism, Buddhisms*. Princeton, N.J.: Princeton University Press.

Kamata Shigeo, ed. 1981. *Chūgoku bukkyōshi jiten*. Tokyo: Tōkyōdō shuppan.

Kimura Eiichi, ed. 1960. *Eon no kenkyū: Yuibunhen*. Tokyo: Sōbunsha.

————, ed. 1962. *Eon no kenkyū: Kenkyūhen*. Tokyo: Sōbunsha.

Kimura Jōyū. 1963. "Darumatara zenkyō settsū kōsho ni tsuite: Hakuin zen no ichi sokumen," *Zengaku kenkyū* 53, pp. 77–81.

Kodama Daien, et al. 1993. "Yugashi to zenkyōten no kenkyū (II): Denshō no mondaiten to bunseki o chūshin ni," *Bukkyō bunka kenkyūsho kiyō* 32, pp. 166–179.

Koga Hidehiko. 1991. *Zengo jiten*. Kyoto: Shibunkaku.

Kojima Noriyuki, ed. 1998. *Nihon shoki*, 3 vols., Shinhen Nihon koten bungaku zenshū 2–4. Tokyo: Shōgakkan.

Lamotte, Etienne, 1944–1981. *Le Traité de la grande vertu de sagesse de Nāgārjuna (Mahāprajñāpāramitaśastra) avec une nouvelle introduction*. 5 vols, *Publications de l'Institut Orientaliste de Louvain*. Louvain: Institut Orientaliste.

Lin, Li-kouang. 1949. *Introduction au Compendium de la Loi (Dharma-samuccaya): L'Aide-mémoire de la Vraie Loi (Saddharma-smṛtyupasthāna-sūtra), Recherches sur un Sutra Développé du Petit Véhicule*, vol. Tome 54, Ministère de l'Éducation Nationale Publications du Musée Guimet Bibliothèque d'Études. Paris: Librairie d'Amérique et d'Orient Adrien-Maisonneuve.

McRae, John R. 1986. *The Northern School and the Formation of Early Ch'an Buddhism*. Honolulu: University of Hawaii Press.

Mohr, Michel. 1997. *Traité sur l'Inépuisable Lampe du Zen: Tōrei (1721–1792) et sa vision de l'éveil*. 2 vols. Vol. 38, *Mélanges chinois et bouddhiques*. Brussels: Institut Belge des Hautes Études Chinoises.

————. 2000. "Emerging from Non-duality: Kōan Practice in the Rinzai Tradition since Hakuin." In *The Kōan: Texts and Contexts in Zen Buddhism*, ed. Steven Heine and Dale S. Wright. New York: Oxford University Press.

————. 2002. "L'héritage contesté de Dokuan Genkō : Traditions et conflits dans le bouddhisme Zen du XVIIᵉ siècle." In *Repenser l'ordre, repenser l'héritage: paysage intellectuel du Japon (XVIIᵉ–XIXᵉ siècles)*, ed. F. Girard, A. Horiuchi and M. Macé. Paris-Genève: Droz.

Mōru Missheru (Mohr Michel). 1987. "Tōrei zenji ni miru Hakuin zen no shinmenmoku," *Zen bunka* 125, pp. 41–54.

————. 1995. "Konton no jikaku kara hyōgen e: Zenbukkyō ni okeru kotoba no toraekata no ichisokumen." In Kajiya Tetsurō et al., eds., *Keiken to kotoba*, pp. 207–238. Tokyo: Taimeidō.

Nakamura Hajime. 2001. *Kōsetsu bukkyōgo daijiten*. Tokyo: Tōkyō shoseki.

Nishimura Eshin. 1982. *Tōrei oshō nenpu*. Kinsei zensōden 8. Kyoto: Shibunkaku.

Nogawa Hiroyuki, 1999–2000. "Sendai kuji daiseikyō o meguru Ōbaku jinmyaku," *Ōbaku bunka* 120, pp. 126–134.

Odani Nobuchiyo. 2000. *Hō to gyō no shisō toshite no bukkyō*. Kyoto: Bun'eidō.

Saigusa Mitsuyoshi. 1987. *Indo bukkyō jinmei jiten*. Kyoto: Hōzōkan.

Sanseidō henshūsho, ed. 1988. *Konsaisu jinmei jiten: Nihon hen*. Tokyo: Sanseidō.

Satō Shunkō. 2002. "Chōon Dōkai no shinkoku ishiki: *Sendai kujihongi daiseikyō* tono deai zengo," *Indogaku bukkyōgaku kenkyū* 50/2: 181–185.

Satō Taishun. 1984. "Darumatara zenkyō kaidai." In Iwano Masao, ed., *Kokuyaku is-saikyō: Indo senjutsubu, kyōshūbu 4.* (rev. ed.), pp. 343–349. Tokyo: Daitō shuppan.

Shintō taikei hensankai, ed. 1999. *Zoku Shintō taikei: Ronsetsu hen: Sendai kujihongi daiseikyō,* 4 vols. Tokyo: Shintō taikei hensankai.

Suzuki Sōchū. 1985. "Ryūtakuji to Hakuin," *Zenbunka* 118, pp. 11–23.

Takao Giken. 1941. "Sōdai ni okeru Tendai to Zen tono kōsō," *Ryūkoku gakuhō* 331, pp. 1–20.

Takasaki Jikidō. 1982. "Yuga gyōha no keisei" In Takasaki Jikidō et al., eds., *Kōza daijō bukkyō 8: Yuishiki shisō,* pp. 2–42. Tokyo: Shunjūsha.

Teeuwen, Mark. 1996. *Watarai Shintō: An Intellectual History of the Outer Shrine of Ise,* vol. 52, *CNWS Publications.* Leiden: Research School CNWS, Leiden University.

Tsukamoto Zenryū, ed. 1973. *Mochizuki bukkyō daijiten.* 10 vols. Tokyo: Sekai seiten kankō kyōkai.

Watson, Burton. 1993. *The Lotus Sūtra, Translations from the Asian Classics.* New York: Columbia University Press.

Wilson, Liz. 1996. *Charming Cadavers: Horrific Figurations of the Feminine in Indian Buddhist Hagiographic Literature,* Women in Culture and Society. Chicago: University of Chicago Press.

Yamabe Nobuyoshi. 1999. "The Sūtra on the Ocean-Like Samādhi of the Visualization of the Buddha: The Interfusion of the Chinese and Indian Cultures in Central Asia as Reflected in a Fifth-Century Apocryphal Sūtra." Ph.D. diss., Yale University.

———. 2000. "Bonmōkyō ni okeru kōsōgyō no kenkyū: Tokuni zenkan kyōten tono kanrensei ni chakumoku shite" In Aramaki Noritoshi, ed., *Hokuchō zuitō chūgoku bukkyō shisōshi.* Kyoto: Hōzōkan, pp. 205–269.

Yanagida Seizan. 1972. *Rinzairoku.* Butten kōza 30. Tokyo: Daizō shuppan.

———. 1983. "The *Li-Tai Fa-Pao Chi* and the Ch'an Doctrine of Sudden Awakening." In *Early Ch'an in China and Tibet,* ed. W. Lai and L. R. Lancaster. Berkeley, Cal.: Asian Humanities Press.

———. 1999. *Yanagida Seizan shū dai ikkan: Zenbukkyō no kenkyū.* Kyoto: Hōzōkan.

Yoshida Michioki. 1996. "Dokuan dokugo, Jikeigo, Hannya kusō zusan, Ben ben waku shinan, Zenshū ben, Dokuan gohōshū saikin, Dokuan zokudan kongenshō kaidai." In Kagamishima Genryū, ed., *Saikin, Kongenshō, Dōja goroku: Bessatsu furoku* (Komazawa daigaku toshokan shozō, Aichi gakuin daigaku toshokan shozō), pp. 155–167. Tokyo: Shigensha.

Yoshino Hiroko. 1995. *Daruma no minzokugaku: Onmyō gogyō kara toku.* Tokyo: Iwanami shoten.

Zürcher, Erik. 1972. *The Buddhist Conquest of China: The Spread and Adaptation of Buddhism in Early Medieval China.* Repr., with additions and corrections, 2 vols, *Sinica Leidensia.* Leiden: E. J. Brill. orig. ed. 1959.

———. 1991. "A New Look at the Earliest Chinese Buddhist Texts." In *From Benares to Beijing: Essays on Buddhism and Chinese Religion,* ed. K. Shinohara and G. Schopen. Oakville, N.Y.: Mosaic Press.

8

Meditation for Laymen and Laywomen: The *Buddha Samādhi* (*Jijuyū Zanmai*) of Menzan Zuihō

David E. Riggs

Some of the best scholarship in the West regarding the Sōtō school of Japanese Zen Buddhism has been about the teachings of meditation, and in this aspect we in the West are much like the Chinese, who in the first years of their contact with Buddhism were very interested in finding out all they could about the techniques of meditation.[1] The Chinese were looking for new mental techniques that might be of practical as well as spiritual use, and in the West the interest in meditation has, at least in part, been due to the hope that it is a powerful practice that has a multitude of benefits. The Zen school itself has long been at pains to impress upon its followers that it is not a meditation school and that its teachings are not limited to this domain. This insistence has had little popular effect, apparently, and today one can hear on any popular tour of Kyoto temples that the Zen school is a meditation school.

   The text discussed in this chapter is about meditative practice and it confronts this misunderstanding in its very title, which emphasizes the ultimate realm of the awakening of the Buddha, not the details of meditation technique. The *Buddha Samādhi* (*Jijuyū zanmai*) is an informal piece written by Menzan Zuihō (1683–1769) during the early years of his teaching career at the request of laymen and laywomen, and it was published some twenty years later in 1737.[2] Menzan was a learned monk and a leading figure in the comprehensive reforms which were sweeping the Sōtō schools during the eighteenth century. The expressed intention of the text is to help ordinary people practice meditation, but the text is in fact an extended sermon in praise of the teaching of Dōgen (1200–1255), who is now regarded as both the founder and the source of all teachings for the Sōtō school.

Dōgen returned from his extended visit to China carrying the approval of a Chinese master and began what has become by far the largest of the contemporary Japanese Zen schools. Menzan's long career of devoted research and teaching was an attempt to focus the Sōtō clerics on the texts of Dōgen, which had not been read as a source of doctrine for many centuries. In the *Buddha Samādhi* he presents Dōgen's way as the highest teaching of Buddhism, far beyond any ordinary practices or understanding. However, Menzan also includes quite detailed and useful summaries of basic Buddhist doctrines, such as causation and the three poisons of greed, anger, and confusion. There is not a single word of practical advice about meditation, certainly nothing that either a contemporary Californian or a fourth-century Chinese would recognize as meditation techniques, or advice about concrete details of posture or breathing. Nonetheless, the text has clear explanations of problems and misunderstandings that can arise in meditation and accessible discussions of some of Dōgen's abstruse teachings that underlie meditation practice. In that sense it is practical. Menzan added to the printed version an appendix which presents passages gleaned from Dōgen's writings that deal with meditation, and at the end of the appendix there is finally some concrete physical advice about meditation posture and environment. It seems as if Menzan was doing everything he could to emphasize that Zen is not meditation in the sense of a particular technique, leaving such details to the very last page of the appendix.

The Changing Role of Dōgen in Sōtō Zen

The *Buddha Samādhi* needs to be read as a single part of Menzan's deep involvement in the Tokugawa era (1603–1867), which was a movement working toward major changes in Zen practice and a wide range of creative reevaluation of Buddhist doctrine. Menzan is remembered as one of the most meticulous in detail as well as the most prolific of all the Sōtō Zen figures of that time, but his creativity was hardly recognized.[3] His approach to learning and his emphasis on historical sources established a precedent of careful scholarship that to this day continues to be characteristic of the Sōtō school. Many of Menzan's doctrine and practice reforms have become so thoroughly incorporated into the contemporary school that they seem to be the way things have always been since the time of Dōgen. Despite his accomplishments, Menzan is not remembered in Sōtō Zen circles as an innovative figure, and in the Tokugawa era, Buddhism in general was for many years regarded as a backward embarrassment by scholars. Among contemporary Sōtō Zen followers and scholars, Dōgen is taken as the source of all authority, and today, as if to emphasize that attitude, the school often refers to itself as Dōgen Zen.

Menzan's writings, although highly respected, are regarded as merely helpful notes and background information with which to gain access to the great insight and awakening of the founder. Not only did Menzan read Dōgen with the greatest attention to textual detail and painstakingly research Dōgen's sources, he used his knowledge of those texts and attempted to put his new understandings into daily practice in a way that Dōgen would have done. In this campaign Menzan was willing to go against both the practices of the established powers of Dōgen's own temple of Eiheiji and what he had been taught by his own teachers, whom he nonetheless held in the greatest respect. Menzan's detailed command of the works of Dōgen is widely remarked on, but it is important to understand that his efforts did not stop there. He filled in areas that Dōgen had left blank, and he attempted to clarify the ambiguities in Dōgen's work by interpreting the texts that Dōgen himself had access to. Menzan certainly used ancient materials to justify his attempts to reform Sōtō practice and doctrine, but the selection and interpretation were very much his own. Although he hid his creativity by presenting his work as merely research and editing, in many ways he was as much a revolutionary as a conservator.

To appreciate how radical Menzan's ideas really were, one needs to revise some stock ideas about Sōtō Zen. Dōgen is present in almost every study of Sōtō Zen, but why is it that he occupies such a dominant position? From the perspective of the modern Sōtō school it is not surprising that Menzan should have devoted his life to the study of Dōgen. Indeed in the last century the vast majority of Sōtō-related studies, both in Japan and in the West, have been focused on some aspect of Dōgen.[4] Dōgen was responsible for the introduction of the Sōtō Zen lineage to Japan, and his writings are now the font of orthodoxy for Sōtō Zen. It is all too easy to assume that this should obviously be the case and that he has always been regarded in this way. Before the Tokugawa era reforms, however, the writings of Dōgen were not the center of Sōtō doctrine and practice. They involved years of painstaking textual scholarship and even more years of often acrimonious discussion about what to do with the results of that work. This era has been meticulously researched by the contemporary scholar-monks of the Sōtō school, but the fact that the focus on Dōgen is a relatively recent development is not something that the contemporary teachers of the school are particularly eager to emphasize. I use their scholarship extensively in my own research, but my conclusions are my own and should not be taken as representative of the mainstream Sōtō view.

In the medieval era Dōgen's role was limited. His writings, especially the collection of essays that is now called the *Shōbōgenzō*, were treated as secret treasures, but there was no commonly accepted version and no commentaries were written about them from about the end of the thirteenth until the seventeenth century.[5] Although Sōtō monks traced their lineage to Dōgen, the content of Sōtō practice and doctrine was determined by teachings passed down from teacher to disciple. Religious authority (and indeed authority in general) relied on this kind of relationship of master and student, and texts and other paraphernalia were used to certify this handing down of authority. In the case of Sōtō Zen, it was the possession of a Dōgen text, not the understanding of its contents, that authenticated the possessor's religious practices and teachings.

In the medieval era merely possessing a text may have been enough, but in the Tokugawa era Sōtō Zen needed something more respectable than secret oral lore for its doctrinal underpinnings. Some of Dōgen's more conventional works had long been available, but it was only in the seventeenth century that the *Shōbōgenzō* and his writings about monastic practice became more widely circulated in manuscript form and were printed for the first time. It gradually became apparent that there were serious discrepancies between Dōgen's writings and contemporary Sōtō customs. Even before Menzan's time there had been attempts to reform customary practices to bring them more into line with the texts of Dōgen. These attempts used the slogan of *fukko*, which means to return to the old [ways], but with the implication that the old ways were the only correct ways. The most prominent attempt was led by Manzan Dōhaku (1636–1741), who succeeded in reforming dharma transmission, the ceremonial authentication of the status of a Zen teacher.[6] Dōhaku, as I will refer to him henceforth to avoid confusion with Menzan, made a creative leap by reinterpreting a 1615 government decree which specified that the house rules of Eiheiji, the temple founded by Dōgen, should also be the rules for all temples of the lineage. Dōhaku made the startling claim that this rather specific legalistic decree meant that the writings of Dōgen should be the source of authority for the entire Sōtō school. Dōhaku then used the "Shisho" and "Menju" fascicles of the *Shōbōgenzō* to justify his campaign to reform dharma transmission.[7] His case for a sweeping transformation was thus based on a text by Dōgen that had been ignored for hundreds of years. Whether or not that was the intent of the 1615 government ruling, Dōhaku's interpretation carried the day and resulted in an enormous expansion of interest in the writings of Dōgen. He succeeded in publishing his own version of the *Shōbōgenzō* in 1686 but, because of the problems arising from disputes about the *Shōbōgenzō*, in 1722 the Sōtō hierarchy requested that the government prohibit its publication, a prohibition that was not lifted until 1796, though manuscript copies continued to be available.[8]

Menzan worked to push the movement far beyond Dōhaku's dharma transmission reform and to focus on just one chapter of the *Shōbōgenzō*. He sought different manuscript versions of the chapters of the *Shōbōgenzō* and investigated the various traditions of organizing them. He also worked on Dōgen's other writings, such as his separate essays in Chinese about monastic regulations as well as a variety of independent pieces. He used these texts as his basis for authority, but he also read extensively in the sources that Dōgen himself relied upon and used these sources to fill in questions that Dōgen had not addressed. On this broader basis, Menzan advocated a much more radical overhaul of Sōtō affairs, including the rollback of some of Dōhaku's reforms that did not actually rely on Dōgen. For example, Dōhaku had created a set of monastic regulations that he claimed were based on Dōgen and Chinese practices of Dōgen's time. Menzan exposed Dōhaku's regulations as being based on the contemporary Chinese practices of the temples that had originally been set up for the Chinese merchant community in the trading port of Nagasaki.

These temples had become very popular in Japan, and many Japanese monks came to Nagasaki to see for themselves this newly imported Chinese Buddhism, which came to be referred to as Ōbaku.[9] Many were strongly impressed by the Ōbaku monks and returned to their own temples inspired by new ideas and practices. Although Menzan had extensive contacts with Ōbaku in his younger days in Kyushu, he came to be a staunch opponent of its practices. His position was that the only true sources of authority were in the writings of Dōgen and the texts on which he drew, and he strenuously objected to contemporary practice (either Chinese or Japanese) as a model. Menzan emphasized that one should read old texts directly and should use texts that were contemporaneous with or earlier than the old text only to support one's reading. He did not rely on the views of living teachers and avoided commentaries. Of course Menzan studied with a variety of teachers and revered his own lineage master, Sonnō Shōeki (1649–1705). Nonetheless, when Menzan attempted to establish authority, he relied neither on customary practice nor on orally transmitted knowledge. Although Menzan and the other reformers insisted that they were merely transmitting the teachings of Dōgen, they can be seen as the founders of a new tradition which derived its authority from textual commentary and scholarship, not from long-established customs and rituals. Although tradition can be thought of as a gradual accumulation of teachings or an organically developing system of practices, it can also be a deliberate construct that is used to bring about change to long-established customary practices.[10] Thanks in great part to the textual work of Menzan, the Edo reform of Sōtō Zen is an example of a well-crafted tradition, that is, a tradition that presents a surface of great authority and antiquity which skillfully conceals the seams and supports used to construct that surface.

Menzan was profoundly influenced by the works of Dōgen, but he was also very much a man of his times in that he used the textual tools and promoted the values of the contemporary trend of returning to the old ways and to the earliest texts. His approach paralleled movements in literature and Chinese studies of this period, in which there was a new interest in the unmediated use of ancient texts. In the Ancient Learning school of Confucian studies, contemporary teachers and their Neo-Confucianism were rejected in favor of reading the texts of Confucius directly.[11] Although the medieval tendency to favor secret lineages in many trades and skills continued, one of the most important intellectual developments in Japan at the time was an emphasis on open discussion within prescribed boundaries of permissible topics. Increasingly, authority based on textual analysis and commentary replaced reliance on secret initiations. The Sōtō reforms have been depicted in sectarian histories as simply a purging of impurities acquired during centuries of degenerate practice, but they can also be seen as a creative application of this new trend in Japanese thought toward emphasizing original texts, adapted to contemporary Sōtō Zen politics and doctrine.

There can be no doubt that Menzan's work promoted a Sōtō Zen that had its own distinct teachings and practices, and one might expect to find that Menzan also practiced the same kind of rigorous separation between Rinzai and Sōtō Zen that is so often noted in modern Japan. In fact, however, he often studied with teachers from outside his Sōtō lineage and, as will be discussed, wrote long commentaries on kōan texts that are now not considered part of the Sōtō sphere of interest. He spent much of his later years as a guest at Rinzai temples and received at least one Shingon lineage ordination. It is true that he was against certain kinds of Zen practice, but there is nothing to suggest a general rejection of Rinzai Zen and there is much evidence of frequent and intimate contact with his brother monks of the Rinzai lineage throughout his life.

Menzan is certainly not alone in his enthusiasm for Dōgen and reforms, but his output is so large and varied that he can hardly be compared to other Sōtō writers. There are over a hundred titles to his credit, including several very large collections of detailed scholarship and philology. One of his works on monastic rules is over 300 pages in the modern typeset edition. He had fifty-five of these titles printed during his lifetime and the number of those included in the standard modern Sōtō Zen collections is greater than those of all other prominent Sōtō authors combined. Although this aspect of his scholarship is not apparent in the *Buddha Samādhi*, in many other works Menzan argued the case for what he characterized as authentic Dōgen Zen with painstaking attention to textual detail and a comprehensive use of materials that set a new level of scholarship.

The History of the Text and Circumstances of Its Composition

Unfortunately, the *Buddha Samādhi* has not been the subject of a scholarly study nor has it been translated into modern Japanese. However, copies of the woodblock edition are still being printed from blocks that date to Menzan's time by the bookstore Baiyu Shoin in Kyoto. The blocks are somewhat worn, but the text is still completely readable, and this inexpensive edition is still used in classes at Komazawa University. The Komazawa library has a photocopy of the manuscript from which the woodblocks were made, in Menzan's very clear hand, and I have yet to find any significant difference between the manuscript and this printed version of the *Zoku Sōtōshū zensho*, which I will use for my citations.[12] The *Buddha Samādhi* is included in collections of Menzan's works as well as in many smaller collections of Sōtō texts, and there has even been an English translation which was privately published in Tokyo.[13]

According to Menzan's afterword, he wrote the *Buddha Samādhi* when he was teaching in Kyushu, because there were laymen and laywomen who were serious students of Zen and practitioners of seated meditation. They could not read Chinese, so in order to provide something in Japanese for them, Menzan searched everywhere in the texts of Japanese Zen teachers. Failing to find any-thing that followed Dōgen's way, he wrote this *Buddha Samādhi* himself in Japanese. The *Buddha Samādhi* is helpful to people interested in meditation, but at the same time, even in this early stage of his career, Menzan was trying to move Sōtō practice toward total reliance on Dōgen. This intent helps to explain why he devotes so much space to discussing what proper Sōtō practice is not and why he is is always bringing the reader back to the teachings of Dōgen. Apparently the text was not really what the laity had in mind, and it seems to have attracted little attention and languished in Menzan's personal library. Nearly twenty years later two Zen teachers came to assist Menzan in his new summer retreat temple north of Kyoto and became very interested in his discussion of Dōgen's practice as taught in the *Bendōwa*. Somehow, they happened upon an old manuscript of the *Buddha Samādhi*, which he had writ-ten many years earlier, and they noticed how much it resonated with what Menzan was teaching about Dōgen. Their interest in the text after so many years of neglect may be due to the advances in the knowledge of Dōgen's teaching that had occurred over the previous twenty years. This growing un-derstanding of Dōgen seems to have made Menzan's writings more accessible and important to them. Also they were advanced practitioners, who had come to fill positions of responsibility in Menzan's training period. They thought so much of the *Buddha Samādhi* that they copied it by hand and studied it during the ninety-day retreat period. At the end they received permission from Men-zan to have it printed that autumn of 1737. Menzan had done much textual research since those earlier days in Kyushu, and he collected the passages from Dōgen's writings that we are now appended to the text. The two teachers re-turned to Menzan's temple and presented him with twenty woodblock printed copies as a token of their gratitude.

Although Menzan approved the printing of the text, the content was some-what of a distraction from the focus of his work. He had been abbot of Kōinji for nearly ten years, and during this time he held regular training sessions and did most of his path-breaking research in monastic rules. For the first time during this period there were records of his lecturing about different chapters of the *Shōbōgenzō*. Earlier in Kyushu, when he spent most of his time traveling and restoring old temples, his talks were on universally admired texts, such as the *Lotus Sūtra* or the *Record of Lin-chi*, that were the standard texts of Zen lecturers of any school. The emphasis of the *Buddha Samādhi* on Dōgen was the exception. At Kōinji, Menzan's talks and monastic style became much more focused on Dōgen. He learned about monastic life in Dōgen's teachings and put what he had learned into practice at his own temple as much as possible, and Taikyo Katsugen (d. 1736), the new abbot of Eiheiji, praised his research on monastic rules. Katsugen brought Menzan to Eiheiji for three weeks in 1732 to look at the manuscripts and edit the abbot's own work on the precepts. Menzan had high hopes of implementing the same reforms at Eiheiji, but Katsugen passed away before anything could be done and his successor at Eiheiji did not seem interested in monastic reform. Menzan's dream of changing Eiheiji practice, which would have been a major step toward changing the standard for Sōtō practice, generally was not realized during his lifetime. It took years of discussion culminating in a bitter dispute that nearly paralyzed major monastic centers before Menzan's vision of the reformed rules became the official standard in 1804.[14]

In contrast to his preoccupation at this time with details of the monk life in a training monastery, the *Buddha Samādhi* is appropriate for almost anyone interested in Dōgen's teaching. As Menzan points out in the last sentence of his opening comments, Dōgen writes in the *Bendōwa* that laypeople too should do this [seated meditation] practice and that attaining the way has nothing to do with being a monk. The texts that Menzan appended to his essay do include pertinent excerpts from the relatively readable *Bendōwa* and the *Shōbōgenzō zuimonki*, which were appropriate for the lay audience. There are, however, also long selections from the "Zanmai ōzanmai" chapter of the *Shōbōgenzō*, including Chinese passages of significant length. These passages praise the practice in the same way that Menzan does in his own *Buddha Samādhi*, and similarly they offer no concrete advice. For the final selection, however, Menzan quotes the entire *Shōbōgenzō* "Zazenshin," which contains detailed instructions on how to select an appropriately quiet place and how to place your legs, hands, and so forth. Thus only at the very end is there a single word that could be concretely helpful for someone who actually wanted to try to do seated meditation. This kind of detail is not mentioned in the *Buddha Samādhi* itself. Originally written without these appended materials, the text may have been inspiring, but it was certainly nothing like a handbook for taking up the practice of seated meditation.

What the *Buddha Samādhi* does provide is a ringing endorsement of the awakened mind. Menzan presents this awakening as the core of Dōgen's teaching, which is also for Menzan the core of Zen, and indeed of Buddhism itself. Unlike the more didactic and down-to-earth writings for which Menzan is well known, most of this work is simply an affirmation of the glorious nature of the ultimate. Often the text is little more than a series of provisional names and epithets for what is beyond all words and names. These passages are similar to the style of Dōgen, though Menzan certainly cannot claim Dōgen's poetic gifts. Between these panegyrics to the ultimate, however, Menzan weaves a series of explanations about core Buddhist teachings that are not beyond words, and warnings about what traps to avoid when one is thinking about Buddhism. Combining these two worlds of discourse gives the *Buddha Samādhi* (*Jijuyū zanmai*) its particular flavor.

The Foreword: Definition and Direction

The Chinese-language foreword begins with an elliptical explanation of *jijuyū*, the key term from which the text takes its name. Menzan says the word derives from the Sanskrit word *vairocana*, which is translated into Chinese using the characters that mean the brilliant light that shines everywhere. As Menzan's audience would have been well aware, this same Sanskrit word is also used to refer to the cosmic Buddha Vairocana, a Buddha that has been important to Japan from its earliest days and that is also an important figure in esoteric Buddhism. Here Menzan indicates *vairocana* in the more fundamental sense of the ultimate manifestation of the Buddha as his awakened teaching, as distinguished, for instance, from his other aspects, including his appearance as the historical Buddha. The term *jijuyū* comes from the first of two meanings of *vairocana*, which is from the internal point of view. It refers to the light of wisdom which illuminates the realm of the truth. The word *jijuyū* is composed of the three characters for self, receive, and activity and is thus self-referential; this wisdom does not depend on others, nor is it for the sake of others. It is used to refer to the ultimate state of the Buddha, as distinct from the way he presents himself to others as a teacher.

Menzan's explanation continues with the second meaning of *vairocana*, which is from the external point of view and refers to the light that shines out from the body of the awakened one and teaches others. This is called the *tajiyū*, and it differs from the first meaning in that it is written using the character for "other" instead of "self." These are the fundamental pair of meanings, but Menzan (following Dōgen) immediately goes beyond the opposition and insists that to split them up in this way is a scholarly mistake. From his point of view, splitting these aspects into internal and external is like "a scholar hesitatingly going over the details, and mired in the gradations between Buddhas and sentient beings. The essential workings of the Buddhas and Patriarchs is surely not like this."[15] He emphasizes the ultimate unity of self and others and the crucial role of this light of wisdom. He does not delve further into this definition in the preface, but the first text in his appendix is a passage from the *Bendōwa*, where Dōgen uses *Buddha Samādhi* (*Jijuyū zanmai*) as an equivalent for the ultimate state of the Buddha and says that *zazen* is the manifestation of this state. Thus for Menzan, *Buddha Samādhi* (*Jijuyū zanmai*) is a way of referring to seated meditation without being trapped by a limited idea of a particular posture practiced at a particular time and place. It is rather surprising that this crucial term is not treated to a fuller discussion in the body of the text.

Menzan concludes the preface with two quotes from Zen literature affirming his interpretation of the relationship between light and this *samādhi* and then laments: "How sad it is that because of the bedazzlement of the heterodox practice of observing the phrase [of the kōan] [*kanna*] of the medieval period, the practice of our school completely changed and the essential working was lost" (463a). Menzan says that only Dōgen kept to the true way of this *Buddha Samādhi* (*Jijuyū zanmai*) and avoided the trap of incorrect *kanna* practices. One of the characteristic features of modern Rinzai Zen is this *kanna* practice that focuses great effort on breaking through to the understanding of a single phrase culled from the kōan. Menzan's text has been linked to the Sōtō school's opposition to this kind of practice, and I will have much more to say about the relationship between *kanna* and Menzan later. The theme of light as the equivalent of awakening appears repeatedly throughout the text. Another central theme, the unity of practice and awakening, is alluded to indirectly in the quotation just cited when Menzan disparages the limited view that there are gradations between the awakened Buddhas and the rest of the world. The unity of practice and awakening is a key topic for Dōgen as well as for Japanese Buddhism in general, but Dōgen emphasizes the practice aspect of the unity, which I interpret as the claim that there can be no awakening except in practice. In this text Menzan frequently uses the term "practice-awakening" (*shushō*) without explaining directly what it means. I prefer to stay with that infelicitous English translation rather than use a more readable English which would force a particular interpretation where Menzan has not given one.[16] These two themes of light and practice-awakening appear repeatedly throughout the text.

What Our School Is Not: Sōtō Zen, Meditation, and *Kanna* Zen

After this brief foreword in Chinese, the body of the text (in Japanese) emphasizes the primacy of awakening and then repeats the standard Zen claim for the authentic transmission from the historical Buddha down through the patriarchs of the school, in this case including Dōgen, who brought the *Buddha Samādhi* to Japan. Then Menzan lists a series of equivalences:

> The practice-awakening of this *samādhi* is the present sitting in
> full cross-legged posture, which is provisionally termed *zazen*
> [seated meditation]. This so-called *zazen* was introduced to China

from India by Bodhidharma, who sat facing the wall at Shaolin Temple of Mount Sung. The teachers of sūtra and commentary, fellows who do not understand the marvelous mind of nirvāṇa nor the *Buddha Samādhi*, saw that the appearance was similar to the eight stages of *dhyāna* and thought that it was the seated meditation (*zazen*) of the Brahmans. And so they called it *zazen*. (464b)

Menzan insists that the passage of the practice-awakening was only provisionally tagged with the name of Zen by outsiders. It is true that in his school this practice-awakening is expressed in the cross-legged posture, but it is the practice-awakening, not the posture that was brought to China by Bodhidharma and by Dōgen to Japan. Despite the fact that the root of the word "Zen" comes from a Chinese transliteration of *dhyāna*, which is one of several words for "meditation," in fact meditation in this sense is not a characteristic of the school, nor even of Buddhism, but a common property of religious life in India. The people who merely read Buddhist texts do not understand this distinction, so they made the mistaken correspondence between the posture and the teaching of the school.

Menzan continues more explicitly:

If Zen indicated nothing but doing *dhyāna*, it would be the *dhyāna* of the six *pāramitā*, or the *samādhi* of the three studies. All bodhisattvas practice these, and since they all practice *zazen*, they would not select just one of those practices and give it the special name of marvelous mind of nirvāṇa, the eye of the storehouse of true dharma, and pass it down. (465)

Menzan is reiterating the distinction between those meditation practices that are the common property of all Buddhist groups, and the practice-awakening of Zen, which he will call *zazen*. Rather than translating *zazen* into English as "seated meditation," I have retained the Japanese term because in this text it becomes one of the key phrases which are repeatedly pushed beyond their fundamental meaning. As is already clear, for Menzan the word *zen* is definitely not meditation alone, and so neither is *zazen* simply seated meditation.

In this beginning section, before Menzan has given the reader any idea of what this practice-awakening might be, he goes into considerable detail about what it is not. He continues with a condemnation of a certain kind of practice involving kōans:

Even though there are many people who are said to be doing *zazen*, all of them are apparently doing the practice of the ordinary deluded followers of the two vehicles or following the provisional bodhisattva [way]. Those who know the *Buddha Samādhi*, the realm of the original awakening of the Buddhas, are rare. Because of this [misunderstanding] people concentrate on a kōan to hasten awakening. They labor the mind to find the subject who sees and hears [kenmon no shujinkō]. They sweep clear the distracted mind [mōnen] and think that no-mind [munen] is good. In addition to these two there are many other kinds of techniques for seated meditation in the Sung, Yüan, and Ming dynasties, but there was not one [teacher] in a hundred who knew the true character of the *Samādhi*, or the true transmission of the buddhas and ancestors. This so-called working on [teizei] kōan started in the Sung. It was never heard of by the ancestors in India or by the Chinese ancestors up to Hui-Neng, nor is it to be found in the old teachings of Ch'ing-yüan and Nan-yüeh. It is merely one kind of thinking of some teachers of the Sung. According to some, it began with Huang-po Hsi-yüan, but actually it was after his death, in the story of Chao-chou and the dog. It is a tiresome thing to say that Huang-po, who had already passed away, would be promoting this kind of working with kōans as Zen practice. Furthermore, not all kōans were originally made for the purpose of encouraging people to practice *zazen*. [In cases such as] inquiring about the one who hears and sees or the one who asks and the one who is asking, inasmuch as there are not two people, it is of no use to make more hardship by just asking and asking. You should know that this is truly nothing but trying to see the eye with the eye. Or trying to stop the arising of the distracted mind with the arising of the mind that wipes it clean is like trying to extinguish the burning fire by pouring oil on it. The fire will only burn more and more. (465a)

The crucial word here for describing the kind of kōan practice under discussion is *teizei*, which literally means "to take up." It occurs in Wu-men's comments on the first case of the *Checkpoint of Wu-men* (C. *Wu-men kuan*; J. *Mumonkan*), one of the most widely used collections of kōans.[17] Wu-men tells his student to concentrate on the single word *wu* (J. *mu*) from the case and to carry it (*teizei*) day and night. *Teizei* later came to have the same meaning as the more common word *teishō*, which refers to the lecture of a Zen teacher on a kōan case.[18] In its older usage, however, it means to guide a student, which is the way Hirata glosses it in his annotated edition of the *Checkpoint of Wu-men*.[19] From the context of the quoted passage, I take the phrase to mean using a kōan to (improperly and forcefully) direct a student's practice. Menzan's teacher Sonnō used *teizei* in a similar way in the *Kenmon hōeiki*.[20] It seems that it is used here in place of *kanna*, a term never used in the body of the *Buddha Samādhi*.

It is rather surprising to find that the brief entry on the *Buddha Samādhi* in the encyclopedia *Zengaku daijiten* characterizes the text as an attack on the

Rinzai practice of *kanna*.[21] Menzan never mentions Rinzai Zen, and as we have seen, the word *kanna* occurs only in the preface. The brief passage quoted here is the only place where an attack on something like *kanna* is found in the text. This example highlights both the importance of rejecting *kanna* for contemporary Sōtō Zen and the strong tendency to assume that the contemporary linkage of *kanna* with Rinzai Zen is found in earlier texts. Even relatively recent texts like this one of Menzan's can be easily misconstrued. It is important to note that the quoted *Zengaku daijiten* is a publication of Komazawa University, which is both a training school for Sōtō priests and a center for textual Buddhist scholarship, especially as it relates to Dōgen.

The practice of *kanna* in modern Rinzai is rooted in the teaching of Hakuin Ekaku (1686–1769), who is regarded as the reviver of Rinzai Zen and the champion of *kanna* Zen by the contemporary members of that lineage. This practice is typically opposed by modern Sōtō Zen teachers, who believe that Dōgen himself opposed it.[22] Hence the interest in finding a premodern text such as the *Buddha Samādhi* is to provide historical background for this position of modern teachers. Since Menzan and Hakuin were contemporaries, it is tempting to assume that Menzan played a role in developments that led to the contemporary disapproval of *kanna* and to the hardening of the separation between Rinzai and Sōtō.

Before saying more about whether or not this assumption might be justified, I need to say a little more about the background of both *kanna* practice and kōans generally. Because the term *kanna* is so laden with sectarian overtones, one needs to be especially careful to specify the time and context of its usage. One should not assume just because the word *kanna* is used that Menzan is referring to the same thing as is meant in modern Rinzai, or for that matter that Menzan's usage is the same as Dōgen's. The Chinese origins of this practice, championed by Ta-hui Tsung-kao (1089–1163), and its importance for the Zen tradition in China, Korea, and Japan have been the subject of much excellent research. There is no need to review these studies here, because my interest is limited to this period in Japan and the relationship between this time and contemporary Japanese Zen thinking about kōans in general and *kanna* in particular.

Kōans are discussed and used throughout the Zen tradition in many different ways; for some time now Western scholars have abandoned the notion that kōans are for Rinzai only, and it is now widely understood that Dōgen and his students made use of kōans. Carl Bielefeldt sees much of Dōgen's *Shōbōgenzō* as a kōan commentary, and Steven Heine has developed an extended analysis of Dōgen's use of kōans and how it contrasts with Ta-hui's style, including a concise system for distinguishing the various kinds of kōan literature.[23] Bielefeldt also points out that in spite of Dōgen's attack on Ta-Hui, the champion of *kanna* practice, the writings of Dōgen contain no direct attack on *kanna* Zen.[24] Bielefeldt makes the case that, however much the kōan, Ta-Hui, and *kanna* are linked in modern polemics, in Dōgen's own writings they are separate topics and one need not imply the other. After Dōgen's time, in the medieval era there was a widespread use of kōans by Sōtō monks in many different ways.²⁵ When Menzan was writing the *Buddha Samādhi*, Sōtō monks were most definitely involved in the study of the kōan, although nowadays those studies do not attract the attention they probably deserve.

Menzan's own positive attitude toward this area of Zen is clearly seen in the extensive work he did in the last years of his life, when he began to work on the classic Chinese collections of commentaries about kōans. In 1758 he composed and put into print his *Explanations of the Old Cases Presented by the Old Buddha of Hsi Province (Shisshō kobutsu juko shōtei)*, a commentary on the collection of 100 old cases by Hung-chih Cheng-chüeh (1091–1157), which is excerpted from Hung-chih's record.²⁶ Hung-chih was the teacher of the Sōtō lineage in China who played a crucial part in the revival of the lineage and has been held in the highest regard by the lineage in Japan. These cases of Hung-chih form the core of the famous compendium of kōan cases and commentary, the *Book of Serenity*, published in 1224.²⁷ There are a number of commentaries on this work, but Menzan's is apparently the only one to be printed in pre-modern times.

Menzan continued this new line of work in spite of his advancing years, and at age eighty-two he published a similar commentary on the 100 kōan cases of Hsüeh-tou Ch'ung-hsien (980–1052), which was the basic text for the *Blue Cliff Record* (C. *Pi-yen lu*; J. *Hekiganroku*) commentary printed in 1128.²⁸ Hsüeh-tou was one of the most celebrated poets of Chinese Zen, and the *Blue Cliff Record* is regarded as perhaps the greatest of the elaborate works of literary kōan commentaries. This was the model for Hung-chih's later work about which Menzan had just written. The *Blue Cliff Record*, in modern Japan at least, has tended to be identified more closely with the Rinzai lineage of its authors. Menzan's commentary, the *Explanations of the One Hundred Old Cases of Zen Teacher Hsüeh-tou Hsien (Hsüeh-tou po-tse sung-ku)*, was printed in 1788 and reprinted in 1833, 1859, and several times in the late nineteenth century by the Baiyū bookstore in Kyoto.²⁹ This commentary is apparently the most frequently reprinted premodern commentary on the kōans of Hsüeh-tou. This kind of work was clearly much in demand, and it appears that there was no expectation that Menzan would confine himself to Dōgen or even to the kōan collection more closely linked to Sōtō. The modern Sōtō school editors decided not to include these two major works in their collections of Sōtō writings. Since they have not been studied, and there is no modern edition, it is very easy to overlook the fact that they exist at all. It is clear that contemporary sectarian thinking makes a much sharper divide between Rinzai and Sōtō Zen than was seen in the Tokugawa era even by Menzan, the champion of Dōgen.

If the case is rather unclear in Dōgen's time, can perhaps the opposition to *kanna*, like so many other details of modern Sōtō Zen, be traced to the Tokugawa-era reforms and Menzan? One of the reasons that this link between Menzan and *kanna* is plausible is that he was a contemporary of Hakuin and it is tempting to think of Tokugawa Zen as some kind of polarity between Hakuin and Menzan. It has been suggested that the modern polemic can be traced back to an opposition between these two, and Steven Heine refers to a "debate" (presumably only figuratively speaking) between Hakuin and Menzan.[30] If one uses the categories of contemporary Rinzai versus Sōtō polemics, *kanna* practice would be an obvious pivot. In this schema Hakuin would be the champion of *kanna* practice and Menzan would be the promoter of the way of Dōgen, which focuses on practice-awakening.

As has been mentioned, Heine suggests this possibility, and Bielefeldt points out (without going into any further detail) that it seems that the anti-*kanna* rhetoric became orthodox only after Menzan.[31] Menzan's contempt for unruly practice is beyond doubt, and there is evidence for this kind of behavior among the people who were associated with the kind of kōan practice championed by Hakuin. This is not, of course, a sufficient basis upon which to argue that Menzan was opposed to Hakuin and *kanna* practice. I can find no evidence for any debate either in person or in writing, nor is there any evidence of which I am aware that Hakuin and Menzan knew of each other in any way. When Menzan was in Kyushu writing this text, Hakuin was utterly unknown (as was Menzan) and was living nearly at the opposite end of the country, not far from present-day Tokyo. Even if they did meet later, Menzan's comments in this early text can scarcely be taken as referring to Hakuin. Indeed, despite some clear attacks on *kanna* Zen, it is difficult to find explicit Rinzai versus Sōtō positions in this period. Hakuin does attack silent illumination (*mokushō*) Zen (a term often used by outsiders to characterize Sōtō practice) and particular Sōtō priests, but he does not attack Sōtō Zen and shows great respect for Dōgen.[32] In the same way, as will be discussed soon, Menzan's apparent opposition to *kanna* does not seem to be directed to Rinzai monks or to *kanna* practice as such, but to particular individuals and their quite outrageous behavior.

It is true that there is some similarity between the behavior that Menzan was objecting to (more examples of which will be given later) and what we know of Hakuin's own life. He was a wild and unruly person in his younger days, with all manner of outrageous behavior associated with his awakening experiences.[33] His story is clear evidence that the picture of the crazy Zen monk is not just a bohemian fantasy of Western lovers of Zen lore. Menzan, in very sharp contrast to Hakuin, was the epitome of probity and order. Much of his writings are concerned with maintaining moral and practical order in the Zen community and, in the passages to be cited here, with keeping order among certain wild monks (whose identity is never entirely clear). If the kind of behavior that is seen in these passages in Menzan and in the record of Hakuin's early days was at all common, then there was good reason for Menzan's emphasis on order.

Although it is unclear in the previously quoted passage from the *Buddha Samādhi* whether or not Menzan was directly attacking *kanna* zen, he is much more explicit in some passages in the collection of talks published in 1765 entitled *Sermons of [the Abbot of the Temple of Mount] Kenkō (Kenkō fusetsu).*[34] The following passage comes from a talk given on the first day of the monastic retreat. He uses the word *watō*, which is an alternate phrase indicating the same practice of *kanna*. After some opening remarks about the transmission from India of the practice of sitting, Menzan launches a sustained attack against

> narrow minded zealots who hold up the flower, blink, smile, laugh, stare at walls, do bows from their place, and mistakenly rely on the wordless teaching. This is a deluded understanding of the mind-to-mind transmission. When I see this, it seems like the vulgar arguing over a puzzle: when they solve it they are satisfied with their accomplishment. This evil has continued so long that they cannot return to the old ways. From the end of the Sung to the Yüan and Ming, many masters affirm this to be the secret essence of the separate transmission outside the teachings. They sweep away the sūtra and the commentaries like old-fashioned calendars that they will never use again. This evil has overflowed [China] and entered Japan, piling evil upon evil. It continues and gets worse and worse. Recently one sees so-called "people of good mind" who have taken up a practice of Zen that entails being given just one word [*watō*] from an old [kōan] case. These tyros are urged on by being told: 'Make it your constant theme: walking, standing, sitting, lying down. Awake now! Wake up now! If you can't achieve awakening, kill yourself. Just stick your neck out and come forward: hear one word and [there are] a thousand awakenings.' I have no space for the rest [of that kind of talk], but concerning the ways of physically driving on students [I can mention that] they bind hands or feet, they force people to sit for long periods, and there is painful sleepiness. The students are hit with the fist, slapped, stepped on, and kicked, even whipped. Really this is nothing but corporal punishment, in some places done by the teachers and in some places by the students to each other. (T 82, no. 2604:723c)

Menzan does not think much of the technique as such, but he is upbraiding these teachers mostly for promoting unruly behavior, for ignoring sūtra and commentaries, and for using rather crude physical and psychological means to force something to happen in a dramatic flash. Menzan did not directly say that this treatment would produce a false awakening, but it is clear that he certainly would not have given his approval. Furthermore, this effort to attain awakening resulted in outrageous behavior toward elders by young monks who ignored precepts and flaunted the wisdom of their elders. There is no hint that these people were followers of Hakuin or were in any way associated with the Rinzai lineage. To Menzan they were not true followers of Dōgen's way of Buddhism, whether they were in the Sōtō lineage or not.

In another section of the same text Menzan makes it even clearer that although this practice may have started with Ta-hui, it is also practiced in the Sōtō lineage:

> After all, the way of *kanna* is easy to enter, and it makes the awakening of the personal self [*korei*] easy, does it not! Of old, when Ta-hui entered the territory of Fukien accompanied by only fifty-three students, before fifty days had passed, thirty of them had attained the way. Since that time, of those in China that have imitated this practice, in the Sōtō lineage there have been seven cases of this sort where there has been something like a great awakening. In Japan these days, before a single summer retreat is finished there are twenty or thirty cases of great awakening. How productive! (T 82, no. 2604:731c)

The crucial term *korei* is used here to disparage *kanna* practice by putting it on the level of what might nowadays be called self-development, as opposed to the true awakening, which transcends any category such as "self" or "development." It is an infrequently seen term even in Zen literature, but it carries a similar meaning in the Zen transmission chronicles, for example in fascicle 5 of the *Ching-te ch'uan-teng lu*.[35] Menzan is not denying that *kanna* practice may have some kind of result, it is just that the results are at a low level.

Although it is true that these are passages in which Menzan clearly disapproves of *kanna* or *watō*, he is condemning mostly the emphasis on productivity of practice retreats, or ridiculing the disruptive behavior, whether it be painful kicking and slapping or noisy "Great Awakenings," not the *kanna* way of meditation practice. By revealing what he claimed to be the true nature of such antics, Menzan encouraged people to embrace Dōgen's quiet way of *zazen*. Menzan himself, like most Zen teachers, used kōans constantly in his texts to illustrate his points and to prompt students to think carefully, and the *Buddha Samādhi* is no exception. His criticism of *kanna* was directed not toward the technique of considering just the critical phrase, but rather at the style of life and the grasping for awakening of people who link themselves to that practice.

The Light of Wisdom and the Mind of Distinctions

Let us now return to the text at hand and its focus on practice-awakening. Menzan concludes his dismissal of incorrect practices with a rejection of the *Tso-ch'an i*, the *Ts'o-ch'an chen*, and the *Ts'o-ch'an ming*, Chinese texts about seated meditation that Dōgen explicitly rejected. Dōgen's reading of these texts has been discussed by Carl Bielefeldt, who provides a full translation of the passage that Menzan is referring to from Dōgen's "Zazenshin" fascicle of the *Shōbōgenzō*:[36]

> Dōgen saw that this was not part of the old way of Pai-chang and that it was an error which had sunk the teachings of the patriarchs into darkness. The *Tso-chan i* that we now see appears at the end of the *Shiburoku*.[37] However much truth there is in it, it is not the correct understanding from the ancient masters of the lineage. From the middle ages we have all been deluded sentient beings, believing that we must put our strength into *zazen* and attain awakening, and then there is no need to do *zazen*. (466a)

For Menzan, the problem with these important Chinese texts is that they make distinctions between the present state and the state one wishes to attain. Dōgen was not trapped by the dichotomy, but between Dōgen and Menzan's time, "we all have been deluded." This section concludes with another long panegyric to *zazen*, that is, directly entering into the realm of the Tathāgata.

Immediately following this affirmation that the teaching of this *Samādhi* is unique, Menzan then breaks out of this realm where there are no distinctions and says:

> And now I will teach in detail about the truth of the clear faith in this *samādhi*. It is nothing more than not hiding one's own wisdom light. When your own wisdom light shines clearly, you are freed both from being sunk in depression and from excess of excited confusion. (467b)

In a stroke he raises the hope of finally getting some detailed explanation, and then immediately returns into the realm of the absolute. He has, however, given us one crucial point: this practice-awakening is a kind of middle way between depression and excitement (though he does not use the term "middle way"). Menzan continues to explain that this is a situation in which a frontal attack results in only a temporary retreat. Striving is always accompanied by discriminative thinking, and hence the harder we charge, the more distant the goal becomes. We are already at the goal and it is only our insistence on thinking otherwise that keeps it distant.

Next Menzan discusses the contrast between the light of *samādhi* and the

ordinary mind, which clings to making discriminations. He says that this ordinary mind in its focus on discrimination is like hard frozen ice, but just like
ice it can also simply melt away of its own accord. All one has to do is stop the
process of constantly making discriminations. The problem with this discrimination, which is our fundamental ignorance, is explained with two sets of
examples. The first set shows how the notion of good and bad is situational
rather than absolute. The bird needs the air to fly through just as much as the
fish needs water to swim in, but for either to switch environments means a
quick death. What we must do is grasp that all of our ideas of good and bad,
and even existence and nonexistence are similarly rooted in our own habits:

> We think the bird flies through the air without being hindered,
> but a fish cannot move if he is in the air. The fish swims freely in
> the water, but the bird will die if it enters the water. Maggots do not
> see the dung as filth, and the bug that lives off a hot pepper plant
> knows nothing of its hot taste. The fire mouse can live in the midst
> of the flames, and there is a crab that lives in the middle of the boil-
> ing hot springs. Our own accustomed way of thinking is just one
> particular way, but we are stuck in taking it to be the way things are.
> This is the fundamental root of delusion, what is called discriminat-
> ing consciousness. The suffering of one world may well be the plea-
> sure of another, just as the upholding of precepts for the śrāvaka
> may be the breaking of precepts for the bodhisattva. The opinions of
> people of all the realms come from contact with countless different
> things; how could they be the same? You should be very clear about
> the fact that originally the countless real things of the world are out-
> side of the discriminating mind, which is certainly nothing more
> than calculations and categorizations. (468b)

This teaching is further driven home by the second set of examples drawn
from the well-known story of how blind men touching various parts of the
elephant never realize the nature of the magnificent beast that is actually present. This example shows that not only is our consciousness relative to our own
situation, it is also very limited. The crux of all of these examples is that the
wisdom light, this *vairocana* with which the text begins, is not something that
can be arrived at by discrimination any more than it can be arrived at by striving. Furthermore, texts in themselves are merely like the printed menu of a
meal, and arguing about the menu will never relieve hunger, which is why
Bodhidharma came to China empty-handed, unlike earlier travelers, who
brought many texts.

Having explained in detail why such discrimination is the root of the dilemma, Menzan begins his next section as follows: "One should begin with a
careful and detailed thinking about the truth of what we consider to be the
human mind" (470a). Clearly, the discrimination that is the problem here is

not something to be overcome by mere faith or by some kind of fuzzy-headed jumping into the unknown. Discrimination is to be confronted by careful thinking about what is involved in discrimination, not by just rejecting it without knowing what is being rejected. The central image that Menzan uses here is the mirror, with particular attention paid to its mysterious nature of being bright while reflecting equally the good and the bad without discrimination. The mirror is a favorite model for the problem of getting caught up in the arising of thoughts and how one must realize that the images that come and go (like our thoughts) is not the most important thing about the mirror. What is important rather is its bright nature, which is to say the fundamental nature of our mind.

The mirror image is also a bridge to Menzan's next major topic: the problem of clinging to having no thoughts. Menzan does not say so here, but Sōtō Zen has been criticized for inactivity and for being caught in a kind of quiescence, which is correlated with this state of no-thought.[38] Menzan's response to this unspoken challenge is that clinging to no-thought is just as bad as clinging to the arising of thoughts, and furthermore it is equivalent to being sunk in the state of mind where one regards everything as neither good nor evil:

> This practice-awakening, which goes beyond having thoughts and having no thoughts, is the face of a mirror, which reflects the beautiful and the ugly. It is the proper functioning of the mirror to be bright. The reflected beauty or ugliness is not, however, in the mirror itself but is the reflection of that form in the mirror. In the same way, we take as our real mind this discrimination of bad and good which we apply to having thoughts or having no thoughts. This is just like when we become confused and take the shape in the mirror for the thing itself, which is a cautionary example of clinging to the confusion of having thoughts. Now consider what happens when we take having no thoughts for the thing itself, which is what happens when we remain in the state of not-the-least-arising of either good or bad thoughts. This is like when we think that the mirror itself is the state when the mirror is not reflecting anything at all, which is like loving the back of the mirror. But of course a mirror that does not reflect the light becomes the same as rocks or tiles. This is the truth of the problem of being sunk in that which is neither good nor evil. However, just as the true light of the brilliant mirror is neither in reflection nor in the back of the mirror, you should clearly know that the truth of the great perfect mirror wisdom of the Buddha-wisdom vision is beyond having thoughts or having no thoughts. For example, when one is sitting in meditation, in the state of no-thought in which there is neither good nor bad,

neither seeing forms nor hearing sounds, so that you are unaware even of being very ill, you are then stuck in this state of neither-good-nor-bad and the emptiness of suffering. On the other hand, if you just see forms and think they are forms, or hear sounds and think they are sounds, and you are fully aware of being very ill, you are still stuck in the confusion of this connectedness. Both of these are discriminating consciousness. (471a–b)

This state of having no thoughts may be quite different from ordinary mind, but it is stuck in a one-sided understanding, just as is ordinary mind. Both are equally far from the true way, like the mirror that is bright but in no way interfering with what it is reflecting.

Thus far, Menzan has followed conventional Buddhist examples making use of the mirror metaphor, but he goes on to explain further in his characteristic, straightforward style. The mirror is only an example, and people have long been confused because not all the details of this example are appropriate to explain the mind. In particular, he says, the images come from outside the mirror: they are two things. But the thoughts of the mind do not come from outside: thoughts of good and bad and so forth; all arise from one's own mind. So, to try to keep the mind free of thoughts makes no sense. It is not like the case of the mirror, which is apart from the images seen in the mirror:

> Since long ago commentators have accepted the metaphor liter-
> ally and taken the arising of thoughts as external afflictions, as being
> things that came alongside and have clung to us. So they take our
> original mind as merely no thoughts and no mind, and try forcibly
> to extinguish the arising of thoughts. This is because they did not
> fully understand the metaphor and so they did not apply it properly
> to the teaching of the Buddha. (472a)

What is the proper understanding? Menzan's answer is by way of an explanation of the celebrated kōan case in which a monk asks Master Chao-chou whether or not a dog has Buddha-nature. Menzan does not stop with the usual reply of "No" (C. *Wu*; J. *Mu*), which is the way this case is often used as an example to work on in *kanna* practice. He continues with the text of the case and quotes Chao-chou's explanation that the reason for his "No" response is that the dog has the nature of ordinary deluded mind. Menzan explains that this means there is no Buddha-nature apart from the ordinary deluded mind, which is called Buddha-nature when it is in thusness:

> The reference to a dog means that apart from this realm of de-
> luded consciousness, which is the world of a body and mind at one
> time, there is no Buddha-nature. This same deluded mind of the
> dog, when it is in thusness, is called Buddha-nature. And so, seen
> from the confusion of ordinary thinking, the realm of the countless

virtues of the Tathāgata seems like the [ordinary] round of birth and
rebirth of living beings are the ever-abiding truth body of the Tatha-
gata. It is said that the afflictions are awakening, birth and death are
nirvāṇa, and that is the truth. As Dōgen says, "In all the realms
there are no afflictions, right here there is no one else." If you do
not study under a true teacher, you will think that cutting off the
arising of thoughts is the true path of the Buddha's teaching.
Among ancient and medieval Zen teachers, as well as among recent
monks of high repute, in both China and Japan, there are countless
ones like this. This is because they explain the meaning based simply on the literal words, and rely on their own personal slanted
views. Though it is true that the arising of a thought unfolds into
the three poisons and that those turn into the six paths of good and
evil, nonetheless, all of these are the changes of our own mind and
it is not right to try to get rid of them. At the time of the good
thought, if you fix upon only the good thought and the result of the
three good paths opens up, you will darken the light that transcends
the good. At the time of the bad thought, if you fix only upon the
bad thought, you are drawn into the results of the bad realms. You
receive the body of the world of suffering and do not know the light
that goes beyond evil. At the time of having no thoughts, at the time
of indeterminacy, if you stop there with the thought that it is a good
place, then you fall into the way of the two vehicles and the heterodox path and will for a long time not attain the realm of the Buddha.
You will not know the light that surpasses indeterminacy. (473a)

This theme is continued with many examples of the importance of not
being stuck in the stage of indeterminacy and of no-thought, which is at best
a trance state belonging to a lower form of Buddhism and at worst a heterodox
view. Next Menzan returns to the theme of light, this time as a springboard to
a discussion of causation. This light is the second kind of light referred to in
the preface: the light that streams from the body of the awakened one, bringing
awakening to all creatures in all conditions. He describes the variety of these
creatures in great detail before coming to the point that this light is the realm
where cause and result are not two. Menzan uses this negation of the view
that cause is different from effect to begin his presentation of the details of
causation, which continues through the remainder of the text. Having described this awakening as being beyond the usual ideas of cause and effect,
Menzan goes on to stress that there is no difference between our *samādhi* and
the *samādhi* of the Tathāgata. Amid the elaborate praises of this *samādhi*, the
details of causation are further developed with a discussion of how the rebirths
through the six paths in the classical teachings of mainstream Buddhism are

caused by the thoughts of an individual. With this fundamental position clearly set out, he adds his own point:

> However, the thoughts are just illusions. When you clearly real- ize that being as well as not being does not go beyond discrimina- tive thinking, thought is not cut off, and there is no more rebirth. Simply do not add discriminative thinking, and you will see clearly. (476a)

In particular, this is not a matter of forcing the mind to stop (what I translate as "thought is not cut off"), because that would be clinging to just one aspect of the mind, the quietist practice that Menzan is so adamantly opposed to, just as he is opposed to the activist forcing of some teachers of *kanna* practice.

Basic Buddhism: Precepts and Causation

From this highly abstract level about cause and effect Menzan jumps without warning into the topic of the three groups of pure precepts of the bodhisattva: to do all good, to not do any evil, and to help all sentient beings to awakening. This is an example of causation which is very pertinent to his thread: following the precepts leads to a good result. Menzan stresses, however, that precepts all need to be understood as a doing away with discrimination, and that to hate evil and love the good, or to cling to the indeterminate state, means to fall to the level of where buddhahood will never be attained. The real way of following the precepts is similar to the way that a bitter persimmon becomes wonderfully sweet as it is dried. If there had never been any astringent flavor, the sweetness would never have emerged:

> This is like the astringent persimmon when it is dried: a splen- didly sweet flavor emerges. If you had somehow squeezed out the astringent part at the beginning, then the sweet flavor would never have emerged. The bitter flavor of the three poisons changes in just this way into the sweet flavor of the three virtues. So when the fol- lowers of the two vehicles squeeze out the bitter flavor of the three poisons, they also get rid of the sweetness of the three virtues. We must get to the real bottom of this truth about this world of our body and mind: if we but let go of our discriminating conscious- ness, then there is no separation, not even as much as the tip of a hair, between body and mind and the world. It is the dharma world of original unity of all aspects. The ancients said, "With the slightest bit of speculative thinking, something extra arises." (477b)

In the same way, following the precepts is not a matter of ensuring that there is never any evil, but of letting go of discrimination, of realizing that there is no separation between good and evil.

The final section returns to the basic teaching of causation, stressing that it is found in no other religion or philosophy and that Buddha's insight was to see both cause and its result as two aspects of one process:

> In addition to all this, you should believe in what is called cause and result. Cause means the seed. Result means the fruit. Just as when you plant a melon you do not get an eggplant, good causes certainly produce good results and bad causes produce bad results. There is absolutely no difference between these two. One can say that this is the primary difference between the teaching of the Buddha and the heterodox ways. Only the Tathāgata clearly explained cause and effect. It is unknown in the various ways of religion, and it does not come up in the teachings of Confucius because he is concerned only with teachings that deal with the world of ordinary men. Cause and effect do not come from outside, they are all made by us. And so you should not stop with seeing cause and effect as two things. When you see cause, there is doubtless effect. For example, suppose you go to a country where there are no poppies and you show people a poppy seed. If you tell them that this seed contains a thousand large flowers in colors as varied as a brocade and also has millions of seeds, not a single person will believe you. If you were to break it open there would be nothing inside, so of course they would doubt you and refuse to believe. But in a country that has poppies, everyone sees this phenomenon for himself every year, and someone who does not believe is just laughed at as a fool. The ignorance of cause and effect in the heterodox philosophies of Indian and the Chinese teachers Confucius and Lao-tsu is like doubting the flowers of the poppy seed. The Buddha taught cause and effect because he looked at the flower and the seeds together and saw the relationship for himself. (479a)

Menzan goes over all the different kinds of causes and their effects in the present life, the next life, or future lives. He gives many examples, mostly textbook examples from Chinese history of either heroes or villains. Throughout all these examples however, there is a continuing background note: this is only a limited understanding. This attitude is expressed most fully at the beginning of the section when he is explaining the importance of not doing evil, and the widespread effect of doing evil:

> This is not to say that we should hate people who do evil and throw them out [of society]. If you cut them off by hating them and

shunning them, then you cannot help the people who are in the three evil rebirths. Evil is as insubstantial as a bubble, and the proper understanding is that it is merely the product of discrimination and thinking, and therefore it should not be despised, but certainly it should not be liked. This is called, not being seen as merely a thing of discriminative thinking, which is not to be liked and clung to. It should not be liked even slightly, and even more it should not be hated. This is called doing [all good]. If we can only separate ourselves from both good and evil, from the discrimination of thinking and classifying, we will just drop evil and practice only good. If we attain this kind of mind and stop doing evil, this attainment is the bodhisattva precept of following all rules and ceremonies; it is the dharma body of the Tathāgata, the virtue of the Tathāgata which cuts off all afflictions. (479b)

These examples, however, are all cases of ordinary limited causes and limited effects. Menzan explains that this is why the cycle of rebirth continues, unlike the case of the limitless abiding in awakening of the Tathāgata, which is the same as the practice-awakening of his (Sōtō) school.

Conclusion

Menzan ends his text with the admonition that one must have the greatest respect and faith in this teaching of cause and effect, and that one should study very carefully the passages from Dōgen that he has appended. The contrast with the opening words of the preface could hardly be greater. From the highest level of the most exalted awakening, understood as being the special property of the Zen school, he has come full circle to the most fundamental teaching of Buddhism, something accepted as central in all Buddhist schools. Never has there been the slightest hint of any mundane advice that the beginning practitioner of this way might follow. The only way is to stop discrimination. Beginning with the ultimate light which is nothing less than the wisdom of the Buddha, Menzan has cycled through explanations of the mind and precepts and causation, each time framing the discussion with affirmations of *samādhi*, which is far beyond such explanations. No sooner does he give the reader something to hold on to than he decisively takes it away.

The *Buddha Samādhi* never relents in its emphasis on the present realization of the ultimate, the practice-realization of Dōgen's way in this very moment. Much of the text, the parts that I have not translated and not much discussed, praises the practice of this realization and often simply lists its transcendent virtues. And yet Menzan continually returns from that level to offer step-by-step explanations and point-by-point arguments that are pertinent to the state of mind of the practitioner. He rejects any limited idea of meditation as a particular technique, and yet his criticism of *kanna* practice is carefully nuanced and emphasizes the problems of the kind of Zen practitioner who is seeking for something outside of himself and is pushing to bring practice to a successful conclusion. Many contemporary Sōtō doctrines have been influenced by Menzan, but the blanket opposition to the Rinzai *kanna* practice cannot be attributed to him. His explanations of the problems of using the mirror as a metaphor for the mind are strikingly clear, a fact that helps explain why woodblock prints of the *Buddha Samādhi* are still being made nearly 300 years after it was written. The discussion he offers of how to understand precepts and causation from the standpoint of nondiscrimination seems to me to be more helpful to people struggling to understand the workings of their own mind than are some of the poetic flights of more renowned writers.

Despite the countless concrete examples and carefully graded explanations, he does not use his skills of detailed explanation to deal with the physical and environmental details of meditation practice. For Menzan there can be no doubt that Zen is not the meditation school and *zazen* is not just seated meditation. *Zazen* is nothing less than the practice-awakening of the Buddha as taught by Dōgen.

ABBREVIATIONS

ZS   Zoku Sōtōshū zensho kankōkai, ed. *Zoku Sōtōshū zensho.* 10 vols. Tokyo: Sōtōshū shūmuchō, 1974–1977.

NOTES

1. The work for this essay began under the kind and patient tutelage of Professor Kosaka Kiyū of Komazawa University and was completed with the generous support of the Japan Society for the Promotion of Science and the International Center for Japanese Studies, Kyoto. For the role of meditation in Sōtō Zen see Carl Bielefeldt, *Dōgen's Manuals of Zen Meditation* (Berkeley, Cal.: University of California Press, 1988). For the early interest in meditation in China, see Eric Zürcher, *The Buddhist Conquest of China: The Spread and Adaptation of Buddhism in Early Medieval China* (Leiden: E. J. Brill, rpt., 1972 [1959]), p. 33.

2. ZS-Hōgo: 463–488.

3. See David E. Riggs, "The Rekindling of a Tradition: Menzan Zuihō and the Reform of Japanese Sōtō Zen in the Tokugawa Era" (Ph.D. diss., University of California, 2002).

4. Carl Bielefeldt, "Recarving the Dragon: History and Dogma in the Study of Dōgen," in William R. LaFleur, ed., *Dōgen Studies* (Honolulu: University of Hawaii Press, 1985), pp. 21–24.

5. William M. Bodiford, *Sōtō Zen in Medieval Japan* (Honolulu: University of Hawaii Press, 1993), pp. 44–50.

6. William M. Bodiford, "Dharma Transmission in Sōtō Zen: Manzan Dōhaku's Reform Movement," *Monumenta Nipponica* 46/4 (1991).

7. S-Shūgen 2, pp. 130–137, 399–404 (SZ Sōtōshū zensho kankōkai, ed. Sōtōshū zensho. rev. and enlarged ed. 18 vols. Tokyo: Sōtōshū shūmuchō, 1970–1973).

8. Kawamura Kōdō, *Shōbōgenzō no seiritsushiteki kenkyū* (Tokyo: Shunjūsha, 1987), pp. 396–397.

9. Helen J. Baroni, *Ōbaku Zen: The Emergence of the Third Sect of Zen in Tokugawa, Japan* (Honolulu: University of Hawaii Press, 2000); Jian Wu, "Orthodoxy, Controversy and the Transformation of Chan Buddhism in Seventeenth-Century China" (Ph. D. diss., Harvard University, 2002).

10. Eric Hobsbawm and Terence Ranger, eds., *The Invention of Tradition* (Cambridge, Mass.: Cambridge University Press, 1983).

11. Maruyama Masao, *Studies in the Intellectual History of Tokugawa, Japan*, trans. M. Hane (Princeton, N.J.: Princeton University Press, 1974), pp. 39–51; Peter Nosco, "Man'yōshū Studies in Tokugawa, Japan," *The Transactions of the Asiatic Society of Japan*, Fourth Series, no. 1 (1986): 109–147.

12. Komazawa University Library (Tokyo) mss. 180-W359.

13. Nagahisa Gakusui, Kawamura Kōdō, and Kosaka Kiyū, eds., *Eifuku Menzan Zenji senshō* (Tokyo: Eifukukai, 1968); Okumura Shōhaku, *Dōgen Zen* (Kyoto: Kyoto Sōtō Zen Center, 1988).

14. Ōkubo Dōshū, *Dōgen zenji shingi* (Tokyo: Iwanami shoten, [1941] rpt., 1987), p. 284.

15. ZS-Hōgo, p. 463a. Subsequent references to the *Buddha Samādhi* will be simply to the page in this edition.

16. For the use of practice-awakening see Stone's concise survey of the background to Dōgen's use of the term and to the contemporary scholarship on the subject. Jacqueline I. Stone, *Original Enlightenment and the Transformation of Medieval Japanese Buddhism* (Honolulu: University of Hawaii Press, 1999), pp. 73–74, 88–89.

17. T 48, no. 2005.

18. Nakamura Hajime, *Bukkyōgo daijiten* (Tokyo: Tokyosho, 1982), p. 976.

19. Hirata Takashi, *Mumonkan* (Tokyo: Chikuma shobō, 1969), p. 19; Iriya Yoshitaka and Koga Hidehiko, *Zengo jiten* (Tokyo: Shibunkan, 1991), p. 320.

20. Z-Hōgo: 413.

21. Komazawa Daigakunai Zengaku Dai Jiten Hensanjo, ed., *Zengaku daijiten* (Tokyo: Taishukan shoten, 1978), p. 434.

22. Kurebayashi Kōdō, *Dōgen zenji no honryū* (Tokyo: Daihōrinkaku, 1980), p. 27.

23. Bielefeldt, "Recarving the Dragon"; Steven Heine, *Dōgen and the Kōan Tradition: A Tale of Two Shōbōgenzō Texts* (Albany, N.Y.: State University of New York Press, 1994).

24. Bielefeldt, "Recarving the Dragon," pp. 36–38. Carl Bielefeldt, "Ch'ang-lu Tsung-tse's Tso-ch'an i and the 'Secret' of Zen Meditation," in *Traditions of Meditation in Chinese Buddhism*, ed. Peter N. Gregory (Honolulu: University of Hawaii Press, 1986), p. 154.

25. Bodiford, *Sōtō Zen in Medieval Japan*, pp. 143–162; Bernard Faure, *Visions of Power: Imagining Medieval Japanese Buddhism* (Stanford, Cal.: Stanford University Press, 1996), pp. 218–219.

26. Komazawa University Library mss. 142–143; T 48, no. 2001.

27. T 48, no. 2004.

28. T 48, no. 2003.

29. Komazawa University Library mss. 141–145.

30. Heine, *Dōgen and the Kōan Tradition*, p. 134.

31. Bielefeldt, "Recarving the Dragon," p. 48.

32. Norman Waddell, *Wild Ivy: The Spiritual Autobiography of Zen Master Hakuin* (Boston: Shambala, 1999), p. xxvi; Philip B. Yampolsky, *Zen Master Hakuin* (New York: Columbia University Press, 1971), p. 26.

33. Waddell, *Wild Ivy: The Spiritual Autobiography of Zen Master Hakuin*, p. 33.

34. ZS-Goroku vol. 2. T 82, no. 2604. Kagamishima Genryū, *Manzan, Menzan* (Tokyo: Kōdansha, 1988).

35. T 51, no. 2076:240b21; Iriya and Koga, *Zengo jiten*, p. 401.

36. Bielefeldt, *Dōgen's Manuals of Zen Meditation*, p. 198.

37. The *Shiburoku* is a set of short Chinese Zen texts collected and widely circulated among Zen monks in Japan (Z 2–18, 19). Even though Menzan is addressing a more popular audience, he cannot refrain from a bibliographic comment now and then. In other writings he often provides detailed references in a nearly modern style, something quite extraordinary at the time.

38. Morton Schlütter, "Silent Illumination, Kung-an Introspection, and the Competition for Lay Patronage in Sung Dynasty Ch'an," in *Buddhism in the Sung*, ed. Peter N. Gregory and Daniel A. Getz, Jr. (Honolulu: University of Hawaii Press, 1999).

Appendix:
Pinyin–Wade-Giles
Conversion Table

PINYIN	WADE-GILES	PINYIN	WADE-GILES
a	a	can	ts'an
ai	ai	cang	ts'ang
an	an	cao	ts'ao
ang	ang	ce	ts'ê
ao	ao	ceng	ts'êng
		cha	ch'a
ba	pa	chai	ch'ai
bai	paj	chan	ch'an
ban	pan	chang	ch'ang
bang	pang	chao	ch'ao
bao	pao	che	ch'ê
bei	pei	chen	ch'ên
ben	pên	cheng	ch'êng
beng	pêng	chi	ch'ih
bi	pi	chong	ch'ung
bian	pien	chou	ch'ou
biao	piao	chu	ch'u
bie	pieh	chua	ch'ua
bin	pin	chuai	ch'uai
bing	ping	chuan	ch'uan
bo	po	chuang	ch'uang
bou	pou	chui	ch'ui
bu	pu	chun	ch'un
		chuo	ch'o
ca	ts'a	ci	tz'ǔ
cai	ts'ai		

PINYIN	WADE-GILES	PINYIN	WADE-GILES
cong	ts'ung	fo	fo
cou	ts'ou	fou	fou
cu	ts'u	fu	fu
cuan	ts'uan		
cui	ts'ui	ga	ka
cun	ts'un	gai	kai
cuo	ts'o	gan	kan
		gang	kang
da	ta	gao	kao
dai	tai	ge	kê, ko
dan	tan	gei	kei
dang	tang	gen	kên
dao	tao	geng	kêng
de	tê	gong	kung
dei	tei	gou	kou
deng	têng	gu	ku
di	ti	gua	kua
dian	tien	guai	kuai
diao	tiao	guan	kuan
die	tieh	guang	kuang
ding	ting	giu	kuei
diu	tiu	gun	kun
dong	tung	guo	kuo
dou	tou		
du	tu	ha	ha
duan	tuan	hai	hai
dui	tui	han	han
dun	tun	hang	hang
duo	to	hao	hao
		he	ho
e	ê, o	hei	hei
en	ên	hen	hên
eng	êng	heng	hêng
er	êrh	hong	hung
		hou	hou
fa	fa	hu	hu
fan	fan	hua	hua
fang	fang	huai	huai
fei	fei	huan	huan
fen	fen	huang	huang
feng	feng	hui	hui

PINYIN	WADE-GILES	PINYIN	WADE-GILES
hun	hun	lao	lao
huo	huo	le	lê
		lei	lei
ji	chi	leng	lêng
jia	chia	li	li
jian	chien	lia	lia
jiang	chiang	lian	lien
jiao	chiao	liang	liang
jie	chieh	liao	liao
jin	chin	lie	lieh
jing	ching	lin	lin
jiong	chiung	ling	ling
jiu	chiu	liu	liu
ju	chü	long	lung
juan	chüan	lou	lou
jue	chüeh	lu	lu
jun	chün	luan	luan
		lun	lun
ka	k'a	luo	lo
kai	k'ai	lü	lü
kan	k'an	lüan	lüan
kang	k'ang	lüe	lüeh
kao	k'ao	lun	lun, lü
ke	k'ê, k'o		
ken	k'ên	ma	ma
keng	k'êng	mai	mai
kong	k'ung	man	man
kou	k'ou	mang	mang
ku	k'u	mao	mao
kua	k'ua	me	mê
kuai	k'uai	mei	mei
kuan	k'uan	men	mên
kuang	k'uang	meng	mêng
kui	k'uei	mi	mi
kun	k'un	mian	mien
kuo	k'uo	miao	miao
		mie	mieh
la	la	min	min
lai	lai	ming	ming
lan	lan	miu	miu
lang	lang	mo	mo

PINYIN	WADE-GILES	PINYIN	WADE-GILES
mou	mou	piao	p'iao
mu	mu	pie	p'ieh
		pin	p'in
na	na	ping	p'ing
nai	nai	po	p'o
nan	nan	pou	p'ou
nang	nang	pu	p'u
nao	nao		
ne	ne	qi	ch'i
nei	nei	qia	ch'ia
nen	nên	qian	ch'ien
neng	nêng	qiang	ch'iang
ni	ni	qiao	ch'iao
nian	nien	qie	ch'ieh
niang	niang	qin	ch'in
niao	niao	qing	ch'ing
nie	nieh	qiong	ch'iung
nin	nin	qiu	ch'iu
ning	ning	qu	ch'ü
niu	niu	quan	ch'üan
nong	nung	que	ch'üeh
nou	nou	qun	ch'ün
nu	nu		
nuan	nuan	ran	jan
nun	nun	rang	jang
nuo	no	rao	jao
nü	nü	re	jê
nüe	nüeh	ren	jên
		reng	jêng
ou	ou	ri	jih
		rong	jung
pa	p'a	rou	jou
pai	p'ai	ru	ju
pan	p'an	ruan	juan
pang	p'ang	rui	jui
pao	p'ao	run	jun
pei	p'ei	ruo	jo
pen	p'ên		
peng	p'êng	sa	sa
pi	p'i	sai	sai
pian	p'ien	san	san

PINYIN	WADE-GILES	PINYIN	WADE-GILES
sang	sang	tian	t'ien
sao	sao	tiao	t'iao
se	sê	tie	t'ieh
sen	sên	ting	t'ing
seng	sêng	tong	t'ung
sha	sha	tou	t'ou
shai	shai	tu	t'u
shan	shan	tuan	t'uan
shang	shang	tui	t'ui
shao	shao	tun	t'un
she	shê	tuo	t'o
shei	shei		
shen	shên	wa	wa
sheng	shêng	wai	wai
shi	shih	wan	wan
shou	shou	wang	wang
shu	shu	wei	wei
shua	shua	wen	wên
shuai	shuai	weng	wêng
shuan	shuan	wo	wo
shuang	shuang	wu	wu
shui	shui		
shun	shun	xi	hsi
shuo	shuo	xia	hsia
si	ssǔ, szǔ	xian	hsien
song	sung	xiang	hsiang
sou	sou	xiao	hsiao
su	su	xie	hsieh
suan	suan	xin	hsin
sui	sui	xing	hsing
sun	sun	xiong	hsiung
suo	so	xiu	hsiu
		xu	hsü
		xuan	hsüan
ta	t'a	xue	hsüeh
tai	t'ai	xun	hsün
tan	t'an		
tang	t'ang	ya	ya
tao	t'ao	yai	yai
te	t'ê	yan	yen
teng	t'êng	yang	yang
ti	t'i	yao	yao

PINYIN	WADE-GILES		PINYIN	WADE-GILES
ye	yeh		zhao	chao
yi	i, yi		zhe	chê
yin	yin		zhei	chei
ying	ying		zhen	chên
yong	yung		zheng	chêng
you	yu		zhi	chih
yu	yü		zhong	chung
yuan	yüan		zhou	chou
yue	yüeh		zhu	chu
yun	yün		zhua	chua
			zhuai	chai
za	tsa		zhuan	chuan
zai	tsai		zhuang	chuang
zan	tsan		zhui	chui
zang	tsang		zhun	chun
zao	tsao		zhuo	cho
ze	tsê		zi	tzǔ
zei	tsei		zong	tsung
zen	tsên		zou	tsou
zeng	tsêng		zu	tsu
zha	cha		zuan	tsuan
zhai	chai		zui	tsui
zhan	chan		zun	tsun
zhang	chang		zuo	tso

Index

Akizuki Ryōmin, 179
An Shih-kao, 218–220

Baizhang. *See* Pai-chang Huai-hai
  (Baizhang)
Bankei, 98
Bielefeldt, Carl, 259, 261, 264
Bodhidharma, 36, 85, 87, 92, 95,
  107 n., 215–236
Buddhabhadra, 217–220, 223

*Chanyuan qinggui (Ch'an-yüan ch'ing-
  kuei)*, 75, 78, 88, 95, 138, 140, 145,
  147, 149, 155
Chih-i. *See* Zhiyi
*Ching-te ch'uan-teng lu (Jingde
  Chuandeng lu)*, 84–85, 128, 263
Ch'i-sung, 229, 233
Chixiu baizhang qingqui, 148–149,
  153, 156
Chung-feng Ming-pen, 194
Colcott, Martin, 159

Dacheng chixin lun, 44
Daiken shingi, 147
Dainichi Nōnin, 68, 85, 88, 91, 94
Daitō Kokushi, 178, 184
Darumatara zenkyō settsū kōsho, 215–
  236
Dharmaraksa, 218

Dharmatrāta, 215, 222–223, 229
Dōgen, 65, 67, 88, 113–133, 138–140,
  142–143, 146, 154, 248–272
Dōhaku, 251
Dokuan Genkō, 225–227
Dumoulin, Heinrich, 134 n.
Dunhuang, 16, 17

Eiheiji, 120–122, 124, 155–156, 160,
  249
Eihei Kōruku, 113–133
Eihei shingi, 155
Eisai, 65–99, 138–139, 141–142, 146
Eizan koki, 147
Enni Ben'en, 139
Erru sixing lun, 36

Fa-hua ching, 89
Fa-yen, 20
Fo-jih Ch'i-sung, 223–224
Foulk, Griffith, 224
Fu Dashi, 59
Fujita Genro, 190
Fushukuhanpō, 140

Genkō shakusho, 225, 228
Gentō Sokuchū, 155
Gesshū Sōko, 154
Gihwa, 45–62
Giin, 120, 122

Guishan jingce, 15–37
Guishan Lingyou, 15–37

Hakuin Ekaku, 98, 154, 227, 231, 259,
    261
Heidegger, Martin, 133
Heine, Steven, 172, 261
Hekiganroku, 114, 174–175, 185–186, 200–
    201
Hōnen, 145
Hongzhou school, 15, 36
Hsü-an Huai-Ch'ang, 85
Hsüeh-tou Ch'ung-hsien, 174, 260
Hsün-ku-hsüeh (*J. Kunkogaku*), 216
Huang Hui-nan, 85
Huang-po Hsi-yun (Huangbo), 31, 39 n.,
    98, 258
Hua-t'ou, 117
Hua-yen, 89, 220
Hui-neng, 47, 56, 58, 60, 85, 87, 98
Hui-yüan, 220, 229–230
Hung-chih, 114, 126, 132
Hung-chih Cheng-chüeh, 260
Hyakunijussoku, 184

Ikkyū, Sojun, 178
Iriya Yoshitaka, 184
Ishii Shūdō, 91–92, 121, 124–125, 127,
    130–131
Isshū Miura, 194
I-yuan, 120, 122, 130

Jakugo, 117, 171–207
Jiaoding qinggui, 139
Jijuyū zanmai, 247–272
Jingang jing, 44–62
Ju-ching, 120, 126, 132

Kanna Zen, 256–259
Keizan shingi, 142
Kenninji, 141–142, 162
Ketelaar, James, 157
Kōan (Kung-an), 46, 83, 151, 171, 258,
    260
Kogetsu Zenzai, 153
Kokugaku, 98
Konkōmyō kyō, 68
Kozen Gokokuron, 65–99, 139, 146
Kraft, Kenneth, 174, 178

Kui-feng Tsung-mi (Zongmi), 32, 47, 49,
    56, 58–60, 231 n.
Kumārajīva, 220–222, 239 n.
Kunchū Zenren Kushū, 192
Kuzōshi, 188, 192

Lanqi Daolong, 143
Linchi I-hsüan, 83, 98, 117, 119
Liu-tsu-t'an ching (*Liuzu danjing*), 44, 45,
    82
Li zhifa, 34

Mahāprajnapāramitā sūtra, 80, 104 n.,
    153, 227
Mahāyanasamgrahabhāsya, 222
Manpukuji, 151
Manzan Dōhaku, 120, 250
Ma-tsu Tao-i (Mazu), 15, 31, 98
Menzan Zuihō, 115, 155, 247–272
Mikkyō, 81
Mujaku Dōchū, 153
Mumonkan (Wu-men kuan), 114, 117, 172,
    174, 177, 179, 186, 205, 258
Myōe Shonin, 225
Myōhō renge kyō, 68, 80
Myōshinji, 152
Myōzen, 67

Nantenbō Rōshi, 159
Nenbutsu, 141, 151, 154
Ninnō kyō, 67–72, 74, 76–79, 86, 96–97,
    102 n.
Nōshū toko-kuzan yōkōzenji gyōji shidai,
    147
Nukariya Kaiten, 158

Obaku shingi, 151, 154–155
Obaku Zen, 150–154, 157, 161
Oga Hae Seorui, 45

Pai-chang Huai-hai (Baizhang), 31, 98
P'an-chiao, 88
Pei Xiu, 39 n.
Pi-yen lu (*J Hekiganroku*), 260
Prajñā-pāramitā, 52, 69
"Pure" Zen, 93, 97, 142, 154

Qing-gui (*Shingi*), 137–134

Rinzai roku, 82
Riyong qinggui, 138
Ruzhong xuzhi, 139

Sākyamuni, 85, 139
Sasaki, Ruth Fuller, 194
Sasaki Sōkei-an, 193
Shen-hui, 223, 224
Shibayama Zenkei, 192
Shikantaza, 43
Shingon, 141
Shinran, 145
Shōbōgenzō, 43, 65, 67, 113–133, 140, 249–250, 264
Shoekō shingi, 149
Shōtoku Taishi, 234
Sōdō shingi, 155
Sōjiji, 160–161
Sōto Kyōkai Shushōgi, 113–116
Sōtōshū gyōji kihan, 162
Sūgawara Yuki, 120, 125, 131
Sung kao-seng chuan, 84
Śuraṅgama-sūtra, 44
Suzuki, Daisetu, 107 n., 111 n., 160

Ta-hui Tsung kao, 83, 118–120, 124
Tathāgatagarbha, 44
Te-shan, 119
T'ien-t'ai, 74, 88, 141, 224, 232, 236
Tōfukuji, 141–142
Tōrei Enji, 215–236
Tōyō Eichō Zenji, 185–186, 183
Tsan-ning, 86–87, 92, 107 n.
Tsuchiya Etsudō, 191
Tsung ching lu, 88, 90–91
Tsuo-ch'an san-mei fa-men ching, 220–221

Ungo Kiyō, 152

Vinaya, 27, 34, 81, 91, 93, 145–146, 158

Wan-shan t'ung-kuei chi, 89–90, 94
Wŏnhyo, 49, 63 n.
Wu-men Hui'kai, 177
Wuzong, 18, 21

Xixin ming, 15, 37 n.

Yamabe Nobuyoshi, 218
Yanagida Seizan, 66, 91, 222
Yefu Daochuan, 47, 52, 57, 59, 61
Yen-shou. *See* Yung-ming Yen-shou
Yinyuan Longqi, 151
Yogācāra, 222
Yogācārabhūmiśāstra, 222
Yuanjue jing, 44, 55
Yüan-wo K'o-ch'in, 175–177
Yülu (J. goroku), 82
Yung-ming Yen-shou, 84, 88, 91–92, 94–96, 107 n.
Yun-men Wen-yuan, 107 n.
Yuzhang Zongjing, 47, 61–62

Zazen, 151, 154, 257
Zengoshū, 191
Zenkyō settsū kōsho, 215
Zenrin kushū, 171, 173, 185–186, 188–189, 193–194
Zenrin segoshū, 178
Zhiyi, 34, 74, 87
Zudokko Kushū, 190
Zutang ji, 39 n.

Printed in the United States
85747LV00001B/109/A

9 780195 175264